Augusta Theodosia Drane

The History of St. Catherine of Siena and her Companions

Vol. II

Augusta Theodosia Drane

The History of St. Catherine of Siena and her Companions
Vol. II

ISBN/EAN: 9783743399112

Manufactured in Europe, USA, Canada, Australia, Japa

Cover: Foto ©ninafisch / pixelio.de

Manufactured and distributed by brebook publishing software (www.brebook.com)

Augusta Theodosia Drane

The History of St. Catherine of Siena and her Companions

THE HISTORY

OF

ST. CATHERINE OF SIENA

AND HER COMPANIONS

With a Translation of her Treatise on Consummate Perfection

BY

AUGUSTA THEODOSIA DRANE

AUTHOR OF "CHRISTIAN SCHOOLS AND SCHOLARS," ETC.

IN TWO VOLUMES

VOL. II.

Second Edition

LONDON: BURNS AND OATES, Limited
NEW YORK: CATHOLIC PUBLICATION SOCIETY CO.

CONTENTS OF VOL. II.

CONTENTS.

ILLUSTRATIONS IN VOL. II.

Part III.

THE RETURN TO SIENA.

CHAPTER I.

THE HOMEWARD JOURNEY.

(OCT. 1376 TO JAN. 1377.)

CATHERINE had received from the Pope a hundred florins for the expenses of her homeward journey, to which sum the Duke of Anjou added a hundred francs. Her motive for directing her course to Toulon rather than to Marseilles was to avoid coming in contact with the Papal cortège, and also because her own journey to Genoa was to be performed by land. She must unavoidably have passed in the near neighbourhood of *La*

Sainte Baume, and it is difficult to believe that she would not have turned aside to visit the sanctuary of her beloved patron and mother St. Mary Magdalen. If so, however, her biographers have neglected to record the fact, and it is at Toulon that we come on the first traces of the travellers. Having reached that city they stopped at an inn, and Catherine, according to her custom, retired at once to her apartment; she wished to observe the strictest privacy, and had charged her companions not to let it be known she was there. "But," says Raymund, "the very stones appeared to announce her arrival. First women, and then men, flocked to our residence, demanding to see the Saint who had come from the Pontifical Court. The landlord having admitted she was there, it became impossible to keep back the crowd, and we were forced to let the women enter. One of them brought an infant whose body was so swollen that it was piteous to behold, and some of those present asked Catherine to hold the child for a moment in her arms. At first she refused, desiring to shun the notice of men, but at last, over-come by compassion, she did as they asked her; and hardly was the infant placed in her arms than it was completely restored. I was not present when this occurred; but it was so well certi-fied that the Bishop of the city sent for me, and relating what had happened, informed me that the child was nephew to his Vicar-General; and he requested me to obtain for him an inter-view with Catherine."

From Toulon it is generally agreed that she and her com-panions travelled to Genoa by land. Nevertheless we learn from a letter written by John of the Cells to William Flete that at one point their land journey suffered a temporary interruption. "A certain prelate," says Don John, "worthy of all credit, related to me as follows: 'I was at Nurcia the same day that Catherine went to the Pope, and such a multitude of men and women ran to receive her blessing, that to my knowledge the heavenly virgin rose by night, and, taking ship, fled from the tumult.'" On the whole sea-coast from Tuscany to Marseilles no place of this name occurs, unless indeed we identify it with Nice, which by the

Italians is called Nizza;[1] but the mention of the Pope's presence there renders it almost certain that some town on the Gulf of Genoa is here intended; and a little experience in the fatality which accompanies the record of names will suffice to explain the fact that Nurcia finds no place in modern geography.

The road which Catherine followed must have been that known as the *Corniche* or *Cornice*, being the remains of the ancient Roman Emilian way. Running along the side of the rocks and in some places overhanging the sea, its dangers were increased by the torrents which rush down from the hills, sometimes rendering even the present coast-road difficult of transit. Its beauties at least equalled its dangers, each turn of that mountain path opening on some new bay or headland, while the waters of the Mediterranean would be seen breaking in jewelled spray on the rocks below. Then as now the eyes of the travellers would have been gladdened with the sight of orange and lemon groves, perfuming the air with their rich blossoms, and mingling their foliage with that of the olives and the stone pines; and at Bordighera Catherine would probably have found a welcome from the Brethren of her Order long established on that lovely spot, sometimes called "the Jericho of Italy" from the abundance of palm trees which still give so Oriental an aspect to the scenery, and which, with other features in the landscape, irresistibly awaken in the heart of the traveller memories of the Holy Land.[2]

---

[1] The theory of their identity has this difficulty. The accurate Bishop of Sinigaglia, in his Itinerary, informs us that the Pope's flotilla passed Nice on the 9th of October. Now on the 3rd of October St. Catherine had gone on to Voragine, and would certainly not have retraced her steps to Nice. (*Notale relative ad alcune visioni avute da Sta. Caterina nella terra di Voragine, ed altrove.* Cod. T. iii. 7 a, carte 295.)

[2] "The noble palm trees of Bordighera almost gird it round on the western and northern sides, and grow in profusion in coppices and woods, of all sizes, from the gnarled giants of one thousand years' reputed age to little suckers that may be pulled up by hand. There are probably now more palms in Bordighera alone than in the whole of the Holy Land" (*Dean Alford*). "The olives here tell us of Olivet and the garden; the lilies carry us to the Sermon on the Mount; the hillside tanks, waving streams, and water-brooks swollen by sudden rain, all speak to us of Palestine" (*J. A. Symonds*).

Continuing her journey, then, along this road (in the course of which one of her companions treacherously abandoned her, taking with him the money which she had given him for their expenses), she arrived on the 3rd of October at Voragine or Varezze, a town on the sea-coast, not far from Genoa. "Described through groves of oranges and palm-trees," says a recent writer, "may still be seen the tower of the church where was probably baptized the Blessed James of Voragine," of the Order of Preachers, who in his day was Archbishop of Genoa, and author of that celebrated collection of Saints' Lives, known as the "Golden Legend." Catherine naturally felt an interest in a spot connected with that holy man, with whose book she was perfectly well acquainted. In fact, the "Golden Legend" was the most popular book of spiritual reading in the Middle Ages, and St. Catherine makes allusions to it in several of her letters. This visit to Voragine is not mentioned by Raymund in his Legend, although it was accompanied by some sufficiently remarkable circumstances. Bartholomew Dominic, however, speaks of it in his deposition ; and certain notes regarding it have been preserved in manuscript in the Communal Library at Siena, from an authentic copy of which I will proceed to restore this missing page of St. Catherine's history.

"A certain Simon Mafei of Voragine, a man of credit, in a document written on parchment and dated in the year 1381, which agrees with others preserved in the Convent of St. Maria Annunciata of the Order of Preachers, declares, that in the year 1376 St. Catherine when returning from Avignon, whither she had gone to transact important affairs regarding the Holy Church with the Sovereign Pontiff, came into the parts of Voragine, that she might visit the country of the Blessed James, Archbishop of Genoa. She was accompanied by F. Raymund of Capua, her confessor, and she found the place, through the destruction caused by the plague, so utterly depopulated, that there remained only a very few people alive. The houses were all deserted, and the grass was growing even over the gates. It was with difficulty she could find any person to take her in and give her hospitality. At last, passing through one street where now stands the hospital, she met, behind the house, a woman of the place, named Costa, who lodged her in her house, and related to her the cause of the depopulation of the said town. And she, horrified by the narrative, as well as by all she had seen in the neighbouring country, was moved by pity to make a special prayer for the people who survived, and for all the inhabitants of the place, recommending them to the Most Holy Trinity and to the Blessed Virgin Mary. Before she left the said town, she told the people who were yet to be found in it, that they must set about building a chapel in honour of the Most Holy Trinity, and that the place would never more be molested by the plague, and that whoever having the plague on him should bring it to the town, should also take it away. In the morning she took the road towards Genoa, in company with the said Raymund her confessor, and passed through another street which led to the Church of our Lady of the Annunciation (called now Our Lady of Graces), founded in the year 1189, which was then under the care of a certain hermit, but is now in the hands of the Friars Preachers; and being accompanied by a few peasants, when she had arrived within a short distance of the spot, she told them, as well as the said F. Raymund, that the town having had a man so illustrious as the Blessed James, their compatriot, they should build a convent for the brethren of the Order of Preachers, which was done many years afterwards by some persons devout to the Order, and among others by the aforesaid Simon Mafei. Then the Saint with her confessor entered into the church and prayed there; which ended, they took their leave, thanking all for the charity shown them; and giving them a blessing, they turned their steps towards the city of Genoa."

To this account we must append that of the most accurate of all the Saint's biographers, F. Bartholomew Dominic, who gives us these additional particulars in his deposition. "Having reached Voragine about the hour of Vespers," he says, "Catherine called F. Raymund to her, and said to him, 'God has even now made known to me that, after some years have passed, you will on this same day, the vigil of St. Francis, with your own hand transfer my body from one tomb to another.' Raymund repeated these words the same evening to Bartholomew, and the prediction was verified by the event. The promise made by the Saint to the unfortunate inhabitants of Voragine has also been fulfilled to the letter, down even to our own times; and that in a manner too remarkable to be passed without notice. The Commune of the town lost no time in carrying out her instructions. They erected a chapel in honour of the Holy Trinity, of the Blessed Virgin Mary, and of the Blessed James of Voragine; and after the canonisation of St. Catherine, they included her name also in the dedication. Never since that time has the plague visited the town, and its immunity from every kind of pestilence is a thing so generally known, that on various occasions, when other places in the neighbourhood have been suffering from this scourge, the inhabitants have taken refuge here; and by so doing have rendered the literal accomplishment of the Saint's words more evident: for coming hither with the infection on them, they have themselves died, but never communicated the disease to any of the citizens of Voragine; and instances of this extraordinary protection enjoyed by them are recorded in the year 1579, 1630, and 1706, and even in the more recent visitations of the cholera. The gratitude of the people to their great protectress is literally unbounded. By a decree of the Magistrates she was declared chief patroness of their city; a mass was ordered to be daily celebrated in her honour within the chapel already mentioned, and her feast is celebrated by processions and other extraordinary devotions, at which persons from all the surrounding districts are accustomed to attend. No inhabitant of Voragine would think of adopting any other means of preservation from pestilence, and they take a pride in showing themselves, above the inhabitants of any other place, her true and loyal clients." (*Relaz. del Passagio di. S. Cath. in Voragine, MS. Siena.*)

On leaving Voragine the little party pursued their way to Genoa, where they were charitably entertained for more than a month in the house of a noble lady named Orietta Scotta.

Caffarini calls her "a devout and noble matron." Her family was in fact one of the most illustrious of the land, and is thought to have been Scottish in origin, and to have first settled in Italy in the time of Charlemagne. The two brothers Amico and Gabriel, sons of William Scott, came to Genoa in 1120, and were given the command of the Genoese troops. From Baldwin, son of Amico, descended Barnabo, the husband of our Saint's hostess. The Scotti afterwards assumed the name and arms of the Centurioni, but they were so proud of the connection of their ancestress with St. Catherine, that the name of Orietta was carefully perpetuated in the family. One letter addressed by the Saint to this lady is printed in the collection of her epistles (No. 334). The original of this letter was preserved by the Centurioni for 300 years as a most precious relic, but it was unfortunately lost in the last century, passing with other valuable property into the possession of another family.

Orietta's house was in the Via Caneto, leading to San Giorgio, and to a very ancient Dominican convent. The letter above spoken of is addressed to " Madonna Orietta Scotta, *at the Cross of Caneto,*" so called because at this particular spot the streets cross. This house was preserved in Burlamacchi's time, though it had then passed into the hands of certain merchants ; and in it was still to be seen St. Catherine's room, converted into a chapel.

Raymund informs us in his Legend that having reached Genoa some days before Gregory, " Catherine stopped there in order to wait for him." These words imply, but do not actually inform us, that they met again at Genoa; but the interesting fact has been carefully recorded by Caffarini in his Supplement. He gives it on the authority of F. Severino of Savona, who related to him how Gregory, being much fatigued by his disastrous sea-voyage, stopped some days at Genoa to rest. How disastrous the voyage had been the Itinerary of Peter d'Amely informs us. Not to speak of the abundant tears shed by all on quitting France, we learn that they were once forced to land on a desert and inhospitable shore to escape the violence of the tempest. On the feast of St. Francis they encountered another storm, and narrowly escaped shipwreck. Peter expresses himself as perfectly astonished at the inhospitable fury of the elements, but at last hits on the happy explanation that it must have been caused by the wickedness of those Romans, to whom the excellent Pontiff was being so barbarously transported.

They at length reached Genoa on the 18th of October, and remained there ten days. During this time the most discouraging rumours reached them from Rome, where the popular leaders, who had possessed themselves of the chief authority in the absence of the Pope, by no means pleased at the prospect of having to resign their power, were stirring up the people to insurrection. Florence, too, was reported to be on the verge of some desperate measures, and the French courtiers failed not to seize the opportunity of representing to Gregory the madness of the enterprise he had undertaken, and to urge him, while there was yet time, to bend back his steps to the more hospitable shores of France. The question of a retreat to Avignon was even debated in Consistory; when learning that Catherine was in Genoa, Gregory resolved to seek an interview with her, for the purpose, as it would seem, of confirming his wavering resolution.

He went, therefore, by night to the residence of Orietta. There were two reasons for this singular arrangement. In the first place, the Pope was unwilling to summon Catherine to come to him, lest he might thereby arouse the watchful jealousy of those who surrounded him; whilst it was equally impossible for him to repair to her house in the daytime without exciting public notice: for, from the dawn of day until the evening, a countless multitude of persons of all ranks flocked to see and consult her, in such sort that she was not left free for a moment. It did not appear suitable to Gregory's dignity to appear in the midst of the crowd, nor did he think it prudent to summon her to his presence, desiring that their interview should be unknown to the members of his suite. He went therefore to her house as a private individual, at an hour when she was less beset by visitors. On seeing the Sovereign Pontiff enter her chamber, Catherine humbly prostrated at his feet. He at once raised her and spoke to her with much affection and kindness ; and after a long conference, begged her to grant him one favour before he departed : it was that she would remember him every day in her prayers. It need hardly be said that she promised to obey his wishes, adding with simplicity and filial confidence, that she trusted he would also not forget her when he offered the Holy Sacrifice. At last they separated, and Gregory withdrew, much edified, after giving her his benediction.[1]

Caffarini, in his narrative of this interesting incident, has dropped no hint that the courage of the Pontiff stood in need of reinforcement, or that Catherine employed her influence with him to counteract that of his courtiers. Nevertheless, the fact is preserved in a note affixed to the third of her Prayers, which runs as follows : " *This prayer was made at Genoa by the said virgin, to dissuade Pope Gregory from the project of returning back : things contrary to the journey to Rome having been deliberated on in the Consistory.*" The prayer itself reveals the circumstances that inspired it ; possibly the words flowed from her lips that same night during the anxious hours which elapsed after Gregory had quitted her. "O Eternal God !" she exclaims, "permit not that Thy Vicar should yield to the counsels of the flesh, nor judge according to the senses and self-love, nor that he suffer himself to be terrified by any opposition. O Immortal Love ! if Thou art offended by his hesitations and delays, punish them on my body which I offer to thee to be tormented and destroyed according to Thy will and pleasure !" Her supplications prevailed. On the 28th of October, Gregory left Genoa and directed his course towards Leghorn. There was no more talk of a retreat ; and thus for the second time had Catherine infused her own strength into his heart, and braced him for his noble purpose. She was herself detained at Genoa for more than a month in consequence of sickness breaking out among her companions. The first who fell ill was Neri di Landoccio, and the pain he suffered was so

---

[1] Sup., Part 2, Trat. 1, § 1.

intense, that unable either to lie in bed or stand upright, he crawled about the room on his hands and knees. Catherine, compassionating his state, desired that a physician should be sent for, and Raymund accordingly summoned two skilful leeches to prescribe for the sick man; but their prescription had no beneficial effect. "They told me plainly," he says, "that they had no hopes of saving the patient. When I announced this sad news to the others who were at table with me, Stephen Maconi rose at once, full of sorrow, and hastened to Catherine's room. Throwing himself at her feet, he begged her with tears not to suffer his brother and companion, who had undertaken this journey for God's sake and hers, to die far from his home, and to be buried in a strange land. Catherine, much moved, said to him with a mother's tenderness, 'My son, why are you thus troubled? If God wishes now to crown your brother Neri's labours, you ought rather to rejoice than to mourn.' But Stephen persisted in his prayer. 'Oh, sweetest, dearest Mother,' he said, 'I conjure you to help him, for I know well enough that you can, if only you will.' Then Catherine, unable to resist his appeal and the movements of her own tender heart, replied: 'I only wished to see you resigned to the will of God; but since you will have it so, remind me of your request before I receive Communion at Mass to-morrow, and I promise to pray to God for him; and you, too, must pray that I may be heard.' Full of joy at having obtained this promise, Stephen failed not to present himself to Catherine the next day as she was going to Mass, and kneeling humbly, he said, 'Mother, do not disappoint me.' She gave him a look of comfort, and passed on to the chapel; and having communicated, remained a long time in ecstasy. At last she returned from her abstraction, and observing Stephen who knelt by her side, she gave him a comforting smile, and whispered, 'You have obtained your grace.' 'What, Mother?' said Stephen; 'will Neri be cured?' 'Yes,' she replied, 'God will assuredly restore him to us.' At these words Stephen hastened to his friend with the good news, and soon afterwards the physicians arrived, and having questioned the patient, began to comment on his wonderful improvement, and to say that though they had given him up the day before, they believed now that he would recover. And so, indeed, he did, and before long was perfectly restored."

Stephen himself was the next to fall ill, worn-out with the sorrow he had gone through, and the fatigue of nursing the others. Every one had warned him that without care he would certainly be ill; and so it came to pass. "He kept his bed," says Raymund, "and we did our best to assist and console him, for he was universally beloved." Catherine hearing of his state came to see him, accompanied by her confessor and companions. "She asked me," says Stephen, "what I was suffering, and I, delighted at her sweet presence, answered cheerfully, 'They tell me that I am suffering, but I know not what.' Then with maternal tenderness she laid her hand on my forehead, and said, shaking her head a little, 'Do you hear what that child says? "They tell me that I suffer, but I know not what," and all the time he has a violent fever.' Then turning to me, she added, 'I will not allow you to follow the example of the others, but I command you in virtue of holy obedience no longer to have this sickness. I will have you completely restored, so that you may serve your companions as before.' Then she began to speak of God, as was her custom, and while she conversed, I found myself perfectly cured. I interrupted her discourse to declare my recovery to all who stood by, who were lost in wonder; and since that time I have enjoyed long years of perfect health. Catherine spoke in the same tone of authority when she cured the venerable John of Vallombrosa, as he affirmed to me when he was in his last agony, at the Abbey of Passignano, near Siena. I heard from the very lips of Catherine a similar order given, in the absence of the same monk, to two of his disciples whom he had sent to her. She commanded him through them to be sick no longer, and to come to her without delay, which he did immediately. The holy religious wrote an admirable letter on this occasion, which I carefully preserve in our convent."[1]

The long delay, caused by the sickness of so many of the party,

---

[1] Letter of Stephen Maconi, forming part of the Process.

was meanwhile exciting great complaints on the part of those who awaited their return to Siena. Lapa, in particular, bitterly complained, and seems to have written to her daughter in a tone of fretful reproach, to which Catherine replied with her usual sweetness and moderation: "My dearest mother in our sweet Jesus" (so she writes), "I, your miserable and unworthy daughter Catherine, desire to comfort you in the Precious Blood of the Son of God. I wish to see you not only the mother of my body, but also of my soul, so that loving my soul more than my body, all inordinate tenderness may die in you, and then you will not suffer so much for the loss of my bodily presence, but be ready for God's honour to endure something, seeing that what I am doing is for His glory. . . . You know that it was His will that I should go, and I am sure you wish me to do His will. . . . So, like a good and sweet mother, you must be content, and not be so disconsolate. Remember how you acted when your children left you on account of temporal affairs, and now when it is a question of eternal life, you say you shall certainly die if I do not soon return. All this comes because you love that part of me which I owe to you (my body) better than the part I received from God. Raise your heart a little to the most sweet and holy Cross, and you will find it assuage every pain. Consent to endure a little passing suffering to avoid the endless punishment which we deserve for our sins. Strengthen yourself in the love of our crucified Jesus, and do not think that you will ever be abandoned either by God or by me. You will presently be consoled, and then the joy will be greater than the pain. We shall soon return, please God; and should have been back before this, had it not been for the serious illness of Neri; Master John and Brother Bartholomew have also been ill. Adieu." (Letter 169.)

But it was not her own mother alone who waxed impatient at the delay. Catherine had to appease the discontent, not un-mingled with jealousy, of a more important personage. This was Donna Giovanna di Corrado Maconi, the mother of Stephen. She had parted with her son, and reluctantly sanctioned his form-ing one of the company who went to Avignon, but she began to be uneasy as month passed after month, and still his return was deferred. Catherine wrote her a letter, in which she exhorted her to use her wealth as the steward of Christ, and to devote herself to the charge of bringing up her children ; mindful that they, no less than her worldly possessions, were lent to her by Him, and must be given to His service. " Make the sacrifice of yourself and of your children to God," she says, " and if you see that God calls them, do not resist His sweet will. If He takes them from you with one hand, do you give them to Him with *two*, like a good and true mother who loves their salvation. Do not choose their state in life *for them ;* mothers in the world sometimes say, 'I wish my children to please God, and I think they will serve Him as well in the world as in any other state ;' but how often it happens that such poor mothers, by insisting on giving their children to the world, keep them neither for the world nor for God." She concludes her beautiful letter (No. 355) as follows : " Take courage, and have patience, and do not be troubled because I have kept your Stephen so long : I have taken good care of him and watched over him well, for the affection between us makes of us two but one and the same thing, and your interests, as you know, are mine. You, his mother, gave him birth once, and I also desire to give to him, and you, and all your family, a spiritual birth, in tears and anguish, offering my prayers to God without ceasing for your salvation and that of all your family. I will say no more ; remember me to Corrado, and bless for me all your family, specially my new little plant, just planted in the garden of the Church.[1] Take good care of her, and bring her up in all virtue, that she may shed forth perfume among the other flowers. May God keep you in His holy grace ! Adieu."

During their stay at Genoa, Catherine effected much for the salvation of souls. Caffarini, in the chapter of his Supplement already quoted, gives some interesting particulars, communicated to him by Fra Severino, the eye-witness of all he relates. " Fra Severino," he says, " told me that during the long stay which Catherine made at Genoa, many men of letters, doctors, and

---

[1] A new-born daughter.

masters in theology came to discourse with her. All who heard her with admiration and respect were visibly favoured by God; but, on the contrary, the proud who contemned and sought to discredit her were severely punished. Among other examples we may name that of a certain doctor of great reputation and eloquence, but of no less presumption and vanity. He audaciously sneered at Catherine, and spoke with contempt of her profound wisdom. But he did not go long without punishment, for the Divine vengeance struck him with a sudden and terrible death. In the same city of Genoa, professors of letters, sacred and profane, lawyers, the chief senators, and other persons of authority and credit were not ashamed to ask and receive her wise counsels. It was observed that all who spoke with her quitted her agitated, and full of a certain kind of terror, as though something extraordinary had happened to them. She exhorted all to penance with much sweetness, and attracted their esteem by the holiness of her life."

Genoa long retained the memory of St. Catherine's visit, and cherished the traces of her presence with jealous care. The Ligurian Academy, addressing its congratulations to Jerome Gigli on his publication of her works in 1707, dwells with pardonable pride on the fact, that next to Siena and Rome no city is richer in its associations with her name. "The streets she went through, the places where she lived, the apartments she occupied, may still be distinctly pointed out. From Capo di Monte towards the east is seen the ancient and solitary monastery of St. Fruttuoso, which gave her shelter both on her way from Tuscany to Avignon and on her return. Towards the west lies the town of Voragine, which she visited. The rural district that leads to the Croce di Caneto was more than any other sanctified by her footsteps. The house of Orietta Scotta still belongs to the descendants of that lady, and in it is the very chamber chosen by the Saint as her place of retirement and prayer." [1]

After remaining at Genoa rather more than a month, the travellers once more took ship and sailed for the coast of

---

[1] *Vocabolario Cateriniano,* p. 395.

Tuscany. Their passage was not unattended with danger, if the circumstances briefly related in the deposition of Peter Ventura belong to this time. "It chanced once," he says, "when the Saint was travelling by sea, that she was overtaken by a violent tempest, so that the vessel in which she was suffered shipwreck and was broken to pieces, but she happily reached the shore safe and sound with all her companions." It would have been more satisfactory to have had fuller details regarding this adventure, but the biographers of the Saint too often observe the rule of retrenching from their narrative the names of places, and persons, and the dates of time. We know of no other occasion when Catherine was exposed to the perils of the sea except her short trip to Gorgona, which was certainly attended by no such disaster to her and her party; though it is barely possible that an incorrect report of the accident which happened to her escort on their return to the island may have furnished ground for the above narrative. Certain it is, that neither Raymund nor any of the other companions of the Saint on the voyage from Genoa have alluded to the shipwreck, though Raymund in his Legend lets us know that they were in real peril. He tells the story, however, more by way of illustrating Catherine's confidence in God, than with any view of describing the incidents of their journey. He does not even inform us in so many words that the circumstances of which he speaks happened at this particular time, though we know it must have been so, this being the only sea-voyage in which he was her companion. "I remember," he says,[1] "that being on board of a ship with her and many other persons, the wind lowered into a dead calm towards midnight, and the pilot became extremely anxious : we were in a dangerous channel ; if the wind had taken us sideways, we might have been thrown on some neighbouring islands or floated into the open sea. I gave notice to Catherine of our danger. She answered in her ordinary tone : ' Why does that trouble you, what have you to do of yourselves ? ' This was her ordinary expression in time of trouble. She considered that a soul which has fixed its thoughts on God should allow no

---

[1] Legend, Part I, ch. ix.

anxiety or distraction to cause it disquiet ; for God knows all, and can do all, and He will watch and provide for the necessities of such as meditate on Him.   Hence, whenever we entertained any fear for ourselves or our brethren, she would often say, ' What have you to do of yourselves ? let God act.   His eye is over you ; and He will protect you.'   When, therefore, I heard her say these words, I took comfort and was somewhat reassured ; but presently the wind changed, and blew in the direction dreaded by the pilot. I mentioned it to Catherine : ' Let him change the helm, in the name of God,' she said, ' and follow the wind that Heaven shall send him.'   The pilot obeyed, while she, meantime, bowed down her head and made her prayer to God.   And we had not kept on that course so far as a man would shoot an arrow, but that there came a gracious wind that brought us to the haven that we desired, where we arrived to our great wonder and gladness about the hour of Matins, singing all, with a joyful voice, *Te Deum laudamus.*" [1]   This "desired haven " was the Port of Leghorn, where they once more set foot on the dear old soil of Tuscany, and where they were met by Lapa, her impatience to embrace her beloved child not suffering her to await her coming to Siena ; for, before returning thither, Catherine was to pay a short visit to Pisa.'   Stephen's joy was a little damped on finding that an arrangement had been made on his behalf, in virtue of which he was to precede the rest of the party, and travel with one companion to Siena, charged with sundry letters and commissions, and feeling not unlike a truant schoolboy to whom the unwelcome hour has come for returning home. [2]

---

[1] In the above passage two paragraphs have been transposed for the sake of clearness, and a few of the picturesque phrases adopted which occur in Father Fen's translation, though his narrative as a whole is less intelligible than the original Legend.

[2] These details, not given in any of the Lives of St. Catherine hitherto published, are not imaginary ; they are furnished by the very interesting collection of " Letters of St. Catherine's Disciples," preserved in MS. at Siena, and published by Signor Grottanelli in 1868, at the end of the *Leggenda Minore.*   From them we learn the fact of the Saint's second visit to Pisa which has hitherto been overlooked.

He lost no time in reporting himself on his arrival at Siena, and consoled himself for the separation by despatching a grumbling sort of epistle to Neri, written half in jest and half in earnest. It is dated from Siena, Nov. 29th, 1376, and runs as follows:—

"DEAREST BROTHER,—You must know that last Friday we reached Siena safe and sound, though we had many alarms on the road, for the route we took by Peccioli is very dangerous by reason of bandits, and all kinds of wicked things are being committed there just now, which had I known I should never have come that way. But it is manifest that the prayers of our dearest Mother have had much to do both with our journey and our safe arrival here. I have given Sano the letters and the other things you sent, and all the sons and daughters of our dearest Mother have had the greatest consolation from them; and they are now impatiently awaiting your return, and I with them, for it seems to me that you delay much too long. Do beg all you can that your return may be soon, otherwise I shall repent having come back, and shall perhaps make up my mind to be the bearer of this letter myself. I will say no more at present, only asking you to salute our dearest Mother for me, and to recommend me to F. Raymund, F. Maestro, F. Thomas, F. Bartholomew, and Fra. Felice; embrace Monna Lapa, and recommend me to my mothers, Monna Cecca, Monna Alessia, and Monna Lisa, begging them to pray for poor miserable me. God knows what I should do with myself, if the hope of the time being short did not keep me up.

"To Neri Landoccio at the Dominican Convent of Sta. Caterina, in Pisa."

His next letter is dated the 8th of December, and from it we find he had written two others which are not preserved. Stephen was certainly a famous correspondent, and as much disposed to rattle in a charming kind of way with his pen as with his tongue. He informs Neri that these two letters (which seem to have miscarried) were pretty long, yet nothing at all in comparison of what he would like to have written. "I do beg of you," he says, by the sincere love I bear you, and which I know you return, reply as soon as you can and tell me how matters stand; whether they are accomplished or about to be accomplished; you can easily write in such a way as that no one but myself will understand. Recommend me to our dearest Mother a thousand times and more, tell her that at last I have obeyed her injunctions in the matter of the *ridotto*.[1] Recommend me to all the good ladies one by one, and tell Monna Alessia that her pretty little cell is waiting for her; and remember me in a special way to Monna Lapa. Also to my fathers, Master John and F. Raymund, and the others, each of them, one by one; and beg of them to have compassion on us poor disconsolate wretches, and to make haste home; and tell them all to pray for wicked me."

We have nothing to show what the business was which took Catherine to Pisa at this time, but it must be remembered that the affairs of Florence were as yet by no means settled, and she was doubtless anxious to secure the fidelity of Pisa and the adherence of Peter Gambacorta to the cause of the Church. In fact, the influence of Florence was so powerful over the other Tuscan republics that though far from desirous of quarrelling with the Pope, both Pisa and Lucca had involved themselves in difficulties, in consequence of their keeping up a friendly intercourse with the rebellious city which lay under the interdict. When Gregory stopped at Leghorn on his way to Corneto, ambassadors from Pisa and Lucca came to meet him bearing magnificent presents, including ample provision of veal, lamb, comfits, new bread, and Greek wine. Pierre d'Amely records the fact, and at the same time reveals the lurking distrust felt by the Pontiff and his court of these fair professions. "Beware, O Pontiff!" he says, "be not seduced by their flattering words! If they had not abjured their fidelity to the Church, would they not have come with their armies to have delivered thee from the Florentines? Yet instead of that, they have contracted an alliance with the guilty city!" We must not, however, judge this conduct too harshly. It was

---

[1] Grottanelli explains in a note that in Siena this word is applied to the entrance-hall of a house; but it appears to have many meanings.

an embarrassing position for the less powerful Tuscan cities, who had to choose their line of conduct between the cross-fire of a double danger. If they took an open part against Florence, she was strong enough to extinguish their independence; and if they kept on terms with her, they ran the risk of being included in the censures of the Church, which were directed against her and all who should take any part in her misdeeds. Questions connected with these circumstances were doubtless the cause of Catherine's journey to Pisa at the present time. They must indeed have been pressing affairs that could prolong her absence from Siena, which had already lasted eight months. Her return took place towards the end of December, or the beginning of January, when she once more found herself in her old home of the Fullonica. How fair must its humble walls have appeared to her after the gaudy splendour of Avignon! Who can doubt that Stephen was waiting there to welcome them home, to exhibit the *ridotto* and Monna Alessia's charming little cell, and everything on which he had expended his superfluous energies during that weary month of suspense? But all this must be left to our imagination, for no traces of such scenes have been preserved by Catherine's biographers. Whatever may have been the joys of that happy moment of reunion, they did not prevent Catherine from following in her heart the progress of Gregory towards his capital. He was then at Corneto, where he arrived on the 5th of December, and before departing for Rome on the 13th of January,[1] Catherine addressed him a letter which reads like a mother's last charge to her son before sending him forth to some glorious and difficult enterprise.

After reminding him that no man can be the servant of God unless he be firm, constant, and patient, and that sensuality and love of ease deprive the soul of constancy, and render our hearts narrow and pusillanimous, she continues thus:

"O most holy Father, and my own sweet Father, open the eye of your understanding, and you will see that if virtue is needed

---

[1] This date enables us to fix that of Catherine's return to Siena; for, as will be seen, her letter to him was written from her own city, and addressed to him while still at Corneto.

by every man in order that he may save his soul, it is doubly needed by you, who have to feed and govern the mystical body of the Church, which is your Spouse. What need you have of constancy, of fortitude, and of patience! Remember you were still young when you were planted in the garden of the Church, and you have to combat against our threefold enemies—the world, the flesh, and the devil. I trust in God's goodness you will resist them all, and fulfil the end for which God created you, namely, to render honour and glory to His Holy Name, and enjoy His goodness hereafter in the beatific vision. Now that you are the Vicar of Christ, who has chosen you to labour for His honour, for the salvation of souls, and for the reform of Holy Church, labours and sufferings are specially destined for you, over and above the ordinary combats which all souls must undergo who would serve God.

" The heavier is your burden, the stronger and more courageous should be your heart, fearless of all that may chance to befall you. You know that in taking the Church to be your Spouse, you pledged yourself to suffer for her sake all contradictions and tribulations. Well, then, go forward, like a brave man, and meet the tempest with strength, patience, and perseverance. Never let suffering make you look back through fear or surprise; but press on and rejoice in the midst of perils and battles, because through all these things you will see the work of God accomplished. It is ever so : the persecutions of the Church, like the tribulations of the just soul, always end in peace, purchased and merited by patience and perseverance, for which is reserved the crown of everlasting glory. I desire then to see your heart firm and unshaken, protected by holy patience : then you will find in suffering peace and consolation, and by suffering out of love for Jesus crucified, you will see this great war end in a great peace.

"Yes, peace, peace, Holy Father! Be pleased to receive back your children who have offended you; your goodness will conquer their malice and pride. It is no shame to stoop in order to raise a repentant child, but rather a thing glorious before God and man. No more war then, Holy Father, but give us peace, and turn the war upon the infidels. My soul desires nothing more in this life save God's honour, your peace, the reform of the Church, and the life of grace for every living soul. Courage then; as far as I can judge, the general disposition is to regard you as a father, specially in this poor little city which has always been the cherished daughter of your Holiness, though circumstances have forced her citizens to do some things that have displeased you. They see now that they acted under constraint, and your Holiness will do well to excuse them; for you may easily draw them with the bait of love. And now I entreat you, go as speedily as possible to the city of the holy Apostles. Go forward in full trust that God on His part will give all that is necessary for you, and for the Church your Spouse. Only have courage, and reckon confidently on the prayers of all true servants of God, and, together with all your other children, I humbly ask your benediction." [1]

Catherine had hardly re-established herself in Siena before messengers arrived from Florence, urging her return to that city, in order that she might make one more effort in the cause of peace. These messengers were Nicolas Soderini, Peter Canigiani, and Bindo Altovito, brave and loyal men, who desired nothing but the good of their country and reconciliation with the Church. Catherine's strong good sense, however, led her to decline their invitation. She saw clearly enough that Florence in the seething effervescence of revolution was no place for a woman. Yet, as it was necessary to communicate to the Magistrates the result of her mission to Avignon, she resolved to send Stephen Maconi back with the three envoys, that he might act in her name. They left Siena, therefore, in the April or May of 1377, and proceeded to lay before the Magistrates of Florence the terms proposed by his Holiness, and to urge their compliance. Stephen used his utmost eloquence in support of peace, but entirely without success. His arguments, instead of convincing his hearers, only irritated them the more. A rumour was spread through the city that one of the "be-Catherined fools of Siena" had been sent,

---

[1] Letter 11.

by his " blessed Catherine," to try and wheedle the Eight of War into surrendering the republic to the court of Rome; and the result was such a tumult that Stephen had to return to Siena with precipitation in order to save his head.

So for the present there was no hope of peace ; and Catherine, seeing the fruitlessness of her efforts in that direction, applied her whole attention to affairs nearer home.

CHAPTER II.

BELCARO, 1377.

FROM the course of our history it will have been seen
that Catherine took no part in the solemn entrance of
Gregory XI. into the holy city, which took place on the 17th of
January 1377. In the great picture of the Sala Regia at the
Vatican, and again on the bas-relief which adorns the Pontiff's
tomb in the Church of Santa Francesca Romana, she appears
walking beside his horse as he rides through the streets in triumphant procession; a representation as false historically, as it is
true in a symbolical sense. Yet in her little chamber in the
Fullonica, she listened with a glad heart to the tidings, that his
galleys had at last ascended the Tiber from Ostia to Rome; that
his feet had first touched the sacred soil at the Basilica of St.
Paul; and that from thence he had ridden to St. Peter's amidst
demonstrations of welcome that seem fairly to have taken him
and his attendants by surprise. The people preceded him not
merely shouting, but dancing for joy; the senators and nobles
appeared clad in such gorgeous silken vestments, that even the
Avignon courtiers admitted they had never seen the like; while
women mounted to the roofs of the houses to get a better view
of the scene, and more conveniently to throw down sweetmeats
and winter flowers on the procession. They did not reach St.
Peter's until evening, and found the whole Piazza illuminated
with torches, and the church blazing with 800 lamps. Whatever
doubts had been raised as to the welcome which Rome would
bestow upon her Pontiff were set at rest that day. "The people,"
says Peter d'Amely, "were delirious with joy; never in my life
did I witness such extravagant transports."

In the meantime Catherine had found one great anxiety awaiting her. Her native city that she loved so well, and that up to
this time had adhered so faithfully to the cause of Gregory, had
through its close alliance with Florence got involved in the interdict. In fact, the case of Siena was one of peculiar difficulty,
for during the quarrel between her nobles and citizens, the intervention of the Florentines had restored peace to the republic;
and hence the obligations of the Sienese to their powerful neighbour were both great and recent. However, though bound to
Florence by ties of gratitude, they had no wish to break with the
Pope; and the question of despatching an embassy to Rome in
order to arrange terms of reconciliation was already under dis-
cussion. Catherine approved of this proposal, and addressed a
letter to Gregory, which she sent by the hands of the ambassadors,[1] supporting the petition of her countrymen. After again
urging him to make peace at any cost, and so to cast coals of
fire on the heads of his revolted children, she continues, "You
know, Holy Father, that all reasonable creatures are more easily
led by love and goodness than by any other means, and this is
particularly true of us Italians of these parts (*Specialmente questi
nostri Italiani di quà*). . . . The ambassadors of Siena are about
to present themselves to your Holiness; there are no people in
the world more easily won by kindness, and I conjure you to
make use of that bait to catch them. Be so indulgent as to listen
to the excuses they will offer for their fault; they repent of it,
but know not what to do. Be pleased then, Holy Father, to
inform them what course they must take which will be most
agreeable to you, without obliging them to go to war with those
to whom they are bound. . . . I humbly ask your blessing, and
would recommend to you the ambassadors of Siena."

Tommasi in his history tells us that "Gregory received the
ambassadors with much kindness, for the sake of Sister Catherine

---

[1] Much difference of opinion exists as to who these ambassadors were.
One was certainly Andrea Piccolomini, and, according to the Aldine edition
of St. Catherine's letters, another was Thomas Guelfaccio, her own disciple,
and the convert of St. John Colombini.

Benincasa, who had sent him a letter by them." The exact object of the embassy was twofold : to make their own submission to the Pope, and to get released from censures ; and also to obtain the restitution of certain important fortresses of which they had been deprived.[1] If any traveller of classical predilections should chance to journey from Leghorn to Città Vecchia by the line of railway which runs along the desolate coast of the Tuscan Maremma, and stopping on his way at the Talamon station, should observe some barren rocks covered with ruins, he may be roused to a momentary interest by being reminded that they mark the site of the ancient Telamon, where Marius landed on his return from Africa, and where Lucius Emilius defeated the Gauls. But the votary of St. Catherine, if hitherwards journeying, will examine those rocks with a keener curiosity. Whether she ever visited the spot in person we cannot tell, but it occupied a good many of her thoughts at the particular time of which we are speaking. Talamon is a town of the Maremma district, which in old time belonged to a Benedictine Abbey, but in 1303 was sold to the republic of Siena. The fortified rock formed an important frontier stronghold, and we have seen its possession demanded in 1368 by the Emperor Charles IV., who was well aware of its strategical value. In 1375 it was seized by one of the Priors of the order of St. John, commonly called "the Prior of Pisa." He was a certain Messer Nicolas or Priam (as he is called, by the Pisan chronicler Tronci), to whom Catherine had some time before written a very stirring letter, which we have already quoted, moving him to join the Crusade. His seizure of Talamon was an unwarrantable act of injustice, but having seized it, he held, or professed to hold it, for the Church, and Peter Gambacorta, to whose family he was related, seems to have favoured the transaction on the ground that Talamon had formerly been Pisan territory. The ambassadors, therefore, were instructed to demand the restoration of Talamon, and Catherine took a particular interest in the success of their application. From what cause does not appear, but in spite of the good recep-

---

[1] See Part I, chap. xvi., p. 205.

tion given them by Gregory, no success attended their mission. Probably more active measures against Florence were demanded of them as a condition of their pardon than they dared agree to ; and they returned to Siena without having obtained either the removal of the interdict, or the restitution of the fortress, the recovery of which was at last due, as we shall hereafter see, to the exertions of St. Catherine.

Meanwhile she was engaged in a rather important undertaking of a more private character. The reader, we hope, has not forgotten Master Nanni di Ser Vanni, who had by her means been induced to make peace with his enemies, and who, in token of gratitude, had made over to her his castle of Belcaro, to be con verted by her into a convent. The various journeys in which she had for the last two years been engaged had deferred the accomplishment of this purpose, though in many of her letters allusions occur which show that the proposed plan was not forgotten. To carry it out, however, two authorisations were required ; one for the foundation of the convent from the Sovereign Pontiff, and another from the Magistrates of Siena to sanction the dismantling, or rather decastellating, of one of the fortresses of the republic. Gregory had given the Saint his sanction to the foundation during the time of her stay at Avignon ; and the Bull to that effect was preserved with some other privileges granted her by the Pontiff in the convent of SS. John and Paul at Venice, where it was seen by Caffarini, as he tells us in his deposition. But there existed in Siena a statute forbidding the alienation of strong places without the consent of the Magistrates. Catherine, therefore, had to present her petition to the Magnificent Lords Defenders of the Republic, and the document is still preserved in the State Archives, and bears date January 25th 1376, that is, in our style 1377.[1]   In it " Catherine, the daughter of Monna Lapa of the Contrada of Fontebranda," declares to the Magnificent Lords that Nanni di Ser Vanni, knowing how the said Catherine desired, for her soul's

---

[1] In Siena at that time the year was not reckoned as beginning until March 25th.   The document above referred to is extracted from the *Consigli della Campana*, vol. cxci. fols. 8, 9.

health, to build and construct a monastery, has determined to make over to her the site of his castle of Belcaro ; that she has procured the necessary powers from the Sovereign Pontiff, and that although the place cannot be called a fortress, inasmuch as it is dismantled and decayed, nevertheless she desires not to begin to build without the license of the Commune. She reminds them that their decree against their alienation of strong places was not intended to forbid the construction of churches or monasteries, but only to prevent evil men from possessing themselves of such places to the danger of the State ; but that in the monastery she intended to erect, there would be received only religious women who would continually pray for the city and inhabitants of Siena ; and that the citizens would be partakers of all their good works. Her petition was put to the vote and granted by 333 white beans against 65 black.

The new monastery was therefore begun, and though we have no particulars left us regarding the subsequent establishment of the Community, yet it is quite certain from various notices in the Legend, in St. Catherine's letters, and in the depositions of more than one witness in the Process, that Catherine occupied herself seriously in its establishment, and that it was the scene of several interesting incidents of her life.

Belcaro became a real fortress once more in 1554 when, during the siege of Siena by Cosmo I., it was occupied by troops, and still exhibits cannon-balls embedded in its walls. After that it became the property of Crescenzio Turamini, a rich banker of Siena, who turned it into a magnificent villa which he caused to be decorated in fresco by Baldassare Peruzzi. It no longer, therefore, presents the same aspect as in St. Catherine's time, yet the site is unchanged, and much of the original castellated edifice is still left standing. Situated about three miles north-west of the city and approached by charming country lanes, it occupies a little hill which, as you draw near, has the appearance of a green mound with a tower just peeping out of the centre. "The hill," says a modern traveller, "is entirely covered with ancient ilexes, which are shorn at the top so as to give the appearance of a level carpet; but on ascending through them by a winding path and entering the gate, what looked like a small tower turns out to be a palace." [1]

Catherine chose for her new foundation the title of "St. Mary of the Angels." Writing to Sano di Maco she says, "I recommend to you the monastery of St. Mary of the Angels. Do not be surprised if I do not come there; good sons do more when their mother is absent than when she is present, wishing thus to show their love for her." She did come there, however, and that pretty often. "I was present at the commencement of the place," says Raymund,[2] "together with all her spiritual sons and daughters. The Commissary appointed by the Pope on this occasion was Fra Giovanni (di Gano of Orvieto), abbot of the monastery of St. Anthimo of the Order of Williamites." This abbot of St. Anthimo was a very holy man, and one of the Saint's great friends and disciples. In him more than in any other person she had confidence in all that regarded the religious life, and to him accordingly she generally referred those who consulted her on the subject of a religious vocation. "Go to the Abbot of St. Anthimo," she says in one of her letters, "he is an earthly angel." He is numbered by Caffarini among those who sometimes acted as her confessor. Catherine, as it would seem, had often conferred with him on the foundation of a convent of strict observance. In one of her letters to him she writes as follows: "The bearer of this will speak to you of Madonna Miranda, wife to Francis of Montalcino. She has in her hands a young girl who wishes to give herself to God, and she wants to put her into a convent which I do not much like. I wish you would see her about it; and when you can find a place suitable for a *real and true* monastery, then put two good heads into it, for we have plenty of subjects. I am sure it would be for God's glory." In these words we see the germ of St. Mary of the Angels, and it explains the selection of the abbot for the office of Papal Commissary. It was probably the journey of Catherine and all her spiritual family to Belcaro on this particular occasion

---

[1] Hare's Cities of Central Italy.   [2] Leg., Part 2, ch. vii.

which is described in the deposition of Mino da Giovanni di Mino Sozzini. "She set out very early one morning," he says, "in company with F. Raymund and several of her spiritual sons and daughters, F. William Flete being of the number. When the party reached the torrent of the Tressa, several of them applied themselves attentively to see how Catherine would cross the stream, which at that time was full of water. According to her usual custom she was walking with her eyes closed and her hands joined; and in this way, even while they had their eyes fixed on her and were carefully watching her movements, they saw her already passed over the stream without their being able to say how. Stupefied with what they had seen they continued their way, and as they approached Belcaro, Pietro di Giovanni Ventura, with some other youths, ran on before the rest, wishing to be the first to cross the ditch, and enter the castle. This ditch was dry and overgrown with bushes and brambles, and as Pietro scrambled along he was wounded by a sharp thorn which entered one of his eyes. Blinded and in great pain he cried out with tears, heedless of all the efforts made by his companions to console him. When Catherine and the rest of the party came up to the spot, Pietro, hearing her voice (for he could not see her), cried out, 'O Mamma (for so she was familiarly called by all her disciples), one of my eyes is blinded!' But she, smiling sweetly, comforted him; and touching the eye with her hand, it was at once healed, and his sight perfectly restored. This incident filled them with joy, and they all entered the castle together, praising God. Mass was then celebrated by F. William Flete; and as he was in the act of giving Communion to the Saint, the same Pietro Ventura saw the consecrated Host fly, as it were, out of the hands of the priest into her mouth. After Mass, Pietro took F. Raymund aside and told him what he had seen; and Raymund replied that it was perfectly true, and that he had seen it also."[1] Possibly it was on the occasion of this same visit that another incident took place related by F. Francesco of St. Pietro, a brother of the Hospital by La Scala, to F. Angelo of

---

[1] Process, fol. 313.

Siena, a Franciscan friar, one of the witnesses in the Process. Francesco declared to him that as he was saying Mass in the castle of Belcaro, he saw the holy virgin raised from the ground in ecstasy, so that between the ground and the border of her garments there was a free space of some distance, to the great wonder of those who saw it. " On this account," says F. Angelo, " I began from that time manfully to resist the detractors of the holy virgin, and to commend myself devoutly to her prayers." Many years later he related what he had heard from F. Francesco to Stephen Maconi, then a Carthusian monk. Stephen listened to him with a smile, and said that the same thing had been witnessed by himself and others, not once merely, but oftener than he could attempt to say.

It was from Belcaro, and some time early in 1377, that Catherine addressed another letter to Gregory, which is remarkable for its unusual tone of sadness. The sorrows of the time weighed heavily on her heart, and it pierced her with anguish to see month after month pass by and still no prospects of peace. She could not hope to see that restoration to the Church of the beauty of holiness, for which her soul longed with the blessed hunger after justice which is the heritage of the saints, or to behold the standard of the Cross displayed, and Christendom united in a noble cause, so long as no measures were taken for putting a stop to the war between the Father and his children. And what a war it was ! We are thankful that the course of our history does not oblige us to inflict on our readers the narrative of the massacre of Cesena, when Count Robert of Geneva[1] led his mercenary troops to the slaughter of unarmed citizens. If in our own days of boasted civilisation the actual facts which attend any war are too shocking to be presented to us in their bare reality, what must it have been in a contest when the combatants on either side were hired brigands, for the time let loose to give full vent to their worst passions ? But if we spare our readers the revolting details, they were not spared to St. Catherine. She knew them in all their grim deformity, and the tales of violence and

____

[1] Afterwards the Anti-pope Clement VII.

sacrilege that met her ears did not reach her as they come to us from the far regions of Bulgaria or the Caucasus—so softened by distance that we listen with comparative indifference to tales that would freeze the blood in our veins with horror if the scene were laid in a neighbouring town or village. To her they were close at hand, and any day the bloody tempest might come still closer, and sweep over the villages which she gazed at from her castle walls, and fill the streets of her beloved city with far worse desolation than the most awful pestilence. Well then might she take the pen with a heavy heart; what more could she say to move the heart of the Pontiff than she had already said? and perhaps there is no thought more sorrowful than that we have done all that is possible for us to do, and all with no result. Catherine was not one, however, who would cease her efforts to remedy a gigantic evil merely because no success had hitherto attended them; so once more she set herself to conjure the Holy Father in grave, tender, and most moving words to let his goodness triumph over the malice of his enemies; not to regard temporal interests or political honour, but to think of nothing but souls. "O Pastor and guardian of the Blood of the Lamb!" she cries, "forget the affronts and injuries you have received, heed not the arguments of the devil who desires to keep up war and disorder. Imitate Christ whose Vicar you are, and bear everything for the salvation of your children. Hunger for that, and consider the evils caused by this horrible war, and the blessings that would flow from peace. Alas! beloved Father, woe be to my unhappy soul, for my sins, perhaps, are the cause of all this misery!"[1] It seems to me as if the demon had verily just now taken possession of the world, not in his own person, indeed, but in that of us who obey him. On whatever side I turn, I see every one making use of his free-will in such a way as to render it a perverse will; all, whether secular, religious, or ecclesiastics, going after pleasures and worldly honours, in the midst of disorder and corruption.

[1] The tenderness of the original cannot be rendered in English. *Ohimè Babbo mio, disavventurata l'anima mia che le mie iniquità sono cagione d'ogni male!*

And what afflicts me more than all, is to see those who should be flowers planted in the garden of the Church to give forth a sweet odour, shedding abroad nothing but the infection of sin. . . . We are at war with God, and the rebellious children are at war both with Him and with your Holiness. God requires you, as far as you can, to snatch the power out of the hands of the devil. Labour then to reform the corruptions of which I speak ; root up those infected flowers, and plant such as will give forth a sweet odour, even just men who fear God. I implore you, then, to agree to peace, and agree to such terms as are possible to be obtained; respecting always the rights of the Church and your own conscience. You must think more of souls than of things temporal. Act generously, and God will be with you, and even if you foresee troubles, fear nothing, but fortify yourself in our Sweet Jesus. It is in the midst of thorns that the rose blossoms, and it will be in the midst of persecutions that the Holy Church will be reformed. You are our instrument. Do what you have to do, then, fearlessly and in love.

"I have a great desire once more to find myself in the presence of your Holiness, and should have many things to say, but I am prevented by pressing affairs. Peace, peace, and no war, that is the only thing we want. I write to you from our new monastery that you have granted me under the title of Our Lady of the Angels. I humbly ask your benediction. Your negligent sons F. Raymund and Master John recommend themselves to your Holiness."[1]

It is probable that Gregory had himself proposed her coming to Rome, and that the concluding sentence in Catherine's letter contains her reply to this proposal. What the particular affairs were, to which she here alludes, we do not know. Raymund with his habitual vagueness says that after their return from Avignon to Siena they "visited in the environs some servants of God to console themselves with them in the Lord, and returned to the city on the feast of St. Mark the Evangelist." This may probably be understood of a visit to Lecceto, which is at an easy distance

----

[1] Letter 12.

from Belcaro.   It would seem, however, that Catherine found on her return much on which to employ her charity in the reconciliation of feuds among her fellow-citizens.   A great undertaking of this nature was to engage her attention during the ensuing autumn, and it was probably the negotiations which had to be gone through in preparation for that important affair which detained her at Siena, and obliged her to defer all present thought of visiting Rome.   She was, therefore, unable to support the arguments in her letter by the more powerful influence of her presence; yet, as will be seen in the sequel, they were not forgotten by Gregory, and it was to her at last that he turned in his perplexity, conferring on her the sublime though perilous office of mediatrix of peace.

CHAPTER III.

THE BREAD OF LIFE.

BEFORE Catherine left Avignon she had received from the hands of the Pope several most important privileges, which were secured to her by formal briefs, some of which are still in existence. By one of these his Holiness appointed three confessors to attend her in her journeys and hear the confessions of such persons as might be won to God by her pious words and exhortations; and to these confessors he granted the fullest powers. Two were named by him in the document; they were F. Raymund of Capua, and F. John Tantucci, the Augustinian. The third was left to her own selection, and she appears to have named F. Bartholomew Dominic, and in his absence, F. Thomas della Fonte.

By another brief, permission was given her wherever she might be, to have a chapel with a portable altar in her house, for Mass to be celebrated there, if need be, before daybreak, and for her to communicate at the Mass without requiring leave from any other person whatsoever, the same permission being extended to all those who assisted at it. This privilege, which in St. Catherine's time was a very unusual one to be enjoyed by any private individual, was granted to her in order to release her from the difficulties made to her frequent Communions, and also to obviate the inconveniences attending those wonderful and habitual ecstasies which rendered it impossible for her to pay her devotions in the public churches without drawing on herself an amount of notice both friendly and adverse. At Avignon, as we have seen, the kindly consideration of Gregory had provided her with a private chapel; and from the time of her return thence she possessed the same boon at Siena.   One of her first cares on finding herself once more at home was to select a suitable room in the house for the purpose; and with her own hands to prepare the necessary vestments and altar furniture.   The room which served as St. Catherine's private chapel is still shown in the Fullonica. You ascend to it by the stairs, those same stairs up which, according to the beautiful old legend, the angels so often carried her as a child; the altar is still there, together with a number of objects formerly used by the Saint, and now preserved as relics.   The altar furniture is preserved, not here, but in the Sacristy of San Domenico, where are shown the corporal, pall, towel, and chalice cover; also the pax and the altar stone, which last is formed of a piece of the stone on which St. Thomas of Canterbury was martyred, and is said by Burlamacchi (in his MS. notes to the Legend) to have been given to her by her English disciple, F. William Flete.   There too is the original Brief of Pope Gregory XI. of which we have just spoken, the whole being preserved in a box covered with velvet.[1]

It need not be said that the possession of this chapel was a blessing most highly prized by Catherine.   The first notice which occurs of its use was on that 25th of April when, as we have said, after some visits paid in the environs of the city, she returned to Siena in company with F. Raymund of Capua, who gives the narrative as follows :—

"When we arrived at Catherine's house, the hour of Tierce had already passed.   She turned towards me and said, '.O Father, did you but know how hungry my poor soul is !'   I understood her meaning, and rejoined, ' The hour of saying Mass is nearly elapsed, and I am so fatigued that it is very difficult for me to prepare myself for it.'   She remained silent a moment; but soon, unable to prevent expressing her desire, she said to me again, ' I

---

[1] *Succinto Ragguaglio della Sacra Testa ed altre reliquie di S. Caterina.* (Lucca. 1713.)   This little book was drawn up by P. Angiolo Carapelli, then Sacristan of San Domenico.   Signor Grottanelli testifies to having seen these objects in the year 1867.

am very hungry.'   I then consented to her request, and repairing
to the chapel in her house which had been granted her by the
Holy Father, I heard her confession, clothed myself in my
sacerdotal vestments, and celebrated the Mass of the day; I
consecrated one small Host for her, and when I had communicated, turning to give her the ordinary absolution, I beheld her
face as it had been the face of an angel, sending forth rays of
light, and so transfigured that it seemed not to be the same.
I thought within myself, 'That is not the face of Catherine!'
Then presently I said, 'Yet, certainly, O Lord, this *is* Thy faithful and beloved spouse!'   Considering these things I turned to
the altar, and said, not with my lips, but as it were in my mind
only, 'Come, O Lord, to Thy spouse!'   And the thought had
hardly been formed in my mind when lo! the sacred Host, before
I had touched It, moved and came towards me (as I could
plainly see) for the space of three fingers or more, till It reached
the paten which I held in my hand."

And here seems the right place to speak of those stupendous
wonders which marked the intercourse of Catherine with her
Lord and Spouse in Holy Communion, and which were, we may
say, daily witnessed and attested by Raymund and others no less
conscientious and worthy of credit.

No one can read the Legend without being struck with the
singular love of truth which seems the characteristic of the writer.
It bears on its pages the proofs of being the testimony of one
timid rather than over ready in accepting the marvellous; of one
who sifted the evidence of others, and was disposed to doubt
and test that of his own senses, and who, far from magnifying the
statements he receives, or repeating them merely as he hears
them, often qualifies them in minute particulars in a way which
reveals the delicacy of his sense of truth.

We may therefore safely trust his narrative, corroborated as
it is by the overwhelming testimony of those who knew Catherine
longer than he, and who had watched and noted down what they
saw day by day as it occurred.   Holy Communion was then to
Catherine, literally, the BREAD OF LIFE.   It was very generally

believed and reported that she communicated daily, but, says Raymund, that was not strictly true; "she did not communicate daily, but very often;" or, as he elsewhere expresses it, "she communicated daily, when not hindered by bodily infirmity, or the necessity of her neighbours; and if deprived of it for any notable time, she suffered visibly, so as to seem in danger of death." She never approached the altar without beholding things above the senses, specially when receiving Holy Communion. Thus she frequently saw in the hands of the priest the figure of an infant or a beautiful child; at other times she beheld a furnace of fire, into which the priest seemed to enter at the moment when he consumed the sacred species. She commonly perceived a delicious and extraordinary odour when communicating; and an ineffable joy took possession of her soul, which caused her heart to beat so as to be even audible to those who were near her. Father Thomas della Fonte, her first confessor, carefully verified this fact, and declares that the noise occasioned by this beating of the heart was unlike anything ordinary; it was of a wholly supernatural character, the jubilee of a heart exulting in the living God. Caffarini collected in his Supplement many other facts which had come to his own knowledge, or which he quotes from the notes of F. Thomas; for the sake of brevity we will give the summary which he makes of them in the *Leggenda Minore:* "Sometimes she saw the holy angels serving around the altar at which the Mass was celebrated, holding in their hands a golden veil, or in company with the saints, praising and blessing God. Sometimes she saw three Faces in one substance, or the altar and the priest wrapt in a flame of fire. At other times a great and marvellous splendour seemed to shine forth from the altar; or again, when the priest divided the sacred Host, it was manifestly shown how all was in each part; and often she beheld the Holy Trinity under various appearances and signs. Sometimes the sacred Host was transformed into the likeness of Jesus Christ Himself, at various ages, or she beheld It consecrated under the appearances of fire, flesh, or blood. Often also she saw above the altar the Queen of Heaven who reverently adored the Blessed Sacrament; besides which, on many occasions, she discerned a consecrated from an unconsecrated Host."[1]

In his Supplement he adds a remark that must not be omitted in this place. "It must be observed," he says, "*that none of the things above mentioned were seen by her with the material eyes of her body, but with those of the mind, supernaturally illuminated by God :* for she could not so much as raise her eyes to look at and adore the Divine Sacrament without being rapt and abstracted from her corporal senses: whence it sometimes happened that at the moment when the Priest raised the holy Body of Christ for the adoration of the faithful, she neither beheld It, nor heard the sound of the bell, and so failed to give those exterior demonstrations of worship which are customary with the faithful. There were not wanting those who wondered and took scandal at this, persuading themselves and others that during the time of the Holy Sacrifice she was indevout and distracted. Others, who better understood her habit of praying in profound ecstasy of mind, would approach and kiss with tenderness the place where she had knelt, which was generally some remote corner of the church where she might as far as possible avoid observation."[2]

The irrepressible sentiments of love and tenderness which the sight of the Blessed Sacrament, or even proximity to the altar or tabernacle, excited in Catherine's heart, were often the occasion of her receiving humiliations and reproofs. The priests who celebrated complained that they were disturbed by the sound of her sighs and weeping; and F. Thomas della Fonte, aware of this, begged her one feast of St. Lawrence to command and suppress these exterior signs as much as possible, or else to keep at a distance from the altar. Catherine obeyed, and remained at a distance; but she besought God to make known to her confessor that the exterior tokens of Divine love cannot always be thus repressed; and her prayer was so perfectly heard and answered, that he never again made her the like admonition.

---

[1] *Leg. Min.*, Part 2, chap. xii, p. 142.
[2] Sup., Part 2, Trat 6, § 1.

" I presume," says Raymund, who tells this story, "that it was out of humility he would say no more; and that he had learnt by a happy experience how impossible it is for a soul smitten with the love of God entirely to repress its transports."

If with some the exterior effects which were thus produced formed matter of complaint, others, and by far the greater number, drew from what they heard and beheld at such moments an increase in their own souls of faith and devotion. Caffarini tells us that he himself saw the Saint on the day when she received that mysterious purification in the Precious Blood of her Divine Spouse, which has been related in a former chapter. "Her face," he says, "was resplendent and bathed in tears; and so she always appeared after Holy Communion, nor is it possible to convey the sentiment which the spectacle inspired. On a certain feast of the Circumcision, sacred to the memory of the first effusion of that Price of our salvation, she assisted at Mass in the chapel of the Sisters of Penance, though at the time so weak that without assistance she was unable to kneel or raise her head. Having communicated, she remained for several hours wholly immersed in God, and at length, rising to return home, she left the church; when at the door she beheld the glorious vision of Him, from Whom her heart was never separated, and Who, casting on her a look of ineffable tenderness, addressed her with these words, ' Come to me, beloved daughter!' She reverently approached, and received from Him that Sacred Kiss of which the Spouse speaks in the Canticles; and for many days afterwards a wonderful and extraordinary fragrance was perceptible, not to herself only, but to all who approached her." F. Bartholomew Dominic tells us, in his deposition, that he frequently gave her Holy Communion, and that often at the moment of doing so he felt the Sacred Host agitated, as it were, in his fingers, and escape from them of Itself. "This at first troubled me," he says, "for I feared lest the Sacred Host should fall to the ground; but It seemed to fly into her mouth. Several persons have told me that the like happened to them when giving her Holy Communion."

Of her condition after Communion, Bartholomew likewise speaks: "Having received the Sacred Host, her mind was immediately rapt in God, so that she lost the use of her exterior senses, and the members of her body became so rigid that you might have broken, but you could not have bent them. Every day she remained thus, for three hours or more, perfectly abstracted and insensible. Often when in such ecstasies, she would speak to God, uttering prayers and profound meditations in a distinct voice, which was audible to those who were present, and moved them to devout and tender tears. These prayers were many of them collected, and written down word for word, some by me, and some by others. None of her words at such times seemed those of a woman, but they were full of the wisdom of learned doctors. For truly it was not she who spoke, but the Holy Spirit who spoke in her." [1]

What passed at such times between her soul and God was known to none but herself, and when she sought to declare it even to her confessor, the power of language failed. "One day," says Raymund, "I saw her ravished out of her senses, and I heard her speaking in an undertone; I approached, and distinctly heard her say in Latin, *Vidi arcana Dei*—'I have seen the secrets of God.' She added nothing to this phrase, but continually repeated, 'I have seen the secrets of God.' Long after, when she was restored to herself, she still repeated the same words. I wished to know the reason. 'Mother,' I said to her, 'why, pray, do you constantly repeat the same words, and not explain them by speaking to us as usual?' 'It is impossible for me,' said she, 'to say anything else, or to say otherwise.' 'But why? you are accustomed to tell us what God has revealed to you when we do not interrogate you, why do you decline answering when we inquire of you?' 'Were I to try and express to you what I saw,' she replied, 'I should reproach myself as guilty of vain words: it seems to me that I should blaspheme God and dishonour Him by my language. The distance is so vast between what my spirit contemplated, when ravished in God, and everything I could

---

[1] Process, 1346.

describe to you, that I feel I should be deceiving you in speaking of these things. I must therefore not attempt their description; all that I can say is, that I saw ineffable things!'"

To these statements we must add one narrative which is given at length by Raymund. He gives no date, but the occurrence evidently belongs to the earlier period of his acquaintance with the Saint. It chanced one morning that Catherine having expressed a great desire to communicate, he went to the church to prepare for Mass, but in the meanwhile, being overwhelmed with an unusual increase in the pain in her side and other infirmities, she sent one of her companions to beg him as a charity to defer doing so for a little while, when she hoped to be sufficiently well to be able to come to the church. "I cheerfully consented," he says, "and went to the choir, where, after reciting my office, I continued to wait. Meanwhile Catherine had come to the church unknown to me, about the hour of Tierce; but her companions seeing that it was late, persuaded her not to communicate that day, for they knew that after Communion she would remain some hours in ecstasy and so cause murmurs, and a great trouble to the brethren who must wait so long a time to shut the church doors. With her usual humility and readiness to obey the will of others, she did not presume to oppose their wishes; nevertheless, she took refuge in prayer, and kneeling at a bench placed at the further end of the church, she entreated her Divine Spouse that since men could not accomplish the desire He had put into her heart, He would Himself in some measure be pleased to satisfy it. Almighty God, Who never despises the prayer of His servants, deigned to hear her in a wonderful manner. I was ignorant of what had passed, and believed her to be at home, when one of the Sisters came to me and told me that Sister Catherine begged me not to delay any longer saying my Mass, as it had been agreed that she should not communicate that day.

"I went at once, therefore, to vest in the Sacristy, and said Mass at the altar of St. Paul at the upper end of the church. Catherine was thus separated from me the whole length of the building, and I was entirely ignorant of her being there. After the consecration and the *Pater Noster* I proceeded, according to the rubrics, to divide the Host. At the first fraction, the sacred Host, instead of separating into two portions, divided into three, two large and one small, which seemed to me about the length of a bean, but not so wide. This particle, which I attentively observed, appeared to fall on the corporal by the side of the chalice above which I had broken the Host; I clearly saw it descend towards the altar, but I could not afterwards distinguish it on the corporal. Presuming that it was the whiteness of the corporal which prevented my discerning this particle, I broke off another, and after saying the *Agnus Dei*, consumed the Sacred Host. As soon as my right hand was at liberty, I felt on the corporal for the particle on the spot where it had fallen ; but I found nothing. Much troubled, I went on with the Mass, and having finished the Communion, I renewed my search, examining the corporal in every possible way, but could discover nothing either by sight or touch. This afflicted me even to tears; but on account of those present, I resolved to finish the Mass, and afterwards carefully to examine the altar. So when every one had withdrawn I minutely examined, not only the corporal, but every part of the altar, but could discover nothing. As I stood before a large picture, it seemed impossible that the particle could have fallen behind the altar; nevertheless, for greater certainty, I looked on both sides and on the floor, but still with no result. I then determined to go and consult the Prior of the convent, and covering the altar, desired the Sacristan to allow no one to approach it till my return.

"I retired to the Sacristy, but had scarcely taken off my vestments when F. Christopher, Prior of the Carthusians, arrived. I knew him well, and had a great esteem for him : his object in coming was to beg me to obtain an interview for him with Catherine. I entreated him to wait a minute while I went and spoke with the Prior, but he replied, 'To-day is a solemn feast with us, and I must absolutely return at once to the monastery, which is, as you know, some distance from the city : I beg of you, therefore, do not detain me, for I must speak with Catherine.'

So I bade the Sacristan stay and watch the altar till my return, and went with the good Prior as far as Catherine's house. There, to my surprise, they told me that she had gone to our church, and had not yet returned. We at once went back, and I found Catherine and her companions kneeling at the far end of the church. I asked one of them where she was; they replied that she was kneeling on one of the benches in an ecstasy, and as I was still troubled at the accident that had occurred, I begged of them to do what they could to rouse her, as we were in great haste. They obeyed, and when we were seated with the Prior, I told her my anxiety in a low voice and in few words. She smiled gently, and replied, just as if she had known all the particulars, 'Did you not search for it diligently?' On my answering that I had done so, 'Why, then, are you so troubled?' she said, and again she smiled. I already felt more tranquil, and said, 'Mother, I verily believe it was *you* who took that consecrated particle.' 'Nay, Father,' she replied, 'do not accuse me of that; it was not me, but *Another;* all I can tell you is, you will never find it again. Then I pressed her to explain what had happened. 'Father,' she said, 'trouble yourself no more about that particle; I will tell you the truth as to my spiritual father; it was brought to me by our Divine Lord Himself. My companions urged me not to communicate this morning in order to avoid certain murmurs. I was unwilling to be troublesome to any one, but I had recourse to our Lord; and He deigned to appear, and gave me with His own Sacred Hands that particle which you had consecrated. Rejoice, therefore, with me, for I have this day received a grace for which I can never sufficiently thank Him!' Her words did indeed turn my sadness into joy, and I no longer experienced the slightest anxiety."[1]

It is perhaps desirable to give a passage from the Saint's own writings, in which she speaks of some of these supernatural favours; as it will greatly assist us in rightly comprehending matters most difficult to render into ordinary language, yet regarding which her own utterances are as exact as they are sublime.

[1] Legend, Part 2, ch. xii.

It occurs in her Dialogue, and the words are spoken as in the Person of the Eternal Father:

"Beloved daughter, open the eye of your intellect, and behold the benefit which you receive in this Sacrament. With what eye can you behold and touch this mystery? Not with mere bodily sight and touch; for here the bodily senses fail. For the eye indeed beholds only the whiteness of the Bread, the hand touches, and the taste discerns nothing else but Bread; so that the grosser senses of the body are deceived, but the senses of the soul cannot be deceived. It is those senses which taste and see and touch the Blessed Sacrament. What is the eye that sees? The eye of the Intellect, the pupil of which is Holy Faith. That eye beholds, under the whiteness of the Bread, all God and all Man; the Divine Nature united to the Human Nature, the Body, the Blood, and the Soul of Christ; the Soul united to the Body, and the Body and the Soul united to My Divine Nature, not apart from Me; as you may remember, in the beginning of your life I manifested to you, not only to the eye of your intellect only, but also to that of your body:[1] although by reason of the great light the bodily eye lost its powers of vision, and the sight of the intellect alone remained. I showed it to you to deliver you from the attack which the enemy brought against you on the matter of this Sacrament, and to make you increase in love for It, in the light of Holy Faith. For you remember how, going one morning to the church at break of day to hear Mass, having been before much tormented by the enemy, you placed yourself before the altar of the Crucifix, and the priest came to the altar of Mary. And reflecting on your sins, you feared lest you had offended Me by reason of the trouble which the demon had caused you; and you thought of My charity whereby you had been counted worthy to

---

[1] These words may seem a contradiction to those previously quoted from Caffarini. But, as will be seen, she presently adds that the corporal sight failed before these stupendous revelations, and that that of the intellect alone remained. If any would argue from this that visions unseen by the bodily eye are no visions at all, we must refer them to St. Theresa for the explanation of a subject which cannot be measured by the perceptions of flesh and blood.

hear that Mass, whereas you reputed yourself as unworthy so much as to enter My Temple. When the priest was about to consecrate, you raised your eyes, and as he pronounced the sacred words, I manifested Myself to you. And you saw coming forth from My Breast a light like the rays of the sun which proceed from the body of the sun, yet without separating from its disc; and in the Light a Dove, all united one with the other, and It smote into the Host, in virtue of the words of Consecration. Then, because your bodily eye could not sustain that light, the eye of your intellect alone remained able to gaze on it, and with it you saw and tasted the Abyss of the Holy Trinity; all God and all Man, hidden and veiled under the whiteness of the bread. And you saw that neither the Light, nor the presence of the Word which intellectually you beheld there, took away the whiteness of the bread; the one did not prevent or interfere with the other; neither the beholding of God and Man in the bread, nor the beholding of the bread, which lost nothing either of its whiteness, or its touch, or its savour." (*Dial. ch.* cxi.)

In another place, after saying that " the soul must make the place of its abode in Christ Crucified, *dwelling and hiding itself in the Cavern of His Side; and finding in His opened Heart the love of God and of our neighbour*," she goes on to speak of an occasion when the sweet odour of the Blessed Sacrament remained sensible to her for many days after receiving.[1]

She also relates how on one of those many occasions when, having asked to communicate, she had been refused by the priest who was about to celebrate, his heart was touched with compunction, and before the end of the Mass he bade her approach. On another occasion, of which she speaks, her longing desires for the Bread of life were satisfied, not by man, but by God. It was on the feast of the Conversion of St. Paul; and having a great desire to communicate on that day in honour of the Apostle so specially dear to her, she was refused in succession by every priest who came to celebrate, God so permitting it that she might know that if men failed her He would not. When the

[1] Dialogo, chap. cxxiv.

last Mass came, she humbly made known her wish to the server, but he would not so much as tell the priest. So when the Mass was over and she remained with the hunger of her soul unsatisfied, Almighty God drew her to Himself in an ineffable manner, so that her soul being united and drawn to Him, her body remained suspended in the air; and in this ecstasy she was communicated in a miraculous manner; and in token of the fact, she was conscious of the same delicious savour which she so often experienced after Communion, and which was continued for several days.

If the reluctance exhibited by so many priests to give Communion to the Saint appears amazing, it must be borne in mind· that the practice of frequent Communion had at that time become rare; even devout persons often contented themselves with approaching the altar once a year, or, at most, at those festivals called in Tuscany "Pasque," for the term *Pasqua* was applied not to Easter alone, but to all the great festivals of our Lord, such as Christmas, the Epiphany, and the Ascension. The custom of frequent Communion, as we understand the term, was not generally revived until the sixteenth century; nevertheless, it is not to be doubted that the practice which was in use among St. Catherine's disciples of weekly Communion,[1] did much to render that devout and salutary habit more common in the Church.

She wearied not of warning her disciples against the delusive humility that would excuse itself from Communion through pretended unworthiness, instead of seeking to render itself worthy. "I say rather," she writes to Ristoro Canigiani, "that we must receive that sweet Sacrament because it is the food of our souls, for without that food we cannot preserve the life of grace. A man should do what he can to remove such things as would hinder his approach; and when he has done all he can, it is enough. It may seem to him that he has not perfect contrition or other dispositions, but he is not to stay away on that account, for his good-will is sufficient, and that is the real disposition

---

[1] See letter 281, addressed to Neri Landoccio : "Be not negligent in prayer, and go to Communion every Sunday."

required of him. I will not therefore have you act like those who neglect to fulfil the precepts of the Church because, as they say, they are not worthy. And so they pass years in mortal sin, and never receive the food of their souls. Oh, what a foolish sort of humility is this! Who does not see that you are not worthy? And when do you expect to become so? You will not be more fit at the end than at the beginning. All the good we could do would never in that sense render us worthy. God alone is worthy of Himself, and He can render us worthy by His own worthiness which never diminishes." [1]

To the same effect she writes to her disciple, Andrea Vanni, in a letter, wherein she speaks not only of the necessity of actual, but of the benefit of spiritual, Communion. The passage is every way remarkable, and may be quoted as a fair specimen of her vigorous style of practical instruction. "You should often wash your soul from every stain of sin by a good and holy confession, feeding it on the Bread of Angels, that is, the sweet Sacrament of the Body and Blood of Jesus Christ, all God and all Man; which every faithful Christian is bound to receive at least once a year. He who desires It oftener may receive It oftener, but not less often; and for no cause may any man entirely neglect it, be he just or a sinner; for if the sinner be not fitly disposed for it, he must make himself fit. If he be just, he must not abstain out of humility, saying, "I am not worthy of so high a mystery; when I am worthy I will communicate." Not so, for of his own merits he will never be worthy, and if he thought himself so, that would suffice to make him unworthy, for pride would conceal itself under the mantle of humility. God alone is capable of making us worthy, and it is clad in His worthiness that we must receive Him. And observe that there are two ways in which we may communicate—actually and spiritually. To communicate spiritually is to do so by true and ardent desire, and this desire ought not to exist only at the moment of Communion, but at all times and in all places; for it is a question of feeding the soul with the food which sustains the life of grace."

[1] Letter 229.

These clear and simple instructions, and the profound and admirable chapters in her Dialogue which treat of the Holy Mystery of the Eucharist, were the fruit of that interior light which she had received from God for the illumination of other souls. Caffarini tells us that the many visions and mysterious signs which were granted to her on this subject filled her with confusion and holy fear.   Her own grand and unquestioning faith demanded no such support ; and in her prayers she was wont lovingly to remon-strate with our Lord, saying, " O Lord, dost Thou then doubt the firmness of my faith?   Knowest Thou not that I believe, without doubting, all, however incomprehensible, that Thou hast revealed to Thy Church, and through her manifested to Thy faithful children?   Why then dost Thou, as it were, daily bestow on me these signs and repeated assurances, as though my faith were weak and vacillating?"   And He replied in order to console her and make her understand the object of these supernatural favours : " Not for thy sake, O my spouse and daughter! do I manifest to thee by these prodigious signs the truth of the high mystery of My Sacrament ; but for the sake of others, that they, by thy means, may be confirmed in faith."

Catherine understood from these words what God demanded of her ; and in all her dealings with the souls of others, there was no one thing that was nearer her heart than to cherish and increase their faith and devotion towards this tremendous Mystery.   Hence the anguish of her soul when she beheld priests, "the Ministers of the Blood," living in a manner unworthy of their sacred calling. Those who are familiar with her Dialogue will have no difficulty in recalling her words on that subject.   But her apostolate was one not merely of words, but of self-sacrifice, and one instance must here be given of her astonishing generosity, in offering her-self to suffer in order to procure the deliverance of another soul from temptation.

" There was a certain priest," says Caffarini,[1] " who in the act of celebrating was accustomed to feel such trouble and sadness, that he had resolved to abstain in future from offering the Holy Sacrifice.

[1] Sup., Part 2, Trat. 6, § 2.

Catherine became aware of his unhappy and foolish resolution, so she contrived that he should come to her, and addressed him, saying, 'I beg of you on no account to give up celebrating the Holy Mass; do not think any more of your troubles, but throw all the weight of them on my shoulders.' From that time the afflicted priest found himself entirely free from his interior disquietude, and resumed his former habit of celebrating with perfect tranquillity of mind. But at the very same moment that he felt himself relieved of his trial, Catherine experienced within herself the same sentiments of weariness and disgust for all things connected with the Divine service; but she accepted these sufferings with heroic charity, and with invincible vigour of soul endured and overcame them, gaining a glorious victory; and she often repeated, in thanksgiving for her own delivery as for that of the soul to whose rescue she had come, 'Oh, how loving and merciful is God to those who hope in Him!'"

It will have been observed that in her instructions to her disciples, Catherine does not omit to recommend the practice of spiritual Communion. She knew its value, and the immense graces which it may be the means of conveying to the soul, by her own experience; for at times when she was hindered from actually approaching the Holy Table, she often made use of this means to satisfy her desires; and not unfrequently these spiritual Communions were attended by circumstances no less wonderful than her actual Communions. On one occasion when the extreme weakness to which she was reduced rendered it impossible for her to set her foot outside her chamber, being thus prevented from going to the church, she resigned herself to the will of God, and began instead to pray in her cell; but she had hardly recollected herself for that purpose, when she seemed to be carried to some place, disposed like a lofty and beautiful sanctuary. She beheld assembled there a great multitude of the saints, who seemed to be assisting at a majestic function, wherein the Holy Sacrifice was offered by one clad like a Bishop, at an altar brilliant with light and magnificent in its adornments, while all around was to be heard the melody of a heavenly chant. When the moment for Communion came, the Celebrant seemed to administer to her the Sacred Host. She understood that this Communion was only spiritual, not actual; nevertheless, as she afterwards declared, she experienced the same interior sweetness of grace, neither more nor less, as she was accustomed to receive in her other Communions.

These are but a few out of the abundant notices which we possess of that which was the heart and centre of St. Catherine's spiritual life; her daily, or all but daily, reception of the Body of her Lord. To her, as to all the saints, the Divine Sacrament was the Life of her life; in her history more remarkably made evident from the fact that she lived in times when, if the faith of men remained unclouded, their charity had grown cold, and the greatest privilege of the Christian soul was for the most part neglected. Among her own disciples, and those whom they in their turn influenced and directed, she may be said *to have revived the custom of frequent Communion*, and this is perhaps not the least title which she possesses to our gratitude and veneration.

CHAPTER IV.

ROCCA D'ORCIA.

IN various parts of the Legend we find allusions to a visit paid by Catherine to the castle of Rocca d'Orcia, one of the strongholds of the Salimbeni family, whose name has so often recurred in the foregoing pages. But whilst relating some of the incidents of this visit, Raymund gives us no information either as to its causes, or the time when it took place. Happily ample materials are to be found in the Process, and in the letters of the Saint, which enable us to set before the reader in a complete form what is undoubtedly one of the most interesting episodes in her life; but to render the story, and the letters which illustrate it more intelligible, we must begin by saying a few words on the family whose members were brought into such close contact with Catherine.

The Salimbeni ranked from very early times among the most powerful lords of Tuscany. The Sienese chroniclers are never weary of extolling their valour, their prudence, and their noble ancestry. A Salimbeni was found in the ranks of those Crusaders who fought with Boemond under the walls of Antioch. Agnolino Avolo Salimbeni was reckoned the richest noble in Italy, and was chosen Captain, or chief ruler of Orvieto. His son, John Agnolino Salimbeni, was head of the Ghibelline, or Imperial party in Siena; "A great and illustrious man," says Malevolti, "who served his country well." For ten years he had exercised such power in the Republic, as to be regarded almost as Lord of the city of Siena. Of the part taken by the family during the Revolution of 1368, we have already spoken; nor would it be fair to allow the fact of their acting as heads of the Ghibelline faction in Siena to prejudice us against them, as though this necessarily implied that they were disloyal to the Holy See. It implied merely that they were opposed to the democracy which had seized exclusive possession of the government, and that they sought, under the protection of the Emperor, to regain for the aristocratic class a certain share of political power. As chiefs of this faction there existed a strong rivalry between them and the Tolomei, who were regarded as the leaders of the Guelphs; and the feud between the two families was promoted in every possible way by the Heads of the republican government, who trusted by this unworthy policy to paralyse the power of both great families. In the petty wars which followed the Revolution, the Salimbeni incurred immense losses; but after peace had been restored through the mediation of the Florentines, they succeeded in winning back a considerable degree of popular confidence, and resumed something of their former footing in the state.

Catherine, as we have seen, devoted herself energetically to the extinction of the party feuds which had either grown out of these unhappy contentions, or been fostered by them to yet more dangerous proportions; and it was probably in the course of such charitable labours that she became introduced to the Salimbeni, though the particulars of their first acquaintance have not been preserved. However it originated, it soon ripened into a friendship in which every member of the family had a share. John Agnolino Salimbeni, of whom mention has been made above, died the year previous to the Revolution, in consequence of a fall from his horse, as he was riding from Siena to Rocca d'Orcia. He left behind him his widow, the Countess Bianchina (a member of the noble house of the Trinci, lords of Foligno), and three children; Agnolino, who succeeded him, and two daughters, Benedetta and Isa. Isa was the widow of Paul Trinci of Foligno: Benedetta had likewise been twice espoused; her first husband dying shortly after their marriage, while the second did not live to complete his nuptials. Agnolino showed himself a wise and valiant man, and took part in many affairs of importance; but besides having suffered much during the troubles of the Revolution and in his feud with the Tolomei, he had to defend himself against his own kinsman Cione Salimbeni, whose restless ambition was always causing trouble. The immediate cause of their present quarrel was the fact that Agnolino, desirous of reconciling himself with the government of the republic, had caused himself to be enrolled among the plebeian families, and had favoured the popular cause; receiving from the Magistrates in token of their restored confidence the castles of Monte Giovi, Montorio, Castiglione di Val d'Orcia, Rocca Federighi, and some others. This aroused the jealousy of Cione, and threatened to cause the outbreak of a fresh feud between the two kinsmen. In Catherine's correspondence with the different members of the family, references are made to all these circumstances. To the Countess Bianchina she writes as to a dear friend and disciple, while the two daughters looked to her for advice and support in their home difficulties. Isa in her widowhood desired to take the habit of Penance, and Benedetta wished to leave the world altogether and retire to a convent. Both proposals were exceedingly distasteful to their brother, with whom Catherine undertook to plead their cause, encouraging them meanwhile to persevere in their holy purposes. She seems to have been successful in clearing away the obstacles which opposed themselves to Isa's design; for in a Brief of Urban VI., granting a Plenary Indulgence in the hour of death to fifty Tertiaries of St. Dominic, and dated March 29th 1380, the name of "Isa, daughter of John Agnolino," heads the list. Two of the Saint's letters to Benedetta are preserved, in which she refers in a very touching manner to the profound experience of the nothingness of earthly joys which had been brought home to the young Countess by her successive bereavements. "The soul that loves and serves the world," she says, "is like a leaf tossed about with the wind; it is made subject to things that are infinitely beneath it. I would not have you subject to such a slavery, but would rather desire to see you the servant of Jesus Crucified, Whose service is perfect sweetness. Oh, love this sweet and glorious Spouse Who can never die! Other spouses die and pass away like the wind. You know the truth of what I say, for in a brief space of time the world has struck you two terrible blows; and God in His goodness permitted it to be so, that you might fly from the world, and take refuge in Him." She concludes by encouraging her to respond to the call of God, and lets us know that Benedetta's design was to enter the Community that was to be established at Belcaro. "The buildings are already begun, and they are hurrying on the works. It is to be called the Monastery of Our Lady of Angels; if you come thither you will enter the promised land."

She next addresses herself to "her son Agnolino," as she calls him, whom she bids to combat with his spiritual foes like a gallant knight who does not fear hard blows. And she warns him that the door by which the enemy will be most apt to enter his soul is the love of the world and its honours. This was probably the exact truth; for Agnolino had it greatly at heart to revive the former splendour and prosperity of his family, and was struggling hard to retrieve its misfortunes, and win back the favour of his countrymen. Catherine did not condemn the course he was taking in public affairs, which seems to have been honourable and worthy of praise; but she saw the danger to his soul which lurked in all these things, and did not fail to give him an affectionate word of warning. "When the enemy would enter by the love of the world and its honours," she says, "open your understanding, and see that there is neither stability nor duration in anything that the world can give. You know it well; you have seen it, you have proved it. Oh, how I long that you should understand that it is not by giving ourselves up to these passing and perishable things that we attain to glory, but often rather to disgrace. For they are all less than we; and if we would attain true honour and greatness, we must love and serve something greater than ourselves. God alone, our Father, the Sovereign and Eternal Goodness, deserves to be so loved and served; all things else are less than man. To despise the world is to be truly rich and honourable, though men think just the contrary. I know all that is being said; and that the Countess (Benedetta) is well tormented on all sides because she wishes to be the servant of the servants of Jesus Christ. Worldly persons seek to persuade her and you to regard *that* as base and disgraceful which is the greatest honour you can receive; an honour not for time, but for eternity. Before God and men your glory will surpass that of all your ancestors. Fools that we are to set our love and hope on a little heap of straw! There was a great blaze at her first espousals, but it soon disappeared, and nothing remained but the smoke of sorrow. Then it seemed as though the fire was about to be rekindled, but it was again extinguished by the cold blast of death. Far better for her and for you that she should obey the call of the Holy Spirit. For you see, the world rejects her, and casts her on Christ Crucified. I do hope, then, that you will not let yourself be influenced by its judgments: impose silence on your vassals; forbid their murmurs, and show yourself firm. To act otherwise would be cowardice unworthy of a brave cavalier. This is why I said I hoped I should see you fight bravely in this new combat that you have to sustain on the subject of the Countess. The devil sees that he is going to lose her, and so he stirs up creatures to torment you. But have courage; despise the opinion of the world, and God will be with you." (Letter 267.) Only one letter is preserved addressed to the Countess Bianchina; it breathes the same spirit, and is written in much the same style. After warning her friend that we cannot serve two masters, and that the heart that desires to be full of God must necessarily first empty itself of the world, Catherine continues: "We go on always forming new attachments; if God cuts off one branch, we make another. We fear to lose perishing creatures more than to lose God. And so keeping them and possessing them against the will of God, we taste even in this life the foretaste of hell: for God so permits that a soul which loves itself with irregular love should become insupportable to itself. It suffers from everything that it possesses because it fears to lose it; and to preserve what it possesses, there is anxiety and fatigue day and night. And it suffers from what it does not possess, because it desires what it cannot get. And so the soul is never at rest in the midst of the things of this world, for they are all less than us; they were made for us, we were not made for them. We were made for God alone, to enjoy His Eternal and Sovereign happiness.

"God alone, then, can satisfy the soul; and all that it can desire it will find in Him. The soul in Him finds peace, for He is He who is the Supreme Riches, the Supreme Power, the Supreme Goodness, the Supreme Beauty, an Ineffable Good which none can rightly appreciate; He alone can comprehend and value Himself. He both can and will satisfy all the holy desires of a soul that desires to strip itself of the world, and to be clothed with Him. Shake off your slumber then, my dearest mother, for the hour of death approaches nearer and nearer. I would have you use all these passing and temporal things as something lent, but not really belonging to you. The way to attain to this is by detaching your heart from them, and this we must do if we would be sharers in the fruit of the Blood of Jesus." (Letter 331.)

These extracts are sufficient to show on what terms Catherine stood with the family of Salimbeni. We will now proceed to unravel the narrative of her visit to Rocca in the autumn of 1377, though it appears probable that this was by no means the only occasion on which she was their guest. In that year a quarrel had broken out, as has been already stated, between Agnolino and Cione Salimbeni. Cione resided at Castiglioncello del Trinoro; and Agnolino at Rocca di Tentennano, now called Rocca d' Orcia. Stricca, the wife of Cione, was also a friend and correspondent of Catherine's, who thus had influence with both the contending parties. The castles of the two kinsmen were about ten miles apart; and (as it would seem), at the request of the noble ladies of the family, Catherine undertook to negotiate the terms of their reconciliation. For greater convenience she first took up her residence at Montepulciano, as being a spot equidistant from both castles, the three places forming a kind of triangle.

Catherine, as we know, was no new guest at Montepulciano. On this occasion she was accompanied by a considerable number of her disciples, both men and women ; among others by Raymund of Capua, F. Thomas della Fonte, F. Bartholomew Dominic, Stephen Maconi, and Don Francis Malevolti ; F. Thomas Caffarini afterwards joined them, coming from Orvieto. There were also F. Matthew Tolomei, the hermit Fra Santi, and several of the Saint's female companions, such as Alexia, Lisa, Cecca, and others. It seems to have been at this time that in the midst of her hard and troublesome negotiations, the peace and tranquillity of the convent enclosure almost gained her heart. " Do you know," she says, writing to Agnes, Donna Malevolti, who after her husband's death had entered among the Sisters of Penance, " I feel half disposed to say, ' Let us make here three tabernacles,' for it seems to me a real paradise to be with these holy religious. They all love us so much, they are hardly willing to let us depart. As to Cecca, she is already half a nun, for she begins to say the office well, in choir with the nuns." (Letter 183.) However, very different duties awaited her from the sweet chanting of the office, and the charms of regular life which she knew so well how to appreciate. Her first expedition was to Castiglioncello, where she was well received by Cione Salimbeni, and found no difficulty in inducing him to come to terms of peace. The next matter was to obtain the like compliance from Agnolino ; and for that purpose Catherine set out for Rocca d'Orcia. " The spot so called," writes Jerome Gigli, in his Preface to the Saint's letters, " stands above the valley of the Orcia, about twenty-three miles distant from Siena, and may be seen by travellers from the Roman road, standing on a sharp and steep rock projecting from the mountain side. The olives flourish here better than anything else that is cultivated. Fitly might a column be erected on this mountain path warning pilgrims to salute that rugged rock where the Dove of Siena brought the olive of peace ! Truly was that rock terrible to Lucifer, discomfited there by the saintly virgin who drove him from the bodies and souls he had so long possessed ! "

The river Orcia, from which the valley takes its name, is one of those many mountain streams which flow into the Ombrone, and divides the hill on which Montalcino stands from the loftier group of Cetona, Radicofani, and Monte Amiata. These are the three highest mountains in the vicinity of Siena, and the scenery among their savage ravines is exceedingly grand. From their summit, and specially from that of Monte Amiata, may be seen the long range of the Apennines, and the whole extent of the Tuscan Maremma. The Roman Campagna also appears in the southern distance ; while to the west is the blue expanse of the Mediterranean, studded with its islands. Even in our own day it is a wild and savage region, and only a century ago, when the celebrated botanist, Peter Antonio Micheli, undertook his scientific journey through the territory of Siena, he found no small difficulty in forcing a way over these mountains ; the thickets of beeches which grow out of the fissures of the rocks on Monte S. Fiora preventing the passage of his horse. It may well be imagined, therefore, that in St. Catherine's time these rocky fastnesses were still more difficult of access, and the prospect of a residence in the stronghold of a mountain chieftain might not have been without its terrors to a less fearless soul. The wild soldiery who gathered around the castles of these chieftains, and formed their garrisons, were little better than banditti, and had spent their lives in murderous feuds, which scarcely deserved the name of civil wars. Among these rude warriors the holy maiden of Siena now came to speak of peace and brotherly love ; strange words which sounded in their ears like an unknown tongue, for the comprehension of which they needed, as it were, new faculties. Long habits of ruthless violence, long years spent without prayer or sacraments, had hardened their hearts and obscured their understandings. The Evil One had indeed laid his grasp on these poor souls, and seemed to claim their wild and desolate region as his own ; and he was to be dispossessed, and rudely put to flight by her, whose fragile form might have been seen one August evening ascending the mountain path that led to the castle, mounted on her little ass,[1] and surrounded by her faithful disciples.

---

[1] *Secondo lei, sopra un asinello.* (Leg., Part 3, ch. vi.)

She was affectionately received both by Agnolino and his mother, who is described as "a lady of great virtue and talent, and most devout to the Saint." Through her influence Catherine found no difficulty in effecting the chief object of her mission; and the reconcilation of the two kinsmen was happily secured. Such an example was not lost on their neighbours, and other lords and chieftains were led to lay down their quarrels at Catherine's feet, so that she was detained for more than four months in these parts, appeasing discords, and restoring peace to many an unhappy family. At the mere sight of her the fiercest hearts were pacified, and the influence of her sanctity and eloquence was greatly increased by the wonders God was pleased to work through her means.

Of some of these a very exact and interesting account has been left by Don Francesco Malevolti, and as his narrative has never yet been published, certain portions of it shall be here extracted, which are the more valuable as being the testimony of an eyewitness. After relating the circumstances which led to Catherine's coming into these parts, and the extraordinary success of her mission, he continues : "The Countess Bianchina bore so great a reverence for the holy virgin that she took care to keep near her day and night. And as her fame for holiness spread far and near, it happened one day that there came a crowd of men, twelve or fourteen in number, from a certain village called Rocca Strada. They had with them a mare, on which was a man bound with many ropes, and with iron shackles on his hands and feet. He was so full of rage and fury, that no one dared approach him, for he tore with his teeth any person who came near him, and his screams and bellowings were rather infernal than human. So these men brought him thus bound to Agnolino's fortress, that they might lay him at the feet of Catherine. When they had entered the court of the castle they laid down the demoniac, bound as he was, with no small fear; which being done, two of those who had brought him went to the place where the Lady Bianchina was in company with Catherine, and drawing the Countess apart, they spoke to her in secret. Then she returned, and addressing

Catherine in coaxing words, 'My sweetest Mamma,' she said (for by this name of *Mamma* they all called her), 'let us go away from hence.' 'Mother,' replied Catherine, with great humility, 'I know very well that this is not the hour when you wish to depart hence; nevertheless, when the hour comes, I will obey your commands.' In fact, she knew perfectly well what the noble lady wished her to do. But after the Countess had, on various pretences, urged her to come, and Catherine, on the other hand, had as repeatedly declined, overcome at last by so many entreaties, as one who knew not how to refuse anything that was asked of her, she bowed her head, and left the room with the Lady Bianchina, and we others followed them, to the number of more than sixteen persons. We all went out into the court where the demoniac lay, still bound; who, when he saw the holy virgin Catherine, uttered such terrific yells that we all remained terrified. Then he rolled on the ground, making unspeakably hideous gestures; and if he had not been bound with many cords, some of the bystanders would have been in no small danger. When the holy virgin beheld him so behaving, she turned to the Countess, saying, 'O lady! what has this poor man done that they have so bound him? For the love of God, bid them loose him, that he may not be thus tortured.' But the Countess replied, 'These men are greatly afraid of him; for with his teeth, and in every way that he can, he attacks those who come near him. Command, however, what you will regarding him, and they will at once do it.' So with many sweet words the holy virgin entreated the men, saying, 'My dearest brothers, do not suffer this creature of God to be thus put to pain; loose him, for there is nothing at all the matter with him, and then, for the love of God, give him some refreshment.' Then they replied, 'O lady! we have hitherto greatly feared him, for he has shockingly maltreated some of our people; nevertheless, we are ready to obey your commands, provided you will engage on no account to depart from us.' So Catherine not only remained there, but drew several paces nearer to the prisoner, and desired them to loose him in the name of Jesus Christ. When she had thus spoken, the man who before seemed like a fierce wild beast, became quite quiet, and stretched himself on the ground like one dead. The men approached, not without fear, and loosed him from his bonds; they also drew the shackles from his hands and feet, and still he made not the smallest movement. Then said the virgin, 'Now, raise him up and give him some food, for he is suffering from nothing but weakness; and you will see that when he is refreshed with food, he will no longer appear the same man.' So they raised him up, and gave him food and drink; and having fully returned to his senses, he was utterly astonished to find himself in that place, and remembered nothing of all that had passed. Humbly commending himself to Catherine, therefore, she made over him the sign of the Cross, and he departed on foot with all the company who had brought him thither, in perfect health, and was never more troubled in the same manner.

"Another man was brought to the same castle from one of the other fortresses of Agnolino. He was possessed by many wicked spirits, and those who brought him feigned that they were taking him in another direction. But the evil spirits perceiving that they were being conducted into the presence of their great adversary, as soon as they drew near the castle caused him to speak with great rage and violence, saying, 'You want to take me to that cruel enemy of mine who is always persecuting me wherever I go. But I promise you this journey shall cost every one of you dear.' Then as he was still crying out in this way, they entered the castle court. Now the Countess Bianchina was in a certain chamber of the castle with Catherine and others of both sexes, of whom I was one. The demoniac, therefore, was brought into our presence bellowing with fury, and entered the room in a very terrible manner;—nevertheless, as soon as he was there, he sprang out of the hands of those who held him, and fell prostrate at the feet of Catherine, who, according to her custom, was sitting on the ground. From that moment he spake no word, small or great, but lay as if dead. Then the holy virgin compassionating him in her heart, began to weep, and taking his head, she supported it on her bosom, whilst we stood round silent and attentive to watch the end. But after the holy virgin had lifted her eyes to heaven, her face became all shining and radiant, whilst she silently conversed with the Eternal Spouse. Then we suddenly beheld coming forth from the form of the demoniac, as he lay on her lap, such a vast multitude of lice that it was a marvel to behold, and they went hither and thither over her garments. We, beholding the exterior but not the interior, began to say, 'O mother! remove this man from us; see you not he is covering us with lice?' But gently and devoutly smiling, she replied, 'Be not uneasy, they will not stay long;' and indeed after a short space they all disappeared, so that not so much as one of them was to be seen. Then Catherine addressing him who still lay on her lap, said, 'Arise, dear brother, and be comforted, thou shalt suffer no evil, but only a little bodily weakness.' So, causing a loaf to be brought to her, and wine, she with her own holy hands made sop in the wine, and gave it him to eat. And so being strengthened and fully delivered, he returned home on foot with his companions, praising God."

To these narratives of Don Francesco we must add the one given by Raymund in his Legend, which becomes more intelligible when we understand the circumstances which brought Catherine into these parts, and the affairs in which she was engaged. It happened that during her stay at Rocca, one of the women of the castle was suddenly seized and tormented by the Evil Spirit, whose rage was excited in a very special manner against all those who took part with Catherine in her charitable mission. The Countess, knowing how greatly averse she was to have any such cases brought to her, took counsel with the Saint's companions, and by their advice had the poor woman brought unexpectedly into her presence, trusting that the pitiful sight would suffice to move her to compassion. Catherine was just on the point of starting for a place where she had appointed to meet two persons whom she was engaged in reconciling.

"When she beheld the wretched woman, and saw that she could by no means escape, she turned to the Lady Bianchina, and said, 'Ah, Madam! God forgive you. Know you what you have done? Know you not that I am disturbed enough by these wicked spirits, that from time to time molest mine own person; wherefore, then, do you increase my trouble by presenting others before me who are vexed with these foul fiends?' With that she turned to the woman that was possessed, and said to the wicked spirit: 'Thou malicious enemy of mankind, I charge thee, lay down thine head in this man's lap, and abide there till I come again.' She had no sooner spoken these words than the woman that was vexed laid down her head in the lap of the hermit, Fra Santi, who chanced to be present, and never moved till she came again. In the meantime, while Catherine was gone to make peace between two nobles that were at variance (whose dwelling was not far from that place), the spirit cried out by the mouth of the miserable woman, leaning her head in the hermit's lap, and said: 'Why do you hold me here? I pray you let me go, for I am very hard holden.' They that stood by made answer, saying: 'And why dost thou not go thy way? Who holdeth thee? Is not the door open?' 'Oh!' said he, 'that cursed woman hath bound me here. She holdeth me that I may not depart.' 'What woman?' said they. 'That cursed woman!' said he; and would not, or peradventure could not, name her, but after a raging manner cried out: 'That cursed creature, that cursed woman, mine enemy!' Then the hermit asked him whether he took her for his great enemy or no? 'Yea,' said he, 'the greatest that I have this day in the world.' Then those that were there present, being much disquieted with his outrageous crying, said to him: 'Hold thy peace, Catherine cometh;' meaning thereby to put him in fear, and so to cause him to cease his crying. 'No, no,' said he, 'she cometh not yet; she is in such a place;' where she was indeed. They asked him what she did there. 'What doth she?' said he; 'she is now doing a thing (as she is at all times) wherein I take small pleasure.' And with that he cried out again very sore, and said, 'Ah! why am I thus holden here?' And it was evidently seen that he never moved from that place where the holy maid charged him to abide till her coming again. At the last he said, 'Now is that cursed woman coming.' They demanded of him where she was. 'She is now,' said he, 'in such a place, and now she is gone from thence, and goeth towards such a place.' And so declared, from time to time, how she passed from place to place, until at length, when she was come to the gate of the house where they were, he said, 'Now, she is come.' When she had entered the house, and began to come towards the chamber wherein they awaited her return, he cried out with a loud voice and said, 'Ah! why hold ye me here by force?' The holy maid made answer and said, 'Arise, wretch, and get thee hence, and leave this creature of God, and from this hour forward see that thou never be so hardy as once to molest her again.' And with that it was seen that the wicked fiend forsook all the other parts of that woman's body, and gathered himself into her throat, where he made such a horrible swelling that it moved as many as were present to great compassion. Then the holy maid made the sign of the Cross over the place that was swollen, and forthwith he departed from the woman, and went his way, and left the woman safe and sound, in the presence of a great many that were there, who saw this evident miracle with their eyes. Now when she was fully come to herself again, and knew the place and persons that were about her, she had great marvel, and asked some of her acquaintance what she did there and how she came thither. They made her answer, and declared unto her in what case she had been, and what had been done by the holy maid about her delivery. When she heard that, she was astonished, and said that in truth she could remember no such thing. Only this she confessed, that her body was very sore shaken and bruised, as if it had been beaten with a club. Of this evident miracle were witnesses the Lady Bianchina, the holy hermit Santi, in whose lap it was done, and more than thirty other persons."[1]

From Rocca, the Saint proceeded to the abbey of St. Anthimo, the abbot of which place, F. Giovanni di Ser Gano di Orvieto, was, as we have seen, the Commissary for the foundation of our Lady of Angels, and one of Catherine's greatest friends. St.

[1] Fen., Part 2, ch. xxxv.

Anthimo was about five miles from Montalcino, which town had formerly been subject to the abbots, but had long before this date been made over to the republic of Siena. In Catherine's time, not only was the temporal authority of the abbots lost, but their spiritual jurisdiction likewise was attacked by the Archpriests of Montalcino. The troubles arising out of these disputes appear to have had some share in bringing the Saint to St. Anthimo, and she took up her residence at the grand old abbey which then stood, with its church with three naves, in a valley between two mountains. A little later it fell into decay, and was finally suppressed by Pius II., so that as Carapelli writes in his *Corso Cronotastico*, a few shepherds only now inhabit the spot formerly peopled with monks. Catherine remained here some weeks, and it was from hence that she addressed a letter to the magistrates of Siena (Letter 201), from which we gather that murmurs had already arisen in the city in consequence of her journey. "I hear," she says, "from the Archpriest of Montalcino and others, that you have passed an unfavourable judgment on the Abbot of St. Anthimo, a great servant of God. He has been here a long time, and if you knew him better you would not suspect him. I beg of you, therefore, not to trouble him, but rather, if necessary, to assist him. You complain that priests and clerics are not corrected, and yet when you find some one willing to do it, you complain of him and raise obstacles. As to my return with my spiritual family, I am told that there are murmurs and suspicions on that score also, but I do not know if I ought to believe it. If you took as much interest in your own affairs as we do for you, you and all the citizens of Siena would close your ears to such things. We are incessantly labouring for your good, sparing ourselves no fatigue. I have so little virtue that I do nothing perfectly, but others who are better than me are doing their utmost, and the ignorance and ingratitude of our fellow-citizens will not prevent them from persevering even unto death. I love you all better than you love yourselves, and desire nothing so much as your peace and welfare; do not suppose that I, or any of my companions, can feel differently. I see that the devil is very angry at the loss of souls which he will suffer by this journey.   I have come here only to feed on souls, and withdraw them out of his hands; and for that I would sacrifice a thousand lives if I had them.   I shall go, therefore, where, and act in whatever way the Holy Spirit may inspire me.   You must not be weary of reading my letters, but bear with me patiently."

Catherine was as good as her word; in spite of the narrow-minded jealousies and reports to her disadvantage which were propagated in Siena, and which from time to time reached her ears, she remained at St. Anthimo for several weeks, and at no period of her life was the fruit of her prayers and exhortations more abundant.   Such was the concourse of those who came to see and hear her, and who flocked from all the country round, that no one who had not seen it (say the witnesses) could have believed it.   Every day they poured over the mountains, not by hundreds, but by thousands.   Raymund, in his Legend (Bk. 2, ch. vii.), has described the extraordinary scenes at which he was present, although he has omitted to tell us when and where they took place; but the omission is supplied by the agreement of his account with that of other witnesses who have been more exact as to the time and locality.   "Often," he says, "I have seen thousands of men and women hastening over the summit of the mountains and all the neighbouring country, as though summoned by the sound of some mysterious trumpet.   They came to see and hear her: her words were not required, her presence alone sufficed to convert souls and inspire them with contrition.   All wept over their sins, and accused themselves of them in the sacred tribunal of penance.   I was witness to the sincerity of their repentance, and it was evident that an extra-ordinary and abundant grace acted on their hearts."   The news of these things reaching the ears of Gregory XI., he granted to Raymund and his companions all the powers usually reserved to bishops for absolving those who presented themselves.   Besides F. Raymund, F. Bartholomew Dominic, and F. Thomas della Fonte, four other confessors were employed, and several other priests were afterwards called to assist; but even so, they could not supply the necessities of the people. For many continuous days they were occupied from dawn till nightfall, not having, like the Apostles, time so much as to eat. "I confess, to my shame," says Raymund, "that I was often tired and discouraged. But Catherine never interrupted her prayers, rejoicing in gaining so many souls to God, and only charging those who were with her to have a care for us who held the nets she knew so well how to fill. It is impossible to depict her joy ; and what we saw in her filled us with such consolation that we forgot our own fatigue."

From St. Anthimo she returned to Rocca, where they were joined by F. Thomas Caffarini. Here the same scenes continued, as he testifies in his deposition. "I came," he says, "from Orvieto to a certain castle of the Salimbeni near Siena, where the virgin then was, and spent some time with her, witnessing the wonderful fruit both of souls and bodies which our Lord wrought by her. I saw how great a number were brought by her to salutary penance, some of whom had spent forty years or more without confession, others brought to make peace, and others delivered from the power of the devil. The lady of the castle, Donna Bianchina, of the noble house of Foligno, was accustomed to say that never had she conversed with any one like her. In my journey thither I had been threatened by many dangers from thieves and other things, all which I and my companions escaped in a manner altogether miraculous, so that we doubted not we must attribute our safety to her prayers."

Peter Ventura in his deposition tells us of one instance in which her exhortations to penance were without success. "While still at Rocca," he says, "she warned a certain man that unless he repented and confessed, he would that night find himself in a place whence he would not be able to get out and return to her. The man went that night to Montalcino, where he was seized and taken to Siena, and there shortly after beheaded."

Meanwhile Catherine's unusually long absence from Siena was exciting complaints among those of her disciples whom she left behind, and in addition to her other labours she had to appease their unreasonable discontent. She writes to Catherine of the

Hospital and Jane di Capo, two of her familiar disciples, whom she had left in charge of her spiritual family : " I know, my dearest daughters, that you are afflicted at my absence, but love and obedience will dissipate your grief . . . What you have not yet done, do now, otherwise you will seriously afflict me. We must do, as the Apostles did when they had received the Holy Spirit ; they separated from each other, and from their sweet Mother Mary. We may well believe that their only happiness was to live all together, and yet they renounced that happiness, in order to seek the honour of God and the salvation of souls ; and when Mary their Mother left them, they did not think her love for them had diminished, or that they were forgotten by her. This must be the rule for us to follow. I know my presence is a consolation to you, but for God's honour and the salvation of souls you ought not to seek your own consolation, and so give an advantage to the devil, who will try and make you believe you have lost my affection. I assure you, I only love you all for God ; why, then, feel such unreasonable pain at what cannot be helped? How shall we behave on great occasions, if we are so weak in little ones ? God unites us, and He separates us, as He sees fit. He wills just now that we should all be separated for His honour. See now ; *you* are at Siena, Cecca and Nonna at Montepulciano ; F. Bartholomew and F. Matthew have gone to join you, and will stay at Siena ; Alexia and Sister Bruno are at Monte Giove, about eighteen miles from Montepulciano—they are staying there with the Countess and Donna Isa ; F. Raymund, F. Thomas, Sister Thomma, Lisa, and myself are here at Rocca among the brigands ; and we have so many incarnate demons to eat,[1] that F. Thomas pretends it gives him the stomach-ache, and nevertheless you cannot satisfy him ; they relish it more and more, and are well rewarded for all their trouble. Pray God in His goodness to give them good morsels, very sweet, and very bitter. What more could you desire ? Courage then, my daughters ; make the sacrifice of your wills to God, and do not always be crying for the milk of babes

[1] St. Catherine's favourite expression of "eating souls," on the table of the Holy Cross signifies, of course, their conversion.

when you ought, with the teeth of holy desire, to be chewing hard bread. Courage! we shall return as soon as we can, according to God's good pleasure."

Catherine was not teaching more than she herself was called on to practise. At this very time, the service of the Church was demanding of her a sacrifice than which none could be more costly. Raymund of Capua was summoned to Rome by Gregory XI., and while there, was for the second time elected Prior of the Minerva; in consequence of which he was unable to rejoin the Saint, and though he retained the title of her confessor, and directed her conscience by letter, they 'never met again in this world save for ten brief days. A letter written by her to Alexia at this time reveals something of what was passing in her soul, and contrasts singularly with the joyous playfulness of the one just quoted. Alexia, as we have just seen, was at Monte Giove, for the Saint seems to have sent her disciples in various directions, to complete and carry out the different missions of peace in which she was engaged. After giving Alexia some good advice as to her conduct she says, "Try particularly to accustom your tongue to silence; I think I have observed that your companion does not keep it very well, and that is a great grief to me. . . . You ask if I am suffering, and if I feel my usual infirmities. God provides for all, both as to the soul and body, and He has provided very well during this Advent, assuaging my suffering by letters. It is true I have suffered more than usual, but on the other hand, Lisa was cured at the same time as Fra Santi, who seemed at the point of death. It seems as if our sweet Spouse wished to give me experience both as to the interior and exterior, as to things that are seen, and things that are not seen . . . I am content that pain should be my food, and tears my drink, and sweat my perfume. Yes, let pain be my food, let pain be my medicine, let pain give me light, let pain strip me of all self-love, temporal and spiritual. The suffering I have experienced from the loss of all consolation from creatures has reminded me of my want of virtue, and made me know my own imperfection. He has not withdrawn His mercy from me, in spite of my ingratitude.

. . . Rejoice, then, on the Cross with me, for the Cross is the bed and the table of the soul, whereon she rests and takes her nourishment, even the fruit of patience in peace and repose . . . . I am here on an island where the wind blows from all quarters. Rejoice in our Jesus ; it is He who keeps us far, one from the other." (Letter 178.) The "island" she here speaks of is the "Isola della Rocca," so called apparently from its detached position. It is evident that the cross which here appears to be weighing on the Saint, by her so generously embraced, and the loss of consolation from creatures, was none other than her separation from Raymund.

But other crosses had to be borne, and among them the one most heavily felt from its injustice, namely, fresh murmurs and suspicions on the part of her fellow-citizens, who began to entertain unworthy doubts of her motives in remaining so many months in the territories of the Salimbeni. Lapa also had set out to join her daughter, but had not got farther than Montepulciano, whence she despatched her complaints to Catherine, who writes a letter conjointly to her and Cecca, who was still a guest of the Community ; and who seems in some degree to have shared in the impatience of her companion. "My dear mother and daughter," writes Catherine, "I wish I could see you both on fire with charity, otherwise you will always be suffering, and make me suffer likewise. Dearest mother, your miserable child is in this world only for one thing, and that is to do the will of her Creator. I do beg of you, if I remain here longer than you like, do not be vexed. I really cannot do otherwise, and I am persuaded if you knew the whole business, you would be the first to tell me to remain. I am here to remedy a great scandal, if I can : it is no fault of the Countess. Pray to God and Our Lady that we may succeed. And as to you, Cecca and Justina,[1] this is the moment to show your virtue. Adieu." Catherine replied in a different strain to the citizens of Siena. It is thus that she expresses herself in writing to Salvi, a goldsmith, and a person of civic authority. "It seems that some who call themselves the

---

[1] Justina was Cecca's daughter and a nun at Montepulciano.

sons of God, have taken scandal, being deluded by the devil, who is always prowling about, seeking how he can tear up the good grain sown by the Holy Spirit. The imprudent have not resisted, and under pretext of virtue have communicated what they felt to others. Now, then, I declare to you that it is the will of God I should remain here. I had a great desire not to offend Him by remaining, on account of the murmurs and suspicions of which I am the object, as well as my spiritual Father, F. Raymund. But He Who is Truth itself, reassured me saying, 'Continue to take thy food at the table where I have placed thee. I have placed thee at the table of the Cross, that in the midst of murmurs and sufferings thou mightest work for the salvation of souls; and I have confided to thee souls in this place, that they might be delivered out of the hands of the devil, and reconciled with Me, and with their neighbour. Finish, therefore, what thou hast begun. It is to hinder so much good that the enemy stirs up so much evil, but go on and fear nothing, for I will be on thy side.' These words restored my peace, and I applied myself with the more zeal to work for God's honour, the salvation of souls, and the good of our city. Negligently as I do it, yet I rejoice to follow the footsteps of my Creator. I do my fellow-citizens good, and they return me evil; I labour for their honour, and they cover me with reproaches; I desire their life, they desire my death: but death is our life, and shame our true glory; the real shame is for them who offend; where there is no fault, there need be no shame. I trust in our Lord Jesus Christ, and not in man. I shall continue therefore, and if they heap on me abuse and persecution, I shall repay them with tears and prayers, if God give me grace. Whether the devil likes it or not, I shall spend my life for God's honour and the salvation of souls, for the entire world, and above all, for my country. What a shame for the citizens of Siena to believe and imagine that we are occupied with affairs of state, either on the lands of the Salimbeni or elsewhere! My fellow-citizens are like Caiaphas who prophesied that one should die for the people, not knowing what he said. They believe that I and my companions are busy with plots, and they say truly, and prophesy as he did, not knowing what they say. We *are* plotting; we seek to triumph over the devil and take away his power, to root hatred out of all hearts, and reconcile them with God and their neighbours. These are our plots, into which I drag every one who is with me. I only complain of their negligence; we work too lazily at our business; pray to God that we may have greater zeal. For the rest, the disciple is not greater than his Master. Brother Raymund, poor calumniated Brother Raymund, recommends himself to you, and asks you to pray for him, that he may be good and patient. Adieu."

But even this was not all. In the letter to Catherine of the Hospital, quoted a few pages back, it will be remembered that she speaks of F. Matthew having gone back to Siena. This was Matthew Tolomei, a Friar Preacher, the younger brother to Francesco and Ghinocchia, and to that " Master James" who, through his young brother's persuasion, visited Catherine, and was by her converted. Their mother, Donna Rabes Tolomei, was a noble and virtuous lady, and a great friend and disciple of Catherine's. But even good persons are not always proof against the spirit of the world, and in the fourteenth century family feuds carried away many a soul otherwise eminently virtuous. The Tolomei, as we know, had long been the mortal enemies of the Salimbeni. The two families headed the rival factions of the republic, and were the Capulets and Montagues of Siena. It is therefore easy to understand how it came about that Donna Rabes lost both patience and common sense when she saw her son borne away with the other disciples of Catherine, and abiding for four long months in the territory of their hereditary enemy. She therefore addressed a letter to the Saint, which is not preserved, but we can gather its tenor from Catherine's reply. (Letter 344.)

" My dearest daughter, I wish you would conquer your sensitive self-love which takes from you the light of reason, and makes you love the world and your children beyond measure. I wish I could see you dead to yourself; but it seems to me that you are very much alive, and I see by the letter you have written that your blind love makes you quite depart from the order of God. You tell me that Francesca is ill, and that you must have Matthew return at once, spite of every obstacle; and that if he does not return, you will give him your malediction; and that if there is no other way for him to return, he is to take a peasant to accompany him. You cannot surely excuse such foolish impatience. Let us judge the matter not merely according to religious rules, but simply according to common-sense, such as we may get from nature; if you had any, you would not act as you do. If it be necessary, in order to satisfy you and your daughter, that Matthew must return, you must ask for two friars to be sent, one to go back with him, and the other to stay here, for you know very well they can none of them come or go alone. But passion blinds you, and your ears are filled with murmurs. You should have closed your ears, both you and the others, and held your tongues. so as not to hear what was said, and not to repeat it. Let there be an end of it all, and encourage Francesca to abide in the sweet love of God." Rabes, however, had her will, and Catherine, to content her, was forced to send back Matthew in company with F. Bartholomew, thus parting from one of her chief supports at a very difficult crisis.

The simplicity and natural style of the letters above quoted will be manifest to every reader. They might be written by one of ourselves, and apply as aptly to any of our own wants or infirmities as they did to those of Cecca, or Rabes Tolomei. We see by them that our Seraphic Mother was not merely the inspired prophetess raised into a region of ecstasy and vision, far above out of the reach of our sympathies and comprehension. She was a woman of like nature and passions with ourselves : she could speak our language and think our thoughts. Over her great soul there passed the same lights and shadows which chequer our little lives; and the playful gaiety of to-day is exchanged to-morrow for the sadder tone of suffering or of reproof. And yet that other life of miraculous power and of Divine favours went on all the while; never for one moment was it interrupted; never was her power with God exhibited on a more marvellous scale. It was at Rocca, as we have seen, that those many cases occurred when the devil was cast out of those whom he tormented by the word and presence of the Saint; it was at Rocca that Francesco Malevolti and many other witnesses beheld the wonders that attended her daily Communions. "I often saw her communicate," says Malevolti, "and always in ecstasy; and I beheld how, when the priest was about to give her the Body of our Lord, before he had drawn more than a palm's length near her, the Sacred Host would depart out of his hands, and like an arrow, shoot into the mouth of the holy virgin. A wise man named Anastasius of Monte Altino, also took notice of this wonderful circumstance, and introduced it into certain rhythmical verses which he composed on things appertaining to her, which he had heard and personally seen." It was at Rocca that the same witness beheld her "times innumerable," raised from the ground in ecstasy as she prayed, and remaining thus suspended in the air more than a cubit above the ground. "I, and some others," he says, "wished to make proof of this; wherefore, passing our hands between her and the floor, we satisfied ourselves that it was true, and that she was altogether lifted up from the ground.[1] Moreover, so long as I remained with her at that time, I saw that she lived on Holy Communion alone, and that no bodily food of any sort would remain within her. . . . I was with her during the whole of that time, both at Montepulciano and St. Anthimo, and in the territories of the Salimbeni, and never did I hear a vain or idle word proceed forth out of her lips."

But one great event of Catherine's residence at Rocca yet remains to be told. It was here, as we know from her own words in a letter written to Raymund, which shall presently be quoted, that *she was miraculously taught to write.* "It chanced by some accident," says Caffarini,[2] "that there fell into her hands one day a certain vessel filled with cinnabar, or *minium,* which a writer

---

[1] We read in the Process (fol. 83) that a certain nobleman having resolved to ascertain how high the Saint was raised at these times, found that there was space enough between her and the ground for him to pass under.

[2] Sup., Part I, Trat. I, § 10.

had made use of to write in red, or rather to illuminate the initial letters of a book, according to the custom of the time. The Saint moved by Divine inspiration, sat down, and taking the artist's pen in hand, though she had never learnt to form letters, or to compose words in regular metre, she wrote, in clear and distinct characters, the following verses :

> ' Spirito Santo, vieni nel mio cuore,
> Per la tua potenza tiralo a te Dio,
> Concedemi carità e timore ;
> Custodiscimi Cristo da ogni mal pensiero,
> Infiammami, e riscaldami del tuo dulcissimo amore,
> Acciò ogni travaglio mi sembri leggiero ;
> Assistenza chiedo, ed ajuto nelle necessità.
> Cristo Amore. Cristo Amore.' "

He testifies to the same fact in his deposition, and affirms that he had seen the paper written in cinnabar, which was kept as a precious relic by F. Jerome of Siena (of the Hermits of St. Augustine), and which was given by him after the Saint's death as a gift of inestimable value to Leonard Pisani, who generously bestowed it on Caffarini; and by him it was laid up with other relics of the Saint in the convent of the Sisters of Penance at Venice. Gigli made every search for the precious original, but unhappily without success. Caffarini concludes his narrative with these words, " In one of her letters to Master Raymund she tells him of the manner in which she learnt to write, which was altogether beyond the course of nature, St. John and St. Thomas Aquinas being her masters, as she attests."

We will now turn to two of the Saint's letters to Raymund, both, as we gather, written by her own hand. The first is No. 89 in Gigli's collection. It is of singular beauty, overflowing with a strain of exquisite poetry. " The soul," she says, " cannot see herself *in* herself, she can only see herself in God. She finds in Him the image of the creature, and Him in His image. She desires to love *herself* in God, and God in herself, as one who sees his image reflected in a fountain, and rejoices to see it ; but if he is wise, loves the fountain better than the image reflected there.　We can never see ourselves and the faults which disfigure the beauty of our souls unless we look into the peaceful mirror of the Divine Essence where we are represented. . . . Let us not separate, then, from our Crucified Jesus ; He is the wall over which we must lean in order to gaze at our reflection in the fountain."　And as we read the words, we almost seem to guess that in one of her expeditions along those mountain paths watered by the streams that descend into the Orcia, Catherine must so have stood, leaning over a wall, and gazing at her reflection in the crystal waters ; and that the image thus imprinted on her memory associated itself with the thought of her Lord, never absent from her mind, and reproduced itself in the page before her.　She continues : "You tell me to rejoice and be glad, and you have sent me good news, which has indeed filled me with joy.　*The day after you left me* the Sweet Truth wished to do for me what the father does for his child, and the spouse for the spouse ; he cannot bear that she should have any sorrow, but always finds some new way of filling her with joy."　Then she speaks of certain wonderful things that had passed in her soul, and of the assaults of the enemy.　"I rose, desiring to make confession to you, but the Divine Goodness no longer gave me what I asked. *I asked for you, and God gave me Himself,* granting me absolution of all my sins, and reminding me of all the lessons He had given me in other days." . . . She concludes this letter in a less exalted strain.　"I must give you news of my good Father Thomas,[1] whose virtue, thank God, has triumphed over the enemy.　He has become quite another man to what he was.　I beg of you, write to him sometimes.　Rejoice with me, for all my lost children have been found and restored to the sheepfold ; they have quitted the darkness, and now nothing hinders the fulfilment of my wishes."　In this letter nothing is said of the Saint's newly-acquired gift, but it is evidently written just after Raymund's departure, to which it refers.　The next letter (Letter 90) is a long spiritual treatise, as it were the first rough draft of the Dialogue she shortly after composed.　It concludes thus : "This letter and

---

[1] After Raymund's departure, F. Thomas again acted as her confessor.

another I have sent you (*i.e.*, the one last quoted) *I have written with my own hand in the Island of Rocca*, in the midst of sighs and so many tears, that I could not see out of my eyes. But I was full of admiration at the goodness of God and the marvels of His Providence in my regard. As my ignorance deprived me of the comfort of trusting any one, He gave me the faculty of being able to write, so that on returning from my ecstasy I might relieve my heart a little, and so prevent its bursting. He would not yet take me out of this life, and He has miraculously given me this power, as a master teaches the child for whom he sets a copy. As soon as he left me with St. John and St. Thomas Aquinas, I began to learn like one asleep. Pardon me for writing at such length, but my hand and my tongue would needs agree with my heart."

Neither of these two letters, however, was actually the first that she wrote. That was addressed to Stephen Maconi, and has unhappily been lost. Caffarini tells us this in his deposition, and also in the Supplement. " The Saint," he says, " learnt to write miraculously. One day, coming out of prayer, she wrote to Stephen Maconi a letter which ended thus, ' Know, my dear son, *that this is the first letter I have written with my own hand.*' Stephen assured me that she afterwards wrote several others, and that many pages of her book which she composed were written by her. Many of her autographs are preserved in the Chartreuse of Pontignano, near Siena."

Before leaving Rocca we must notice one other subject which has left its traces in the records of this time. We have said that Neri di Landoccio was one of those who accompanied Catherine to the castle of the Salimbeni. While there, he received two sad and terrible letters, the contents of which could not but make a profound impression on his sensitive heart. In order to explain these letters we must unfold a melancholy page in the history of St. Catherine and her spiritual family. In the midst of that group of chosen and innocent souls there was, as there had been in the company of the Apostles, an apostate—we do not know his name, for it has been carefully effaced from all records. Raymund, indeed, has told us in the Legend, the miserable story of one unhappy man who, moved by a strange malice against the holy virgin, had kicked her, cast her out of the church doors, and even attempted her life, and who a few days later was seized with frenzy and tried to commit suicide. His friends, believing his senses were gone, watched him carefully, but as he grew calmer, released their vigilance; when, escaping from their hands, he hung himself like a second Judas. This story simply reads like the account of a maniac, and we should so regard it but for the precise narrative given at length by the author of the *Miracoli*, which reveals the fact that the unhappy man was one of the Friars, who first resorted to Catherine, attracted by her holy conversation, but in process of time conceived for her a profane affection. " But she persevering in her holy life, and showing herself an utter stranger to all such sentiments, his love turned to hatred, and in his mad passion he tried to kill her in the public church, when her life was saved by a man who chanced to be present. Wherefore a few days later this man left the Order, cast off the habit of religion, and returning to his home in a village near Siena, lived there almost in despair. Catherine knew of his departure out of the Order, and always prayed God to have mercy on his soul. But at last the unhappy man, persevering in his despair, hanged himself."

The two accounts differ in several important particulars; nevertheless, it would seem most probable that they refer to the same person. And there can be little doubt that the miserable apostate, " living in his own home, almost in despair," after having once been numbered among those who listened with innocent admiration to the teaching of the Saint, must have been the writer of the two letters addressed to Neri, which he received at Rocca, and which we are now about to quote.

1.—*From F. S. to Neri di Landoccio de' Paglieresi.*

DEAREST BROTHER,—I heard how you were from Gabriel, who came to me and gave me many messages of comfort from you; for which cause and because of your extreme importunity I write; not that I had any wish to do so, yet I am moved to write in reply to your many salutations. I marvel how you can so much as re-member a wretch like me, for God knows I am become a vessel of contumely, no longer exhaling the sweet odour on which in old times I was nourished : but now I am cast out of every good way. But know that if it were with me now as in the happy old times we once had together, I could not refrain from often writing to you. But as it is, I am ashamed to write either to you or to any friend or servant of God, considering my utter misery. God preserve you in His grace, you and your Mother.   F. S.

"To Neri di Landoccio, at Rocca."

2.—From the Same to the Same.

"To Neri, my dearest Brother, of all the friends and servants of
          God—

"Although you have many times sent to me, saluting and try-ing to comfort me, who was once your brother, both in the com-mon life we led together and in the bonds of charity, yet now for a long time past I have been cut off, and extinguished, and blotted out of the book where once I dwelt so sweetly ; for which cause I no longer number myself as a brother among you and your dear friends and brethren. Wonder not, therefore, that I have not written, or if I never write again, until I return to gather the fruit of obedience and patience and humility. But I have wandered so far out of the right way that I count it almost a thing impos-sible that I should ever return and feed in the old pastures, and find a place of rest. And this has come upon me, because I shut fast in darkness the eye of my understanding, and cast the light out of my soul. So I am driven from the table, and I know my-self to be clothed in darkness. No hunger or desire of good is left in me any more. I make neither beginning nor end to this letter, for there is none in me. Neither will I put my name to it, for I know not if I have a name. God grant *you* perseverance, and a good end."[1]

These are indeed terrible letters, and give us a glimpse into a melancholy history. It was probably the one dark spot in

[1] Lettere dei discepoli di Santo Caterina, No. 7 and 8.

Catherine's memory; and if, as we can hardly doubt, she read these letters, they must have had their part in the sadness which clouded the last days of her stay at Rocca. If the writer had really at one time been of the number of Catherine's disciples, how are we to reconcile this fact with the promise which we are told she had received from our Lord, that all her spiritual children should persevere to the end? The probable answer to this difficulty is, that the promise was given after, or even on the occasion of this one apostasy. Or again, we may understand it by recalling our Lord's words in the Gospels: "Of them whom Thou hast given Me I have lost none," as compared with those other words: "None of them is lost, save the son of perdition." "She always prayed for him," says the author just quoted. But did she ever allude to his fall, or make any personal effort to reclaim him? In reply to the first inquiry we may turn to one of her letters to Neri, in which she is striving to rouse him from the sadness and discouragement which so often beset him. "My dearest son," she says, "I write to you in the Precious Blood, desiring to see you grow in virtue until you reach the ocean of peace where you may never more fear to be separated from God. Then the evil law of corruption which is ever fighting against the spirit will be destroyed, and the debt will be paid. So long as you are in this world, my sweet son, you must try and live dead to self-will, and so you will conquer the law of our evil will. *You need not fear that God will permit that to happen to you which He has permitted to happen to others;* and you will not afflict yourself any more because you are for a short time separated from me and from the others. Courage, and remember what the Truth has said, that not one shall be snatched out of His hands. I say *His* hands, for all belong to Him, and I know you will understand me without many words. Adieu."

We know from Christofano di Gano that Catherine had received the promise from our Lord that none of her disciples should perish; but in her exquisite humility whilst referring to it here, she so expresses herself as to speak of them as rather His disciples than hers: " not one shall be snatched out of *His* hands, for all belong to Him." The idea suggests itself that this promise was probably given her at a time when she was mourning the fall of this one soul; that she had been given to understand that none of the others who called her mother should ever be separated from the bond of charity, and that, therefore, having received such a promise, she was able to assure Neri that what had happened to this one soul should never happen to him. The fact of this passage occurring in a letter to Neri, rather than to any of her other spiritual children, increases the probability that she is here alluding to the unhappy apostate, towards whom he had shown so persevering a charity, and who even in his gloomy despair still kept up some intercourse with him. That she herself held any communication with him is extremely doubtful, though among her letters is one addressed "To a religious who had quitted his Order;" and it is barely possible that this may have been the person in question.

Catherine returned to Siena some time in the winter : probably in the January of 1378, for as we have seen by her letter to Alexia she had spent the whole of Advent at Rocca. She did not long enjoy the quiet of home, for circumstances were already preparing the way for that second mission to Florence, in the course of which she showed herself ready to lay down her life in very deed for the cause of peace and reconciliation. But of this we shall have to speak in another chapter.

ST. CATHERINE IN THE GARDEN.

CHAPTER V.

CATHERINE'S SECOND EMBASSY TO FLORENCE.

JANUARY TO AUGUST, 1378.

RAYMUND of Capua's presence in Rome, whither we have seen him summoned whilst Catherine was still at Rocca, was destined to produce some important and unexpected results. He has related all the circumstances in his Legend with that unpretentious simplicity which characterises his entire narrative.

"Before quitting Tuscany," he says, "I held an interview with Nicolas Soderini, a citizen of Florence, a man most faithful to God and the Church, and strongly attached to Catherine; we spoke of the affairs of the republic, and in particular of the ill-will of those who pretended to desire reconciliation with the Church, but who did all they could to prevent peace. As I complained of this course of conduct, that excellent man answered me thus : 'Be convinced that the people of Florence and every honest man in the town desire peace : it is only a few obstinate men by whom we are governed who offer obstacles.' I said : 'Could no remedy be applied to this evil?' He rejoined : 'Yes, it could be done, if some respectable citizens took to heart the cause of God, and had an understanding with the Guelphs, in order to deprive those intermeddlers of their power, for they are enemies of the public good, and it would be sufficient to remove four or five of them.' When I went to fulfil my commission to the Sovereign Pontiff, I related to him the conversation which I had held with Nicolas Soderini.

"I had been occupied several months in fulfilling my charge of Prior, and announcing the Word of God, when one Sunday morning a messenger from the Pope came to inform me that his Holiness awaited my presence at dinner. I obeyed this command, and after the repast the Holy Father said to me, 'I am told that if Catherine of Siena repairs to Florence, peace will be concluded.' I replied, 'Not only Catherine, but all of us are ready to obey your Holiness, and, if need be, to suffer martyrdom.' The Holy Father said to me : 'I do not wish that *you* should go to Florence, because they would maltreat you ; but for *her*, she is a woman, and they have a great veneration for her ; I do not think she would incur any danger. Consider the matter over, and what powers she would require ; then bring them to-morrow morning for my signature, so that the business may be concluded at once.' I obeyed, and forwarded the letters to the Saint, who submitted, and set out without delay." Never was an important affair more rapidly decided, and never has such an affair been more briefly chronicled. We are even disposed to think that on this as on other occasions, Raymund's memory failed him in the details, and that Catherine's departure for Florence did not take place as immediately as he represents. That a letter was sent by Gregory to Catherine while she was still at Rocca, may be gathered from one of her own to Raymund. (Letter 90.) In it she expresses her grief at all the miseries under which the Church was then groaning. "However," she continues, "after sorrow will come sweetness; that is the consolation I felt on receiving your letter and that of our sweet Father; for I had suffered much since St. Francis' day, and your letter drew me out of my sad thoughts." Whether in this letter Gregory had expressed his wish that the Saint should return to Florence, and whether her engagements at Rocca prevented her immediate compliance with this desire we cannot say; but it is certain that there was something in her conduct at this time which had displeased him, and drawn from him a sharp rebuke. Possessing as we do only one side of the correspondence, and that but imperfectly preserved, it is impossible to decide either the exact cause of his displeasure, or the terms in which he expressed it; but whatever they were, they pierced deep into Catherine's heart. In fact, Gregory at Rome was not the same man he had been at Avignon. The discontent of his French courtiers, the strangeness of the language, and the melancholy of the half-ruined city, which contrasted unfavourably enough with the brilliant capital he had left on the shores of the Rhone, weighed on his spirits, and made him feel daily more and more the difficulties of his position, while he lacked the brave heart that could have made head against them. Add to this his failing health and the disappointment he felt at the rejection by the Florentines of all his overtures for peace, and we shall understand that tinge of fretfulness which was apparent in his words towards the close of his life. Though ignorant of the cause of his displeasure with Catherine we have her reply; and we do not know our holy Mother—the sensitiveness of her heart, or the depth of her humility—until we have read that touching page in her correspondence. Let us remember who it is that writes; she whose dauntless courage had sustained the timidity of the Pontiff in more than one moment of trial, and to whose energy his return to Rome was mainly to be attributed. She does not address her letter to him, but to Raymund, whom she charges to stand by the Pope and support him loyally to the last. "If you chance to find yourself in the presence of his Holiness, our sweet Father," she continues, "recommend me humbly to him and ask his pardon on my part for the many faults which I have committed by my ignorance and negligence. I fear it is my sins that are the cause of the persecution he suffers, and all the woes of the Church may justly be attributed to me. He has therefore good reason to complain of me, and to punish me for my faults; but tell him I will use every effort to correct myself and to obey him better. May God give him the grace to be courageous and never to turn back on account of any difficulty, or any persecution raised against him by his rebellious children; may he be firm and constant, not fearing labour, but casting himself like a lamb into the midst of those wolves, hungering only for God and for souls, and not troubling himself about temporal losses. If he acts thus, the lamb will become the master of the wolves, and the wolves will turn into lambs, and we shall see peace, and the good estate of holy Church restored." Then changing her style, and addressing herself directly to Gregory, she adds, "Ah! Holy Father, it was so you acted the first day you returned to your post; and now all these miseries have arisen because of me, from my lack of virtue, and my many faults of disobedience. But, Holy Father, see in the light of reason and truth what you have to reproach me with, not to punish, but to pity me. To whom can I turn if you abandon me? Who will help me, where will be my refuge, if you drive me away? My persecutors pursue me, and I take refuge with you, and with the other servants and children of God; and if you abandon me, and are irritated and angry with me, I can but hide myself in the Wounds of Jesus Crucified, Whose Vicar you are; and I know that He will receive me, because He desires not the death of a sinner. And when *He* has received me, surely *you* will not drive me away, and we shall still remain at our post, fighting generously for the Sweet Spouse of Christ. It is so that I desire to end my life in tears and sighs, giving my blood, if need be, yea, and the very marrow of my bones for her. And if all the world drive me away, I will not torment myself, but will repose, weeping and suffering, on the bosom of the Sweet Spouse. Most Holy Father, pardon my ignorance and the many offences I commit against God and your Holiness. It is the Eternal Truth Who excuses me and reassures me whilst I humbly ask your benediction." And these, so far as we know, were her last written words to him who in old time she had addressed with a child's fondness as *Babbo mio dolce.* She concludes with a word to Raymund : " Dear Father, stand by his Holiness and be full of courage, and have no disquietude or servile fear. Be faithful to your cell, in presence of Mary and of the holy Cross ; persevere in prayer and self-knowledge ; be firm in faith, and willing to suffer, and then go on confidently and do all you can for God and for souls, until death." But Catherine's relations with Gregory XI. were not so to end. Perhaps she overrated the tenor of his words ; and as often enough happens, the reproof which was felt so keenly by her who received it, had been forgotten by him who gave it almost before it reached her. Anyhow, Gregory still leant on her aid, and was impatient to employ it ; and the necessary powers and instructions having been sent to her, she prepared to depart on the gravest and most difficult mission that had yet been entrusted to her.

Before leaving Siena, however, she prepared the way for her coming by a letter addressed to the Signoria of Florence (Letter 181), in which she goes over all the old arguments for peace and submission, and thus concludes : " Rise, then, and cast yourself into the arms of your Father, and he will receive you with goodness. If you do this you will have peace, both spiritual and temporal, and all Tuscany with you. The war will be turned against the infidels, and all will follow the standard of the holy Cross. But if you will not conclude peace, you and all Tuscany will have to suffer what none of your ancestors have ever yet suffered. I should greatly prefer speaking to writing to you. Believe me, I am ready to lay down my life itself if that were needed, and if thereby I could advance God's glory, or obtain your reconciliation with Holy Church." The event proved that these were not empty words, and that in accepting this mission, she was in reality risking her life.

Catherine set out for Florence some time early in the year 1378. She travelled with several companions, among whom were Stephen Maconi, Christofano di Gano, Jane di Capo, and her mother Lapa. They found the city in a truly miserable state. For seventeen months the interdict had weighed on the inhabitants, nor can we in these days of cold faith fitly realise in what way the deprivation of all religious rites was then regarded by a believing population. And though Florence had exhibited a spirit of profanity and contempt of ecclesiastical authority, which seems to imply that the instincts of faith were not very keen among her citizens, the sentiments of the whole body must not be judged by the revolutionary excesses of a minority which had seized on the executive power. When first the terrible sentence had been fulminated, the intrepid Archbishop, Angelo di Ricasoli, quitted the city in order not to be compelled by violence to disobey the commands of the Pope. He thereby earned a word of sympathy and encouragement from Catherine. "I have heard," she writes, "of your firmness and noble conduct, and I beg of you, persevere in it to the end." But the Government seeing the great discontent felt by the people at the closing of the churches, and the suspension of all holy offices, feared lest in consequence they should insist on a policy of submission to the Holy See, which was of course the result aimed at by the infliction of the sentence. They therefore issued a decree setting the Pope's authority at defiance, and commanding all ecclesiastics to return to the city under penalty of a fine of 10,000 florins. Their intention was to enforce the non-observance of the interdict, and in fact it was openly violated in many places, an extremity of contempt which their own historian, Scipio Ammirato, is foremost to condemn.

On her arrival, Catherine was received, not as before in Soderini's own house, but in one which he had caused to be built expressly for her. Scipio Ammirato informs us of this fact. "Soderini," he says, "partly at his own expense, partly helped by the contributions of friends, built her a little house at the foot of St.

George's (hill), where she retired. Afterwards when his own house was burnt in the insurrection he took this house for his own residence." Some writers represent this house as built by Peter Canigiani, which probably means that he was one of those who contributed towards the expense.

A few days after her arrival at Florence, Catherine wrote to the Cardinal Peter de Luna, whom she had known at Avignon, and from whom better things might have been hoped than that he should eventually become the abettor of the schism, and accept the miserable dignity of Antipope. Catherine, who had quickly discerned the superior qualities of his mind, had trusted that he would prove a firm support to Gregory, who so greatly needed able councillors. "Things go badly here," she writes (Letter 25), "not to speak of seculars of whom there are many bad and few good, even priests and religious, specially among the Friars Minors, are found who outrage the truth even from their pulpits, saying that the interdict may be violated, and the offices celebrated with a free conscience, and that seculars who assist at them commit no sin. They have thus thrown the people into a confusion dreadful to think of." In fact, in the very month she came to Florence, the Government had obliged the priests to say Mass on the feast of St. Reparata, the patron Saint of the Cathedral, and not a few were found who did so willingly, and defended this act of contempt. Before this, the offices had been celebrated, but with closed doors; but after the return from Rome of the last envoys, sent thither to treat for peace, the Magistrates were so enraged at the rejection of their terms, that they determined on breaking with the Pope altogether, and ordered the churches to be thrown open, and all priests to take part in the violation of the interdict under severe penalties.

The first thing, then, that Catherine had to do, was to put a stop to this grave disorder. It was to little purpose to talk of making peace with the Pope so long as his lawful commands were being thus flagrantly disobeyed. She therefore lost no time, and on the very day of her arrival met the chiefs of the republic, in the halls of the Palazzo Vecchio, and made them three orations, no doubt to three distinct bodies of Magistrates. We learn this fact from Stephen Maconi, in some valuable notes which he left in MS., and which were preserved in the monastery of Pontignano. "By the grace of God," he says, "such was her success that although before that they had broken the interdict and shown great contempt towards the Apostolic See, yet after hearing the exhortation of this holy virgin, they once more obeyed and observed it."

Here we may properly notice an interesting circumstance which illustrates the kind of effects which flowed from St. Catherine's influence and teaching. It has been said above that all the Florentines were certainly not partakers in the guilt of their rulers, and many exposed themselves to great obloquy on the part of the faction which was in power, in consequence of their firmness in adhering to the Pope's authority. In this they were supported and encouraged by St. Catherine's disciples, who were numerous in Florence, and who devised means for keeping up the piety of the people at the same time that they held them back from frequenting the forbidden Church offices. In the ancient Chronicles of Manni we read that "the Florentines, being unable during the interdict to assist at the Church offices like good Catholics, began to make processions of secular persons, who went about singing lauds, and litanies, and other prayers; and with them went the Companies of the Disciplinati. Many other such Companies were also formed, of men, boys and children; and other Companies for the express purpose of singing lauds and hymns at eventide in the churches of Florence, to do honour to God." The "lauds" here spoken of were not any part of the Divine Office, which could not be celebrated publicly, but certain devout hymns in the vernacular; nor is it a random conjecture that attributes the origin of these pious practices to Catherine's disciples, for some of these identical lauds have been preserved, and have lately been printed, their author being Giannozzo Sachetti, one of her devout followers. and a great friend of Peter and Ristoro Canigiani, as well as of Buonacorso di Lapo, and Nicolas Soderini; and his verses, which are of high merit in a literary point of view, express in a poetical form the doctrine he had heard from the lips of the Saint.[1]

Stephen Maconi's words, which we have quoted above, were the testimony of an eye-witness. He accompanied the Saint into the halls of the Palazzo Vecchio, and stood by her side while she addressed the very men on whom, in the year previous, he had spent his own eloquence with so little fruit. What a scene was that ! One woman facing with unconscious heroism the leaders of a revolution ! We should have been glad to have known more of her "orations," and of the manner in which they were received, but nothing more is told us. However, we have two of her own letters of this date addressed to F. William Flete and to Alexia, who had not this time accompanied her to Florence.[2] To the first she says, "I think the first dawn of the Aurora is appearing and that our Lord is enlightening these people, and withdrawing them from the guilty darkness into which they had fallen, by enforcing the celebration of the Holy Mysteries. *Now, thank God, they observe the interdict*, and are beginning to return to the obedience of their Father. I beg of you, and of the Master (Tantucci), Brother Anthony, Brother Felix, and the rest, to pray earnestly that the Divine Goodness will send them the full sun of His mercy, that so peace may be made ; that indeed would be a sweet and blessed Sun." Here she names the two objects of her mission—the observance of the interdict, and the restoration of peace. One brief hour of her inspired eloquence had already gained the first of these objects, and opened the way to the second ; yet not a word in her announcement of the fact refers the success to herself. To Alexia she speaks in the same terms ; you can see that the two letters were written on the

---

[1] The *lauds* of Sachetti were published at Naples in 1862 by Francesco Palermo, from a Florentine manuscript. The learned editor has enriched the publication with notes, showing the exact correspondence between the doctrine and language of his author and those of St. Catherine in various passages of the Dialogo. The identity of ideas and expression could hardly be more complete.

[2] Letters 126 and 181.

same day. "Now is the time to pray, for the dawn is appearing, and the sun will soon arise. The Aurora is come, and the darkness of mortal sin is being chased away. Those who celebrated and assisted at the holy offices do so no longer; and the interdict is observed in spite of those who seek to prevent it. Pray then that God may soon send peace, so that He may be glorified, and all evils cease, and that we may soon be together again to relate the wonderful works of God. Get special prayers said in all the monasteries, and ask our Prioress [1] to make all her daughters pray for peace, *for I shall not come back till that is gained.* Ask her also to pray for me, her poor daughter, that God may teach me to love Him, and that I may always be ready to speak the truth, and to die for it."

The interdict was then enforced, and this point being gained, Catherine next concentrated her efforts on the great question of peace. But here she encountered graver difficulties. We have already spoken of the extraordinary constitution of the Florentine government, made up of several distinct bodies of Magistrates, whose views and interests were often opposed. The "Eight of War," whose political existence depended on the maintenance of hostilities, were supported by the powerful family of the Ricci. On the other hand, there was another body called "the Captains of the Guelphs," the singular nature of whose authority requires a word of explanation. Florence, it must be remembered, was pre-eminently a Guelph city. She had somewhat departed from her Guelph traditions in declaring war against the Sovereign Pontiff, yet the dominant party still gloried in the name, and detested every Ghibelline as a kind of outcast. The Guelph party-spirit in Florence was one of actual fanaticism. When about to raise the great Palazzo of the republic, it was discovered that the architect had planned to place a portion of the edifice on the site formerly occupied by the Uberti palace. But the Uberti had been Ghibellines, and after their banishment from the

---

[1] *Our Prioress,* that is the Prioress of the Sisters of Penance in Siena. Catherine addressed a letter to her during her residence at Rocca. She was called Sister Nera di Gano, and her name is to be found in the Register.

city, the ground on which their palace stood was declared accursed. "Never shall our Palazzo stand on that unholy ground!" exclaimed the citizens; and in spite of the remonstrances of the architect, the plans were altered, and the palace deprived of its symmetrical proportions. The same uncompromising hatred to Ghibellines in every form or shape had led to the establishment of a body of officials, who were invested by a republic, jealous of its liberties, with powers which in their odious tyranny set all principles of freedom at defiance. "The Captains of the Guelphs" were chosen for the express purpose of excluding from every public office or employment any person suspected of entertaining Ghibelline opinions, or tainted in the most distant degree with Ghibelline blood. These formidable powers were, for the most part, entrusted to the hands of good and honest men—for example, Soderini and Peter Canigiani were of the number of those who had filled this office. They were naturally the advocates of peace, being of the party most attached to the Church, and opposed therefore to the policy of the "Eight of War." Catherine was introduced by Soderini to these Captains, and to many other good citizens, with whom she held long conferences, and soon succeeded in convincing them of the necessity of putting a stop to the existing state of things. "The chiefs of the Guelphs," says Raymund, "and a great many good citizens yielded to her persuasions, and demanded of the governors of the city that they should labour for peace, not by their words only, but also by deeds."

In the November of the previous year it had been agreed that a Congress for the pacification of Italy should meet at Sarzana, a city on the northern boundary of Tuscany, whither deputies should be sent from all the states united in the league against the Church, as well as from the Pope and the King of France, Bernabò Visconti acting as arbitrator. This important step was most unwelcome to the war party, and though they could not hinder the assembly of the Congress, they used every endeavour to render its deliberations fruitless. Their factious intrigues at last became so troublesome, that the necessity of some decisive measure to check them was evident to all. Catherine pressed this on the Captains of the Guelphs, who had it in their power to restrain the excesses of the eight, owing to the singular nature of their official privileges. They were able to " warn," as it was called, those appointed to any public office; and if their warnings were neglected, they could proscribe the *Ammoniti* (or persons who had received the warnings), as convicted Ghibellines. It was an odious kind of ostracism, and had often been used as a mere pretext for crushing personal enemies. Soderini, in his conversation with Raymund, already quoted, had first suggested the removal from office of some of the war party, as affording the only reasonable hope of obtaining peace ; and Catherine, following up this idea, endeavoured to persuade the Captains that instead of using their powers in order to punish suspected Ghibellines, they would do better to exclude those real enemies of the state who sought for selfish purposes to keep up the breach between the Father and his children. This advice appeared so valuable, that the Guelph Captains at once determined to put it in practice ; nor was their determination to check the tyranny of the " Eight " at all weakened by the news which reached them towards the end of March 1378, of the death of Gregory XI. It is remarkable that no reference to this event is to be found in any of the letters of Catherine that are preserved. And although it broke up the Congress of Sarzana, and appeared therefore to ruin all the hopes of peace that had been built on that assembly, it in no way affected Catherine's mission at Florence. She had come with the firm resolution of staying until peace should have been made, and this resolution she kept, in spite of every discouragement.

Meanwhile the Captains of the Guelphs, supported by a great number of the citizens, had gone to the Priors of the city to demand that the peace negotiations should not be abandoned ; and a little later, ventured on the bold step of using their powers to put out of office John Dino, one of the most conspicuous members of the " Eight of War." This first success emboldened them to follow up the blow with other "admonitions," and in doing so, they unhappily suffered themselves to be guided, less by the patriotic desire of serving their country, than by that of satisfying their private resentments. An immense number of unoffending citizens found themselves made the victims of this proceeding, the whole odium of which was thrown on Catherine; for such was the prestige attaching to her name, that the Guelph Captains took pains to have it proclaimed as less the fruit of their councils than of her exhortations. The city was therefore in great agitation when, in the month of May, Silvestro de Medicis was elected Gonfalonier of Justice. He was a man of firmness and good repute, and he at once set himself to oppose the excesses of the Guelph party. They themselves hastened to make terms with him, and it was agreed, first, that no one should in future be "admonished" unless he were a notorious Ghibelline; and, secondly, that no one, whoever he might be, should have his name put to the vote for exclusion more than three times. Catherine had exerted herself actively to keep the Guelphs within bounds; so far was it from being true that she had exhorted them to make these reckless "admonitions," that she had severely blamed them, and we have the written evidence of Stephen Maconi to prove the fact. In one of the MS. notes left by him at Pontignano we read as follows: "I, Stephen Maconi, the unworthy writer, was at Florence at this time with Catherine, who ordered me, as well as others, to speak against the scandals which arose out of the 'admonitions,' in order that they might be remedied without delay. And I was actively occupied in this business, but without success." It is surmised that Catherine had exerted her influence over Silvestro to obtain his support in the cause of peace, and he certainly adhered to her policy in despatching fresh ambassadors to the newly-elected Pontiff, Urban VI., to reopen the negotiations.

Meanwhile, new elections had to be made of the Guelph Captains, for none of these offices were held for a longer term than two months at a time. The newly-elected captains were none of them disciples of the Saint. Capecelatro gives the names of all eight (from Marchione dei Stefani), and not one on the list was in any way associated with her. They were some of the most fanatical members of their party, and instead of keeping to the rules that had been agreed on with the Gonfalonier, they recommenced the "admonitions," and not being able to obtain the exclusion of two citizens against whom they had a special grudge, after three scrutinies, they closed the palace doors, forbade any to quit the chamber, and continued to the twenty-third scrutiny, until they had obtained the vote they desired. This lawless proceeding put the whole city in a ferment; and on the 22nd of June, Silvestro, not finding himself strong enough to withstand the Captains alone, in a fatal moment excited the populace to rise in insurrection against them. The *Popolani* obeyed his invitation only too willingly, and the city was for some days in their hands, while scenes of frightful disorder were perpetrated. Naturally enough, the storm chiefly broke over the heads of the Guelph party and their Captains. Nicolas Soderini and Peter Canigiani were no longer in office, and had no part in the transactions which immediately led to this insurrection. But they had formerly been captains, and as such had "warned" many citizens; and they were therefore included among those against whom the fury of the *Popolani* was directed. Raymund says that many of the Guelphs and of their leaders had been already massacred, and their houses given up to pillage, when the cry arose to attack "the false traitor and hypocrite, Soderini, who thought of nothing but building a house for his blessed Catherine."[1] Soderini escaped, but his house was burnt and sacked, as was also that of Ristoro Canigiani, the son of Peter, and one of Catherine's most devoted disciples. Then the crowd, glutted with blood and pillage, and joined by a number of the lowest ruffians from the other side of the Arno, proposed to seek out Catherine herself, whom they represented as the author of the whole business, and against whom their leaders sought to direct their utmost violence. For it must be remembered the senseless and irrational passions of the multitude were being guided by the party headed by the "Eight of War," who were perfectly well aware that they had no

[1] Scip. Am. Lib., 14, p. 719.

firmer adversary to the continuance of their tyranny than the holy maid who was come to Florence exclusively on a mission of peace. We will relate the well-known story of what followed in the words of Raymund : " The leaders (of the revolt) pointed her out to the people, and everywhere was heard the cry, 'Let us take that wicked woman and burn her ; let us cut her in pieces !' Then those who had given her shelter in their houses were afraid, and sent her away with all her companions. Catherine, conscious of her innocence, was perfectly tranquil, rejoicing to suffer in the cause of the Church. She encouraged those who were with her, and made them an exhortation, and then after the example of her Spouse, retired to a place where there was a garden, and began to pray.

" As she was praying in this garden, the followers of Satan came in great tumult, armed with swords and sticks, and crying, 'Where is that cursed woman, where is she ?' Catherine heard them, and prepared for martyrdom as for a joyous feast. She rose, and went to meet one furious man who carried a sword, and cried louder than the rest, 'Where is Catherine ?' Then kneeling humbly and joyfully before him, she said ' I am Catherine ; in God's Name do to me whatever He may permit ; but I charge you, do not touch any of my companions.' At these words the man appeared troubled, and so lost all power, that he could not so much as endure her presence ; he wished her to depart, and said to her, ' Fly, I say, fly !' But she replied, ' I am very well where I am ; where would you have me go? I am ready and willing to suffer for God and the Church, and I desire nothing better. If, therefore, you are charged to kill me, do so ; I shall not resist, but let these go unharmed.' The man, however, withdrew confused, with all his companions. Catherine's children surrounded her, congratulating her on having escaped the hands of the ruffians ; but she, full of sorrow, only wept, saying, ' Alas, how unhappy I am ! I thought to-day that God would place the crown on my happiness. In His mercy He has granted me the white rose of virginity, and I had hoped He would add to it the red rose of martyrdom ; but I am disappointed of my hope, and doubtless it is my innumerable sins that are the cause!'" (Legend, Part 3, chap. viii.).

"Although the tumult was appeased, Catherine and her companions were not yet safe from danger. The terror which reigned in the city was so great that no one would receive her into their houses. Her friends advised her to return to Siena, but Catherine's lofty spirit refused so much as to entertain the thought. 'I have received the command of God to remain here,' she said, 'and never will I quit the territory of Florence until peace is restored between the Father and the children.' They dared not contradict her, and at last found an honest man who feared none but God, and who concealed her in his house. Some days later the excitement calmed down. Catherine was then taken out of the city, but not out of the territory of Florence, and retired with her disciples to a solitary place inhabited by hermits."

It is thus that Raymund relates this story in the sixth chapter of the third part of his Legend. In a former chapter (part 2, chap. iii.) he says that Catherine refused to leave the territory of Florence, because God had forbidden her to do so until peace was concluded between Florence and the Sovereign Pontiff. He does not name more particularly where the "solitary place inhabited by hermits" was, but it is always understood to have been Vallombrosa, where she had many friends. As she prepared to set out, Jane di Capo, one of the Mantellate who accompanied her, was found to be seriously unwell. Her foot was much swollen, and she had a violent fever, so that she was quite unfit to move. Catherine, not choosing to leave her alone, exposed to the ill treatment of the populace if she should chance to be recognised, had recourse to prayer; and very soon the invalid fell into a quiet sleep, from which she awoke perfectly cured, and able to set out with the rest.

It appears to have been from Vallombrosa that Catherine wrote the letter to Raymund in which she gives her own account of these events (Letter 96): "To-day," she says, "I wish to begin a new life, for I see clearly it has been through my fault that I have been deprived of the happiness of giving my life for

Jesus Crucified. I was consumed with the desire of suffering, and my heart was bursting with this desire, at once so sweet and so painful; sweet because I was united to the Word; and painful, because I saw God offended, and a multitude of demons that obscured all the city and darkened the minds of the people; and it seemed as if God had permitted them to do as they willed in order to punish sinners. I feared lest something might happen which would hinder the peace; but God and our sweet Lady have protected us, and in this tumult the only harm done has been to those who were executed by the hand of justice.

"But the desire I had to give my life for Christ was not heard. The Eternal Spouse of my soul has well disappointed me, as Christofano will tell you by word of mouth. And so I weep because my sins have prevented me giving my blood to obtain light for these blind souls; my blood has not reconciled the Father with His children; my blood has not cemented the stones of the mystical Body of the Church. It seemed as if the hands of him who wished to strike were bound. I said, 'Here I am, strike me, but let the others go their way;' and my words seemed to pierce their hearts like a dagger. Never could I tell you the happiness I felt at that moment. I felt so clearly what I owed to my Creator, that if I could have delivered my body to the flames, it seemed to me I should not sufficiently have acknowledged all the graces that I and my children have received. Oh, how happy I should have been if I could have given my blood for the love of the Blood, and for the salvation of souls! I will say no more on the subject, Christofano will tell you all about it. Only beg the Christ on earth (Urban VI.) not to delay the peace on account of what has happened. On the contrary, let him make all the more haste, that he may occupy himself with the great designs he has for the reformation of Holy Church; for these events have changed nothing, and now the city is quite quiet. Ask him to release me soon out of my prison, for until peace is made it is impossible for me to leave this place, and yet I long to go and taste the blood of the martyrs, and to visit his Holiness, and to see you once more, that I may tell you all the wonderful things God has wrought in these past days, and that we all may rejoice together."

Here we see the visit to Rome already projected. One sentence above quoted deserves remark. Raymund in his narrative says that some of the Guelph party were slain by the mob. Catherine says no harm was done to any, except those *chi fece la Giustizia*, and Scipio Ammirato's history confirms the accuracy of her statement. The Magistrates sent soldiers into each quarter of the town with orders to hang the first five rioters who should fall into their hands, but to choose *foreigners* by preference; "and those who suffered," he adds, "were mostly Flemings."

Three other letters seem to have been written by Catherine from Vallombrosa. Nicolas Soderini accompanied her to that retreat, as did also Christofano di Gano; but the former returned to Florence, where he found his house burnt and pillaged. Catherine wrote to him to console him for his losses. "It seems to me," she says, "that God in His great goodness is showing you His love of predilection by rendering you worthy of suffering something for Him; do not be impatient, therefore, or faint under His mighty hand. Later we shall receive in heaven the reward for all our losses, but only if we are patient. Be confirmed, then, in patience, that when you enter the holy city of Jerusalem you may, in the vision of peace, receive all that you have merited in this time of pilgrimage. Strengthen Donna Constanza in the name of Jesus; tell her to examine who has suffered most, and she will see that God will bring back calm by means of this tempest." Her letters to Peter Canigiani and his son Ristoro are in the same strain; to the latter she says, "Rejoice at what has happened, for it is the life of your soul. If sensuality and the language of the world says otherwise, do not listen to them, but be firm and courageous, and remember that worldly men cannot answer for you before the Supreme Judge at the moment of death, and that then your only help will be a good conscience."

In fact, both Soderini and the Canigiani incurred severe penalties for their share, real or supposed, in the late troubles. Soderini was exiled fifty miles from the city, Peter Canigiani was fined 2000 gold florins, and his son Ristoro, who had been enrolled among the *Popolani*, was declared a *Grandee*, and even a *High Grandee* (Sopragrando), and as such, altogether ineligible to any office in the republic.

As soon as calm was restored, Catherine returned to the city, and thence addressed her first letter to Urban VI. The month of June was coming to a close, and Catherine had already heard of his projects of reform ; perhaps also she had received hints to the effect that the zeal of the new Pontiff was not always tempered with discretion. Her letter begins by touching, in the gentlest possible manner, on the necessity of uniting justice with mercy. Then she says, "Most Holy Father, God has established you Pastor of His sheep throughout Christendom, and He has chosen you to dispense the Blood of Jesus, Whose Vicar you are, at a time when the iniquities of the faithful abound more than they ever did before, whether in the clergy or the whole body ; therefore it is most necessary that you should be established in charity and justice. Be not disturbed at what the world may say ; like a good Pastor reform with courage, root out vice, plant virtue, and be ready, if need be, to give your life. Most Holy Father, I see no other way of succeeding than by entirely renewing the garden of the holy Church, and surrounding yourself with holy persons who will not fear death. Do not look to birth, provided they are good pastors. Create a college of good Cardinals, who will be as firm columns, and with God's grace will help you to support your burden." Then she passes on to the affairs of Florence. "I recommend to you all these poor sheep who are out of the sheepfold, doubtless because of my sins. For the sake of the Blood of which you are the minister, do not delay receiving them to mercy. Let your Holiness triumph over their hardness of heart, and bring them back to the sheepfold. If they do not ask it with perfect humility, yet supply for their weakness, and do not ask more of them than they have strength to perform. Have pity on the souls that perish ; do not think of the scandals that have lately taken place in this city, where it seemed for a moment as if all the demons of hell had done their utmost to hinder peace : but, through God's goodness, no great harm has come of it ; and now all is quiet again, and your children ask of you the oil of mercy. We will grant that they do not ask it with all the suitable forms and sorrow of heart that you might desire ; yet do not refuse them. Alas, *Babbo mio*, I do not wish to remain here any longer, nevertheless, do with me what you like, only grant me the favour that I ask of you, miserable as I am. Do not refuse me this little sweetmeat." (Letter 15.)

Whilst the result of this appeal was still uncertain, St. Catherine found a new object on which to expend her zeal. Florence was at that time the headquarters of the heretical sect of the Fraticelli, against whose errors and misdeeds it had often fallen to her lot to warn her disciples. They were pretended pietists, who under the cloak of devotion concealed an abandoned life, and endeavoured to propagate their false doctrines chiefly by insinuating themselves into the confidence of nuns, through the appearance of a sanctimonious rigour. They were particularly addicted to the profession of poverty, and on this account many other religious societies that embraced poverty had, in their beginnings (like the Gesuati), fallen under the suspicion of being tainted with their errors. We learn from Nicolas Manerbio in his addition to the Legend, and in the Proemio affixed to Gigli's second volume, that Catherine, when at Florence, publicly disputed with these heretics, and put them to silence, but no further particulars on this interesting subject have been preserved.

At last the object of her long prayers and labours was granted, and in the beginning of July the terms of peace between Florence and the Holy See were definitively agreed to. The city was to pay 150,000 gold florins, and everything was to return to the condition in which it was before the war. Even Talamon was not forgotten ; and it was to be restored to Siena, though considerable delays attended the fulfilment of this condition, due at last to Catherine's personal exertions. This peace was signed at Florence towards the end of July 1378, and ratified at Rome in the October following. As one happy result, the city of Florence was released from the interdict, the Bishop of Volterra and F.

Francis Orvieto, an Augustinian hermit, being deputed by the Pope to absolve the citizens. This joyful event filled the heart of Catherine with inexpressible joy, and she thus announces the happy news to her children at Siena. She writes to Sano di Maco: "Oh, my dear son! God has heard the prayers of His servants who have so long cried to Him, and the long groanings they have uttered over His dead children! Now they have risen again, and returned from death to life, and from darkness to light. Yes, my dear sons, the lame walk, the deaf hear, the blind see, the dumb speak, and cry in a loud voice, 'Peace, peace!' Oh, what immense joy to see them return to the obedience of their Father! As those who begin to see, they say, 'Thanks be to Thee, O Lord, Who hast reconciled us with our Holy Father!' Yes, *he* is now called holy, the sweet Lamb, the Christ on earth, the same whom awhile ago they called heretic and *patarin;*[1] now they accept him for their Father whom hitherto they rejected. The clouds are dispersed, and the sky is once more serene. Rejoice then, my beloved children, rejoice, and shed sweet tears of gratitude before our Eternal Father; but do not yet be satisfied until the standard of the holy Cross is displayed, and that right soon. Rejoice, and be transported with joy in our Lord Jesus. Peace is made at last in spite of those who sought to hinder it. It was on Saturday evening that the Olive arrived, at one in the night, and to-day at vespers the other also came . . . I send you some of the Olive of peace."

Catherine's allusion to the "Olive of peace," is not a mere metaphor; in those days, at any rate in Italy, as Dante tells us, ambassadors of peace actually carried one as the symbol of their mission; and it was a real substantial olive branch which had gladdened her eyes that Saturday evening, and of which, it would seem, she sent a leaf as a welcome present to her Sienese children. Raymund, in relating the close of these events, dwells on the courageous firmness which St. Catherine displayed to the very end. When at last the peace was signed, she said to her spiritual children, "*Now*, we may quit Florence, for, by the grace

---

[1] *Paterin*, a kind of heretic; equivalent to Vaudois.

of my Saviour Jesus Christ, I have followed His commands and those of His Vicar; those whom I found revolted against the Church I leave subject to that sweet and tender Mother. Now, therefore, let us return to Siena."

She returned about the end of July or the beginning of August, for we have a letter written by her to Louisa di Grannello, dated "Siena, August 27, 1378." She brought with her from Florence one new disciple, who from that time until the day of her death never quitted her : it was Barduccio Canigiani, the younger brother of Ristoro, who had been a spiritual son of Don John of Vallombrosa, and who with the other followers of that holy man had adhered to Catherine throughout the whole of her troublesome residence at Florence. He now joined her "family," and acted as one of her secretaries. Raymund speaks of him as "a young Florentine, who had enriched his youth with the wisdom of age, and adorned it with all the virtues. They called him Barduccio. He left his parents, his brethren, and his country, to follow Catherine, and remained with her till her death. I have learnt since that the Saint had a special affection for him, and I think it was on account of his angelic purity, nor is it wonderful that a virgin soul should be dear to a virgin."

Here then we close this heroic chapter in the life of St. Catherine. To few women has such a moment been granted as that which saw her calmly facing the maddened mob who thirsted for her blood, more ready to give her life for the cause of God and the Church than they were to take it. To her deep sorrow she was denied "the red rose of martyrdom;" yet if ever there was one who merited to be regarded as a martyr in desire it was she, before whose kneeling form the cowardly ruffians shrank with terror, and who wept that she had not been counted worthy to die for the honour of her Lord. But she had gained the palm, if not of martyrdom, yet of victory. She had achieved the difficult mission entrusted to her, and made peace between the Father and the children, and there was no cloud to shadow the joy with which, for the last time in her life, she returned to her old home in her native city.

CHAPTER VI.

THE MONKS OF VALLOMBROSA AND MONTE OLIVETO.

IN the foregoing chapters the name of Don John of the Cells of Vallombrosa has more than once occurred in connection with various affairs in which St. Catherine took part; and it will be remembered that in our account of her last mission to Florence she is spoken of as having taken refuge in that celebrated sanctuary, when her life was threatened during the insurrection of the "Ammoniti." Not to interrupt the thread of our narrative we have abstained from many a tempting episode, but some account of this remarkable man must now be given, and of his valorous championship of her whom he was proud of denominating his spiritual Mother.

There is, perhaps, no example in the history of great penitents more remarkable than that of Don John of the Cells, who during the latter portion of his life was deservedly regarded as the Socrates of his country and a great luminary of the Church; yet whose earlier career was only remarkable for its extraordinary depravity. He was a Florentine of noble birth, and entering when young into the Order of Vallombrosa, he greatly distinguished himself as a man of letters, and became Superior of the Convent of the Holy Trinity, then existing within the city walls. But whilst still filling that office, he came to lead a life of the utmost iniquity, the long catalogue of his crimes including the practice of magic. The General of his Order caused him to be deposed and imprisoned for a year in a darksome dungeon. There, by a wonderful stroke of Divine grace, his heart became touched with true penance; and on his release, refusing to be reinstated in his charge, he retired to a hermitage in the holy solitude of Vallombrosa. He did not take up his residence in the larger monastery, but in a small building which still stands on an insolated rock overlooking the deep wooded ravine, and bears the name of the *Paradisino*, or of "the Cells;" from which last John received the surname by which he has become known to posterity. Here, then, he gave himself up to a life of prayer, study, and penance, and was soon as renowned for his austere sanctity as he had before been for his grievous excesses. He was not content with burying himself in his hermitage, and letting his name become effaced from the memory of men; he had the courage to expose himself to the notice of those who knew his history, and to endure their scorn and reproach, while devoting his great gifts to the cause of truth, and the salvation of souls. In the last chapter we have spoken of the *Fraticelli*, that pestilent sect of hypocrites whom Catherine, among her other good deeds, defeated and put to confusion. Don John also opposed a manful opposition to their errors, and succeeded in delivering many young men from their dangerous influence. Those who followed his direction he formed into a kind of devout society, not very unlike that which gathered around St. Catherine, and whom she called "her family." Living in the world, they withdrew from its follies and occupied themselves in good works; and people called them the *Spirituali*. Some persons were to be found who, confounding them with the very Fraticelli to whom they were opposed, came to regard them as hypocrites, and tainted with the same errors; but this was a gross calumny. Barduccio Canigiani, as has been already stated, began by being one of these disciples of John of the Cells; but after forming the acquaintance of St. Catherine, he enrolled himself among her spiritual sons, together with most of his companions, and headed by their venerable director himself.

When Catherine left Florence after her first visit, she wrote to Don John in affectionate confidence, begging him to have a watchful care over these young souls so dear to both of them. " I entreat you," she says, "take good care of your children and mine; provide for the needs of each one; and make them all as perfect as you can." She also wrote a joint letter to the youths themselves, which is addressed, "To some young men of Florence, the adopted sons of Don John" (Letter 308), which reads as if written in reply to one asking her advice as to the choice of a state of life. She answers them with great tenderness and moderation, dwelling on the virtue of obedience, which she calls "the soul's best friend." "It is most easily practised," she says, "in some approved Order; and though it is true we see many relaxed religious who do not keep their rule, yet the rule itself is not the less good on that account, being inspired by the Holy Spirit. So if you think yourselves called by God to this state, answer His call, and do not be hindered by the consideration of those Orders which have fallen into tepidity and scandals. There are many monasteries where these abuses have been reformed. Among them I will specially recommend that of St. Anthimo; the abbot, as Don John will tell you, is the model of humility, charity, and poverty. May God guide you as is best for His glory and your own sanctification. Meanwhile, my children, be united together in the bonds of charity. Bear with each other's faults, for you know that was the sign which our Lord gave whereby we we should know His true disciples. It will be a real consolation to me to hear that you are all united; let me be able to say with St. Paul that 'you are my joy and my crown.'"

How much Don John loved and reverenced St. Catherine will be apparent both from the open-hearted way in which he allowed his "adopted sons" to rank themselves as her disciples, and by the terms in which he wrote and spoke of her, both whilst living and after her death. Nevertheless, busy tongues did their best to cause a breach between them, and did actually raise a storm which is among the most curious episodes of St. Catherine's life. It has been said that at the time of her first introduction to Don John she was much taken up with the project of the Crusade. The letters she wrote, and the exhortations which she addressed to her friends on this subject, not only had the effect of gaining many to take the Cross, and promise effectual aid in men and money, but were likewise laid hold of by certain weak heads among her female hearers, who loudly declared their intention of joining the Crusaders, and going across the seas, whether to fight the infidels or to convert them, does not very clearly appear. However, they made themselves ridiculous, and thought fit to quote the authority of Catherine in justification of their folly. The matter reached the ears of John of the Cells, and he addressed a letter to one of these devout ladies named Domitilla, in which he read her a lesson of common sense.[1] "I hear," he says, "that you, with many other virgins and youths, wish to go across the seas. A pious desire in the husk, no doubt, but the kernel is altogether bad, and proceeds from the enemy of the human race who deceived Eve by an appearance of good, and drove her out of Paradise. Perhaps you will tell me that the holy virgin Catherine preaches that you should go across the seas. I reply, that if she advises you to do such a thing, because there you will find Christ, I deny it, with all the saints. In the first place, our Lord said that the kingdom of God is within." And after further expostulations with her, he continues, "If you are more disposed to trust your St. Catherine than the holy doctors, go to her, and ask her by what road she reached such perfection; she will tell you it was by the road of prayer and silence, for according to what is said of her, she kept silence three years, and always remained shut up in her room, praying. Do that first of all, and when you have attained a sanctity like hers, I will certainly give you permission to cross the seas."

It is evident that Don John had no intention by this letter to blame Catherine, but only to check the indiscretion of those who quoted her in support of the excesses of their own pious enthusiasm. But the rumour got abroad that he had severely condemned her, and reaching Lecceto, F. William Flete, of all persons in the world, took fire at the supposed affront to his venerated Mother, and addressed a most lively remonstrance to his brother solitary, which unfortunately is not preserved. However, we may judge of its character from Don John's replies, which are printed by Gigli at the end of the first volume of St. Catherine's letters. If

---

[1] The letter is printed in the *Lettere di Sancti e Beati Fiorentini*, No. xx.

F. William's contemplative soul was roused to indignation by the bare thought of Catherine having been calumniated, Don John was no less troubled at being supposed capable of uttering a word of blame against one whom he regarded with so much veneration. Monks were in those days prodigious letter-writers ; they spared neither their words nor their figures of speech, and on this occasion the hermit of Vallombrosa condemned the hermit of Lecceto to the penance of reading two extremely long letters, of which we shall inflict on our readers no more than a few short extracts.

"To the Venerable Father, Brother William ; Don John the sinner wishes health in Christ to your charity at the Oak of Mambre. O happy fault, to which such a corrector was granted, whom I have deserved to hear admonishing me after having so long desired to see him ! I beg you to understand, my father, that I have never written any letter to the Venerable Catherine of Siena, nor have I ever been foolish enough to use rash or jesting language concerning the Spouse of Christ. I only wrote to a certain damsel at Florence, fearing she might expose herself to danger in her endeavours to convert the Saracens, and knowing how easily a weak woman may fall, I desired her to ask the blessed Catherine if she had found Christ by praying, or by gadding about. I hear that you have no great knowledge of our vulgar tongue, whence this error may easily have arisen. As to Catherine, I will make known to your piety what I feel about her in the innermost recesses of my heart. I consider her to be that angel who sounded the sixth trumpet." Then after some very singular adaptations of Holy Scripture, he continues : "I say all this that you may understand how much I love her, and everywhere praise her ; and I beg of you to receive me as your son, since I understand that your will is her will, and her will yours. Now, I will tell you a secret. When she was in Florence,[1] it happened that being in an ecstasy she was seen by a certain virgin, who, quite beside herself with wonder, ran to her, and cutting off some of her hair wrapt it in a piece of silk which she had in her hand. I went to Florence about that time for certain business, and the

____

[1] That is, on the occasion of her first embassy.

damsel seeing my devotion to Catherine, gave me some of this hair as a precious treasure. I received it with joy, and placed it among my choicest relics, kissing it reverently, as if it belonged to a saint of Paradise."

Father William answered this letter in so friendly a way as to call forth from Don John a second, yet fuller of Scriptural quotations and protestations of fidelity to Catherine. In it he alludes to having received a letter from her, which is not preserved; but we gather that the Saint, hearing of the dispute which had arisen between her two good friends, had interfered to adjust their differences. Don John's second letter has the rare merit of bearing a date. It was written on the 10th of October 1376, just at the time when, as we have seen, Catherine was returning to Italy after her visit to Avignon. But if the rumours which had so roused the indignation of F. William had entailed some little annoyance on John of the Cells, Providence so ordered it that he had his revenge. Will it be believed that even among the Oaks of Lecceto a traitor could be found to asperse Catherine's reputation, and to circulate injurious criticisms of her conduct? We know nothing of him but his name and the castigation which he received: he was called John of Salerno; and Landucci, the historian of the Augustinian hermits, has very prudently told us nothing at all about him, whence it may be concluded he was not very eminent among his brethren. Still he had a tongue and a pen, and he seems to have used both for the purpose of representing Catherine as altogether unworthy of the praises so lavishly bestowed on her by the public. One would have thought he might safely have been trusted to the tender mercies of Prior John III. and Father William Flete. But Don John did not think so, or perhaps he was not sorry of the opportunity thus afforded him of turning the tables on his brother hermits. Lecceto had taken Vallombrosa to task for the very same misdemeanour, and it was now the time for Vallombrosa to return the debt with interest. So once more did John of the Cells draw his pen; and this time we are very glad he did so; for however contemptible an adversary John of Salerno may have been, the letter in which

Don John demolished him has preserved some very interesting facts regarding Catherine, which would not otherwise have come to our knowledge. We will quote the letter, therefore, with certain merciful abridgments. He begins by repudiating several most unjust charges brought against him by Brother John of Salerno, to the effect that he encouraged and corresponded with some of the heretical and excommunicated Fraticelli. After having defended himself at considerable length on this head, he goes on to notice the different points of the attack against Catherine. They were briefly, that she offered to do penance for the sins of others, that she allowed people to kiss her hands and feet, and that before she had been approved as a saint by the Church she ought not to be so extolled. Don John replies to each and all of these objections, and then bursts forth in a strain of that peculiar kind of eloquence fashionable in the fourteenth century. "But who am I who dare to touch this mountain of the Lord? *Montem coagulatum, Montem pinguem, Montem in quo beneplacitum est Deo habitare,* the burning mountain of Sinai, of which it is written, ' And if a beast touch this mountain, let him be stoned with stones!' Far from me be such stones! . . . You say that we ought not to venerate her till she has been approved by the Church. This I dispute not; yet only lately the Pope having sent for her, caused her to be prudently examined, and finding her just and holy, sent her back with many gifts and graces, so that we have not believed every spirit, but one that has been tried. You say that the city of Florence abounds in fools, and the city of Siena in fantastical persons. Pray, why do you leave out Pisa, Lucca, Genoa, and many other cities, in all which men have been seized with such admiration for her, and such innumerable crowds have run for her blessing, that she could only go through these cities secretly, and by night?" Then follows the narrative of her visit to Nurcia, already quoted, and he concludes with a eulogy on her admirable doctrine, declaring that the spirit of Paul seems verily to dwell in the body of Catherine.

John of the Cells was twice cured of dangerous sickness by the command, so to speak, of Catherine. He himself related all the circumstances of his cure to Stephen Maconi, when lying in his agony at the Abbey of Passignano, near the lake of Thrasimene, about thirteen miles from Siena. This monastery was only second in repute to that of Vallombrosa, for it was the burial-place of the founder of the Order, St. John Gualbert, who died here in 1073. St. Catherine often visited this abbey, and had many disciples among its hermits. She corresponded in particular with Don Martin, the abbot, a great friend of John of the Cells. The manner of life followed by the religious did not greatly differ from that of the Carthusians. Each hermit occupied his own cell and cultivated his own little garden. So when Catherine writes to the Abbot Martin, she talks to him of the best way of cultivating the garden of our soul; how we must turn up the soil, and clear away the briars, and plant the virtues, and bring forth sweet flowers. "Fulfil my desires," she says, "and be a good gardener to your own soul and those of your brethren." In another letter she bids him graft himself on the Tree of the Cross. We must not be barren trees, grafted on the dead stock of this world, but living trees, grafted into the one fertile Tree, Jesus Christ. She writes as one to whom the woody solitudes of Vallombrosa and Passignano were familiar spots. And, indeed, she had seen with her own eyes the deep shadowy vale down which pours the torrent of the Ellero. She had walked under those dark pines, and listened to the music of the wind among their branches. She had beheld the same scenes which entranced the eyes of Milton—the mountains clothed to their summit with beech trees, the lawns and meadows which preserve a perpetual green from the countless streams with which they are watered, and the blossoms of a thousand hues which could not fail to delight the eye of such a lover of flowers as she was. Like him, too, she had watched the fall of those

> "Autumnal leaves that strew the brooks
> In Vallombrosa, where the Etrurian shades,
> High over-arched, embower."

But whilst *he* retained the image in his mind, to liken it to the fallen host of rebel angels, *she* carried away a memory of the gardens and meadows, the brooks and the luxuriant foliage, to weave it all into a beautiful picture—a parable of the order and loveliness of a faithful religious soul.

One other thing she had also in all probability seen, namely, the miraculous beech tree of Vallombrosa growing over the little cabin which served St. John Gualbert as his first place of retreat. This beech begins to put forth its leaves before all the others in the forest, and retains them long after the foliage has fallen from every other bough. And the good monks (when there were such things at Vallombrosa, for in the late Revolution all have been swept away) used to make crosses out of the wood of this tree, which they distributed as objects of piety. Catherine had one of these crosses, which was given her by Abbot Martin of Passignano, and it was thus she thanked him for it : " You have sent me a cross, reverend Father ; I shall value it more than any I have, and I am greatly touched by your having had the thought of sending it to me. You offer to the eyes of my body that which I ought ever to have present to the eyes of my soul, but, unhappily, I do not do it. I earnestly beg you to pray to our sweet Lord that I may be entirely changed. I will return you cross for cross, inviting you to suffer that of holy desire and bodily suffering for the love of God and the salvation of souls." She wrote a very beautiful letter to the monks of Passignano in common, exhorting them to strict observance of their rule. " You know, my beloved sons," she says, " what sort of persons those monks are who do not follow their rule, but their own irregular desires, and who are weary of their obligations, and seek after the pleasures of the world, desiring its honours, riches, and distinctions which are the death of the soul, and should be the shame and disgrace of a religious. These are stinking flowers which shed forth no perfume, but an odour of infection. . . . The soul that loves prayer is a perfumed flower, and such a soul enjoys all the treasures which can be enjoyed in this life. My dear sons, look on yourselves as novices who have just entered the Order, that you may keep the rule with devotion. Since God has placed you among *angels*, do not you seek to remain among *men;* I mean, by men, seculars who are called only to the common way ; *but you are called to the perfect state, and if in it you are not perfect, you will be less than men and you will descend to the level of irrational brutes.* So be faithful to your cell, love the choir, be obedient, fly conversation, and apply yourselves to watching and prayer." (Letter 69.) John of the Cells survived St. Catherine, and lived to extreme old age. He died, at length, worn out by his penances even more than by his years. The chroniclers of his Order speak of them as "something incredible, whereby his body was, as it were, broken to pieces." He is called by them "a second Socrates," "a beautiful soul," and he was honoured among his brethren, after death, with the title of "the Blessed."

Another religious body with whose members Catherine had very close relations, was the congregation of the Olivetan monks. The Olivetans might indeed be called a Sienese Order, having been founded in 1319 by the Blessed Bernard Tolomei and the Blessed Ambrose Piccolomini, members of the two illustrious families of Siena already often mentioned. Bernard was a learned doctor in the university, who, having become blind, was miraculously cured, and thenceforth renouncing the world, retired to a wild desert about sixteen miles to the south of the city, called Monte di Accona ; and there building a little clay hut, he lived for a time with two friends, until the vision of a silver ladder reaching from earth to heaven, up which he saw the angels leading a company of white-robed monks, put it into his heart to found a religious Congregation. His design being approved by Pope John XXII., they took the Benedictine rule, and founded their first monastery in the same desert tract of country above spoken of. This monastery was erected on the hill of Monte di Accona, which thenceforth received the name of Monte Oliveto. Three other houses of the same Congregation were founded in the Sienese territory, which were all in a state of excellent discipline in St. Catherine's time, in this respect presenting a great and favourable contrast to other religious institutes. During the plague of 1348, Bernard and a considerable number of his monks left their solitude and came into Siena to serve the plague-stricken, himself and eighty of his religious children falling victims to their devoted charity. Catherine was well acquainted both with the Olivetan monks and with their convents, specially with the Mother-house of Monte Oliveto Maggiore, spoken of above,[1] and with that of St. Benedict, situated nearer to the city, outside the Porta Tufi, where lay the body of the holy founder. No fewer than twelve of her letters are preserved, addressed, some to the General, some to the other superiors and some to the novices, of whom several would seem to have been directed in their choice of this Congregation by her advice. Writing to the Prior of St. Benedict's, she says: "I send you two more sheep; give them the repose of their cells and of study. They are two whom you will have no difficulty in feeding, and they will give you much joy and consolation." In St. Catherine's time *study* formed no part of the life of these monks. She was pleading for an exception, which afterwards became the rule. One of the novices so recommended by her appears to have been a son of her friend Nanni di Ser Vanni; and there was a certain Nicholas di Ghida,

---

[1] "Scarcely do we pass the rose-hung walls which encircle the fortifications (of Siena) than we are in an upland desert piteously bleak in winter, but most lovely when spring has come to clothe it. The volcanic nature of the soil gives a softer tint to the colouring. Miles upon miles of open grey-green country—treeless, hedgeless, and houseless,—swoop towards one another with the strangest sinuosities of volcanic earth, till at last they sink away in pink and blue distances, so far off, so pale and aerial that they can scarcely be distinguished from the atmosphere itself. Only here and there a lonely convent, with a few black cypresses around it, cuts the pellucid sky. Here, in these great uplands where all is so immense that the very sky itself seems more full of space than elsewhere, it looks as if it were the very heaven itself, only far away. The steep ascent leads to Monte Oliveto through a barren desert, but about half a mile from the gates the scene changes, and the desert becomes an oasis. The immense depths below the buildings are covered with wood, while the road is fringed with cypresses and the ancient olive trees which gave the place its name."—(Hare's *Cities of Italy*, vol. iii. p. 300). Æneas Sylvius, afterwards Pope Pius II., visited this spot and speaks of the figs and almonds, pears and apples, and the groves of cypresses; vineyards, too, and walks in the shade of vine leaves, a perennial spring of water with tanks and wells, and fine groves of oak and juniper; and a number of walks winding about the hill with borders of vines, roses, and rosemary.

a famous physician of Siena, who, joining himself to the company
of the Saint's disciples, was led to renounce the world and all its
attractions, and by her advice took the white habit of the
Olivetans. Her letters to all these religious are remarkable for
their appreciation of the duties of a monastic life, and specially
for their admirable instructions on that virtue of religious obedience on which depends the preservation of true observance. In
one of these she develops the thought (so truly Dominican) that
he who observes the vow of obedience, virtually observes all the
other vows. "His bark," she says, "sails straight to the port of
Eternal Life, without striking on any rock. For many rocks are
to be found in the stormy sea of this life, and we shall make shipwreck on them unless we are directed by the safe wind of obedience. The malice of the enemy seeks nothing so much as to
disgust us with prayer and holy obedience, and to make us
believe it impossible to persevere, or to support the obligations of
our rule. He persuades us to take a straw for a beam, and a
hasty word for the blow of a dagger. Again, there is the rock of
the world, ever presenting itself to us decked in the fair show of
riches, honours, and pleasures. And yet in reality it affords
nothing but bitter regrets. It has no solidity, no duration, and
all its seeming joys quickly vanish. Their beauty is like that of
flowers; when we behold them in the meadows they rejoice the
eye and the smell, but as soon as they are gathered, their beauty
and their sweet smell disappear. And so the things of this world
attract and deceive us; they look beautiful; but the soul which
gathers them out of an irregular love finds them empty, without
colour, and without perfume: for the perfume of earthly things
comes from the holy thought of God, from Whom they proceed;
but it is lost to him who would gather and possess them unlawfully. Is it not the fault of the things themselves, or of their
Creator; but only of him who has gathered them, and would not
leave them where he found them growing, and where they ought
to remain: I mean, who has not loved them only for the sake of
God." Then she shows how this irregular love of earthly things
is destroyed by the practice of poverty; and poverty is only truly

practised by him who is obedient to his rule. "He cares for no sensible loss or suffering, because self-will is dead in him, and to him who has no will of his own, pain is a pleasure, and tears a delicious drink. Yes, obedience is truly a queen crowned as with a royal diadem ! She holds the sceptre of perseverance, and bears on her bosom the flowers of all the virtues ; and she gives to mortal men the foretaste of heaven, so that a man becomes an earthly angel !" [1]

[1] Letter 77.

CHAPTER VII.

THE DIALOGUE AND THE LETTERS.

EVERY life has its brief seasons of repose and consolation. For the most part such moments intervene between more troubled periods, as though granted to recruit the soul exhausted by past trials, and to prepare her for yet harder ones. Yet, brief as they are, such times have an unspeakable sweetness; we dare not trust them, for we know too well their fleeting nature, but they come to us like a momentary foretaste of our blessed rest hereafter.

Such a season there was in the life of St. Catherine; a lull granted to her between the stormy scenes of her Florentine mission, and the rising of another tempest of which she did not live to see the close. She returned to Siena towards the end of the summer of 1378, with her heart full of joy and gratitude, rejoicing to be the bearer of good tidings, and singing with the angels, " Peace on earth to men of good-will ! " And she chose the season of comparative leisure which at last she was able to command, in order to put into writing some of those secrets of the Spiritual Life which she had learnt in her long hours of communing with God.

" As soon as Urban VI. had concluded peace with Florence," says Raymund, "Catherine returned home and occupied herself actively in the composition of a book which she dictated under the inspiration of the Holy Ghost. She recommended her secretaries to be present during her ecstasies, and carefully to write down whatever she might then dictate : they did it faithfully, and collected a book full of great and useful truths. She dictated this work while her soul was abstracted from her bodily senses, so that she neither saw, nor heard, nor was sensible to touch; God desiring to make known that this work did not resemble that of man, but was inspired by the Holy Spirit."[1] The book here spoken of is the Dialogue, and we feel a desire to know some more particulars of its composition than are here given—Where was it dictated? Who were the secretaries? Were any pages written by her own hand?

It is stated in the Process that it was written "at different times and in different places!" but we have indisputable evidence as to the place where, at least, a great portion of it was composed, and where it was undoubtedly finished. Our readers will remember the good hermit Fra Santi, whom Catherine twice restored to health, once at Siena, and once at Rocca, at which last place he was present at the exorcism of the possessed woman. In company with some of her disciples, Catherine often visited him in his hermitage, attached to which was a little chapel, where she loved to retire out of the noise and bustle of the city. In particular, she often came there between the months of July and October 1378, accompanied by one or other of her secretaries and sisters. Here in this oratory or chapel, as Caffarini informs us in the Third part of his Supplement, a good part of the Dialogue was written; and here it was finished on the 13th October of that same year. He attests this fact as an ocular witness, and says he often saw how, when she retired to that spot and began to pray, she was rapt in ecstasy, and began to speak with God as in a dialogue. No vestige now remains of this little oratory, nor does any certain tradition exist as to where it was situated ; a matter to be regretted, for, had it been preserved, it would have been justly regarded as one of the most venerable sanctuaries consecrated by the presence of the Saint.

The secretaries who wrote the Dialogue from her dictation were

[1] Leg., Part 3, chap. i. Our readers will, of course, understand that the term "inspired" as here applied to the writings of St. Catherine, must not be interpreted in its rigorous sense. Raymund's real meaning is probably identical with that expressed by Pius II. in the Bull of Canonisation ; *Doctrina ejus infusa, non acquisita fuit.*

Neri Landoccio, Stephen Maconi, and Barduccio Canigiani, to whose number was sometimes added the faithful Christofano. Caffarini, in his deposition, has very exactly described the manner in which she dictated it. " Sometimes she held her hands clasped on her breast, sometimes she walked about the room, or knelt down for a while, always however keeping her eyes turned towards heaven. And if, from accidental interruptions, she allowed some days to pass without having dictated anything, she would take up the subject as exactly as if she had only just left off, and had everything in her mind."

Stephen speaks for himself in his " Letter to Caffarini," which forms part of the Process. Referring to Catherine's ecstasies, which he had often witnessed, he says, "She gives the explanation of these things in *her Book*, great part of which I wrote from her dictation." But was *all* written by the hand of her secretaries ? for by this time she had herself acquired the art of writing. Caffarini assures us that far from its being true that, as Raymund expresses it, "her body was all the time in a complete state of insensibility," she wrote several pages of the Book with her own hand. After relating the story of the verses written in cinnabar at Rocca, he says that this was not a faculty granted for the moment only, but permanently. "The Venerable Don Stephen Maconi, who among others served as her secretary, and was one of those most dear to her, has assured me that she wrote him a letter in the vulgar tongue, as a sign of her partial affection to a most dear son ; for it was the first letter she ever wrote. He also assured me that *he had seen her write with her own hands (besides not a few important letters) many sheets of the Book by her composed in the vulgar tongue.* And he freely confesses out of love and devotion having gathered up some of those sheets ; and in order to preserve them in a safe place, he deposited them in the Carthusian Monastery of Pontignano, two miles from Siena, which was the house of his profession " (Sup., Part 1, Trat. 1, § 10).

Gigli, when editing the Saint's works in 1707, made every inquiry to ascertain if these precious autographs were yet in existence, but without success ; and he could only suppose that they had been conveyed to the great Chartreuse a few years previously, at a time when all the smaller Carthusian houses were required to send thither their most valuable manuscripts.[1] But if these pages have been lost, a happier fate has awaited some of the original copies of the Dialogue, written by the hands of her secretaries. One of these which still exists formed the text which Gigli edited. It was at that time preserved in the private chapel of Signor Silvio Gori Pannellini of Siena, and an exact description of the manuscript will probably be interesting to the reader. It is written on parchment, and in the margin appear certain Latin notes, set down by the disciples to whom the Saint dictated. It runs on continuously; the division into chapters, however, being noted in the margin, and, as it would seem, at a later period. Gigli supposes this copy to be in the handwriting of Stephen Maconi. For at the end of the manuscript appear the identical words which Stephen was in the habit of putting at the conclusion of his letters, "Pray for your useless and sinful brother." The same disciple has also added some of her letters, and the *Transito*, or account of her death, to which he prefixes the following introduction: "I will not write part of the order of the happy and glorious end of this most sweet Virgin, according as our base intellects can understand the same, pre-occupied as they are with immense grief." Whence it appears that the writer was one of her faithful followers, and as Gigli supposes, none other than Stephen Maconi himself.

The Dialogue was translated into Latin by Christofano di Gano, who gives the following account of the matter in his Memoirs: "This servant of Christ," he says, "made a notable thing, namely a book about the size of a missal. She composed it all being in ecstasy abstracted from the use of all her senses, except her tongue. God the Father spoke to her,[2] and she

---

[1] Whilst the present work has been in compilation, application has been made to the Superior of the Grande Chartreuse, to ascertain what had become of these inestimable relics of our holy Mother: but nothing was there known about them.

[2] We must again remind the reader not to attach too rigorous a sense to these expressions. Christofano's addiction to matter of fact led him to make

replied and made her demands of Him; and she repeated His words and her own likewise, and all in the vulgar tongue. She dictated, and another wrote, sometimes Barduccio, sometimes Don Stephen, and sometimes Neri di Landoccio. This is a thing difficult to believe, but to those who heard and wrote it, it does not seem so, *and I was one of these.* Then as the book was in the vulgar tongue, and as those who know grammar or have any learning do not so much care to read things thus written, as they do to read Latin, I, for my own satisfaction and that of my neighbours, translated it into Latin, according to the text, adding nothing; and I tried to do it as well as ever I could, and spent several years over it as a matter of pleasure, now on one part, now on another. And when by the grace of God I had finished it, I sent it to Don Stephen, then at Pontignano, that he might correct it, for it was he who wrote down the greater part of it at Catherine's dictation. And when it was corrected, I caused it to be copied by a good writer, and bound. And it was hardly finished when a certain Bishop, of the Order of Preachers belonging to France, who had seen and spoken with Catherine at Avignon, came to Siena with Master Raymund, then General of the Order. I had not had the book in my house one night before I carried it to the Bishop, who was so pleased with it that he would not let it go out of his hands. And he begged me to give it him, which I did. He assured me that he found some things set forth in that Book better than in any of the Doctors, and declared that he should preach its doctrine in his own country, and gain great fruit of souls."

We cannot attempt in this place anything like an analysis of this celebrated work. Those who would desire to know something of St. Catherine's doctrine must study it in her own pages; nor would it be easy to name any writings which combine in equal proportions the practical with the sublime. In whatever qualified sense we understand the expressions used by her disciples, when speaking of the source whence she derived her doctrine, no

no distinction between the literal and the mystic; and the extreme simplicity of his language must not be measured by rules of theological exactitude.

one can read the Dialogue without feeling that she who dictated those words, uttered them with her own soul absorbed in the presence and the sense of God. This, in fact, was the special grace and privilege which she enjoyed through life; she was never for one moment separated from the Divine Presence; and it is a grace which has stamped its character on every page of her book. Hence it would be difficult for any one to imbibe her teaching without a certain sensible increase in the virtue of faith. Not that she treats of the different revealed doctrines by way of controversy, but with her own soul filled to overflowing with the perfection of that fundamental virtue, she ever sets before us the rock on which it rests, namely, the Truth of God. We might say that she worshipped the very name of truth, as was befitting a daughter of the glorious Order which bears the word VERITAS as its motto. Did we possess such a thing as a concordance of St. Catherine, it would be a marvel to see how often and how lovingly she uttered it.[1] Her understanding was illuminated by that divine light, of which she discourses so wonderfully and in so many places,—the Light of Faith—which communicates to a finite mortal intellect the whole Truth of God.[2] Although, then, St.

[1] We will give but one example from her twelfth prayer. *O Verità, Verità, e chi son' io, che Tu dai a me la Verità tua? La Verità tua è quella che porge la Verità, e con la Verità tua dico la Verità. Non è separata da Te la Verità tua, anco tu sei essa Verità. Tu Deità Eterna, Figliuolo di Dio, venisti di Dio per adempire la Verità del Padre Eterno, e nauno può avere Verità, se non da Te Verità.*

[2] A recent biographer of St. Catherine has hazarded the assertion that in her writings the Saint makes little or no allusion to points of doctrine, specially those "rejected by the reformed churches." If by doctrine is meant controversy, the remark is true; the reformers not having yet arisen, she could hardly be expected to enter the lists against them. But if intended to convey the idea that St. Catherine's teaching is vague on those points of revealed truth, on which the reformers have since differed from the teaching of the Church, its inaccuracy is amazing. We will notice only her words on Faith as first infused into the soul in Holy Baptism (pp. 44, 52, 154). Of the three kinds of Baptism (p. 111). On the necessity of the Holy Sacrament, (p. 184,) the virtue of which is not diminished by the sins of the ministers (pp. 25, 37). On Sacramental Confession (p. 111; also Prayer vii.) On Sacramental and Spiritual Communion (p. 96). On the Holy Eucharist (p. 175-178). On the Dignity and Office of the Pope, as successor of St.

Catherine's language is never that of controversy, yet it is worthy of remark, how naturally some of her phrases seem almost to anticipate certain expressions in our " Abridgment of Christian Doctrine ;" as when she reminds a man of the world to whom she is writing that "the end of our creation is to love and serve God here, and to enjoy Him hereafter," or speaks of the likeness which our soul bears to the Blessed Trinity in its three powers, namely, the memory, the understanding, and the will.

Nevertheless, it is doubtless true that in speaking of the *doctrine* of St. Catherine we generally have in our mind something distinct from theological teaching.   We understand rather her idea of the spiritual life as a path, a bridge by which the soul reaches God by union with Jesus Christ, by the surrender of self-will, by the practice of obedience, and by perseverance in prayer.   On all these subjects she tells us the old truths in words so strong and massive, that they seem like huge columns supporting our puny conceptions.   While her own spirit of adoring reverence builds up our faith and our sense of God, she teaches us also to understand the value of our own immortal souls.   When, indeed, she speaks on that subject, her language may fitly be termed inspired. "The soul in which God dwells by grace," she says, "is a heaven " (p. 49), "when united to Him by charity, it is another Christ " (p. 38); "it cannot live without love, for it was created for love and by love" (p. 76).   "Herein is its amazing dignity, that it is able to love God" (p. 77).   "It lives to God in proportion as it dies to self" (p. 333).   She truly writes as one to whom the gift was given of *seeing souls.*   Indeed, certain as it is that St. Catherine knew nothing of the science of human nature from study, she may nevertheless be said to have been an eminent psychologist. Those who are versed in mental science bear witness to her wonderful knowledge of the human soul in all its operations.   She sees its nature, its faculties, and its powers as with the vision of

Peter, and Vicar of Christ (p. 183).   On Free-Will (p. 62 ; also Prayer vii.) On the foreknowledge of God (*ibid.*) On the Blessed Virgin, who co-operated by her Dolours in the redemption of the world (Prayer 11) ; and who obtains from God eternal life for those who are her faithful clients (p. 251).

the eyes, and all their mutual relations and interactions, under whatever influence, whether human or divine. She is equally conversant with the effects of every action of soul on body, or body on soul. This science had its origin from the clear intuition which she possessed into her own soul,—an intuition which taught her all the ways of human nature, and which she derived from contemplating herself in the mirror of God's Light. This wonderful knowledge is manifested in every page of the Dialogue, in the opening paragraph of which she expresses the source of her knowledge in these terms :

"A certain soul being full of great and fervent desires for God's honour and the salvation of souls, exercised herself for some space of time in the habit of Virtue, abiding continually in the cell of self-knowledge, in order that she might better come to know the goodness of God. For from knowledge proceeds love, and he who loves seeks to follow the truth and to clothe himself with it. But there is no means by which a creature can so taste and be illuminated by truth as that of humble and continual prayer, founded on the knowledge of self and of God. For prayer thus exercised unites the soul to God, following the footsteps of Christ crucified ; and so by the desire, and affection, and union of love He makes her one with Himself. This appears by the very words of Christ Himself, ' If any man love Me and keep My word I will manifest Myself to him, and he shall be one with Me, and I with Him.' And in other places we find similar words, whence we may gather that He is the Truth, and that by the affection of Love the soul becomes one with Him."

In other words, the illumination of Divine Truth which St. Catherine enjoyed was derived from no human source, but was the effect of her union with God by Love,—a union effected by prayer, and which rendering her one with the Object beloved, put her in possession of the Truth which He Himself manifested to her. Next to her magnificent utterances on God and the soul, we should be disposed to single out the passages in her writings which treat of the Will as among those most remarkable and most useful in these our days. One of the weapons with which she combated the powers of evil was the earnest warning she gave to her disciples, that their wills, when made strong by grace in the Blood of Christ, are fortresses which cannot be stormed unless we basely open the gates to the enemy. In these weak days, when men are hardly willing to believe in their own possession of a faculty which they have no heart to use, her exhortations on this subject are a true spiritual tonic. "Your will," she writes, "strengthened by the Blood of Christ, is given you by God. You can keep, or you can lose, that fortress, as you please. It is a weapon, which if you choose to make over into the hands of the devil is a knife that will slay you. We call our wills weak; they are weak when they are opposed to God's will; united to His, they are strong." For, far from her was the thought that our human wills have any strength for good apart from the grace of God! Let us hear her own beautiful words: "Thou seest, O Lord, the law of our perverse nature, ever apt to rebel against Thy will. Thou seest how weak, and frail, and miserable it is. But in all things Thou providest for Thy creature, and hast found a remedy for all. Thou givest him the rock and fortress of Thy Will, to make his will strong; for Thou permittest the will of thy creature to share in the strength of Thy will; and hence we see that our will is strong in proportion as it is conformed to Thine, and weak in proportion as it is opposed to Thine : for Thou hast created our wills in the likeness of Thy Will, and abiding in Thee, they are strong." [1]

The subject is of sufficient interest to excuse our adding a few extracts from her letters in which the same teaching is conveyed in a more familiar style. "We may be sure of this that God permits us trials only to exercise us in patience, strength, and perseverance. These virtues all spring out of self-knowledge, for it is in the hour of combat that we learn our own nothingness. If I were anything, I should be able to deliver myself, but of myself I am powerless alike over the tempests of the soul, or the maladies of the body. *We can only conquer by a will that knows how to resist ;* and such a will we must seek in the goodness of God." (Letter 56.) "You

---

[1] Prayer 7.

will say to me, 'I lack the weapons with which to fight, how am I to procure them?' I answer, Every reasonable creature may have them, if he chooses, by divine grace. Both good and evil are effected by the will; it is the consent alone which makes a thing to be either vice or virtue; for without the will, sin would not be sin, or virtue virtue. And this will is so strong that nothing has power to move it without its own consent. Hear St. Paul, who says, 'Neither hunger nor thirst, nor persecution, nor the sword, nor things present, nor things to come, can separate me from the charity of God.' In these words he shows us what is the strength of that will which God in His mercy has given us. Let no one, therefore, say *I cannot*, for no person can be excused from wilful sin." (Letter 85.) Again she presses home the truth that the disordered will is the only source of all our sufferings. " To have what we would not have, is indeed the source of suffering; but when we are clothed with the eternal will of God and not our own, we become one with Him, and judge all things in love, according to His most holy Will." (Letter 53.) "The servant is not greater than his Lord; he suffers in love, bathing himself in the Blood of Jesus, *and there his self-will dies.* And when once the will is dead, all suffering disappears, for it is our self-will alone that makes our tribulations painful; when that is dead, and we are clothed with God's will, suffering is a pleasure, and sensual pleasure becomes a pain. This is the way by which the saints travelled; they knew that the eternal kingdom was not to be bought with pleasure; but when our will is one with God's will, then indeed we enjoy the foretaste of eternal life." (Letter 55.)

But this sensitive self-will is always in rebellion, how then are we to master and kill it, and bring it into subjection? Here is her recipe, strong and heroic teaching indeed, and, as we know, one she had made trial of by her own experience. " Let reason sit on the tribunal of your conscience, and pass over not so much as the least thought opposed to God. Let a man know how to distinguish between his reason and his sensuality, and let reason take a two-edged knife and put sensuality to death. Let him reduce it to slavery by never giving it what it cries for. If it asks to sleep, let him watch; if it would eat, let him fast; if it seek any other indulgence, let him take the discipline; if it would give way to sloth and negligence, let him persevere in holy exercises; if it would yield to imaginations inspired by the devil, let him terrify it with the thought of death." (Letter 296.)

The Dialogue, as we at present possess it, is divided into four Treatises, namely, those on Discretion, Prayer, Divine Providence, and Obedience. We would venture the surmise that although the work forms one whole, yet not only were these divisions made from the first, but that certain other portions also, which treat on particular subjects, were written separately, and received distinct titles. This at least seems to explain the Saint's own allusion (in a letter to Francis Tebaldi) to her " Treatise on Tears," by which we understand the 87th to the 97th chapters of the Dialogue. The Treatise on Obedience contains some of the finest passages of the whole composition ; as, when she comes to speak of the different religious Orders in the Church and their distinct object and spirit, unable to restrain the enthusiasm of a loyal daughter of St. Dominic, she describes the glorious Father guiding the ship of his Order, and "desiring that his sons should seek no other thing than the glory of God and the salvation of souls . . . And he made his Order a royal Order, large, joyous, and odoriferous, as a delightful garden." [1]

We cannot close this chapter without saying a little more on the subject of the Saint's letters, which in style and variety are not inferior to the Dialogue.

And first, it may be of interest to compare with the account which Caffarini has given of her method of dictating the Dialogue, another description which is given by Francesco Malevolti in his deposition, of what he himself witnessed when writing her letters ; for he frequently acted as her secretary : " I saw her dictate many letters at the same time to several writers," he says, "and particularly to three at once, and this not once only, but innumer-

---

[1] *La sua religione, tutta larga, tutta gioconda, tutta odorifera, è uno giardino dilettissimo in sè.* Dial., chap. clviii.

able times, and during the course of many years. . . . When she so dictated, her dictation never required correction, addition, or retrenchment, unless from some fault on our part. Once we were all three writing at the same time, one was engaged on a letter to be sent to Pope Gregory XI., another on one to be sent to the Lord Bernabò Visconti, and the third to another great personage, whose name I now forget. She dictated now to one and now to another; now with her face covered, now looking to heaven with her hands crossed, and many times in ecstasy, yet in that state still continuing to dictate. It happened as she did so, that as she said some words only to one of us, we each wrote down the same words, each one believing they had been spoken to himself. When we perceived this, we supposed we had committed an error, so asked her to which of us she had spoken those words, because each of us had written them down. But she answered kindly, 'Do not be uneasy, you have done right; we shall see when the letters are finished that the words will answer the purpose of all.' And wonderful to say, although the letters were addressed on various subjects and to persons so different, yet when we read over these words, they were so much to the point of each of the three letters, that not one of them could have done well without the words in question." [1]

The many extracts which have been already given of these wonderful compositions may have furnished the reader with some idea of their general character; but it is only after a close and long perusal, assisted by a study of the circumstances under which they were written, and the persons to whom they were addressed, that we can gain a real insight into the mind and heart of St. Catherine, a mind illuminated by its continual contemplation of the Eternal truth; a heart made one with the Heart of Christ. Setting aside their value as a body of spiritual instructions, how unspeakable is their beauty! the freshness of their illustrations, the vigour of their style! Open them at hazard where you will, and you are sure to light on some passage flooded with intellectual splendour. "God manifests Himself in many ways," she

---

[1] Dep. Fran. Mal., chap. vii.

says, writing to a Carthusian of Pontignano, "for has not the Blessed Christ told us that in His Father's house there are many mansions? Who could number up the diversity of gifts and graces which are to be found, not merely in all creatures, but in one soul! For though all must have the virtue of charity, and without it all the other virtues are nothing, yet each has some one virtue which predominates over the rest, and this makes up the differences of life. The saints who have attained eternal life did not all attain it in the same way. They do not all resemble one another; and there is the same difference among the Angels; they are not all equal. One of the great joys of the soul in eternity will be to contemplate the greatness of God in the variety of rewards which He dispenses to His saints. We find the same variety in created things, which all differ one from another, yet were all created for the same end; for God created them all for love. He who would know God's glory and greatness may find it in the contemplation of all these things, whether visible or invisible." (Letter 55.)

Let us hear her addressing Rainaldo of Capua, of whom we are told that he was "a man of subtle genius and a great investigator of the mysteries of God and of the Holy Scriptures." Proud of his intellect, he considered himself to be thereby an enlightened man; and Catherine, without presuming to rebuke him for his conceit, endeavours to set before him the grand truth that the real light of the soul is not knowledge, but Faith; and that without it we walk in darkness. "If we consider by what means we may lose the eye of the body," she says, "we find that it may be lost by the blow of a sword or a stone, or by dust which enters and injures it, or by heat, as happens to those who are blinded by the glare of a red-hot vessel, which destroys the pupil;[1] by all these ways we lose our bodily sight. And the eye of our understanding is in like manner destroyed by the sword of vice, or the

---

[1] She is here alluding to a cruel method of blinding criminals by compelling them to fix their eyes on brazen vessels, made red hot. This punishment was practised in the Middle Ages at Constantinople. The eyes of the victims were thereby destroyed without disfigurement.

dust of earthly pleasure ; by the glare of vainglory, or the scorching heat of pride. . . . Yet a man may recover his sight by somewhat the same means as that which caused its loss. What is that burning vessel which, placed before the eyes of our intelligence, will restore their sight? even Jesus, who entering the vessel of our Humanity, displayed there the burning fire of God's ineffable charity, and the splendour of the Divine nature united to the nature of man. That is the object on which if our eye be fixed, it will dry up our self-love, and dissipate our darkness, and diffuse a supernatural light into our understanding." Then she goes on patiently unfolding the idea that is in her mind, how when the supernatural illumination of Faith is substituted for the natural light of our own purblind intellect, it produces all the virtues ; first, love, because we cannot love until we know ; and then humility, and the desire to be like what we love, and therefore the desire of suffering. And thus at last the soul attains the sublime virtue of Patience, understanding that God gives us tribulations and temptations only that we may be sanctified in Him ; and accepting them sweetly "because it cannot complain of that which is its good." Having got thus far, it is not difficult for her to remind Rainaldo that the humble believer seeks not to penetrate the secret mysteries of God, but rather to know himself, to see in all things God's will, and to taste the fire of His charity. "But unlike Him, the proud and presumptuous man before he will enter the valley of humility pretends to examine the conduct of God and to ask, 'Why does He act thus? Why does He give to me what He has not given to another?' As though he would lay down laws to God instead of adoring His goodness.

" And there are some who, destitute alike of humility and self-knowledge, would subtilise, and with the darkened eye of their own understanding would seek to understand and explain the Holy Scriptures and the Apocalypse, and so draw death out of life, and out of light, darkness. The soul that should be full of God, is full of vain phantoms, and all because, instead of descending, it has sought to exalt itself. What folly ! I do not know myself, and I presume to investigate the secrets of God ! *But if we would see the stars of His mysteries, we must first descend into the deep well of humility;*[1] for the humble soul casts herself upon the earth in acknowledgment of her own baseness, and then God raises her up." Then she goes on to speak of prayer, as the means by which the soul may unceasingly gaze upon the Truth ; and all this is the work of Faith which inspires humility and sorrow for sin, and chases away despair, and establishes us in Hope. Then at the sound of that word, like one on whose ears there bursts a sudden strain of exquisite music, she breaks forth into one of those passages to which it is hard to refuse the name of poetry, only because not written in the metre of versification :—

"O Hope ! Sweet Sister of Faith ! 'tis thou that with the Key of the Blood dost open the portals of Eternal Life ! Thou guardest the city of the soul against the enemy of confusion : thou slackenest not thy steps when the demon would seek to trouble the soul with the thought of her sins, and so to cast her into despair; but generously pressing on in the path of virtue, and putting in the balance the Price of the Blood, thou placest the crown of victory on the brow of perseverance !" (Letter 236.)

It is difficult in looking over the large collection of St. Catherine's letters to know which to select as best worthy of our study. Those addressed to the religious houses of various Orders with which she was connected are wonderfully solid in their instructions. No less solid, though written from a totally different point of view, are her letters of direction to persons living in the world ; and of these we would choose the five addressed to Ristoro Canigiani as models of prudence and persuasive eloquence. Ristoro, the son of Peter, and the elder brother of Barduccio Canigiani, was a man of uncommon gifts and endowments. He was a skilful advocate, and cultivated a taste for literature, showing himself no mean poet, if we may judge from

---

[1] This exquisite illustration is founded on a fact well known to men of science, even in St. Catherine's days, namely, that even at noon the stars may be discerned from the bottom of a deep well, or the shaft of a mine. Such excavations have been made for the purpose of astronomical observations at various times and places ; one of the most famous was to be seen in the Paris observatory built by Louis XIV.

his poem of the "Ristorato," which is still preserved. He had incurred great losses in the insurrection of the Ammoniti, but his intercourse with Catherine during her residence in Florence had inspired him with a certain indifference to worldly prosperity, and after her departure he wrote to her to say that he forgave those who had injured him in the late troubles, and that he felt a desire in his soul to spend the remainder of his life more entirely for God. But here was his difficulty. His place was in the world, for he was married and the father of a young family; and his profession obliged him to mix with public affairs; and how was all this to be harmonised with a devout life? Then in the matter of his worldly property; did the Gospel rule require him not to demand what was justly his, but to abandon his lawful rights? and was his profession of advocate really one in which a man could serve God? In fact, he laid before her exactly the ordinary perplexities which are continually arising in the consciences of those whose vocation is to sanctify themselves in a secular state of life.

Catherine replies with a discretion and moderation which exacted from him no more than he was able to perform, while at the same time she leads him gradually on to perfection, in proportion as his firmness of purpose becomes strengthened, and his spiritual instincts have grown keener. He may certainly claim what is justly due to him; for no man is required to renounce what justly belongs to him. If he feels inspired to keep away from the Palazzo and other places of public resort, that is well. It is best to fly occasions of disturbance and temptation, and to remain in the quiet of his own home. "Nevertheless," she says, "I make one exception; if the poor have need of some one to plead their cause, you will greatly please God by exerting yourself for them out of charity, as St. Ivo did in his time, and so earned the title of the advocate of the poor." Then if he wants some easy way of sanctifying his every-day duties, let him take the exercise of the presence of God. "Think that the eye of God is ever on you and that you must die, and you know not when. Labour for the peace and happiness of your soul, that is your first duty. Relieve your conscience of everything that can burden it, forgiving injuries and repairing wrongs. Sell some of your superfluities, your sumptuous clothing, for instance, which is of no use, but rather dangerous, for it puffs up the soul with foolish pride. Nevertheless, I would have you dress becomingly, only with less expense, and, as far as you can, persuade your wife and children to observe the same rule, for a father is in duty bound to bring up his children according to the laws of reason and virtue. I think you are right in refusing state offices, for the experience you have had of them shows their danger."

Then she passes to his religious duties, and recommends monthly confession; if more often, so much the better, but not less. Communion on great feasts, or at least once in the year; and if he possibly can, let him hear Mass daily. Then prayer, and at certain times in the day a few moments of recollection; so as to recall the thought of our sins and God's goodness, and to remind ourselves how much He loves us. "Say every day the Office of our Lady, if you do not do so already, that she may be your refuge and advocate before God; and fast in her honour on Saturdays, as well as on the other days prescribed by the Church. And at all times live simply, and renounce excessive banqueting, for no man can long preserve innocence if he does not know how to mortify himself in eating and drinking." Then from the level of this ordinary rule of life, she leads him on, step by step, to higher things, till in her last letter we plainly see that he and his wife have generously embraced a life of perfection. There is no longer question of Communion "once a year," but frequently; he has come to understand what is meant by the "continual prayer of holy thoughts and desires," and to "love often to find himself with God in actual prayer;" and his eyes have opened to that interior light which draws him powerfully to the love of virtue "in all times and places and positions wherever God places us, conforming ourselves in all things to the sweet will of Him who desires nothing but our sanctification. Oh, what immense joy fills my heart!" she exclaims, "when I think of your salvation; for I see by your letter that this light has not been obscured in your soul. Otherwise you could not see so clearly the misery and inconstancy of the world, or despise it so truly, and so earnestly follow after perfection. Oh, how happy I shall be to see you advancing still from virtue to virtue, spite of the attacks of the enemy who will not fail to surround you with snares; and to cherish and augment that light, I would have you ever keep before your mind four things. First, remember how much God loves you; secondly, reflect how generously we ought to love God; in the third place, consider how detestable sin is to God and man; and fourthly, think of that everlasting reward of which St. Paul says, 'that the sufferings of this life are not to be compared to the eternal weight of glory which God has prepared for those who love Him.' Courage, then," she says in conclusion, "courage in the Precious Blood! It is ever near you. Love to be alone with God in prayer, and repeat all these things to your wife. Quit the common way, and embrace the life of angels; God calls you to it. Respond generously to His call, and you will indeed, even in this world, be a family of Angels."

Occasionally there fall from her pen expressions of amazing beauty, which show how richly her mind was stored with graceful images. Writing to the Cardinal del Porto, she says, "I said just now that you must be a lamb in order to follow the true Lamb. But you must be a lion also, and utter your roar over the Holy Church, to the end that you may raise to life again the children who lie dead in her bosom.[1] If you ask, 'Where am I to learn that cry?' I answer, From the Immaculate Lamb, Who though in His Humanity He uttered no cry, but remained meek and silent, yet in His Divinity He gave forth the cry of His measureless compassion. For in the power of that love which united God and man the Lamb became a Lion; and from the Cross He sent forth His cry over His dead child—humanity;— a cry which destroyed death, and restored life to the whole human race." Writing to another Cardinal, James Orsini, she speaks of the folly of pride, a fault into which men fall through

---

[1] It was a poetical notion of the Middle Ages that the lion could raise its dead cubs to life again by roaring over them.

lack of self-knowledge. "For if men knew their own nothingness, they could not be proud. The being we have, we received from God. We did not ask Him to create us: He was moved to do it out of the love which He had for His creature, whom regarding in Himself, He became enamoured of its beauty. The soul that looks within sees there God's goodness. She sees that she was the real rock in which His Cross was fastened; for neither the rock nor the nails would have kept it there without the force of love. I remember what was once said to a certain servant of God, who cried out in fervour of spirit, saying: 'O Lord, would that I had been the stones, and the earth in which your Cross was planted! What grace should I not have received when your Precious Blood flowed down from the Cross!' And the Sweet and Sovereign Truth replied: 'My daughter, thou and all reasonable creatures were indeed the stones that held Me fast; for it could only be My love for you that so held me; nothing else was capable of holding the Incarnate God!'"

Of her more familiar letters the many quotations already given in different parts of the present volume may perhaps suffice as specimens. It is difficult, if not impossible, however, to render the beauties of her style in a translation, and particularly the tenderness which, like a true woman, she usually reserves for those of her disciples who gave her most trouble. Thus in writing to Francesco Malevolti, whose complete conversion was not effected until some time after her death, and who was always making good resolutions and as often breaking them, she addresses him as *Carissimo e sopra carissimo figlio;* and adds, "I may well call you dear, for you have cost me many tears and much anguish; but console my soul, and do not refuse to come to me." Brother Simon of Cortona was a novice, and as such comes in for the youngest child's portion in the shape of messages such as a mother sends to her nursery, "Bless my son Simon for me, and tell him to open his mouth for some milk which his mother is going to send him." "Bless my dear son Simon for me, and tell him he must learn to run with the stick of good desires." Messages of this sort often occur in her letters to F.

Bartholomew Dominic, with whom she was completely at her ease. When at Asciano he wrote to her, begging her to come there and take part in the good work that was going on. "I would come willingly," she replies, "were it only to please you; but the weather does nothing but rain, and I have been so weak for ten days past, that I have scarce been able to get to the church except on Sunday. Father Thomas feels compassion for me, and does not think me fit to come so far. . . . I must therefore help you invisibly by praying for you and all the people, though, had it been possible, I would gladly have helped you visibly also. Tell Brother Simon, my son in Jesus Christ, that a son should never be afraid of coming to his mother, and that he should run to her, specially when he has been hurt. Then his mother opens her arms and takes him to her bosom; and though I admit that I am but a bad mother, yet I will always carry him on the bosom of charity. So now remember, no negligence but zeal, and then my soul will be joyful before God." As was natural, one who could be so tender in encouragement, could equally use a mother's familiarity when it was necessary to give a rebuke. "Respond, negligent son, respond to God's grace," she writes to Stephen Maconi; "it is a shame to see God always standing at the door of your soul, and you not opening it to Him." In fact, she generally contrives to give Stephen a little motherly admonition even in the titles of her letters, which are addressed to "Stephen, my worthless and ungrateful son;" or to "Stephen, poor in all virtue." Writing to Neri, she says, "Encourage and bless my son Simon from me a thousand and a thousand times; tell him to pray for all his brothers, who send him their compliments, specially that negligent Stephen." Probably Stephen himself was acting on this occasion as secretary.

Our limits warn us to stop, though to do so we must close the volumes that solicit us to linger over their pages. We will but add that both the Dialogue and the Letters are accepted by all critics as models of pure Italian; that the most learned academies have ranged them amongst their *Tesli di Lingua;* and that the dyer's daughter of Siena has taken her place in the literature of her native land by the side of Petrarch and Bocaccio.

Part II.

THE GREAT SCHISM.

CHAPTER I.

URBAN VI., 1378.

GREGORY XI. died at Rome on the 27th of March, 1378. The College of Cardinals, on whom devolved the duty of electing his successor, consisted of twenty-three members, of whom one was a Spaniard, four were Italians, and the remaining nineteen were Frenchmen. Only sixteen Cardinals were present in Rome, six remaining at Avignon, and one being absent at Sarzana, where the Congress was then sitting. They entered the conclave immediately after the funeral obsequies of the late Pope had been concluded, and had hardly commenced their proceedings when a tremendous uproar was raised in the city by the populace, who demanded that a Roman, or at least an Italian Pope should be given to them. The Cardinals themselves were divided in their wishes; seven of the French Cardinals desired a Limousin; the others were as hotly opposed to this proposal; till, seeing the impossibility of carrying the election according to their own views, they determined on fixing their choice on some Italian prelate, renowned for virtue, who should be equally independent of either party among the electors. Their choice fell on Bartholomew Prignano, Archbishop of Bari, and a Neapolitan by birth. This latter circumstance seemed to secure his favourable acceptance by the Roman people, as well as the support of the Queen of Naples, whose close alliance with France would also, it was hoped, secure the good-will of the French nation. The election was unanimous, with the exception of Cardinal Orsini, who contented himself with declaring that he gave his vote to whoever should be elected by the majority. The Archbishop was therefore admitted into the conclave; and his election being made known to him, he was declared Pope in the usual manner, taking the name of Urban VI. Knowing the turbulence of the populace, however, the Cardinals hesitated at once to publish the election, lest they should provoke a riot when it was known that they had not elected a Roman. They were considering how best to act, when some report of what had passed having transpired, the mob surrounded the conclave with cries and threats of violence. To gain time until they should be able to effect their retreat to a place of safety, the Cardinals allowed the rumour to be put in circulation that Tebaldeschi, the old Cardinal of St. Peter's, had been elected Pope, but that he had declined the dignity; and in fact, his name had been proposed by Cardinal Orsini, and rejected on account of his great age. At the mention of his name the excited crowds at one rushed to his house, and according to what was considered their privilege in such cases, began to pillage it; others forced their way into the conclave, as though to compel Tebaldeschi to accept the papal dignity. The terrified Cardinals implored him not to undeceive the excited people until they should have had time to effect their escape; and the poor old man found himself against his will clad with pontifical vestments, and half suffocated by the crowds of citizens who came to kiss his hands and feet with every boisterous demonstration of delight. At last he succeeded in delivering himself from their hands, and made known to them the fact that it was not he, but the Archbishop of Bari, who was elected Pope; on hearing which, there was a burst of indignation. "We will not have him!" they cried, "we will have none but a Roman!" The tocsin was sounded, and the whole city was thrown into a state of excitement and alarm.

Next day, however, calm was restored; and the Cardinals reassembled to confirm their election of Urban. This was done, and the customary acts of homage were paid him with all possible solemnity. On Easter Day he was crowned at St. John Lateran's with great pomp, after which he despatched letters to all the reigning sovereigns of Europe, announcing his election; and received in return their respectful acknowledgments and congratulations. As to the part taken by the Cardinals, a few facts will suffice to show how entirely the election was recognised to be their own free act. Cardinal Robert of Geneva had been one of the first to offer his spontaneous act of homage; Cardinal Gerard of Amiens, on his return from Sarzana, followed the example of his colleagues. They all addressed letters to the Emperor and other sovereigns, declaring the election they had made; Robert of Geneva himself writing other letters to the same effect to the Emperor, the Count of Flanders, and the Duke of Brittany. Finally, all the members of the Sacred College present in Rome addressed a joint letter to the six Cardinals at Avignon, in which, after declaring Urban VI. to have been lawfully and canonically elected, they use the following words: "At the hour when the Divine Paraclete descended into the hearts of the Apostles at Jerusalem, we freely, and by common consent, united our votes on the person of the most reverend Father in Christ, Bartholomew, Archbishop of Bari; a man eminent for his great merits, whose virtues shine like the lamp of the Sanctuary. . . . We announce these things to you, that if the death of Pope Gregory has filled you with sadness, the gift which God has given to us of such a Father may inspire you with joy."[1] We may add to this the significant facts that the same Cardinals officiated with the Pope at all the great feasts of Easter, the Ascension, Pentecost, and Corpus Christi; that they took part in many of his official acts, such as the conclusion of peace with Florence; and that they applied to him for not a few dispensations and favours for themselves or their friends; Robert of Geneva, in particular, petitioning for, and receiving several special graces; and we gather from the whole narrative, variously as it is related by various historians, three conclusive facts in which all agree. First, that the election of Urban was unanimous. Secondly, that so far from its having been made through fear of the turbulent people, the violence of the populace had been excited by hearing that their demands of a Roman Pope had not been granted. Thirdly, that after making the election, the Cardinals confirmed it; and again and again declared by act and in writing that it had been truly and lawfully made.

The character of the new Pope differed greatly from that of his predecessor. He was a man of great learning and equally great austerity of life, well known as holding in detestation both the habits of luxury and the simoniacal practices too common at that time among ecclesiastics. · Maimbourg, whose authority may certainly be trusted as that of an adverse partisan, says of him in his "History of the Great Schism," that before his elevation to the Chair of St. Peter he appeared to be humble, modest, the friend of good and learned men, pious and mortified, given to practices of penance, and very zealous for the glory of God and the good of the Church. That the severity of his temper was also well known is apparent from a letter written to St. Catherine by Dom Bartholomew, Prior of Gorgona, and dated April 27th, 1378. It seems that the Cardinal of Amiens was at Pisa on his way to Sarzana, when he was summoned back to Rome by the death of Gregory, being escorted thither by Andrew Gambacorta. "Know," writes Dom Bartholomew, "that Master Andrew Gambacorta returned to Pisa last Sunday. According to what he says, this Holy Father of ours is *a terrible man*, and greatly

---

[1] Rinaldi, An. 1378.

frightens people by his acts and words: he says he will have peace, but with the honour of Holy Church; that he does not care for money, and that the Florentines must come to him with truth, and not with lies. . . . He shows great confidence in God; and on that account fears no man in the world, and openly proclaims his resolve to banish the simonies and pomps that reign in the Church of God; and himself shows the example by living moderately with all his Court." This letter fairly represents the character which Urban then bore, and justifies St. Catherine, when writing to her friends at Lecceto, in speaking of him as "a good and just Pastor, who is resolved to purge and root up vices, and to plant virtues; fearing no one, but acting justly and bravely." (Letter 127.)

And, in fact, Urban deserved these commendations; he was a man of unspotted virtue, and had resolved on devoting himself to the difficult task of reform; but he had a stern and inflexible temper, and pursued his purpose with more determination than prudence. Catherine, who had first made his acquaintance at Avignon, and with whom he had since then kept up his relations by correspondence, had early discerned the one defect in his character; and in the first letter she addressed him after his elevation, she drops a few gentle words on the prudence of mingling mercy with justice, which else would rather become injustice. (Letter 15.) Writing at the same time to Cardinal Peter de Luna, she urges him to support the Pope in his measures of reform, but to advise him to employ methods of gentleness and sweetness. (Letter 25.) A little later, when perhaps the rumour had reached her that the first steps taken by the new Pontiff were of a character likely to estrange from him the hearts of his Cardinals, she ventures to address him in yet plainer language. " Act with benevolence and a tranquil heart," she says, "and for the love of Jesus, *restrain a little those too quick movements with which nature inspires you.* God has given you by nature a great heart; I beg of you act so that it may become great supernaturally, and that full of zeal for virtue and the reform of Holy Church, you may also acquire a manly heart, founded in true humility; then you will have both the natural and the super-natural; for without that, mere nature will accomplish but little; it will rather be apt to find expression in movements of pride and anger, and then, perhaps, when there is question of correcting those near to us, it will relax and become cowardly. But joined to the hunger for virtue, whereby a man seeks nothing but the honour of God without thought of self, it will acquire a light, a strength, a constancy, and a perseverance which are above nature, and which will never relax, but will always remain firm and courageous." (Letter 21.)

Happy would it have been for Urban, and for the Church at large, had he listened to the wise counsel suggested by the words above quoted. But following the dictates of a zeal untempered by discretion, he had already begun by making enemies of those whom he sought to reform. On the very day that followed his coronation, after the termination of solemn Vespers, he repri-manded several bishops who were present, reproaching them as guilty of perjury in having left their bishoprics in order to reside in Rome. The severity of his language provoked a haughty reply from the Bishop of Pampeluna, which might have shown Urban how little was to be gained by this method of procedure. However, some days later, having assembled the Cardinals in Consistory, he made them an address on the text, "I am the good pastor," in which he denounced their vices in terrific language, which struck dismay into the hearts of his hearers. When the Cardinal of Amiens presented himself at Court, Urban reproached him with fomenting the hostilities between the kings of France and England for his own private ends; adding other injurious accusations, to which the Cardinal responded by a gesture of indignation, exclaiming at the same time, "Archbishop of Bari, thou liest!" after which he abruptly quitted the council chamber.[1] Nor was this all. The new Pope showed himself equally insensible to the necessity of conciliating the good-will of temporal sovereigns. The news of his election had been re-ceived with every demonstration of joy at Naples, and the queen

---

[1] Rinaldi, An. 1378, No. 45; Baluze, p. 1159.

had despatched to Rome her husband, Otho of Brunswick, to offer her congratulations as an extraordinary mark of respect. He found himself received at Court, however, with scanty courtesy; while at the same time the Pope is said to have opposed certain negotiations which were in progress for a marriage between the heiress of the king of Sicily and a relative of Queen Joanna's; and the result was deeply to offend that powerful princess, who thenceforward became his bitter enemy. Nor was he more happy in his dealings with the susceptibilities of his French Cardinals; for in the zeal which he expressed (in common with all his predecessors) for the conclusion of peace between France and England, he was careful to declare his resolution, that "the king of England should have justice shown him," in terms which were too readily interpreted in a sense hostile to France.

The immediate cause which led to the breach between Urban and the Cardinals is differently related by different historians. Theodoric of Niem, his secretary, says that he made certain constitutions for reforming the Sacred College, and obliging them to a more canonical manner of life. Thomas Petra, Pro-notary of the Apostolic See, and a fervent disciple of St. Catherine, writes to the following effect: "At the time of the disputes between the Cardinals and Pope Urban, I went to the latter, and humbly besought him to tell me the real cause of the quarrel. He replied, 'Indeed, my son, it has not been my fault. They pressed me to restore the Court to Avignon, but we excused ourselves, saying that we neither could nor would do this, seeing that both Urban V. and our predecessor Gregory had come hither to restore the sanctuaries of this city, to revive the devotion of the people towards the Church, and to pacify Italy, which was not yet done; and that, moreover, even if we wished it, we had neither galleys nor other requisite means. To which they replied that Italy had never been ruled by the See Apostolic; and they proposed that we should sell the possessions of the Order of St. John of Jerusalem all over the world, which would furnish us with means ample for all purposes. Hearing which we shuddered, and said we would die a thousand deaths sooner than so destroy the right arm of Christendom; and this was the real ground of quarrel."[1]

It can hardly be matter of surprise that no great tie of sympathy should have existed between Urban and his Cardinals. Independent of the fact that they had elected him rather with the view of excluding other parties in the conclave to whom they were hostile, than out of any decided preference for himself, the fact that he was not a member of the Sacred College considerably diminished his prestige, and rendered it more imperative that he should have sought to win their confidence; or, failing that, that he should have counterbalanced their influence by the creation of other Cardinals eminent for their merits, and devoted to his person. This latter policy was repeatedly pressed by St. Catherine both on Gregory and Urban, but by both it had hitherto been neglected; and to this neglect must mainly be attributed the misfortunes which afterwards ensued.

The month of June had now arrived, a season notoriously unhealthy in Rome; and the French Cardinals seized the pretext for leaving the city and retiring to Anagni. They appear already to have concerted their measures, and began by attempting to draw the Pope thither also, with the intention, had he come, of extorting from him an abdication. Disappointed of this hope, they next began to set afloat doubts as to the validity of his election, and engaged Honorius Gaetano, Count of Fondi and governor of the province, to take into their pay certain Companies of the Breton Free Lances; at the same time securing to their side Peter de Rostaing, the French Commandant of the Castle of St. Angelo. On the 26th of June, Urban, who by this time had become aware of his danger, repaired to Tivoli, whence negotiations were opened between him and the French Cardinals with a view to reconciliation, but without success. Catherine in her retirement heard rumours of what was going on, and at once addressed herself to those who seemed to have it most in their power to avert the threatened calamity. In her letters to the two

---

[1] Thomas Petra, Tom. 4 De Schism: Rinaldi, 1378, No. 25.

Cardinals Orsini and Peter de Luna, she urges them to fidelity to their Head. "I hear," she says, "that discord has broken out between the Christ on earth and his followers. I feel an inexpressible pain, through the fear I have of its producing a heresy. I conjure you, by the Precious Blood that has redeemed you, do not separate from your Head. . . . Alas what misery! all the rest seems but a straw, a mere shadow, compared to the danger of schism." [1]

But Peter de Luna had already suffered himself to be gained over to the party of the rebellious Cardinals, and as cannot be doubted, through a motive of ambition. In fact, the French Cardinals, to whom the adhesion of their Spanish and Italian colleagues was of the utmost consequence, scrupled not to write separately to each one, promising him the tiara if he would desert the party of Urban, and join them at Anagni. At first their intrigues were unsuccessful; the Italian Cardinals remained with the Pope, and took part in several of his official acts; they also endeavoured to mediate between the two parties, and proposed submitting the question in dispute to a general council. Urban would have consented to this proposal, which was, however, scornfully rejected by the French Cardinals; and one by one, the Cardinals Peter de Luna with the three Italians, James Orsini, Simon de Borzano, and Peter di Porto, joined the rest of the deserters at Anagni, and thence proceeded with them to Fondi. One Italian Cardinal, and one only, remained faithful to Urban; it was Tebaldeschi, the aged Cardinal of St. Peter's, who, then lying on his death-bed, solemnly called God to witness that the election of the reigning Pontiff had been made lawfully and freely. The act by which he did this was dated the 22nd of August; shortly after which he expired, and Urban was left alone and unsupported.

Finding himself thus deserted, Urban resolved on filling up the

---

[1] Letters 28, 29. The Saint here uses the words *heresy* and *schism* as equivalents. But in speaking to Raymund in 1375, when she predicted these events, she accurately distinguished the difference, and declared that the scandal that would fall on the Church would in reality be, not a heresy but schism.

ranks of the Sacred College with men of his own choice ; and on the 18th of September nominated twenty-six new Cardinals, of whom two were Frenchmen, and the rest Italians.   Possibly this step hastened the action of the rebellious party, as convincing them that there was no alternative between submission and an entire breach.   They decided on the latter course, and having assembled at Fondi under the protection of Count Honorius Gaetano, they proceeded to consummate the crime on which they had resolved, urged on by the triple motives of fear, resentment, and ambition.

They began by citing Urban to appear before them, and on his non-appearance, drew up a manifesto, in which they declared him to have unlawfully intruded into the Holy See, to which they had elected him, urged solely by their fears of the populace, and in the conviction that as soon as the tumult was over, he would have been moved by his own conscience to have declined the papal dignity ; that they had, it is true, enthroned and crowned him, but still through the sole motive of fear ; wherefore he was no true Pope, but deserving rather of the titles of Apostate and Antichrist.   This extraordinary statement they embodied in an Encyclical letter, which was sent to the reigning European sovereigns, and otherwise circulated among the faithful.   Finally, on the 20th of September, they proceeded to the election of an anti-Pope.   Their choice was as disgraceful as the act itself was criminal; they selected one whose name was notorious throughout Europe as "a man of blood," and who, in Italy particularly, had earned himself an unenviable reputation as leader of those Breton troops by whom had been perpetrated the massacre of Cesena.   This was Cardinal Count Robert of Geneva, a man not without some princely qualities, for he was possessed of graceful manners and a taste for magnificence ; but one who seemed to embody all the faults which were charged against the ecclesiastics of the day; and whose achievements up to that time had been exclusively military.   He took the name of Clement VII. ; and his election was at once notified to the various courts of Christendom.   And thus was inaugurated that guilty and unhappy Schism which was destined for forty years to rend the seamless robe of Christ. This atrocious proceeding seems partly to have opened the eyes of the three Italian Cardinals, who perceived, too late, that they had been duped by their French colleagues. Nothing could have been more foreign to their wishes and intentions than the election of another French Pope, specially of such a Pope as Robert of Geneva. They therefore at once withdrew from Fondi to a castle belonging to the Orsini, and there remained to watch the course of events, and hold a neutral position between the two parties.

Such was the terrible intelligence which fell on the ears of Catherine at the close of that brief interval of tranquillity which she had enjoyed at Siena after her last return from Florence. Although she had long ago foreseen the event in the spirit of prophecy, it did not on that account cause her a less lively grief. She did not, however, give way to discouragement, but at once addressing herself to Urban, she exhorted him to stand fast in courage and confidence; to remember that nothing great in this world is accomplished without suffering; to cast himself fearlessly into the midst of the thorns, clad in the armour of charity; and to be ready, if need be, to lay down his life for the flock of Christ. " I hear," she says, " that those incarnate demons have elected an anti-Christ, whom they have exalted against you, the Christ on earth, for I confess, and deny not, that you are the Vicar of Christ." Then she set herself to expostulate with those who supported the schism, among whom there was reason to fear that Joanna of Naples was likely to be foremost. On the 7th of October, therefore, Catherine addressed her a letter (Letter 315), in which she admirably sums up the whole question at issue, and shows how false were the pretences put forth by the rebellious Cardinals, that they had acted out of fear in making their election; concluding by an apostrophe to the Cardinals themselves, as vigorous as it is touching.

But while thus engaged, she herself received commands from Urban, summoning her to Rome. He communicated them to her through Raymund of Capua, who throughout this difficult time gave him his firm and loyal support. On this subject we have Raymund's own precise statement. "The Sovereign Pontiff, Urban VI.," he says, "who had seen Catherine at Avignon, and had there formed a high idea of her wisdom and virtue, desired me to write to her, and bid her come to Rome. I obeyed, but with her usual prudence she replied to me as follows : ' My Father, many persons at Siena, and some even of the Sisters of my Order, consider that I travel about too much ; they are scandalised at it, and say that a religious ought not to be always thus on the road. I do not think that these reproaches ought to trouble me, for indeed I have never undertaken any journey except at the command of God and His Vicar, and for the salvation of souls ; but to avoid all cause of scandal, I had no purpose of again leaving home. Nevertheless, if the Vicar of Christ desires it, it must be as he wishes. Only in that case be so good as to send me his commands in writing, that those who complain may see and understand that I do not undertake this journey of myself.' Having received this answer," continues Raymund, "I went to the Pope and humbly communicated it to him. He charged me to desire Catherine to come, in the name of holy obedience, and Catherine, as an obedient daughter, did so without delay." On this occasion, as on all those that preceded it, we see that Catherine only left the retirement of her home at the call of obedience, and with manifest reluctance. But when once the will of God and of His Vicar was made manifest to her, her own wishes were laid aside. And thus it was that she once more left her native place and directed her steps to the capital of Christendom, which was to be illuminated with the last setting rays of her earthly existence.

CHAPTER II.

CATHERINE IN ROME, NOVEMBER 1378.

WE do not know the precise date of Catherine's departure
from Siena, but it must have been during the latter part
of November 1378, as on the 28th of that month she reached the
Holy City. She set out with a sorrowful heart, for the woes of
the Church, and the coming calamities which three years previously she had so clearly foreseen and predicted, weighed heavily
on her spirits. Nor can we doubt that her last farewell to her
own home cost her "some natural tears," as she passed with her
little company out of the Porta Romana, and took the well-known
road so often traversed on former missions of peace and charity.
That road is easy to be traced, as it carried her past Asciano, and
the great convent of Monte Oliveto, among whose brethren she
numbered so many faithful disciples. It led her to the mountain
district through the valley of the Orcia, marked by a thousand
recollections most sweet and consoling to her heart. And as she
climbed the steep ascent of Radicofani, there must have been
some spot, some turning-point on that wild and desolate road,
whence looking back over the intervening hills she would have
caught the last distant view of the towers of Siena. It is probable
that St. Catherine passed through Orvieto on her way to Rome.
Writing to her disciple, Sister Daniella of Orvieto, just before she
started, she says, " As to my coming to you, pray God that all may
be for His honour and the salvation of souls ; specially now when
I am about to set out for Rome, to accomplish the Will of Christ
Crucified, and His Vicar. I know not what route I shall take."
(Letter 165.)

We know by a letter addressed to Stephen Maconi[1] that she reached Rome on the 1st Sunday in Advent, which that year fell on the 28th of November. Her suite was numerous, and would have been yet more so but for her express prohibition. It is certain, however, that she was accompanied by at least seven Sisters of Penance, among whom were Lisa, Alexia, Cecca, and Jane di Capo;[2] and that the entire party numbered about twenty-five persons. It included among others her two secretaries, Neri di Landoccio and Barduccio Canigiani. Stephen Maconi was detained at Siena by family affairs, to his own bitter regret, but greatly to our gain, as the correspondence between him and the rest of his fellow disciples furnishes us with much interesting information which would otherwise have been lost. F. Bartholomew Dominic seems to have escorted her to Rome and then returned to Siena, where he was at that time Prior. Fra Santi, Alphonsus di Vadaterra, and Master John the Third were certainly also of the party. Catherine lodged first in the Rione di Colonna, removing thence to a house between the Church of the Minerva and the Campo di Fiore in the Via di Papa.[3] The whole company of pilgrims seem to have formed one community, and to have lived on alms. "They voluntarily made themselves the poor of Divine Providence," says Raymund, "choosing rather to beg alms with the Saint, than to enjoy an abundance of all things at home, deprived of her sweet and pious company." A letter is preserved from Lando Ungaro, a citizen of Siena who had been despatched to Rome by the Magistrates of the Republic to conclude the negotiations for the restoration of Talamon. It is

---

[1] Letter 255.

[2] At the time that Catherine left Siena, her mother Lapa was at Florence. She did not therefore accompany, though she afterwards joined her daughter in Rome. Lapa had, it seems, about this time taken the habit of Penance. "Tell the Prior to do as he thinks best about *Sister Lapa*," writes Catherine to Stephen, "if she comes to Siena, I recommend her to you." (Letter 256.)

[3] Caffarini, *Leg. Min.*, p. 131. It is the second of these residences which is shown as Catherine's house, being now converted into a chapel used by the Confraternity of the Nunziatelle.

dated the 30th of November, two days after the arrival of the Saint in Rome, an event he does not fail to notice. "Catherine of Monna Lapa has arrived here," he says, "and our Lord the Pope has seen and spoken with her; I do not know what he has said to her, but only that he was much pleased to see her." He adds: "Everything goes on as before at the castle of St. Angelo: they are battering it all day long." In fact, almost immediately on Catherine's arrival she was summoned to the presence of the Holy Father, where, says Raymund, "he willed that in the presence of the Cardinals [1] she should deliver an address, and particularly that she should speak to them concerning the Schism, then just beginning. She did this with much wisdom and at some length, exhorting them all to courage and constancy, showing that Divine Providence watches over all, but specially over those who suffer for the Church, and concluding by saying that none ought to lose heart because of these untoward events, but that they should all do God's work and fear nothing. When she had finished, Urban, much encouraged, exclaimed to the Cardinals, 'Behold, my brethren, how contemptible we are before God when we give way to fear. This poor woman (Donnicciuola) puts us to shame; whom I call so, not out of contempt, but by reason of the weakness of her sex, which should make her timid even if we were confident; whereas, on the contrary, it is she who now encourages us. Is not this matter of confusion to us?' and he added, 'What need the Vicar of Christ fear, even if the entire world be against him? Is not Christ more powerful than the world? and He can never abandon His Church.' It was thus the Sovereign Pontiff spoke, encouraging his brethren; after which he praised Catherine much in the Lord, and granted many spiritual favours both to her and to her disciples." [2] In the advice which Catherine offered to Urban at this juncture, she adhered faithfully to the same policy of which

[1] That is, of course, of those newly created, for none others were then in Rome. Urban was at this time residing at Santa Maria in Trastevere; he was unable to live at the Vatican, owing to the vicinity of the castle of St. Angelo, then in the hands of a hostile French garrison.

[2] Leg., Part 3, chap. i.

she had been the unflinching advocate during the quarrel with the Florentines. To him, as to Gregory, she constantly represented that the Vicar of Christ should seek to conquer his enemies by no other weapons save those of patience and charity. Her admiration for the pure intentions of the Pontiff and his freedom from all human respect, and her hearty sympathy with his zeal for the reformation of abuses, did not prevent her seeing and lamenting that asperity of temper which often rendered his best efforts fruitless; and perceiving that the gentle hints she had from time to time dropped on the subject had not produced much practical result, she hit on a graceful and ingenious method of suggesting to him the necessity of somewhat sweetening the bitterness of his zeal. About Christmas time she sent him a little *regalo*, namely, five oranges preserved in sugar and gilded, which she had prepared with her own hands; accompanied with a letter in which she expresses the profound concern she feels at the bitter sorrows which overwhelm his soul, and draws a distinction between two kinds of sorrow; that which darkens and clouds the soul, and that which, even while it afflicts us, has yet a sweetness about it which supports and consoles. "Those who feel this sweet sorrow," she says, "are careful to drive from them all bitterness, because they seek not themselves, but God. It seems to me, Holy Father, that Jesus the Eternal Truth wishes to make you entirely like Himself. You are His Vicar, and He wishes that in bitterness and suffering you should reform His Spouse the Church. He would make you His instrument, that by a patient endurance of persecution His Church may be perfectly renewed, and come forth pure as a newborn child. All that is old must be renewed in the new man. Give yourself up then to this sweet bitterness, which will be followed by consolation full of sweetness; and be a tree of love grafted on the Tree of life. The love of virtue shall be the flower of that tree; and its ripe fruit, a prayer for God's honour and the salvation of your flock.

"That fruit seems bitter when first we taste it; but when the soul is resolved to suffer until death for Jesus crucified, it becomes truly sweet. I have often remarked this in the orange, which seems to taste so bitter; but when its pulp is taken out, and it is preserved after being steeped in water, the bitterness disappears. Then you fill it within with strengthening things, whilst you gild its exterior. Where has all the bitterness gone which at first was so disagreeable to the taste? Into the water and the fire. And so it is with the soul that loves virtue. The beginnings are bitter, so long as the soul is imperfect, but the water of grace will draw out the bitterness of self-love, that bitterness which is the only cause of suffering. And so the bitterness is all taken away, and it is filled with the strength of perseverance, whilst it is preserved in the honey of patience mingled with humility. Then when the fruit is finished and prepared, it is gilded outside with the gold of an ardent charity; I say *outside*, for this charity appears exteriorly in the patience with which the soul serves its neighbour, bearing with him with great tenderness, and steeping us in that sweet bitterness which we cannot but feel when we see God offended and souls perishing. And so, Holy Father, we shall come to produce fruits free from all bitterness, and shall overcome that which has been caused by the late mischance, brought about by guilty men who have afflicted your Holiness by the offences they have committed against God." (Letter 19.)

The "mischance" to which she here refers, was the lamentable commencement of bloodshed. Sylvester de Budes, Captain of the Breton Free Lances whom Clement had taken into his pay, had made his appearance under the walls of Rome; and finding the gate of St. John Lateran badly guarded, he entered the city and penetrated as far as the Capitol. The principal nobles and magistrates were assembled, unarmed, in the Piazza outside the palace; Sylvester fell upon them and slaughtered two hundred defenceless citizens, among whom were seven bannerets, or chiefs of the city quarters. After this atrocious and cowardly massacre, he withdrew to a place of security outside the walls. But the enraged populace took up arms, and unable to wreak their vengeance on the Breton assassins, they attacked the houses of all the foreigners then in Rome, and slew a great number without distinction of sex, age, or condition; directing their violence particularly against some English priests who were living at the Pontifical Court, and who, in common with all their countrymen, remained faithful to Urban.

It will be seen, then, that the first blood spilt in this unhappy quarrel was shed by the brutal followers of the Antipope; and Catherine's solicitude was directed to prevent the miserable policy of retaliation. She would not hear of an appeal to arms until every other means had been tried and exhausted: and deeply convinced of the fact that what the rulers of the Church most needed at this crisis was the counsel and support of all true servants of God, she suggested to Urban the plan of summoning to Rome a number of men of known piety and virtue, that he might strengthen himself by their holy presence, and infuse into his Court more and more of the spirit of Christ. The proposal was most acceptable to the Pontiff, who issued a Brief, dated December 13th, 1378, summoning to Rome, amongst other persons, Dom Bartholomew Serafini, Prior of Gorgona, Dom John of the Cells, three hermits of Spoleto renowned for sanctity, and the Augustinian hermits, Brother Anthony of Nizza, and Father William Flete. Catherine supported the summons of the Pope by her own letters, in which she called on all these good men, after the example of the ancient hermits, to make the sacrifice of their peaceful solitude, and to come to the assistance of the suffering Church of God.

Wonderful to say, she met with resistance where we might have supposed she would least have expected it. F. William and Brother Anthony, her two disciples of Lecceto, refused to leave their hermitages; and Catherine, learning the fact, at once wrote two letters, one addressed to them conjointly, which is dated December 15th, 1378, the other to Brother Anthony only, who seems to have been the least refractory of the two. "My dear sons," she says, "I desire to see you lose yourselves and seek no repose save in the salvation of souls and the reform of the Church. At this moment she is in such urgent need that in order to help her you must quit your solitude, and abandon yourselves. If you would do any good it will not do for you to stand still and say, ' I shall lose my peace.' God has given us a good and holy Pastor who loves his servants and summons them to his side; we ought then to hasten to his aid. Follow the call of God and of His Vicar; quit your solitude and run to the field of battle. I beg of you not to hesitate, and do not be afraid of losing your solitude, for here you will find plenty of woods." This first letter producing no effect, she despatched a second, addressed to Brother Anthony. " My dear Brother," she says, " we have two wills, one sensitive and the other spiritual; but sometimes this last, under the appearance of virtue, holds to its own sense, and likes to choose times and places, and says, ' I like this way best, because in it I can best enjoy God.' It is a great mistake and a delusion of the enemy, who not being able to deceive the servants of God in the first-named will, because they have mortified it, tries to do so in the second, and tempts them by means of spiritual things. This is the time for all true servants of God to show their fidelity, and for us to see the difference between those who love God for Himself, and those who only love Him for their own consolation. When the true servant of God is called on to give up his solitude and labour for God's service, he does it, and appears in public like the glorious St. Anthony, who certainly loved solitude as well as you do, but who nevertheless quitted it in order to strengthen those who were weak in the faith. . . . It seems from the letter which F. William has sent me, that neither he nor you intend to come. I shall not answer that letter; but I groan from my heart at his simplicity, and to see how little he cares for God's honour or the good of his neighbour. If it is out of humility and the fear of losing his peace, he should ask permission of the Vicar of Christ, and beg him to be so good as to leave him undisturbed in his solitude, and then leave the decision in his hands. But your devotion cannot be very solid, or you would not lose it by a change of place. Father Andrew of Lucca, and Father Paulinus, have not acted so ; they are old and infirm, but they set out at once. They are come; they have obeyed, and though they wish very much to return to their cells, yet they will not cast off the yoke of obedience : they have come to suffer, and to perfect themselves in the midst of prayers and tears. This is the right way of acting." (Letters 127, 130.)

Landucci tells us that Brother Anthony obeyed the Saint's injunctions, and came to Rome, where he suffered much for the Church, and died in 1392. But we do not find that F. William followed his example. In fact he retired to the yet more solitary convent called the Selva di Lago, his favourite retreat, which is separated from Lecceto by the forest. It must be believed that he obtained the Pope's excuses for his non-appearance at Rome ; and Urban was probably persuaded that the good hermit would do more for his cause by his prayers and writings, than by more active exertions in public, as indeed proved to be the case. Nor are we to suppose that Catherine was very seriously displeased with "the Bachelor," in spite of the scolding she administered to him, for, as we shall see, it was to his care that she recommended her spiritual children as she lay on her bed of death.

In answer to Urban's letters, a considerable number of excellent religious hastened to Rome, and it would seem that Catherine's house became their *rendezvous*. She was not unfrequently called upon to provide even for their temporal wants, a thing which seems a little unreasonable when we remember that she and her own little company were living on alms. "At the time when she was living at Rome in the Rione di Colonna," says Raymund, "she had with her a great number of her spiritual sons and daughters. They had followed her from Tuscany almost against her will, some to make the pilgrimage and visit the holy places, others to petition the Pope for spiritual graces, but all in order to enjoy the sweet conversation of Catherine. Moreover, the Holy Father, at her instance, had called to the city of Rome a number of other servants of God, all of whom she received at her house out of her great love of hospitality. For though she possessed neither lands, nor gold, nor silver, and lived with all her family on daily alms, yet was she as ready to receive and entertain a hundred pilgrims as if they had been but one, confiding with all her heart in God and never doubting but that His liberality would provide. So that the very least number who dwelt in her house at that time was sixteen men and eight women; sometimes even they amounted to as many as thirty, or even forty. Nevertheless, she had established such good order in her household, that each of the Sisters took it by turns, week by week, to provide and dispense for the rest, so that they might give themselves to God and to the pilgrimages or other affairs for which they had come to the city.

"Now it happened one week that it fell to Jane di Capo to discharge this office. But as the bread which they ate was procured by daily alms, Catherine had desired the Sister who should be in charge always to let her know a day in advance if the bread were failing, in order that she might either send some one out on the quest, or else go herself. But this week (God so permitting it) Jane forgot this order, and so when the dinner hour came, it was found that there was no more bread left in the house than would barely suffice for four persons. Jane, perceiving her negligence, went, full of shame and sorrow, to Catherine, and told her trouble. 'God pardon you, my Sister,' she replied, 'for bringing us into this embarrassment in spite of the directions I gave you. You see all our family are hungry, for the hour is late; where shall we now find bread enough for all who want it?' Jane could only lament over her forgetfulness, and own that she deserved a good penance; so Catherine said, 'Tell the servants of God to sit down to table,' and when her companion represented that there was so little bread to place before them, that if they divided it no one would have sufficient, Catherine only replied, 'Tell them to begin with that little, and God will provide the rest,' and so saying she began to pray.

"Jane did as she was ordered, and divided her small stock of bread among the guests. Hungry and exhausted by the long fasts which for the most part they observed, they found their portions very small, and expected them soon to disappear; but though they ate, and that with a good appetite, they did not come to the end of their provisions, but something was still left on the table. Nor is this surprising, seeing it was the work of Him Who fed 5000 men in the desert with only five loaves. Everybody, however, was astonished; they asked one another what Catherine was then doing; and hearing she was in prayer, the sixteen persons who were at table said with one voice, 'It is her prayer that has brought us bread from heaven; for we are all satisfied, and the little that has been served to us is rather increased than diminished.' After dinner there remained bread enough on the table to supply the Sisters that were in the house, who all ate abundantly, and they were able also to give a large alms of it to the poor. Lisa and Jane, both of whom were witnesses of this miracle, related to me a similar one, which God worked by the hands of Catherine in the same house, and the same year during Lent,[1] in the week when Cecca was in charge."

It is evident that Catherine's grand spirit of faith awoke to a sense of devout exaltation during her residence within the walls of the Holy City. To her, as to all the faithful when first they tread that consecrated soil, it seemed like home. She saw herself surrounded by the memorials of those whom for years she had most loved and venerated; of St. Paul, the standard-bearer of Christ, whose name was so often on her lips, *Paoloccio mio*, as she sweetly and familiarly called him; of "that sweet virgin St. Lucy of Rome,"[2] her devotion to whom has been noticed by one of her poetical biographers; and of all the countless virgin martyrs in whose steps she longed to tread, and whose glories she reckoned as her own. In fact, it was as the *City of Martyrs* that Rome was so dear to her who truly inherited the martyr spirit. Corne-

---

[1] That is, during the Lent of 1379. The above miracle probably took place in January of that year (Leg., Part 2, chap. xi.).

[2] The history of this Saint was first published, says Gigli, in the fourteenth century by Pietro de Natalibus. Catherine had probably read it, for in a letter to the Abbess of St. Martha's Convent, she says, "I have just found a new and beautiful light; it is the sweet virgin St. Lucy of Rome who gives it to us." (Letter 150.) This Saint (who is not to be confounded with St. Lucy of Syracuse) is believed to have suffered martyrdom at Rome on the 25th of June.

lius a Lapide tells us that whilst in Rome she was accustomed to perform the devotion of the Stations, going to all the holy sanctuaries in turn, and exclaiming as she did so, "I tread on the blood of the martyrs!"[1] In one of her first letters to Stephen Maconi she gives utterance to something of this pious enthusiasm : " The blood of the glorious martyrs who have died here in Rome, who gave their lives for the love of the Life, and whose bodies here lie buried, seems to live again, and to invite you and the others to come here and suffer for God's glory and for His Holy Church ; to come and practise virtue here, on this holy soil where He displays all His greatness, and which He chooses as His ' garden,' calling hither all His servants that he may try them as gold ;" and in all her future letters from the Holy City we find her speaking of it under the name of the " Garden."

Although we possess no more distinct notice of the sanctuaries which she visited, our knowledge of the fact that she performed the devotion of the Stations gives us a very sufficient guide in following her footsteps ; for, as the reader will remember, this devotion consists in visiting certain of the more ancient Basilicas and churches of Rome, one of which is assigned to each day in Lent, and other holy days in the course of the year ; we know, therefore, not only the sanctuaries that she visited, but also the days on which she repaired thither. On the Ash Wednesday of 1379 she would have ascended the Aventine, and paid her devotions in the Church of Santa Sabina, still fragrant with the memory of St. Dominic. There we can picture her spending an hour of ecstatic prayer on the stone where he spent his nightly vigils, or in that chapel of the Rosary, where many years later was to be placed the master-piece of Sassoferrato, which represents her, in company with her glorious Father, kneeling at the foot of the Madonna and receiving from the Divine Child the Crown of Thorns. Not once only, but many times, as we cannot doubt, she must have bent her steps to that spot so rich in sacred recollections, as well as to the neighbouring sanctuary of St. Sixtus, which is the church of the Station for Wednesday in the third week of Lent. St. Sixtus

---

[1] Commentary on Isaias, chap. xxvi.

in Catherine's time was still occupied by the community of nuns first placed there by St. Dominic, and it even yet retains evidence that she was known and venerated by its inmates. For on one of the walls behind the choir is to be seen an ancient picture, representing our Lord drawing out of the Wound in His side a garment which He is bestowing on St. Catherine who kneels at His feet, clad in the black mantle and white veil of her Order. Near to her, in much smaller proportions, appears (as a votary) the figure of a nun, who is supposed to be the Prioress of St. Sixtus, by whose order this picture must have been executed shortly after the death of the Saint; for she is represented, not with the aureole of a canonised saint, but with her head surrounded simply with rays.[1]

Catherine had not been long in Rome before the proposal was made to despatch her on a fresh embassy of the greatest difficulty and danger. Queen Joanna of Naples had by this time openly joined the party of the schismatics, and her intrigues placed the Pope in a position of much peril. Urban, however, hoped to conciliate her; and the thought suggested itself to him of placing the negotiations in the hands of Catherine and of another holy virgin of the same name then present in Rome. This was St. Catherine of Sweden, the daughter of St. Bridget, who was personally well known to Joanna. When our Saint heard what was proposed, she declared herself ready to set out at once; but Catherine of Sweden, whose recollections of Naples were sad and recent, had no desire to accept the mission to one whose treacherous and abandoned character she knew too well by experience.[2] Raymund of Capua, too, discouraged the project,

---

[1] This interesting painting was discovered in July 1852, by the Rev. Père Aussaut, and is considered by experienced judges as certainly as old as the fourteenth century. We have the testimony of F. Thomas Caffarini that these pictures of Catherine without the aureole were greatly multiplied almost immediately after her death. "Her portrait," he says, "represented after the manner of those Saints not yet solemnly canonised by the Church, is to be found multiplied in every province." (Process, 1291.)

[2] St. Catherine of Sweden, celebrated for her extraordinary personal beauty, as well as for her sanctity and wisdom, had been present in Rome at the time

for he believed Joanna to be capable of any crime, and he hesitated to trust the life and honour of two unprotected women in her hands. He stated his objections to the Holy Father, who, after a brief moment of reflection, replied, "You are right; it is better that they should not go." Raymund hastened to communicate this decision to Catherine, who was then lying ill at her house. It deeply disappointed her, nor could she enter into the reasons of prudence which had dictated it. "If Agnes and Margaret and so many other holy virgins had made all these reasonings," she said, "they would never have obtained the crown of martyrdom. Have we not a Spouse Who is willing and able to protect us? Believe me, such objections proceed from a want of faith, rather than from real prudence." However, the proposal was for the time laid aside, though we find from the letters of the Saint's disciples that it was not entirely abandoned until the July of the year following.

But there was another embassy, the accomplishment of which was yet more urgent, and the carrying out of which was to impose on Catherine a new sacrifice. In coming to Rome she had naturally looked forward to a reunion with Raymund of Capua, whose separation from her had been the greatest loss which, humanly, she was capable of feeling. But it seemed as though this last portion of the Saint's life was destined by Divine Providence to be rich in such sacrifices, as though to teach us that it is from the sharp tool of detachment that even the most exalted sanctity must receive its perfect finish. Raymund and Catherine did indeed meet at Rome; and it was on the occasion of their meeting that Raymund, alluding to the troubles of the Church which just then absorbed all minds, reminded her of the words she had spoken some years previously at Pisa, and owned that what they were now witnessing was the realisation of that prophecy. She had not forgotten the circumstance. "I told you,"

of Urban's election, and was intimately acquainted with every incident attending it. In 1379 she was examined on the subject before a regular tribunal, and gave important evidence on matters which she had herself witnessed, and which the Cardinals could not deny. See Rinaldi, 1379, No. 20.

she said, "that what we were then enduring was but honey and milk compared to what would follow; and now I will add that what you witness to-day is but child's play compared to what will soon take place in some neighbouring countries." "She was alluding," says Raymund, "to the dreadful woes which were so soon to fall on the kingdom of Naples, and which perfectly realised her words. Then I added, 'Dearest Mother, tell me what wil happen in the Church after all these miseries shall have passed away?' She replied, 'When all these troubles have come to an end, God will purify His Church in ways unknown by men. He will rouse the souls of His elect, and the renewal of life in the Church will be so perfect, that even to think of it thrills my soul with exceeding joy. I have often deplored with you the wounds and nakedness of the Spouse of Christ; but then she will appear brilliant in beauty, covered with precious jewels, and crowned with a diadem of virtues; all the faithful shall rejoice in the possession of good and holy pastors; and unbelievers, attracted by the good odour of Jesus Christ, shall return to the true Fold, and yield themselves to the Head and Bishop of their souls. Give thanks to God, then, for the blessed peace which He will surely grant His Church when this furious tempest is over." She said no more; and knowing that the Most High is more prodigal of His goodness than of His rigours, I have a firm hope that after our present troubles those good things will come which have been foretold to us by the blessed Catherine; and that it will be made manifest to all men that she was truly a prophetess of the Lord."[1]

This remarkable conversation was one of the very last that ever took place between Raymund and his saintly penitent. He quitted Rome a fortnight after her arrival there; and to explain the causes of their fresh separation we must return to the history of the schism which day by day was making an alarming progress. The man in Europe who might have interfered to check it in its commencement with the best chance of success was King Charles V. of France. The promoters of the conspiracy were all French-

---

[1] Leg., Part 2, chap. x.

men by birth, and the grand object at which they aimed was the re-establishment of the Papacy on their native soil. They naturally felt that the support of Charles was essential to the success of their design, and with this view they are said, before making their election, to have offered him the tiara. He had the good sense to decline this preposterous proposal, and he did not at first promise them any active support. But the course he determined on was one almost equally fatal to the interests of the Church. He assembled his councillors, and agreed with them to observe an absolute neutrality, neither approving nor rejecting the election of Urban VI. The schismatics were not slow in interpreting this decision to their advantage, and found no great difficulty in convincing the king and his councillors that the political interests of France were on the side of the party which advocated a return to Avignon. It was the old and fatal mistake which ignores the fact that the real political interests of a country must ever be identical with truth and justice. Charles listened to their plausible arguments, and to the representations so busily set afloat, that Urban had resolved to espouse the claims of the king of England; and when, after the election of the Antipope, he despatched envoys to Italy who should report to him on the true state of the case, these envoys were easily gained over to the side of Clement, and on their return laid before the king a statement entirely in his favour. On this it was resolved, in an assembly held at Vincennes, that the election of Robert of Geneva should be received as lawful and canonical, and that throughout the kingdom of France he should be obeyed as true Pope. Yet even after this, with a singular inconsistency which proves how little Charles was really satisfied in conscience on the point in question, he directed that the whole matter should be laid before the University of Paris, and thoroughly examined by its most learned doctors.

The manifest hesitation of the French king gave hopes at Rome, that he might even yet be held back from hopelessly committing himself and his country to the cause of the schism. His known piety and zeal for the faith rendered it difficult to regard him as one likely to be the promoter of such a crime ; and Urban resolved to despatch to him some trustworthy envoy who might succeed in putting the real facts before him and gaining him to be the champion, and not the enemy, of the Holy See. For this office none seemed better fitted than Raymund of Capua, who was perfectly well informed of the whole case, and whose uprightness of character and zeal for justice were united to a moderation and discretion which eminently qualified him for gaining the goodwill of such a monarch as Charles the Wise.

Raymund's narrative shall be given in his own words : "It seemed good to the Sovereign Pontiff to send me into France, for he had been told that it would be possible to detach Charles V., King of France, from the cause of the schism which he had himself excited. As soon as I heard of this project, I went to take counsel with Catherine. In spite of the sorrow which the prospect of my departure caused her, she urged me at once to comply with the Holy Father's wishes. 'Be sure, my Father,' she said, 'that he is truly the Vicar of Jesus Christ : therefore, I would have you expose yourself in his defence as you would do in that of the Church herself.' I myself felt no doubt on the subject ; but her words so encouraged me to combat the schism, that from that time I entirely consecrated myself to defend the right of the Sovereign Pontiff, and I often recalled them to strengthen me in my trials and difficulties. I did then what she advised, and bowed my head to the yoke of obedience. A few days before my departure, knowing what would take place, she desired to confer with me on the subject of her interior, and allowed no other person to be present during our interview. Having spoken to me for several hours, she said at length : 'Now, go where God calls you. I think in this life we shall never again speak together as we have just now done.' And it was, indeed, even as she said, for I departed, and she remained behind ; and before my return she had passed to heaven, and I never again listened to her admirable exhortations. No doubt it was because she knew it would be so that, desiring to bid me a last adieu, she came to the place where I embarked, and when we had set forth, she knelt down in prayer and, weeping as she did so, made over us the sign of the Cross, as though she had said, 'Go, my son, in all confidence under the protection of this sacred sign: but know that in this life you will never more behold your Mother.'[1] The exact spot where this touching parting took place is not indicated, but it was evidently on the shores of the Tiber; for as we have seen in a former chapter, the journey from the city to the seashore was then performed by water, the river being still navigable. And thus in the supreme moment of her life, Catherine was left, if not alone, yet deprived of the society of the two persons who, each in their own way, enjoyed her closest confidence, Raymund of Capua and Stephen Maconi. Moreover, as she well knew, Raymund's mission was one of no small difficulty and danger, and on her would fall the duty of encouraging him to brave the perils to which he was exposed. Accordingly, they had hardly parted when she despatched a letter for the purpose of cheering the hearts of him and his companions, and inspiring them with a joyous confidence. 'Courage, my Father and my beloved sons,' she writes; 'go forth like the Apostles, poor, yet bearing with you the riches of faith and hope, and the fortitude of charity. Remember the words that were spoken by the Sweet Word of Truth, "Send forth thy sons as sheep in the midst of wolves! Let them go with confidence, for I will be with them, and if human help fail, My help shall never fail."

"'Oh, my Father and my children, what more help and consolation can you wish for? Who could fear? He who has no confidence may do so: but not he who hungers for God's honour

---

[1] Raymund does not give the date of his leaving Rome, but we know that it must have been between the 28th of November, on which day Catherine arrived, and the 13th of December, the date of the Pope's Brief to Dom Bartholomew Serafini and the others. For in her letter to the Prior of Gorgona, forwarding this Brief, Catherine says, "F. Raymund has gone to labour elsewhere: the Pope has sent him to the King of France. Pray for him that, if need be, he may give his life for the Church." (Letter 54.) The two persons associated with Raymund in this embassy were James Ceva Marshal of the Pontifical Court, and William, Bishop of Valence. The Brief appointing them is preserved in the Archives of S. Domenico, Siena.

and the salvation of souls. Such an one will be consumed in the fire of Divine charity; bathed, annihilated, consumed, in the Blood of the Lamb. Alas! I die, and cannot die! My heart breaks because the long-wished-for moment does not come. The Eternal Truth begins to produce flowers, but they do not satisfy me, for we cannot live on flowers; we want fruits. Help me then, my Father and my children, and pray Him soon to send me these fruits.' (Letter 98.) Another letter met the travellers at Pisa. 'It is no longer the time to slumber,' she wrote, 'we must shake off the drowsiness of negligence, and espouse the truth with the ring of fidelity. We must declare the truth, and not keep silence out of fear, but be ready generously to give our life for the Holy Church. We see her now dismembered; but I hope in the Eternal and Sovereign goodness of God that He will heal her infirmities, so that these members may be reunited and renewed on the shoulders of God's saints. Yes! we shall be consoled for all our sufferings by the joy of beholding the renewal of that Sweet Spouse. But silence, my soul, and say no more. I will not speak what is difficult either to say or to write about,— you know all I mean. May you soon return to this sweet garden, and help me to root out the thorns.'" (Letter 99.)

CHAPTER III.

PROGRESS OF THE SCHISM, 1379.

I T is not our purpose to present the reader with anything like a complete history of the Great Schism, but only to notice those facts which are indissolubly connected with the history of St. Catherine, and a clear comprehension of which is necessary, in order to understand the affairs in which she was now engaged. There were three distinct parties who, though at the moment hostile to Urban's cause, appeared nevertheless to offer some hopes of being won over by words of reason to take a better course. These were, the French King, the Italian Cardinals, and the Queen of Naples. Raymund having been despatched to the first of these, Catherine made it her business to try what could be effected with the other two. With the Queen of Naples she had long been in correspondence, and it is evident that in spite of the vices of Joanna's character, Catherine felt a singular interest in her and an ardent desire to gain her soul to God.[1] She had already written her a letter of expostulation before leaving Siena for Rome; she now reiterated her warnings in a yet more solemn tone. "O my mother!" she says, "for so I will call you, if you still love truth and are subject to the Holy Church, otherwise I can no longer give you the name of Mother; I see a great change in you. You have abandoned the counsels of the Holy Spirit to

---

[1] It must be remembered in judging of Joanna's conduct that she held her kingdom as a fief of the Holy See, and therefore, according to what was universally recognised as the common law of the time, was bound to fidelity by a double obligation. Nor did this obligation rest on any ancient or obsolete transaction of the old Norman sovereigns, for the act had been solemnly renewed by Joanna and her nobles at the beginning of her reign.

listen to the Evil One; you were a branch of the true Vine, and you have cut yourself off with the knife of self-love. You were the beloved daughter of your Father, the Vicar of Christ, and now you have abandoned him. Alas! we may weep over you as over one that is dead, dead as to the soul, dead in the body too, if you do not quit your error. And you will have no excuse; you cannot say when you come to die, 'I thought I was doing right,' for you knew full well you were doing wrong. But I am persuaded this counsel has not come from you. Try then, I conjure you, to know the truth, and who those are who would deceive you by saying that Pope Urban VI. is not the true Pope, and that the Antipope is the Christ on earth, whereas in truth he is an Antichrist. What can these perverse men say for themselves? If it were true that Pope Urban was not lawfully elected, they would deserve a thousand deaths, being thus convicted out of their own mouths as impostors. For if they elected him out of fear, and not by a valid election, and nevertheless presented him to us as being the true and lawful Pope, they gave us a lie in the place of the truth, and obliged us to do homage to one who had no right to it. They had already acknowledged him, asked favours from him, and accepted him as the Sovereign Pontiff; so that, if it were true that they knew all the while he was not the lawful Pope, no punishment could be too bad for them. Every one knows that the person whom they named out of fear, after they had elected the Archishop of Bari, was the Cardinal of St. Peter's, who, like a brave and honest man, declared to the people that it was not he who had been elected, but the Archbishop of Bari. And whom have they now chosen in his place, if Pope Urban VI. be not the true Vicar of Christ? Is it a man of holy life? No; indeed, we may rather call him a demon, for he is truly discharging the office of the demon. . . . They knew well enough that any just man would have preferred to die a thousand deaths rather than accept their proffered dignity; but now, demons have elected a demon. I say it with profound sorrow, for I love your salvation with my whole soul; but if you do not repent, the Sovereign Judge will punish you in a manner which will terrify all who would revolt against His Church. Do not wait for His blows, for it is hard to resist Divine justice. You must die, and you know not when. Neither your riches, nor your power, nor your worldly honours, nor the barons and people subject to you, can defend you against the Sovereign Judge, Who sometimes makes even these very persons to be His executioners, in order to punish His enemies. You are exciting against you your own people, who have found in you not a manly, generous heart, but the heart of a mere woman, without strength or firmness, tossed about like a leaf by the wind. They remember how, when Pope Urban VI. was first elected and crowned, you celebrated the event with great festivities, as a child does at the exaltation of its father, and a mother at that of her son ; for indeed he was both your father and your son,—your father, by the dignity to which he was raised, and your son as being born the subject of your realm ; and now all this is changed, and you command them to take the opposite way. Oh unhappy passion ! The evil you have embraced yourself you wish to impart to them, and instead of truth you would give them a lie. Oh, do so no more, for the love of Jesus ! You are calling down on you the Divine judgments, and I shudder to see that you seek not to avoid the storm which threatens to fall on you. But there is yet time, my most dear mother, to escape the vengeance of God ; return to the obedience of Holy Church ; humble yourself and acknowledge your fault, and God will show you mercy. I conjure you, accomplish the will of God and my desire, for indeed I do desire your salvation with all my heart, and soul, and strength ; and gladly would I have come in person to tell you the truth with my tongue, for your salvation and God's honour. It is the goodness of God, Who loves you with an immense love, which urges me thus to write to you in profound sorrow. . . . . Alas, my mother, have you no compassion for yourself? Willingly would I give my life to save you ! Oh, how happy should I be to go and give my life to restore to you all the blessings of heaven and earth, and to take from you the weapon with which you are killing yourself. Alas ! alas ! let not my eyes have to shed torrents of tears over your poor soul and body! I love your soul as though it were my own, and I see that it is dead; for it strikes a blow, not at Pope Urban only, but at the truth, at our Holy Faith!—that faith which I once thought to see carried to the infidels through your means!" (Letters 316, 317.)

In addressing the three Italian Cardinals, who, as we have seen, had endeavoured to hold themselves neutral after the election of the Antipope, Catherine used the same arguments as those which she had laid before the Queen. But in addition she set before them the special duties which might have been expected from them in their exceptional position. "When the others abandoned their Father," she says, "you, as his children, should have remained to be his support. Even though he made you some few reproaches, you ought not on that account to have given the example of revolt. In the eyes of God we are all equal, but to speak in the language of men, the Christ on earth is an Italian, and you are Italians also. The love of country, then, did not lead you astray as it did the Ultramontane Cardinals; and I can see no other explanation of your conduct but wounded self-love. You abandoned the truth out of resentment; you could not endure,—I will not say a just correction, but not so much as one rough word. You lifted your heads on high, and that was the cause of your revolt. Yes, we know and see the truth; before the Holy Father reproved you, you acknowledged him and did him homage as the Vicar of Christ; but your tree was planted in pride and nourished by self-love; and it is this that has deprived you of the light of reason."

Among others whom Catherine was most anxious to gain was Honorius Gaetano, Count of Fondi, whose adhesion to the cause of the Antipope had been entirely caused by private pique and resentment. He was governor both of the province of Campania and the city of Anagni, and Urban had deprived him of both offices, which he conferred on the Count's bitterest enemy, Thomas Santa Severina. This affront, offered to one of the most powerful nobles in Italy, had borne disastrous fruits, and Catherine, while reproaching him for his ungenerous way of seeking revenge, was careful to assure him of the loving pardon which he would receive on his return to his allegiance. "We know," she says, "that Urban VI. is the true Pope; so that were he the most cruel father possible, and had he chased us from one end of the world to the other, we ought not to forget, or to persecute the truth. But your self-love has conceived indignation and brought forth wrath. Surely you must suffer in your conscience, for you were once an obedient son and firm support of Holy Church. . . . It is not only yourself on whom you inflict a deadly blow; but think of all the souls and bodies whose loss you will have to account for to the Sovereign Judge! For God's sake, do so no more; *to sin is human, but to persevere in sin is the part of the devil.* Be sure no fault committed against the Holy Church will ever remain unpunished. That is always clearly seen. Then I implore you, for the love of the Blood shed for you, return to your Father who will await you with open arms; for indeed he desires to show mercy to you and to all others who may seek for it." (Letter 192.)

Catherine's appeals to the Queen of Naples, to the Italian Cardinals, and to Honorius Gaetano, were fruitless in their result, but she was more successful in her efforts to hold to their allegiance the cities of Florence, Siena, Bologna, Perugia, and Venice, to all whose Magistrates she addressed letters as fervent as they were argumentative. During the early months of 1379 she was, in fact, devoting all her extraordinary energies to the support of Urban's cause, and when not engaged in more active labours on his behalf, she poured forth her soul in prayer, that God would defend his cause, and deliver the Church from the new and terrible calamity that had fallen on it. If we look at the collection of her Prayers printed at the end of the Dialogue, we find no fewer than six dated in the months of February and March of this year, and taken down from her lips by her disciples. The increasing difficulties of Urban's position in Rome, and the rapid spread of the dark cloud which overshadowed the Church, wrung her heart with agony unspeakable, and drew from her these ardent intercessions; and, in truth, the aspect of affairs was daily growing more and more alarming.

Whilst Catherine was using her influence with Urban to induce him to hold back from all violent measures, the Antipope Clement was busily engaged collecting troops and preparing for hostilities.   He had the talents and the ardent military spirit of a secular prince; and badly as such accomplishments suited his sacred profession, they gained him favour among the wild soldiery whom he sought to gather round his standard.   Tall of stature, with a handsome countenance and captivating address, Robert of Geneva was just the man to win popularity with the multitude; and his openhanded prodigality contrasted favourably enough in their eyes with the austere and simple habits of Pope Urban.   By the commencement of the year 1379, therefore, he had succeeded in gathering together a considerable number of Gascon and Breton mercenaries, who audaciously entered the Roman territories and encamped at Marino, at a short distance from the city.   Urban, on his part, had been fortunate enough to secure the services of Count Alberic di Balbiano, a man of low birth who had acquired the reputation of a skilful captain, and whose not inglorious ambition it was to command none but native Italians, and by their means to drive out of his country those hordes of foreign mercaries who preyed upon her vitals.   His Company, which bore the title of the " Company of St. George," numbered no more than four thousand foot-soldiers, and as many horse, but they were all well-trained veterans, and being joined by Sir John Hawkwood, they appeared fairly able to cope with their opponents. The schismatics, meanwhile, were ravaging the whole surrounding country, and driving before them the terrified inhabitants, who took refuge within the city walls, thus increasing the alarm and confusion of the citizens.   Catherine beheld it all in profound affliction, and tears became her bread day and night, as she ceased not to cry to God that He would restore peace to His Church. The danger was augmented by the fact, that the Castle of St. Angelo was still in the hands of the partisans of Clement; but acting by Catherine's advice, John Cenci, Senator of Rome, had already opened negotiations with Rostaing for its surrender. Deeply as the Saint lamented the necessity of having recourse to the sword in defence of the cause of God, yet, when warlike operations became inevitable, she did not withhold her words of encouragement to the combatants. With Hawkwood she had already had relations, and both by him and his wild comrades her name was held in the utmost veneration. And she now addressed herself to Alberic likewise, and promised him that she and the other servants of God would not cease to offer their prayers for a blessing on his arms.

On the 29th of April a double attack on the Schismatic forces was concerted. While the Roman citizens attempted an assault on the Castle of St. Angelo, Alberic and his troops sallied forth from the gates and fell on the Bretons encamped at Marino. Though far outnumbered by their adversaries, the Urbanists gained a complete victory; and Alberic re-entering Rome in triumph, such consternation took possession of Rostaing and his garrison, that they at once surrendered the fortress into the hands of the conqueror. This double victory, gained on the same day, filled the hearts of the Romans with inexpressible joy, nor did they hesitate to ascribe their success as due to the prayers of St. Catherine. Only a few hours previously they had been ready to abandon themselves to despair, beholding the city surrounded on all sides by their enemies ; and now they saw themselves delivered as by a miracle, and the citadel, whence their peace and safety had so long been threatened, restored to their own keeping. It was a success which might well rouse the coldest hearts to gratitude, and Catherine was resolved that the devotion of the people should be moved in the right direction. She saw in the late victory an occasion for raising their hearts to God, of confirming them in sentiments of loyalty to His Vicar, and of rendering to His Holy Name a tribute of honour, in reparation for the thousand outrages it had endured during this disastrous time. She therefore entreated the Pope to order a special and solemn act of thanksgiving, and himself to take part in it before the eyes of all the people. Urban was then living at Santa Maria in Trastevere, and Catherine proposed that he should make thence a solemn procession to the church of St. Peter's, walking barefoot, and attended by a great number, both of clergy and of the faithful. It was a touching spectacle, and the populace failed not to remark that no Roman Pontiff had been known to perform such an act of penance and devotion since the time of Stephen IV. in the eighth century. And whilst the pious were edified, the hearts of all were filled with joyful satisfaction at seeing the Pontiff once more able to take up his residence in his own palace, secure from the insults and attacks of an intrusive foreign garrison. Catherine also was full of joy at the accomplishment of this devout ceremony, and she expressed her sentiments in a letter to the Pontiff, dated the 30th of May, in which she says, "We have witnessed within the last four weeks what admirable things have been worked by the power of God by means of a vile creature; and we have seen clearly that they were wrought by Him, and not by the power of man. Let us give Him glory, and testify our gratitude. And, indeed, I have been filled with joy at beholding with my eyes that holy procession, the like of which has not been performed since the most remote ages. I rejoice that our sweet Mother Mary and St. Peter, the Prince of the Apostles, have restored you to your rightful residence. May the Eternal Truth grant you to make in your garden a garden of the servants of God, who may have nothing else to do than to pray for the prosperity of the Church and of your Holiness; for these are the soldiers who will obtain for you a complete victory."

She also exerted herself to obtain a proper acknowledgment from the Roman Magistrates and people, of the services rendered both by the troops and by John Cenci. "I desire," she says, "that you should be grateful to the Company whose members have been the instruments of Christ; assist them in their wants, specially the poor wounded. Be kind and charitable to them that you may preserve their aid, and not give them occasion to turn against you. You are bound to this as well from motives of gratitude as of prudence. . . . I think you have been a little ungrateful in respect of John Cenci. I know with what zeal and generosity, merely to please God and serve us, he abandoned everything in order to deliver you from the danger that threatened you on the side of the Castle of St. Angelo. He acted with great prudence; yet now, not only does no one show him the least gratitude, but there are envious calumnies raised against him. This is not right." (Letter 196.)

At the same time, she addressed herself to Alberic and his companions in a letter written on the 6th of May, which is one of four which she is known to have dictated on that same day, so marvellous was the activity of her mind, and her continual application to the affairs to which she had devoted herself. Her letter is addressed " To Count Alberic of Balbiano, Captain General of the Company of St. George, and to the other Chiefs." After expressing her hopes that they may be rewarded for their sufferings in the good cause, she continues, "Who is the Master for whom you went forth to the field of battle? It was Christ crucified, the Eternal Sovereign whose greatness none but Himself can understand. Oh, my sons, you came to the battle-field like good knights, to give your life for the love of the Life, and to shed your blood for love of the Blood of Christ. Behold a time of new martyrs! You have been the first to shed your blood, and what will be your reward? Even life eternal. Courage, then, you serve the Truth, and the Truth will make you free! and the better to call down God's blessing on your holy enterprise, have a good intention; take for the motive of your actions God's honour, and the defence of the faith of Holy Church; and prepare yourselves by a good confession, for you know sin calls down God's anger, and hinders the success of our works. In your position as Chief, give your followers an example of the fear of God. If all whom you command have not time to go to confession, let them at least do so in desire. Surround yourself with good advisers. Choose for your officers brave men, as faithful and conscientious as you can find, for it is good officers who make good soldiers. Be on your guard against treason both within and without; and the first thing morning and evening, offer yourselves to our sweet Mother Mary, begging her to be your advocate and defence, and to let no treason harm you, for the love of her dear Son. Courage then in Christ Jesus!

Always have His Blood present to your minds! Fight under the banner of the Cross, and think that the blood of the martyrs cries for you in the presence of God. Be grateful for the benefits you have received from Him and from the glorious knight, St. George, whose name you bear, and who will guard and defend you till death! We, on our part, will do as Moses did: whilst the people fought, Moses prayed, and whilst he prayed, the people triumphed over their enemies—we will do the same.[1] Be pleased to read this yourself, and also to the Captains." (Letter 219.)

It has been said above that this letter was one of four, written or dictated by Catherine on the same day. The other three were addressed to the Roman Magistrates, to the Queen of Naples, and to King Charles of France. This last-named epistle is one of the most remarkable of her compositions; and to explain the occasion on which it was written, we must retrace our history a little, and see what success had attended Raymund of Capua after his departure from Rome. In spite of the numerous galleys of the Schismatics and of the Queen of Naples which scoured the seas with the purpose of intercepting any envoys who might be sent by Urban to the King of France, he managed to get safely to Genoa, stopping on his way at Pisa, where he received a letter of encouragement from Catherine. From Genoa he got as far as Ventimiglia, where he was warned by one of the fathers of his own Order not to proceed farther, as an ambuscade had been laid for him which it was impossible for him to escape. Indeed, one of his companions did actually fall into the hands of the enemy; and on inquiry, it proved, that every road to France was so strictly guarded by troops, as to exclude all hope of his being able to elude their vigilance; for he could not make his way into the French

---

[1] The last paragraph in this letter is quoted by Rinaldi, in proof that the victory of Marino was due to St. Catherine's prayers. He overlooked the circumstance that it was written a whole week after that event. Maimbourg, the partisan of the Schism, takes occasion from this blunder to cast discredit on the authenticity of the letter altogether; but it is evident that the Saint is not referring to prayers offered before the battle of Marino, but to those with which she promises to help Alberic in his *future* undertakings in defence of the Church.

dominions without passing through Provence, which at that time was subject to Joanna of Naples, and filled with her spies and emissaries. In this perplexity he determined on returning to Genoa; whence he wrote to Urban, stating the facts, and asking for further instructions. He also sent a letter to Catherine, relating his adventures, and rejoicing with great simplicity over his late providential escape. From Urban he received a command to remain where he was for the present, and use his eloquence to keep the people of Genoa from joining the Schism; but Catherine's reply was not precisely a congratulation. Had he been cut to pieces by the Schismatics, or cast into a dungeon, she would have rejoiced over him with holy exultation. But that he, a man, the Envoy of the Christ on earth, should have cared for his life in the cause of God, and turned his steps backward in order to save it; and most of all, that he should have rejoiced, and asked her to rejoice with him over his escape, was more than she could endure or understand; and she addressed a letter to the poor Father, which must have greatly qualified his satisfaction. "God," she says, "has desired to make you know your imperfection, and to show you that you were a child at the breast, and not a man who feeds on bread; for if you had had teeth with which to eat that bread, He would have given it to you, as He did to your companion. But you were not found worthy of fighting on the field of battle, so you were put aside like a child; you fled of your own accord, and now you rejoice at the escape which God has granted to your weakness. Oh, my poor Father! what a happiness it would have been for your soul, and for mine also, if with your blood you had consolidated but one stone of the Holy Church! Truly we have reason to groan and lament that our want of virtue has deprived us of such a grace! Ah, let us lose our milk teeth, and try to get the good strong teeth of hatred and of love." (Letter 100.)

In his reply Raymund seems to have urged the insurmountable obstacles in the way of his journey and the impossibility of escaping detection; but Catherine could not accept the excuse. "If you could not pursue your way walking," she says, "you should have crawled on hands and feet; if you could not travel as a friar you should have done so as a pilgrim; if you had no money, you should have begged your way." (Letter 101.)

The failure of Raymund's attempt for a moment suggested the thought that Catherine herself should undertake the journey to Paris. Many things seemed to indicate that she was the most likely person to gain a favourable hearing from Charles and his councillors. She had already been invited to his Court; and her words to him at the very moment when she was using her influence to carry out a policy to which he was strongly opposed, had been received with respect and favour. The Duke of Anjou had professed himself her firm friend and disciple, and as to the dangers to be apprehended on the journey on the part of the Schismatics and their Neapolitan allies, it is perhaps the truest statement to say that they attracted rather than dismayed her. The chance they offered her of steeping her white robe in the blood of martyrdom was in her eyes the most glorious privilege to which any mortal could aspire, and she therefore cheerfully placed herself at the disposal of the Sovereign Pontiff. We are ignorant of the obstacles which opposed themselves to this project. Probably Urban felt her presence necessary to him, but however it was, Catherine submitted with her usual self-abandonment, and set herself to supply by writing what she was unable to say by word of mouth. She therefore addressed to king Charles the letter of which we have spoken, and which has drawn from Papirio Massonio an eloquent word of admiration.[1]

The letter is of great length, and we shall give but a summary of its contents. She endeavours to show first how self-love is the real root of injustice, and the cause why men in power who seek human interests persecute the Church. She expresses her wonder how a prince so renowned for his Catholic piety could have suffered himself to be guided by false councillors in a matter of such grave importance. Then she sets before him the chain of arguments which proved beyond the possibility of doubt that the election of Urban had been true and valid. The ground on

---

[1] *Nihil gravius, nihil elegantius, aut concipi animo, aut scribi ab ullo illius temporis viro certe potuisset* (*Annal ad.* 1378 : *Lib.* 4).

which they pretended to call it invalid was that it had been made out of fear. But the person whom, under the influence of fear, they had put forth to the people as having been elected was the Cardinal of St. Peter's, who himself declared that Urban had been lawfully elected. Then for five months afterwards they confirmed their election by repeated public acts. They announced the elevation of Urban to the Sovereigns; they did him homage; they crowned him, and asked favours of him. If they did all this, knowing that he was not really Pope, they convicted themselves of a prodigious crime. "How! they, the columns of the Church, they who are established to spread the faith; *they*, out of fear of temporal death to drag us with them to death eternal! But the fact is, that they acknowledged him as true Pope until he began to reprove their vices. As soon as he showed that he was resolved to correct scandalous abuses, they revolted and became renegades. If I speak thus of them," she continues, "I speak not against their persons, but against the Schism which they have brought into the world; against their cruelty to their own poor souls and the souls of those who will perish by their means. Had they feared God, Pope Urban might have done more than he did do, and they would have borne it patiently, and died a thousand deaths rather than have rebelled against him. And you may see that all the true servants of God remain obedient to him and acknowledge him as Sovereign Pontiff. Call such persons to your councils to explain the truth to you and enlighten your ignorance. Do not let yourself be moved by temporal interests; if you do, the result will be more fatal to you than to any one else. Have compassion on the many souls whom you are delivering up to error. Yet if you desire, you need not be deceived, for you have near you the fountain of science;[1] have recourse to it, and you know what will become of your kingdom if you consult conscientious men, free from servile fear, and caring only for the truth. Oh, my dear Father, enter into yourself; you must die, and you know not how soon,[2] think

---

[1] The University of Paris.

[2] Charles, in fact, died the next year, protesting on his death-bed that he

only of God and the truth, not of private passion or national interests. Before God there is no distinction of nations, for we all came forth from the same thought; we were all created in His image and likeness, and were all redeemed in the Precious Blood of His Son. Pardon me if I have said too much; I would far rather speak than write to you, for the love that I have of your salvation." (Letter 187.)

Charles was probably never suffered to receive this letter. Almost as the Saint was writing it, the Royal Brief was sent to the University of Paris, requiring them to consider and decide on the claims of the rival Pontiffs in terms that could hardly be interpreted in any other sense than a command to give their verdict in favour of the Antipope. The too facile instruments of the royal will knew well what was expected of them. The College of the Sorbonne indeed had already pronounced in favour of Urban, but on the 30th of May, pressed by fresh letters from the king, the majority declared that Clement VII. was to be accepted as true and lawful Pontiff; the English "nation" in the University, to their eternal honour, withholding all part in the transaction. Had the decision been unanimous, which it was far from being, it is obvious to observe that the University was not a tribunal that could dictate laws to the Church. But at that period immense weight attached to its decisions; and from the miserable day when this decree was promulgated, the Great Schism of the West may be said to have been fairly accomplished. There can be no doubt that had Charles from the first firmly opposed the rebellious Cardinals, their scheme would have been nipped in the bud. His vacillation in the first instance, followed by his actual adherence to their party, gave them the most formidable support; and hence, by most writers, he is represented as the chief promoter, if not the actual author of the Schism. In any case, this defection was so serious a blow to the cause of Urban, that it became necessary for him to seek among

had adhered to the cause of Clement through the advice of the Cardinals, and that in case he were mistaken, he desired to abide by the decision of the Universal Church, as expressed by a general Council.

the other Christian princes for some who would support his claims. There was one then reigning who seemed by his chivalrous character and tried devotion to be eminently fitted for being chosen as the champion of the Faith. This was Louis, King of Hungary and Poland, great grandson of Charles of Anjou, the brother of St. Louis of France. Thus he was closely connected with the Queen of Naples, and was brother to that Andrew of Hungary, the first husband of Joanna, whom she had caused to be smothered in the Castle dell' Uovo ; while his cousin Charles Durazzo had been declared heir to the kingdom of Naples by the Queen and the States General ; though since then she had given her preference to the Duke of Anjou. By his wisdom and valour Louis had earned the surname of the Great : he had been victorious against the Tartars and other enemies of the faith, and had received from Pope Innocent VI. the title of "Gonfalonier of Holy Church." The Schismatic Cardinals had made every effort to gain him over to their side, but without success ; he would never depart from the obedience of Urban, and at the first outbreak of the Schism had greatly exerted himself to stop its further progress. To him Urban naturally turned for help. The sentence of excommunication was still hanging suspended over the head of Joanna of Naples ; should she by her obstinacy incur that sentence she would forfeit her kingdom, which was a fief of the Holy See ; and Urban proposed to invest Prince Charles at once with the royal dignity, and invited both him and his cousin King Louis to come into Italy and act in defence of the Church. Catherine likewise wrote to both these princes ; and whilst soliciting their support, it is worthy of notice that she seems to deprecate extreme measures, and clings to the lingering hope that even yet Joanna may be spared. " Much good," she says, writing to the King, " will result from your coming hither ; *perhaps even the truth will triumph without the necessity of using human force, and this poor queen may be delivered from her obstinacy either by fear or love.* You well know how she has been spared by the Christ on earth, who was unwilling to deprive her actually of what by her conduct she had forfeited ; he awaited her repentance, and that out of consideration for you." (Letter 188.) To Charles Durazzo she also writes inviting him to come to the aid of the Church, as was becoming one in whose veins ran the blood of St. Louis; but she makes no allusion to the proposal for investing him with the forfeited kingdom; and it is probable that she yet hoped by her influence with Urban, and by fresh appeals to Joanna, to avert so terrible a calamity as a warlike invasion.

In the meanwhile that princess was far from evincing any signs of repentance; on the contrary, she was acting as the open partisan and protector of the Antipope. After the defeat of his troops at Marino, Clement felt himself no longer safe in the Roman provinces, and took refuge in the kingdom of Naples. His military spirit deserted him in the hour of need, and he arrived at the Castle of Spelonca half crazed with terror. Joanna received him with a great display of respect, and conducted him to her famous Castle dell' Uovo, causing a bridge to be constructed in the sea, on the spot where he was to disembark from his galley. He was treated with royal pomp, and received the homage of the queen and her brilliant court; and amid a series of splendid and costly festivities, consoled himself as well as he might for his late disaster.

But the Neapolitan people were far from sharing the sentiments of their sovereign. They clung to the obedience of Urban, venerating him as true Pope, and loving him as their own fellow-countryman; and they regarded the honours shown his rival as nothing short of sacrilegious. Andrea Ravignano, one of the queen's courtiers, hearing an artisan giving vent to his indignation in no measured terms, commanded him to be silent, and his command not being attended to, he had the base cowardice to ride down the poor fellow, and strike out one of his eyes. This was the signal for the people to rise; they assembled in crowds, shouting, "Long live Pope Urban!" and in a few hours Naples was in their hands. The Archbishop appointed by Urban, who had been thrust out of his see, was brought back in triumph, and the schismatic intruder chased out of the city. Clement, terrified at so unexpected a storm, again took flight, and hurried first to Gaeta, and thence to the shores of Provence ; where establishing himself at Avignon with the Cardinals of his party, he felt at last in safety, and did not again return to Italy.

The revolt of the Neapolitans seemed to cause a momentary hesitation in the mind of the unhappy Joanna. Civil war had broken out in her dominions, and there were plenty of ambitious and unscrupulous princes who would be likely to take advantage of such a crisis to possess themselves of the territories of an heirless queen. In her doubts and fears her thoughts turned towards Catherine, to whom she addressed several letters, assuring her that "the words of a Saint had not been lost on her, and that now she clearly recognised Urban to be the lawful Pope." To satisfy her revolted subjects whose loyalty to the Holy See it was impossible to tamper with, she even despatched ambassadors to Rome to negotiate her reconciliation, and everywhere circulated the report that she had separated from the party of the Antipope. Catherine's singular interest in this princess made her receive the intelligence of her retractation with extraordinary joy. She wrote to some of her disciples, bidding them rejoice with her, because "the heart of Pharaoh was at last softened, and God was working admirable things in her regard." And with the view of confirming her in her good resolutions she despatched to Naples two of her most trustworthy disciples, the Abbot Lisolo and Neri di Landoccio, who seem to have reached their destination in the August of 1379.

But it soon became apparent that Joanna's submission had been feigned. With the detestable bad faith which marked her character, she had only sought to gain time, while her husband Otho was collecting a body of German troops in order to quell the insurgents. She had equally deceived the Pope and her own subjects ; and so soon as she believed herself secure against insurrection she threw off the mask, recalled her ambassadors from Rome, where Urban had given them the most gracious reception, and again declared herself the partisan of Clement. Catherine saw with profound sorrow that she could no longer interfere to save the unhappy queen from the fate which she so blindly courted, yet she could not abandon her without a last parting word. In this sublime letter Catherine's entire heart appears unveiled. She is pleading with the queen for her own soul; and not for her own soul only, but for her subjects, on whom her persistence in rebellion would entail all the horrors of a bloody war. There is not a word of bitterness or reproach in the whole letter; she still gives her the sweet name of *mother*, and reminds her of the many years during which she had governed her people wisely. "If you care not for your own salvation," she says, "think of them who have enjoyed so many years of peace under your wise rule, and who are now miserably divided, making war on each other, and tearing each other like wild beasts. Does it not break your heart to see such divisions? One holds for the White Rose, and another for the Red,[1] one for the truth, and the other for falsehood: yet all were created alike by the unspotted Rose of God's Eternal Will, and all were regenerated to grace in the Red Rose of the Blood of Christ. Neither you nor any one else can give them those two glorious Roses; none can do that but our Mother the Holy Church and he who holds the keys of the Blood; how then can you consent to deprive them of that which you cannot give them? The second fault you committed after your repentance was worse than the first, for you had acknowledged the truth and your error, and you had sought as an obedient daughter the mercy and pardon of your Father; and after that you did even worse than before. Is it that your heart was not sincere, and that you only dissimulated? for I received a letter from you in which you confessed that Pope Urban was truly the Sovereign Pontiff, and that you desired to submit to him. Oh, for the love of God, confess your fault sincerely; for confession to be good must be accompanied with contrition and satisfaction.

---

[1] The White and Red Roses were the symbols of the Urbanists and Clementists in the kingdom of Naples, and it is supposed that from thence these same symbols were carried into England by some of Hawkwood's followers, and adopted in the civil wars which broke out so soon afterwards in that country.

Where is the truth that should always be found on the lips of a Queen? Her word should be as sure and trustworthy as the Gospel, and when she has made a promise to God, she should not change." Then she assures her that the Pope is even yet desirous to spare her and treat her with indulgence; she reminds her that she is no longer young, and that the world therefore must soon pass away; that death is not far off, and what kind of death? "Be not cruel to yourself, lest at the last moment you hear the terrible words, 'Thou hast not remembered Me in life, and in death I will not remember thee; thou didst not answer to My call when there was yet time, and now the time is past, and no hope remains.'" (Letter 318.)

The sentence of excommunication was in fact pronounced against Joanna, though not until the early part of 1380, a very short time before the death of the Saint. Catherine's charitable advocacy, and Urban's own desire to give her every chance of repentance, delayed the stroke of justice until, in the solemn words above quoted, "no hope remained." Nor was it even then pronounced until Joanna had actually conspired against the life of Urban, and despatched Rinaldo Orsini to Rome at the head of an armed force to seize his person. Raymund speaks of this in the Legend, and informs us of the atrocious cruelties which were perpetrated by the Queen's emissaries on all the unoffending inhabitants who fell into their hands. Some were fastened to trees, and left there to perish by famine; others loaded with chains and carried captives to the camp, in hopes of obtaining a ransom.[1] These facts must be taken into consideration, as well as the peculiar relations of Naples with the Holy See, before we can estimate the act by which Urban finally declared the queen to have forfeited her kingdom, and bestowed it on Charles Durazzo. The history of his expedition against Naples does not properly belong to our present subject, for it took place two years after Catherine's death, and is only here alluded to as displaying the fulfilment of those

---

[1] Leg., Part 3, ch. v. Raymund says that many of those thus tortured obtained their deliverance in a miraculous manner after invoking the aid of St. Catherine.

repeated warnings which she had urged on Joanna as to the terrible fate which most surely awaited her, unless she repented while there was yet time. Charles was received with enthusiasm by the people of Naples, and found himself master of the kingdom almost without a blow. Joanna fell into the hands of the conqueror, who, as a stern act of justice, became the avenger of his cousin's murder; and in the very Castle dell' Uovo, where that crime had been committed, the guilty and unhappy princess suffered the same ignominious death.

CHAPTER IV.

ENGLAND AND THE SCHISM, 1378-1379.

WE have reserved for a separate chapter a brief notice of the part taken by our own country in the affairs of the Schism, which is not without some points of special interest, as connected, in a certain way, with the history of St. Catherine: and we shall set these facts before the reader with the more satisfaction, because it is impossible to deny that, on this occasion at least, the King, the Parliament, and the clergy of England, acted with a good faith and clear-sighted justice which even in Catholic times did not always distinguish our national dealings with the Apostolic See.

The Bull in which Pope Urban announced to the sovereign and clergy of England his election (which he calls *communis et concors electio*) is dated April 19th, 1378. Various documents in exercise of his authority were issued by him during the following month, and are to be found printed in the third volume of Wilkins' Concilia. On the 9th of August in the same year the Encyclical letter addressed to the faithful by the rebellious Cardinals was received in England, declaring that they had elected Urban "to avoid peril of death, which was imminent by reason of the fury of the people." In the following October a Parliament was held at Gloucester, to which there came envoys from the Pope, declaring the great straits he was in, and the injuries he was suffering from the apostate Cardinals, and beseeching the king and lords of England to succour him. There likewise came thither other envoys from the Cardinals, bearing letters sealed with ten seals; making strong allegations on their side, and also petitioning for succour. "By the favour of God who disposes all things justly," says the monk of St. Alban's, "the apostate envoys were refused admittance, and the Papal envoys were received, and aid promised to the Pope in due time. Then the Archbishop of Canterbury, considering the falsehoods made public through the writings of the Cardinals, and the manifest errors into which they had fallen, moved by the Spirit of God, took up this theme, 'There shall be one Shepherd' (Ezech. xxxvii. 24), and he so clearly declared their error to the people as evidenced by their own words, that their malice became evident to all, and their execrable crime unveiled."[1]

Meanwhile a reply was despatched to the Cardinals written in the king's name, and equally decisive in its terms. It runs as follows:[2]

"Richard, King of England, and Lord of Ireland, &c., to such Cardinals: not as you write to us, by the Divine mercy, Cardinals of the Holy Roman Church, but rather by the Divine malediction thundering over you, who as ravenous wolves are attacking the whole flock of Christ, and as crafty foxes who desire to destroy the vineyard of the Lord of Hosts. The foolish tenor of your letters, which at the instigation of the enemy you have rashly addressed to each and all of the provinces of Christendom, wounding thereby our inmost souls, has in no way injured our faith; but has filled us with sorrow of heart at so horrible a scandal, newly raised in the Church of God. But woe to you by whom this scandal has been brought about! *For the face of our Mother the Church has become pale;* and we believe that this pallor, caused by trouble, is owing to your crime, a crime unheard of in all past ages. For you who were regarded as the teachers of the law, have not shown yourselves the true servants of God, but sacrilegious men. The blush of your shame is spread abroad,

---

[1] *Chronicon Angliæ*, by a monk of St. Alban's, p. 212.

[2] Walsingham, *in Richard II.*, 1378, quoted by Rinaldi. The whole letter (which we have given abridged) is also printed by Baluze (*Vitæ Paparum Avenionensium*, Tom. i., p. 554), but with the error of substituting for the name *Richard* that of *Edward* who had died a year previously.

whilst the very confines of Christendom are set on fire by your scandalous acts. Oh, that unhappy and detestable ambition of yours, which seeks to rend the seamless garment of the Lord, which has not fallen by lot to your disposal; and to part that which suffers no division, but rather rejoices in unity! Wicked servants! You shall be judged out of your own mouths! For you have declared to us by your letters the manner in which the recent election of the Sovereign Pontiff was celebrated; saying that a lawless multitude of armed men surrounded your conclave, uttering terrible and deadly threats against you unless you elected an Italian or a Roman; but not limiting you to any person whom they compelled you to elect. It is therefore manifest that the person whom you yourselves grant that you elected, was elected freely and not under compulsion. And we therefore firmly hold, and will hold, that his election was, and is rightly and canonically celebrated; and we firmly adhere to him who was thus elected, enthroned, and crowned, as to the true Head of Holy Church, and successor of St. Peter, and the true Vicar of Christ on earth; and we humbly promise to obey his words and admonitions. And we detest your pernicious rebellion and sacrilegious and heretical contumacy, which led many to follow your damnable example and share your disgrace; for whereas you were placed in the battle-array of the Church, as warriors and champions of the orthodox Christian faith and of the liberty of the Church, wearing red hats upon your heads in token of the constancy and boldness wherewith you ought fearlessly to fight for justice even unto death, how has the fear of death so suddenly come upon you and conquered you, as that you should suffer justice to perish? How is it that you who call yourselves pillars of the Church are become infirm and weak, so that you cannot support the roof and prevent it from falling? . . . For the rest, let not your foolish blindness and blind folly imagine that those words in your letters which seem to savour of piety and zeal for the house of God will move or persuade us in any way to take part with you. We have sufficiently understood that those words are seasoned with the leaven of the Scribes and Pharisees. You name to us the place which you have chosen as suitable for your crime, clearly showing that you have left the true Head of the Church, *and have become members of the devil.*"

Rinaldi, who quotes this letter from Walsingham, observes that "the English burnt with pious zeal against the traitors to the Church, the justice of Urban's election being made evident to them by clear proofs, *drawn from the very testimony of the Schismatics, which we adduce from their own records.*" He then proceeds to give a document which we shall quote, in spite of its length, as it furnishes a notable and valuable contribution to our ecclesiastical history.

Reasons of the English.

1. Because the Romans did not press the Cardinals to elect any person in particular; they demanded only what was reasonable—that a Roman or an Italian should be given them.   Therefore, as regarded the person to be elected the Cardinals were free. Having then elected the Archbishop of Bari, *whom the Romans had not demanded*, it is clear that they elected him freely.   He is then Pope.   It may be stated thus: the Cardinals were not forced by the Romans to elect any one in particular, for they demanded no one in particular.   They elected Bartholomew of Bari, therefore they elected him freely; they were constrained as to the nation, but not as to the person, of him who was to be elected.

2. Because the Archbishop refused earnestly to accept the Papal dignity, and only accepted it at last at the instance of the Cardinals.   Since then they prayed him to accept it, they did not elect him unwillingly; therefore they elected him freely.   He is then Pope.

3. Because according to the relation of the Archbishops, Bishops, masters in theology, and other doctors then in Rome, the English have learnt that even before entering the conclave they unanimously named him Pope, not having been able to agree on any of the Cardinals.

4. And because, after they had entered the conclave, they made a *triple* election of him, in order that there might be no doubt on the matter.   His election was therefore perfectly free.

5. Because they also freely crowned him, as is manifest from the fact that the Cardinals who were out of the city returned to be present at his coronation.

6. Because, moreover, the Cardinals remained in peace with him for several months, received Holy Communion from his hands, and asked him for benefices and other favours for themselves and their friends.   Now, it is not likely that they would have done this if they had known he was not Pope.   He therefore is so truly.

7. Because the Roman populace did not certainly force the Cardinals to write letters commendatory of the said Archbishop. Those which they wrote and sent to the princes and great personages, to announce that he had been elected Pope, and to declare his praises, were written freely.   Therefore he is truly Pope.

8. Because, for no earthly reason ought the Cardinals to deceive the Church of God.   Now, one of these two things must be true : either the Cardinals knew that Bartholomew Prignano was Pope, or they knew that he was not.   If the first be true, we have proved our point ; if the second, they have deceived the whole Church of God.   The consequence is manifest ; for there is no fear that can compel a man of constancy to sin mortally.   But to deceive the Holy Church of God is to sin mortally.   Therefore, they are no longer worthy of credit.

9. Because the Grand Penitentiary sealed the letters of his tribunal with his seal, bearing the inscription : "Given at Rome, in the first year of Pope Urban VI."   He has thus given evidence with all possible authority that Urban is Pope.

10. Because the Cardinal electors wrote unanimously to the Parliament of the King of England that they had elected the Archbishop of Bari, saying, "We *elected* the Archbishop of Bari, only we did it out of fear."   Then they did elect him.   Now such fear would not vitiate their election, because it was not impressed upon them with a view to their electing this particular person for

whom the Romans did not ask : for no one can be forced to *elect ;* election being an act of free will to which no man can be forced ;[1] and even before they incurred that fear, they had named the Archbishop as the person they intended to elect.

11. Because the Romans did not demand that the Cardinals should affirm by their own seals, and by their public acts, that the Archbishop Bartholomew was Pope. If they did this, they did it freely. Therefore, the English people are obliged to believe him to be Pope.

12. Because one of the canons says, "If any one be elected Pope, either by money, or by a military or popular tumult, *without the unanimous consent of the clergy,*" &c. If, therefore, the consent be unanimous, the election is made, even though there may have been a popular or military tumult. We see this in the case of Gregory V., who was elected Pope at the instance of the Emperor, and acknowledged to be duly elected. We may equally say of the Archbishop of Bari that, even though there was a popular tumult at the time of his election, there was, nevertheless, the unanimous consent of the Cardinals to his election.

13. Because, moreover, it was revealed to a certain holy hermit of England, who dwells in the place where the Brother Hermits of St. Augustine took their origin, that Bartholomew of Bari ought to be received as Pope. For it is said that he wrote three letters to England, urged by the Holy Spirit ; one for the government of the kingdom, another for the reformation of his Order, and a third, in which he relates that whilst he was celebrating Mass it was shown him in the Sacred Host that Bartholomew of Bari was the true Pope ; and in that letter he exhorts all persons whom his letters shall reach, to hold as true Pope the said Bartholomew

---

[1] The meaning here seems to be that, in saying " We *elected* the Archbishop of Bari," the Cardinals had unconsciously committed themselves. For they might have been forced to *name,* but not to *elect, i.e.,* not to make choice of any one, which is an interior act of the mind to which they could not be compelled. Yet in saying they had *elected* him, they implied that they had thus made choice of him.

of Bari, putting aside all doubts according to what has been divinely revealed to him.

14. Because, moreover, the common people say we ought to believe as our prelates, the Archbishops and Bishops, masters in theology, and doctors of the sacred canons inform us. But these tell us that under pain of the greater excommunication, and pain of deprivation of all our goods, spiritual and temporal, we are bound to believe Bartholomew of Bari to be Pope. Therefore we hold him to be Pope. Moreover he was the first elected; therefore he is Pope.

15. Because, if, after having elected him, the Cardinals have now separated from him, it is said to be for three causes. First, because he was determined to maintain the rights of the King of England, and to show him justice, and not unjustly to favour the King of France against him. Secondly, because he desired that each Cardinal should restore the title of his Cardinalate to Rome. Thirdly, because he would prevent them from going about with excessive pomp, and living dissolutely, irreligiously, and prodigally, as they had been wont to do. Moved, therefore, by these things, the Cardinals withdrew themselves from so much holiness and justice.

16. Because, moreover, it is commonly said, that the Antipope Clement is a man of blood, having ordered many persons to be put to death, and made himself a leader of armed men. Therefore it seems to us that he ought not to have been elected Pope, according to the 22nd chapter of the First Book of Paralipomenon, wherein it is said: " The word of the Lord came unto David, saying, thou hast shed much blood and fought many battles; therefore thou canst not build a house to My Name, after shedding so much blood." [1]

Rinaldi, who quotes these " Reasons " at length, considers it probable that the last five were added somewhat later than the rest. If we take the first eleven and consider them simply in the

---

[1] Rinaldi, 1378, No. 51, quoted from Tom. i. De Schis. p. 32. Rohrbacher has cited this remarkable document (Vol. xxi. pp. 22, 23), omitting, however, four of the "reasons," and considerably abridging the remainder.

light of a logical argument, it is impossible not to be struck by their force and lucidity. It is manifest that those who guided the English councils of State had not drawn up these reasons without thoroughly and accurately acquainting themselves with the history of the whole transaction. Rohrbacher has observed that "the nation whose zeal most resembled the zeal of St. Catherine of Siena, was undoubtedly England." But they not only resembled her by their zeal; they exactly reproduced her line of argument. There is an identity in the very language used, and the points taken notice of in this State document of England, and in the letters of the Saint which, to say the least, indicates some common source of information. This similarity is also observable in the letter addressed to the Cardinals by the King and Parliament of England, which has been quoted a few pages back, in which we find the expression of "the face of the Church growing pale," the Sovereign Pontiff spoken of as "Christ," and the Schismatics as "members of the devil," all which terms recall, in a striking manner, the language of St. Catherine.

We have seen her addressing her closely-reasoned arguments to kings and princes, magistrates and republics; and the question suggests itself, did she despatch any such letters to England, and if she did, may they not have had their influence, as in other quarters, so also in the English Parliament? The inquiry is one of great interest, and in reply we are able to affirm positively that such a letter was despatched to the King of England. The proof of this assertion is contained in a letter addressed by Stephen Maconi, from Siena, to Neri di Landoccio, then with St. Catherine in Rome. It is dated June 22, 1379, and speaking of certain letters which he has asked his brother secretary to send to him, he says: "That was the third letter; the second contained the news of the Emperor, of which you promised to send me the copy; but I never had it. I also wrote to Richard at Florence, as you told me; but that other letter, *together with the copy of that which went to the King of England,* I have never had. You tell me to procure it, but I do not know from whom." [1]

---

[1] Lettere dei discepoli di Sta. Caterina, No. 13.

Many researches have been made among the English State papers with a view of recovering this letter, but hitherto without success. But the fact remains that St. Catherine did hold communication with Richard II. or his councillors at this momentous crisis, nor is it to be supposed that they who attached such weight to the authority of an anonymous hermit as to adduce his testimony before the Parliament of the realm in support of their arguments, should not have given due consideration to the words of one who enjoyed so great a reputation as St. Catherine. But the hermit, if anonymous in the Parliamentary document, is no stranger to us. Our readers will at once have recognised in him our old friend F. William Flete, who from his solitude at Lecceto ("the place where the Brother Hermits of St. Augustine took their origin") had sent his letters of admonition and warning to his countrymen; and whose fame for learning and sanctity had secured from them so respectful a hearing. Here then is the link which unites this page in our national history with the story of St. Catherine. Her words, and those of her most devoted disciple, were heard and listened to in the Councils of England: they had their weight in keeping the English steady in their loyalty to the See Apostolic; and we hold it as indisputable, that they communicated to those who drew up this remarkable document, some of the arguments which are there put forth in terms identical with those which we have seen used by St. Catherine herself.

It is a little remarkable that the " Rationes Anglicorum " are not to be found preserved in any of the English State records, and that the originals exist only among the papers of the Schismatics. How they came there it is not difficult to explain; for they were felt to be so forcible, and so damaging to the cause of Clement, that the best French legists were engaged to frame a reply. This reply, however, was an utter failure. It was solely based on the testimony of the Cardinals, and thus they were brought back to this terrible dilemma; these Cardinals, the sole witnesses that Urban's election was *invalid*, themselves, for five months, by act and deed had declared it *valid* to every court and nation in Europe. Could such witnesses be received as worthy of credit?

But though we do not find the "Rationes" preserved in our State records, we find reference made to them in one of the Statutes of the realm. We shall give it verbatim, as it stands in the Rolls of Parliament, wherein some words have been injured and effaced by time.

"Item, pur ce q̃ nr̃e Sr̃ le Roi ad entenduz si bien par certains Lettres patentes nouvellement venues, de certains cardinalx rebeulx contre nostre seint Pere Urban a ore Pape, come autrement par cõe fame, q̃ division et discord etoit p entre nr̃e dit seint Pere et les ditz Cardinalx, lesqueux s'afforcent a toute leur pouir a deposer nr̃e dit seint Pere de l'estat de Pape, et de exciter et comoever par leur meins vraies sugestions les Rois, Princes, et le poeple Christien encontre lui a grant peril de leurs almes et a tres mal example: notre dit Sr̃ le Roi fist moustre les dc̃es lr̃es ax Prelatz, Seignrs, et autres grantz et sages esteantz au dit Parlement, et venes et entenduz les Lettres avant dc̃es, et ene meure deliberation sur la matiere, estoit par les ditz Prelatz pr̃unciez et publiez *par plusours grantz et notables resons* illoc̃qs monstrez en plein parlement sibien par matire trovez en dc̃es lettres come autrement, q̃ le dit Urban estoit duement esluz en Pape, et q̃ enzi il est et doit estre verraie pape et chef de seinte Eglise, et l'en doit accepter et obeir. Et a ce faire s'accorderent toutz les Prelatz Seignrs et Coẽs en le parlement a vaunt dit. Et en outtre est assentuz que toutes les Benefices et autres possessions q les ditz cardinalx rebellautz et toux autres leurs coadjutours, fautours, adherentz ou aucuns autres enemys de nr̃e dit Sr̃ le Roi et de son roialme ont denez leur pouir nr̃e dit Sr̃ le Roy Soient seisez es mains de mesme nre Sr̃ le Roi et q̃ nr̃e Sr̃ le Roi soit responduz des fruitz et profitz de mesmes les Benefices et possessions tant come ils dem ront en ses meins p la cause avant dit. Et auxent est ordenez q̃ si aucun lege du Roi ou autre deinz son Poair purchace provision, Benefice, ou autre grce d'aucun autre par nonn de Pape q̃ del dit nr̃e seint Pere Urban ou soit obeisant a aucun autre persone come a pape soit suis hors de la protection nr̃e S̃r̃ le Roi et ses biens et chatexx seisez come for factes."[1]

In the last portion of this statute is embodied the answer to a petition which the Commons presented in this same Parliament, to the effect that, whereas the realm had been greatly impoverished by so many rich benefices being given to foreigners, and that those who drew large sums out of these benefices let the houses attached to them go to ruin, &c., it will please our Lord the King to provide some remedy. To this petition the following answer was returned : "Ordeine est, et assentuz q̃ tous les Bene-fices de Cardinalx et autres rebelx au Pape Urban q'on est soient seisiz."

These proceedings took place in the second year of Richard II., that is in 1378, whence we see how prompt and vigorous was the action taken by the English Legislature, and that it can in no way be attributed, as Maimbourg represents, to the spiteful determination to take a course opposite to that taken by France ; for France delayed any decisive action until the following year. But England at that time possessed great and patriotic statesmen, such as those whose measures of justice had procured for the Parliament of 1376 its title of "the Good Parliament," at the head of which was William of Wykeham, at that time Chancellor of the realm. And though he and the other members of the Good Parliament had suffered a temporary disgrace towards the close of the reign of Edward III., yet the first act of the new sovereign had been to restore him to favour ; so that it is not to be doubted that his voice was heard in the Parliament which rejected and condemned the Schismatics ; possibly, even his hand may have

---

[1] The above is copied from the Rolls of Parliament. It is likewise to be found printed with an English translation, in the "Statutes of the Realm," Vol. i., fol. ii. This English translation is likewise given in Myddleton's "Great Boke of Statutes ;" but it appears there with one notable alteration, showing the translation to have been made in the time of Henry VIII., and after the passing of the Act against acknowledgment of the Pope's supremacy ; for wherever the word *Pope* occurs in the original, the expression is exchanged for *Bishop of Rome.* So far as we know, the document has not been inserted in any other printed edition or translation of the Statutes.

been employed in drawing up those "great and notable reasons" which have been laid before the reader.

Nor were the English statesmen content with securing the allegiance of their own country to the rightful Pontiff. They exerted the powerful influence which England then possessed throughout the States of Europe, to obtain the adhesion of other potentates to the cause of Urban. There were two sovereigns in particular, with whom England was closely allied, they were the Emperor Wenceslaus, and Peter, king of Arragon. The Emperor's decision in favour of Urban was announced to that Pontiff, together with the intelligence that England and Hungary likewise remained faithful; and Catherine, writing from Rome on the 1st of January 1379, to Stephen Maconi, who was still at Siena, refers to this piece of good news, saying, "Holy Church and Pope Urban VI., by the sweet goodness of God, have received the best news during the last few days, that they have had for a long time. I send with this a letter for the Bachelor (W. Flete), in which you will see what graces God is beginning to pour out on His Spouse, and I trust through His mercy that they will go on multiplying" (Letter 264). This "good news" was the fidelity of England and the other northern nations; and it is noteworthy that Catherine at once communicated the intelligence to F. William Flete, who, as we have seen, had his own share in the business. As to Peter of Arragon, he had declared his intention of remaining neutral until he should have taken counsel with other Christian kings. He particularly consulted his English allies, with what result will appear in the following letter, which we quote (abridged) from Rinaldi:

"*To the august Prince the King of Arragon, and our well-beloved Cousin.*

"Cousin, beloved beyond that which we can express in writing, —You are aware how two persons are now contending for the Papacy, namely, the one who was first elected and who lives at Rome, named Urban, and another elected afterwards, named Clement, who is living at Avignon; and though you have been solicited by both parties to declare for one or the other, yet you would not do this, until you were assured which of the two was the true Pontiff. . . . You have begged Us to acquaint you with what We have deliberated concerning this matter, and of what mind We are. . . . Be it known to you, that from many persons worthy of credit, who were present at the election made at Rome of the aforesaid Lord Urban, We have learnt that he was lawfully and canonically elected by the College of Cardinals then in Rome, previous to any popular tumult alleged by the Cardinals as having taken place. Therefore they afterwards enthroned and crowned him, and obeyed him as true, canonical, Sovereign Pontiff, and rendered him Pontifical honours. They also received Holy Communion from his hands, asked and obtained various favours from him, and for some considerable time acknowledged him as true Pope; until on account of certain things which he proposed to do out of just and honourable zeal, the Cardinals themselves went backwards, led astray by the malignant spirit, and rebelled maliciously against him. Having therefore maturely considered these things, and held council with the bishops and clergy of Our realm, and those skilled in the laws recently convoked in Parliament, by their advice and that of the peers and nobles and commons of the realm assembled in Parliament, We have decided that We ought to adhere to the said Lord Urban as true and Canonical Pope, and We hope that you and all other Catholic princes will do the same for justice's sake. And that you may know in what manner the illustrious King of the Romans and Bohemia (Wenceslaus),[1] as also the King of Hungary, conduct

---

[1] Wenceslaus, King of Bohemia elected Emperor, but not being yet crowned, he as yet only assumed the title of King of the Romans. His daughter, Anne of Bohemia, became the queen of Richard II. : hence the strict alliance between those two sovereigns. Urban VI. confirmed Wenceslaus in the Imperial dignity, to which cause Maimbourg attributes his adherence to that Pontiff; though he might more correctly have reversed the statement, and said that Urban's confirmation was granted in acknowledgment of the fidelity shown by the King of the Romans to the Apostolic See. Letters similar to the above were sent by Richard to the Count of Flanders, another close ally of England.

themselves in this behalf, We transmit to you a number of letters of the said King of the Romans and Bohemia addressed to Us on this subject.

"May the Most High preserve your Majesty in prosperity unto length of days.

"Given under Our private seal, at our palace of Westminster, on the 14th day of September (1378).[1]

"Richard, *by the grace of God,*

"*King of England and France.*"

From the position they had thus taken up, the King, Clergy, and Parliament of England never swerved. In the March of 1379 a process was instituted against the rebellious Cardinals, in form of a Brief addressed by Simon of Sudbury, Archbishop of Canterbury, to the Bishop of London, communicating the copy of a letter received from the Pope, in which the whole history of the Schism is carefully drawn up. By this Brief all the Schismatics and those who support them are excommunicated, and the letters ordered to be read in all churches;[2] and when after the calamitous death of Simon (who was slaughtered in the Tower by the insurgents under Wat Tyler), Courtenay, Bishop of London, was promoted to the Primacy, on receiving the Pall he not only swore fidelity to the Holy See, but formally abjured all connection with Robert of Geneva and his schismatical adherents.

When actual hostilities began between the two parties, the English were no less forward with their aid, and Henry Knighton gives an amusing account of the zeal which the devout ladies of England in particular manifested in making collections for the Holy Father. One lady gave as much as £100, a large sum in those days. Others contributed jewels, necklaces, rings, combs, and a variety of other female ornaments in great abundance, so that, to use the words of the historian, *all the secret treasure of the kingdom, which was in the hands of the women, was risked.* This extraordinary liberality was in no small degree due to the large

---

[1] Rinaldi, 1378, No. 42, quoting from tom. 18, De Schis., p. 152.
[2] Wilkin's Conc., vol. iii.

indulgences granted by Urban to those who should come to the aid of the See Apostolic, the preaching of the so-called Crusade being committed to the care of the brave, chivalrous, popular, and most able Henry de Spenser, Bishop of Norwich.[1]

But we shall not be tempted to further digressions into the English annals of the period, interesting as they are, and certainly more full of edification at this particular juncture than those of the Continental States. In England, as elsewhere, there were doubtless plenty of abuses both among clergy and laity; but we observe one marked superiority which the Church in this country possessed at this time over other lands. She could boast of many great, wise, and holy prelates; men who stood as bulwarks against both the spread of heresy and the encroachments of the Crown. Looking over the annals of other kingdoms we find as remarkable an absence of great names among the bishops and prelates of the period. The history of St. Catherine does not bring us in contact with a single French or Italian bishop of any eminence in the Church. This quite exceptional poverty in the Episcopal staff of that period seems to afford an explanation of the otherwise incomprehensible enigma, how a scandal so monstrous as that of the Great Schism could ever have come about. The Church was weak precisely in that point wherein should lie her greatest strength; she lacked "those faithful guardians of the Lord's flock" who in other times of grievous trial stood forth as Defenders of the Faith. Had it been otherwise, it would have been impossible that the eyes of the faithful should have been scandalised by the spectacle of a clergy rebelling against their Head, and rebelling on the distinct and unmistakable ground that he desired to reform their abuses.

And this remark suggests another with which we will conclude our imperfect sketch of this dark and sorrowful time. St. Catherine did not only predict the Schism; she likewise foretold a time of renewal and consolation, when the Church, then covered, as it were, with rags, should appear adorned with jewels, and all the faithful should rejoice at seeing themselves governed by good

---

[1] Knighton's Chronicle, p. 2671.

and holy pastors.[1] Have not we been reserved to witness the fulfilment of this prophecy, and do we not with our own eyes behold the accomplishment of her further prediction of a time *when even unbelievers, attracted by the good odour of Christ, shall return to the true fold, and yield themselves to the true Bishop and Pastor of their souls ?*"

"In truth," says Rohrbacher, "we are witnessing the very marvels, the mere prophetic view of which thrilled the heart of St. Catherine of Siena with joy unutterable. We see the faithful in every land, at home and abroad, rejoicing in the government of good and holy bishops. We see God everywhere renewing His elect : on the Apostolic Chair we behold the spirit of St. Gregory and St. Leo ; in the Episcopate we see the spirit of St. Athanasius and St. Ambrose ; among priests and religious we see reviving the spirit of St. Jerome, St. Benedict, St. Francis, St. Dominic, St. Ignatius, and St. Vincent of Paul ; we see the Church, beautiful as in the days of her youth, adorned with a diadem of virtues, with the lilies of a countless number of holy virgins, with the palms of a noble army of martyrs of every age, sex, rank, and nation ; from those multitudes of the faithful, seculars and ecclesiastics, who confessed the faith in the last century on the scaffolds of France, to those of our brethren and sisters who have confessed and are at this moment confessing it in the prisons and torture-rooms of Tonquin, China, and Corea. Holland, Scotland, England and Germany, countries which for so many years persecuted the children of the Church, are beginning to look towards her with revived tenderness, to grant her bishops liberty of action, and often to second the efforts of her missionaries more effectually than is done in France. The best heads of Protestant England are labouring to justify the Roman Church and the Roman Pontiff from national prejudices ; while the savages of America and Oceania are crying to us for priests, to procure whom, the faithful of all lands unite in contributing their prayers and their alms : new Apostolic congregations are being formed, old ones are being revived, and the chance of martyrdom

---

[1] Leg. Part 2, ch. x.

only offers an additional attraction to those who would emulate the glories of St. Francis Xavier ! "[1]

To us in England who have witnessed the marvellous resurrection of the faith in these latter days, these eloquent words, far from seeming excessive, fall short of the actual truth. It is impossible for us to read St. Catherine's prediction, and not give thanks to God that we have lived to behold and take part in that great revival of which she spoke ; it is impossible for us not to see all around us the fulfilment of our glorious Mother's words, and not to rejoice in acknowledging that among ourselves the days have truly come "when unbelievers, attracted by the good odour of Christ, have returned by thousands to the true Fold," and submitting with loving joy to the Chair of St. Peter, "have acknowledged their true Head, and yielded themselves to the guidance of the Bishop and Pastor of their souls."

NOTE.—The letters quoted in the above chapter as written by Richard II. could scarcely have been his actual composition, he being then no more than twelve years of age. They were, of course, drawn up by those ministers in whose hands the government of the kingdom was vested during his minority ; but he steadily adhered to the policy inaugurated by them. It may not be uninteresting to the reader to know that this Prince is supposed to have been himself a Brother of the Third Order of St. Dominic ; and that so early as the year 1375 he obtained a Bull from Rome whereby the chaplains who accompanied him on his journeys, and with whom he was accustomed to recite the Divine Office, received permission to do so according to the Dominican Rite, and to use the Breviary of the Order. A translation of this Bull will be found in Appendix C.

---

[1] Rohrbacher. Hist. de l'Eglise, vol. xxi. pp. 26, 27.

CHAPTER V.

FAMILY LETTERS, 1379.

IN the preceding chapters we have endeavoured to give so much of the history of the Schism as is needed for the understanding of this latter portion of St. Catherine's public life; and we shall now gladly return to its more private records, and to the correspondence kept up between her and her companions in Rome with their absent friends at Genoa and Siena. The reader, it is hoped, has not forgotten that Stephen Maconi was left at the latter place, detained by business, and as it would seem, also, in compliance with the wishes of his family. He would gladly have accompanied the Saint to Rome, and failing that, desired speedily to have followed her; but she would not allow it. "As to your journey," she says, "it is not necessary for the affairs in question; I do not therefore ask you to come. I should have been very glad if you could have done so, and shall be still more glad when you are able to come; but it must be without giving occasion of complaint to any one. You must not irritate or trouble your parents more than can be helped. Avoid this as much as possible; I am sure that when God sees it best, He will put a stop to all murmuring, and enable you to come in peace. So only come if you can do so without giving offence." (Letter 256.) Barduccio, to whom this letter was dictated, added a concluding paragraph on his own account, to say that he wanted Stephen so badly about some business on which he was engaged, that if his friend did not make haste and come, he should go and fetch him. This was only another way of saying that the little family terribly missed their gay and charming comrade; and he, on his part, felt

Siena equally dull without them. So, as they were mutually deprived of one another's society, they made up for the loss by frequent letterwriting; the absentees in Rome charging Stephen with all sorts of messages and commissions, and he giving vent to his dissatisfaction at being left at home, by characteristic grumbling. They kept him well employed: Catherine writes to him about a horse which she is supposed to have ordered, and bids him see that the mistake is rectified, for she knows nothing whatever about the animal. He is to send to the Countess Bianchina for the copy of the Dialogue that had been lent her, and not returned. "I have expected it daily, but it has never come. If you go, be sure and tell her to send it to me as soon as possible, and see that whoever goes does not forget it." He is also charged with several missions of charity. If Lapa returns to Siena, he is to see after her; and he is to be very kind to Catherine (of the Hospital), who is poor, alone, and friendless. Then there are messages to Master Matthew, who has been ill, and wants them to do some commissions for him in Rome; and to Peter Ventura, who is to join them as soon as he possibly can. And there are generally a number of sealed letters enclosed for him to distribute to their respective owners.

In one of his replies Stephen has to communicate the unpleasant intelligence that a certain person named Megliorino, would not evacuate Catherine's house, in which he seems to have taken up his abode uninvited, in the absence of its rightful owners. However he may have got in, neither Father Thomas nor Stephen Maconi could succeed in getting him out. "I wrote to our Mother to say that he was going out," says Stephen, "and, indeed, he had solemnly promised me to do so, in presence of Ser Christofano, saying that as she was not willing he should remain there, he would leave by next St. Agnes' feast. I spoke to him again to-day, in presence of Sano di Bartholomew, reminding him of his promise, and telling him that, as a man of honour, he was bound to keep his word, &c. And although it seemed to me that he had made up his mind not to go, it ended by my getting Sano to speak to him, and I think he will manage, so that I may be satisfied.   I think Sano wished I had spoken to *him* about it, and I know he wants him to go."   There are also two allusions to a singular, and one would say a rather troublesome, commission which Stephen had to discharge for his friends in Rome.   They wanted him to procure and send them a *capretto raso*.   That *a whole kid*, alive or dead, shaven or unshaven, should have been sent from Siena to Rome for the use of Catherine and her disciples, is difficult of belief; and the probable explanation seems to be, that not the kid itself, but its *skin*,[1] stripped of the hair and otherwise prepared, was sent to the little party; possibly to supply them with shoe-leather.   Why they could not procure this necessary article in Rome is a mystery, of which we can suggest no explanation ; but that there was a difficulty in the case appears from another of the letters, in which Master Thomas Petra, the Pope's secretary, asks Neri to get some *shoes* made for him in Naples.   Catherine and her family lived on alms, and as poor persons, they probably proposed to get their kid-skin from home, and convert it into shoes and sandals with their own fingers.   The obliging Stephen at once set to work.   " As to the *capretto raso* you asked me for, I inquired of Paul in order to know what, and how much to get, and he says that one will be sufficient for your purpose ; so we are sending it to you by that wood-master of ours, a Sienese, and a friend of Paul's, who is son to Master Francesco del Tonghio."   The *wood-master ;* a curious expression, but one which is not without its interesting explanation, too; for Master Francesco del Tonghio, father to the " wood-master," was none other than the artist who carved the wooden stalls in the choir of the Duomo, and presided over the *tarsia*, or inlaid woodwork, then being executed in that building. One sees that Stephen had plenty to do in quality of general agent for the rest of the " family," and all these affairs kept him busy, and were the trifles out of which he contrived to find matter for scribbling his lengthy and amusing letters.   Not less amusing

---

[1] *Chevreau* in French stands not merely for a kid, but a *kid-skin*, and the expression *Carta di capretto* is used for Vellum in one of Stephen Maconi's letters.

in its way is the contrast between these letters written in charming familiar Tuscan, and a Latin epistle, the only one preserved, from Brother Simon of Cortona, the young Dominican, whom as a novice Catherine had treated somewhat like a pet child. He was evidently studying hard to acquire that peculiar epistolary style which in those days was *de règle* between religious men ; and an extreme example of which has been presented in the correspondence between William Flete and John of the Cells. There is a theory current among some persons, that the clergy of the Middle Ages were ignorant of the Scriptures : the biographer of Luther has (I believe) represented that historical personage as startled and overwhelmed, when at an advanced age there for the first time fell into his hands an unknown book called the Bible. But when one reads the compositions—historical, epistolary, or hortatory—in which the religious men of those ages endeavoured to convey their sentiments on the most ordinary subjects by means of a string of Scripture texts ingeniously adapted to the occasion, one is tempted to wish, I will not say that they had been less familiar with the letter of Scripture, but at least that they had been guided by better taste in its adaptation. However, Brother Simon, no doubt, had no choice in the matter ; and he addresses Neri a solemn little letter, in which, when he wants to express that he does not forget his good friends, he quotes the Gospel precept, "Thou shalt love the Lord thy God with all thy heart, and thy neighbour as thyself ;" and is unable to say that he longs to see them all again without referring to that of the Psalmist, "As the hart desireth the water-brooks, so does my soul," &c., adding, "But woe is me, that my sojourning is prolonged," by which he means to say that he cannot get leave of absence to pay them a visit.

Some of the correspondence is more serious, bearing reference to the troubles of the times, and specially of their own city. Owing to circumstances that are nowhere explained, Siena had not yet been relieved from the interdict which she had incurred through her alliance with the Florentines ; and considerable embarrassment was thus caused to the consciences of the faithful.

Giacomo Tolomei, Bishop of Narni, having been sent to Siena for the purpose of arranging for the absolution of the city and the final restoration of Talamon, some persons endeavoured to evade the difficulties of their position by enrolling themselves as members of his household, and so sharing the privilege he and his servants of course enjoyed of being able to assist at the Holy Sacrifice. Stephen, among others, had been persuaded to do this; but he did not venture to hear Mass until he had written to consult the Saint. She did not like the proposition at all: there was a want of straightforward adhesion to the plain line of duty in it, which was repugnant to her sense of truth; and she writes at once in reply: "About the Mass, you did quite right not to go. As to your having made yourselves the 'familiars' of Monsignore Giacomo, if I had known of it, you would not have done so; you should have been humble and obedient, and patiently waited the moment of peace. However, if you think now you may go with a safe conscience, do so, but not otherwise. I do not know if his rank gives him such extensive privileges, or if by his 'familiars,' we are justified in including any besides those actually in his service. Can we take the title of 'familiars,' if we are not, and have no intention of becoming so? Does his rank allow of it, and who has assured you that it does?" (Letter 256.)

Meanwhile Catherine was not backward in procuring indulgences and privileges from Urban for her friends in Siena, and exerting herself to hasten the conclusion of this painful business. But this was not all. She was naturally full of solicitude as to what part Siena might take in the question of the Schism. What she could not do in person to confirm their fidelity she tried to effect by her letters, and through the influence of her disciples, whom she charged to keep her accurately informed of the state of public opinion. On the 14th January, 1379, a letter from Christofano to Neri di Landoccio gave assurance that so far as he could ascertain there was not a man in Siena who entertained the least doubt that Urban was the rightful Pope. "If the ambassadors of the Antipope come here," he says, "they will not be listened to; we must pray much for the Spouse of Christ whom they seek to deprive of her Bridegroom, and in which so much cockle is being sown. But she is founded on a rock which cannot fail, even the Rock that said to Peter, *Rogabo pro te ut non deficiat fides tua, igitur confundantur qui eam persequantur.* The more she is abased the more she is exalted, *Quia dictum fuit sibi: Tu es Petrus, et super hanc petram edificabo ecclesiam meam."* He has a few words on his own affairs; he has been appointed Notary to the Institution for Orphans, and though sorry on some accounts, is glad to stay at Siena. He wants to come to Rome before Easter, if his colleague will let him. Then after the usual salutations which, according to the custom of the time, were somewhat lengthy, he says, " All our brethren salute you. Tell Mamma that *we are rather falling to pieces;* I wish she would give us some sort of a rule, which for her sake we would obey, and meet together at certain times in her name; and beg her to write to her wandering sheep, though we are all well assured she does not forget us in her prayers."

This request for " some sort of a rule," Catherine did not refuse, and we are disposed to think that one of her letters addressed " to Sano di Maco and other seculars, her sons in Christ," was written by way of reply. After some long and very beautiful spiritual instructions on the light of faith, without which they cannot accomplish the will of God, she says, " I desire to see you all serving Him without measure, not in your own way, but His; not choosing times and places, or seeking consolation, or refusing trials, but embracing sufferings for the honour of God. Follow Christ crucified, macerating your bodies by watching, fasting, and prayer. Resign your wills to the sweet will of God, and let your Society be a society of His servants. When you assemble together,[1] do not lose your time in idle words, criticising the

---

[1] " From these words," says Burlamacchi, " we see that the disciples of the Saint were formed into a sort of Spiritual Society, as is still the custom in many cities of Tuscany, assembling to confer on spiritual things, spending part of festival days in pious conversation, spiritual reading, or the singing of God's praises; and as most of these disciples belonged to the Company of Mary (under the Hospital), she is probably referring to their meetings held in that holy place."

conduct of others, or tearing your neighbour's reputation to pieces with murmurs and rash judgments; for God alone is the Sovereign judge of all. But show that you have assembled in the name of Christ, to confer together on His goodness, on the virtues of the Saints, and your own faults. Be strong, constant, and persevering; it is perseverance alone that will obtain the crown. The memory of the Precious Blood will entirely detach you from all things contrary to the will of God; be faithful to Him and to my miserable self. If I do not write to you, I nevertheless always love you, and occupy myself about your salvation in the presence of God. Have courage then, and love one another. I desire more than ever to see all your names written in the Book of Life." (Letter 247.)

In another letter she particularly warns them on the subject of uncharitable conversation. "On this head," she says, "I do not think you are, as yet, all perfect. Often under colour of zeal or compassion you murmur and judge others. Now this must be displeasing to God, and it is not the teaching you have received; you should mutually love one another and bear each other's faults. No one is faultless; that belongs to God only. If you were His faithful servants, we should see no murmurs, or ridicule, or scandal, or disobedience among you, whether in joke or earnest. I have often noticed this imperfection in you." (Letter 248.) The day after Christofano's letter was received, came one from Stephen, somewhat different in style. He also writes to Neri; and indeed it is remarkable that among all the letters preserved, none, or nearly none, are addressed directly to Catherine.

"Dearest Brother in Jesus Christ,—I have been wonderfully pleased with the contents of the two letters you have written to me since you left Siena, and they comforted me so much that I was not content with reading them once, or even twice. As to what you say of our sweet and venerable Mother, it is no sort of surprise to me; I have no doubt about it, knowing many facts, beyond comparison greater, which I cannot write. Indeed I believe and confess that our sweetest Mamma *is* Mamma; and every day I hope to believe and confess it more earnestly.

" The other great and good news [1] which you send, touching
the exaltation of Holy Church and of the true successor of St.
Peter, Pope Urban VI., has been a sort of mitigating unguent to
the pain I have felt, and am still feeling; and though it is much
alleviated, yet I don't think I shall be quite cured till I find myself
once more at the feet of my dearest Mother. I hope, in God's
goodness, soon to be free. I have done what you desired, narrating
and spreading about the news as much as possible, so that good
folk who believe Pope Urban to be the true Pope may rejoice,
and that the wicked who believe the contrary may be put to confusion. Every one who has heard it up till now has shown the
greatest joy. On this point at least you may give a good report
to the Holy Father; for I assure you that everybody, universally
and with one voice, declare he is true Pope, and that they will
hold to his obedience; nor have I heard of any one who holds
the contrary view. And in proof of this I will tell you further
that, a few days since, it was said that an ambassador of the
Antidemon,[2] who was at Fondi, was coming here : for which cause,
suspecting he would get no hearing here, many who were zealous
for God's honour (from which number I do not wish to exclude
myself, however tepidly I may seek it) buzzed the matter about
in the Palazzo, and in the ears of the people outside, who might
be able to devise some remedy; showing them that this demon
was coming here to sow heresy among us, and to contaminate our
faith, and suggesting that it would be a good work done to burn
him, &c. Moreover, Peter (Ventura) and I went at once to
Messer di Narni, offering ourselves as his lordship's humble
servants to be the first to lay hands on him. And I promise you
we found the people so well disposed, it would have been a real

---

[1] *i.e.* The fidelity to Urban, of England, Hungary, and the Empire, which
Catherine had already communicated to Stephen and William Flete.

[2] Stephen very often calls the Antipope the *Antidemon*, a palpable blunder ;
for if one who opposes the Pope is an *Antipope*, and one who opposes Christ
is an *Antichrist*, an *Antidemon* can mean no other than one opposed to the
demon ; *i.e.*, a true servant of Christ. He probably meant either an *Antichrist*, or an *Archdemon ;* but his pen, like his tongue, often outran his
thoughts.

pleasure to you to have seen them ; specially those at the Palazzo, who immediately gave orders that he was not to be suffered to enter the gates. The children declared they would stone him, and I verily believe that had he come, one way or another he would not have escaped with his life. I write this to show the good dispositions of our poor little city, and to comfort you for the pain you felt some time back when it was opposed to the obedience of the Church.

"I will say no more except to ask you, my sweet brother, not to forget me, but to pray for me who certainly needs your prayers, that God in His goodness may deliver me from the miserable bondage of the world, and show me in what way I may best serve Him. And there are two signs by which you can show that you do not forget me ; one is, that you very often recommend me to our dear and venerable Mother; and be so good as to do that at once, before this letter goes out of your hands, so that you may not forget it. The other is, that you write to me very, very often, a thing I entreat as earnestly as I can, specially about what you promised, and also when you have any good news to tell me about the Church. I am sure you would do so if you knew what a great charity it is.

"Remember me to all our poor family, each one in order, bearing in mind that the head and every member is fixed in the very centre of my heart. Tell Gabriel (Piccolomini), who shows very little charity to his brethren, that I will do as he asks, and that I have not been once to sit by his fireside this year, except when I read them his letter, which was listened to very gladly. God keep us all in His love, and grant that we may soon meet again. Your useless and unworthy brother Stephen, poor in all virtue. Jan. 15, 1378 (79)."

The "Peter" mentioned in this letter, who seems at this time to have been Stephen's constant companion, was Peter Ventura, the same whose eye had been cured by Catherine at Belcaro, and who, when he and his horse had ridden by mistake into the lake, got out again after invoking her. His character was very sympathetic with Stephen's, and he often came in for a share in the scoldings which Catherine bestowed on his friend. She not unfrequently wrote one letter addressed to both, and seems to have thought her exhortations against carelessness and tepidity as applicable to one as to the other.

Stephen's friends in Rome took rather a serious view of the letter we have just quoted, and not only thought it a little giddy, but considered that in his tales about the desire of the Sienese to stone or burn the envoy of the Antipope, he was, to use a common phrase, "drawing the long bow." Neri wrote and told him so plainly, and we shall see presently in what way he justified himself. Meanwhile a difficult negotiation was placed in Catherine's hands. Pope Urban was in want of substantial aid to defend himself against the forces of the Antipope, which were beginning to establish themselves at Marino. He therefore engaged Catherine to appeal, in his name, to her countrymen, and she obeyed. But though the Magistrates showed every wish to hold firmly to their allegiance, yet when there was question of proving their loyalty by contributing supplies of men and money, difficulties not unnaturally arose. Catherine, therefore, in obedience to the Pope's wishes, addressed a letter to the Defenders of the Republic (Letter 203), in which she urged, among other arguments, the motive of gratitude to Pope Urban who had absolved their city, and prevented Talamon from remaining in the hands of the Pisans; yet now, she complains, when it had come to giving proof of their gratitude, they treated him like a child, putting him off with fair words, and giving him no substantial aid. The Sienese, who had already paid down 8000 gold florins for the restoration of Talamon, perhaps felt the further demand on their exchequer somewhat a hardship; and as they were slow in their response, the Saint thought it well to appeal to the devotion of that association, whose influence in Siena was powerful with persons of all ranks, and whose words and example were sure to carry respect. This was the Company of the Blessed Virgin, which has already been spoken of as holding its assemblies in the subterranean vaults of the hospital of La Scala, and most, if not all, of whose members were her fervent disciples.

So she writes to them that it is time to see if they are indeed branches of the true Vine. If so, in this time of calamity they will come to the aid of the Master of the Vineyard both spiritually and temporally; spiritually by their prayers, temporally by doing what they can to induce the Magistrates of the republic to send him supplies. "We certainly ought to do this," she continues; "have we so little love for the Faith as not to be ready to make some sacrifice for it? Can we forget the great benefits we have received from God and his Holiness? I beg of you, therefore, put your hand to the work and that without delay." (Letter 144.) Then she writes to Stephen Maconi to tell him what she has done, and charges him to support her appeal by all means in his power. "I send you a letter I have written to the Lords Defenders, and another to the Company of Mary. Read them, and profit by them; then have them delivered, and speak to each one as occasion serves, according to the tenor of these letters, enjoining everybody, in God's name and mine also, to labour with all their power in concert with the Magistrates, to do what can be done for the help of the Church and of the Holy Father. For my part, I only regret that so much trouble is necessary when there is question of God's honour and the spiritual and temporal interests of our city. Try not to be tepid, but stir up the brethren and chiefs of the Company that they may do their utmost. If you and your brethren were what you ought to be, you would kindle all Italy; the thing is not so difficult." (Letter 261.)

To this appeal Stephen replied, and his letter, addressed to Neri, shows that he somewhat shared the sentiments of the Magistrates; at any rate, he frankly exposed their difficulties. At the same time, he took occasion to defend himself from the charge of levity and exaggeration which his grave friend had brought against him on occasion of his January letter.

"DEAREST BROTHER IN JESUS CHRIST,—On the 21st of June I received your letter written on Ascension Day (May 19th), in which you give me good news [1] as to the affairs of the successor

---

[1] This fresh "good news," written on May 19th, was no doubt an account of the victory gained over the forces of the Antipope on the 29th of April.

of St. Peter, and the Vicar of Jesus Christ, and the confusion of that Antidemon, all which gave me great and singular joy. Although I had already some weeks back heard something of what you wrote, yet not so particularly; so it caused me a new pleasure. . . . You say, that to please no one, ought I to tell lies, and I suppose you think what I wrote in my last letter was all lies. But to this I reply that I wrote nothing but the truth as to what *had* happened; as to what was going to happen in the future, granting it was not all true, yet I don't consider I told any lie, for I did not say anything contrary to what was in my mind,[1] and I said it at no human being's suggestion. Possibly the great wish I had that it might be as I said, made me believe more than was true. But I seemed to see the villain coming and sowing his cockle among the good seed in the field of the Lord. And I say again, that as far as I know or have heard, there are certainly not more than nine or ten at the most who do not hold with Pope Urban, and few as they are, they are all regarded as thieves. In spiritual matters particularly all will obey the Pope as their true Pastor, but as to temporals they allege their poverty and the misery in which we are. Just think, every month the soldiers here require six thousand gold florins; and only the day before yesterday, the Company[2] demanded fifteen thousand; and even so, we could not prevent their scouring the Maremma and surrounding country. I don't say this by way of excuse. I have spoken to them on the subject many times; and both in the Signoria and elsewhere, I do not yield them an inch, and pretend not to believe them, saying that for God's honour and for the maintenance of the faith we ought willingly to pay something; and if we are too poor, we should pledge the goods of the

---

[1] After the lapse of six months, such a madcap as Stephen may be pardoned if he had no very clear remembrance of what he had written expressive of the delight he would have felt in burning the envoy of Clement, which seems to have been the point disapproved of by Neri.

[2] We learn from the Chronicle of Neri di Donato, that to protect themselves from the ravages of the Free Lances, the cities of Lucca, Siena, Pisa, Perugia, and Florence came to an agreement with them, paying them a regular sum in money.

Commune; and that if we cannot send many men, we should at least send a few,[1] and that the Holy Father will accept the little that is possible for us. For, believe me, dear brother, it grieves me to my heart that the Holy Father should not have what he desires from this city, and I have said so much about it, that I have often been told I say more than becomes me. But for that I care but little." Then follows the passage already quoted in which he asks for a copy of the letter written to the king of England, and complains that F. Thomas, who had gone to Rome, had given him no news of anybody, except what he knew before. He continues, "If I had time, I would give you a good laugh; not the others only, but even Master Matthew was ready to split with laughter." Then come messages to "Our sweetest Mother, whom he would die for rather than displease," to Monna Lisa, and Alexia, and Cecca, and the other Sisters, and to Master John III., and Fra Santi, and F. Bartholomew, "and a great deal very specially to Master Thomas Petra, and to all the family, whom though I am not worthy to be with them in the body, yet in heart I am ever with them. I was just finishing this letter in our room at the Misericordia, when who should come in but Master Matthew himself, and finding I was writing to you, he desires me to send this message to our Mother,—that he has written so many letters he does not think he can write any more, but he begs her, and you, and everybody to remember him in such a way as that some effects may follow. We are certainly much indebted to him, and I include myself, for he has made me, I may say, one of his family, and has given me a room here, which I use day and night. Farewell. If you cannot write yourself, get Barduccio or Cecca to do so; I am sure they will do it willingly."

Meanwhile Neri had been sent to Naples, and F. Bartholomew Dominic came to Rome. We have one of his letters to Neri, which is interesting as setting before us, in a commonplace, matter-of-fact way, some of the circumstances of St. Catherine's

---

[1] Eventually a body of troops was sent by Siena to the aid of Urban, under the command of Sozzo Bandinelli.

daily life in Rome: her interviews with Urban, the weighty business in which she was as constantly engaged as if she had been a Secretary of State, the projected expedition to Naples talked over and finally given up, and how she and her family were supported on alms. "We have received two of your letters," writes Bartholomew, "one written to our Mother, the other to me. You tell me I am to get those two letters sealed; I will do so as soon as I can; but when I spoke of it to Master Thomas (Petra) a few days after you left, he said that his Holiness would not seal any of them unless he first had assurance of the good life of the persons concerned. He was then ill, but is better again now, though somewhat weak. To-day, Master John wishing to get his and Peter's sealed, Master Thomas spoke to his Holiness, our Mother and Master John being present: and his Holiness replied that they must draw up the petition afresh, and then he would sign it. So Master John does not know what to do, and Master Thomas is so weary of it all that he will have nothing more to do with it. None the less I will do what I can. Master Thomas says you may have the shoes made by whoever you please, and sent to him. To-day we received six gold florins from the Countess Joanna (d'Aquino) and from Madonna Catilla and her companions at Naples. It is all we have had. Our Mother has several times thought she was coming; but it does not seem to be the will of God, and the Pope does not consent, though at first he said that he wished it. I fancy now we must think no more about it.

"At Rome, Sept. 1st, (1379). Thy brother Bartholomew Dominic."

Are we not right in calling these "family letters"? They bring before us Catherine and her companions in the aspect of ordinary mortals, not however to the exclusion of the fact that the extraordinary mingled with the ordinary, as Stephen's casual remark [1] lets us see. The messages about horses, kid-skins, shoes, and refractory tenants, Stephen's careless rattle, and Neri's grave rebuke; good Master Matthew looking into the room at the

[1] See p. 518.

Misericordia, and compelled to split with laughter at some joke related by his irresistible guest; the letter from Rome read at Gabriel's fireside, and Christofano's solemn confession that in the absence of their spiritual Mother her disciples were getting rather careless and relaxed,—does it not bring before us each individual of this beloved "family," and make them live again, as we hear them tell their own story in their own natural unaffected words?   Concerning one of the party, however, we have a good deal more to say.   In spite of his light-hearted exterior, and a certain carelessness which seems to have been the fault which Catherine was always trying to correct in her "tepid" and "negligent" son, Stephen Maconi was not entirely happy.   As in most men of his temperament the outward seeming was not altogether a trustworthy index of the inward self.   Even in the correspondence which has been quoted, the reader may have observed the passing hint he drops to Neri, that he is tired of the world, and longs to know what God demanded of him.   Catherine had long ago penetrated to the most secret recesses of his heart, and understood him far better than he understood himself.   In the very earliest letter from her to Stephen which has been preserved, she says, "Follow the guidance of the Holy Spirit.   I feel a difficulty in not saying to you one *word of Christ;* but I hope to be able to say it some day in the right time and place; and then you will hasten to fill the vessel of your heart with the Precious Blood."   This "word of Christ" was doubtless His word to the young man in the Gospel, "Go, sell all that thou hast, and follow Me."   Catherine saw where God was leading this soul; but in her prudence she kept back the word till the right moment should come: when that was will appear in the sequel.   In the meantime she watched him with a mother's tenderness, and sought to train him for something better than any career the world could offer.   Sometimes she writes to him about the city of his soul, and reminds him that one day the Master will call on him to surrender it to Him, adorned with true and solid virtues.   Once he fell into the hands of some roving Free Lances and escaped almost miraculously, and Catherine takes occasion to examine whether in his moment of danger he had not experienced a strange interior peace. "This was but the Aurora," she adds, "the full light of the sun has not yet risen upon you, when you will be free from all your enemies. Nevertheless, take courage, from this hour of dawn, for the sun will soon arise, and then you will hear the sweet word, 'Let the dead bury their dead.' But on that subject I will say no more at present." Another time she speaks more urgently. "You must cut your bonds and not fasten them; he who does not know how to cut a knot will always remain bound; if he cannot fly, he will always be a prisoner. O negligent son, respond to God's call: it is a shame to see you always keeping God waiting at the door of your heart and never opening it to Him. I say again, you must cut the ties that keep you outside of the will of God, and stop you in the path of perfection. Fly the world, then, go forth from your father's house, retire into the open Side of Jesus crucified. If you will act decidedly, suffering will be your glory; but otherwise you will always be ill at ease, and afraid of your own shadow." These and other similar words show us that Catherine perfectly understood what was working in the heart of her favourite disciple. He was torn to pieces by two contrary emotions: a secret disgust of a worldly life, and a longing after perfection, on the one hand; and on the other, that horror which flesh and blood must inevitably feel at the thought of renunciation. Who, by nature, could have seemed more suited to the world, and more likely to become its spoilt child than the brilliant and volatile Stephen who was everybody's favourite, whom, separated from us by five centuries, we cannot help loving as if we had known him face to face; and to whose feet the world was ready to flow at his first word of invitation? The interior conflict was severe; and in that unsettled mood which betrays itself in variations of temper and changes of purpose, Stephen was just then an enigma to his best friends. Even at a distance from him Catherine discerned what was going on: and now, far from forbidding him to leave Siena, she urged him to come to her, and to "come quickly." "I received a letter from you yesterday," she writes, "which I will answer in a few words. As to the indulgences I promised to get for you, do not expect them, or anything else from me until you come yourself. I do not say that I will refuse to help you in your spiritual needs: God knows I never desired to do so more ardently than now; never have I more earnestly offered you to God, for I never knew you need it more. You say that your present state displeases you : when it *really* displeases you, you will quit it. Then you will show that you know your state, which up to the present time you have been ignorant of. I trust in God that as the veil is beginning to fall from your eyes it will soon be taken away altogether; then you will see your real state, and it will be soon, too, provided you do not resist, and that my sins do not prove an obstacle." She seems to have been still engaged on this letter (in the middle of which occur some broken and imperfect phrases which indicate an interruption) when another was placed in her hands from the Abbot of Mount Oliveto, near Siena, telling her that Stephen and several of his companions were about to join his Community. And this without a word to her, her counsel not asked, their confidence not given ! The report seemed confirmed by all that had appeared so unaccountable in Stephen's late conduct. And yet, after all, it was merely a report founded on words which Stephen had almost unconsciously dropped in conversation, and which had led the Abbot to draw a somewhat hasty conclusion. Startled with the unexpected intelligence, however, Catherine finished her letter to Stephen, and wrote as follows : " I have just received a letter from the Abbot, who talks to me of the plants he has planted in *his* garden and *mine*. He says that he hopes to plant some others, among whom he reckons on *you*,—you and your companions, and says that you have already engaged yourselves ! Of course it is a great happiness to me to see you coming out of your state of imperfection and embracing a perfect state ; but I confess I am greatly surprised that you should have engaged yourself without letting us know a word about it here. There is something in all this I do not understand : but I pray the Divine Goodness to do whatever may be best for His honour and your salvation.

" You know I have never wished or desired anything else since I first knew you, than that you should be delivered from the corruptions of the world. I have the same wish still, and I hope, please God, to keep it to the end. If you think the Holy Spirit calls you to this state, you have done well not to resist, and I shall be content. When He calls, we must answer. I should have many things to say, but I cannot and will not say them now." (Letter 263.)

And after all the Abbot had made a mistake, and interpreted Stephen's intentions by his own hopes. And he had been a little imprudent and a little premature in communicating his hopes to Catherine, for in reality they had no foundation in fact. So it was all a misunderstanding from beginning to end, such as often takes place in this world of mistakes and imperfections. Yet it inflicted a wound on Catherine's heart, which she had enough of human sensibility to feel acutely; and at that moment with how many wounds was her sensitive nature being pierced! Raymund was at Genoa, Neri at Naples, Stephen at Siena: and now it almost seemed as if he, the child of her predilection, were withdrawing his confidence from her, and deciding his vocation without so much as a reference to the Mother who loved him so tenderly. She did not complain; she rejoiced that he should be set free from the shackles of the world; but the thorn pricked sharp. Nor in saying this are we (as we may hope) representing our holy Mother in too natural a light. They surely do real injustice to the Saints who represent them as strangers to human emotions, whereas we judge that the Saint of saints Himself suffered beyond our utmost capacity of comprehension, precisely because, above all men, He possessed most of that keen sensibility which gives the power of suffering. Catherine then suffered in her woman's heart, and in the decrees of Divine Providence she was intended thus to suffer. In these last months of her mortal life she was to undergo her Passion, and to endure, not merely the extremity of bodily pain and the assault of evil spirits, but, after the pattern of her Divine Spouse, the loss of all human consolation. No letters are preserved which show in what way

Stephen explained this misunderstanding, nor are we able to conjecture why he did not go at once to Rome whither the Saint had so earnestly summoned him.   His biographer gives us to understand that he was really detained by important affairs, and that "he was ready to move heaven and earth" to get them finished, that so he might hasten to his beloved Mother, the accounts of whose state of health were beginning to alarm him.   But for the present we must leave Stephen and his budding vocation, and see a little what sort of intercourse had been kept up during the same period between Catherine at Rome and Raymund of Capua at Genoa.

It is not every heart that is able to share its love with many friends, and yet to love them all with any degree of intensity. The common verdict of mankind is in favour of the theory that affection, to be worth anything, must be limited to few, if not to one ; and that what it gains by diffusion, it loses in force.   Those, however, who hold that the perfection of love on earth must be found in its resemblance to the charity which reigns in heaven, will not readily yield the point that in the heart of man, as in the house of God, there are " many mansions;" and that if once such a heart be purified from selfishness, there is absolutely no limit to its power of loving.   Such a heart was St. Catherine's ; and she whom we have seen writing so eloquently on the variety which makes up the beauty of God's works, presented an example of that same beauty in the variety of her human affections. Thomas, Bartholomew, Raymund, and Stephen; Lisa, Alexia, and Cecca,—she loved them all, and each with their own individual love.   Her letters show that they each had their own separate place in her heart, and she did not write to one as to another.   To Raymund she reserved the most intimate outpourings of her confidence ; he was the depositary of her secret intercourse with God.   Their mutual friendship had only strengthened with time, though the wonderful simplicity of Catherine's character led her sometimes to speak to him with a frankness quite free from human respect.   We have seen one specimen of this in her letter to him after his return to Genoa ;

he himself has given us other instances not a little amusing. "At the time that I knew her," he says, "I am certain that if she had had an opportunity of speaking on Divine things with persons who understood her, she would have gone on for a hundred days and nights without eating or drinking, and never have been tired, but rather refreshed thereby. I may say this, albeit to my own confusion, that frequently when she spoke to me of God, and His profound mysteries, for a long time together, I, who was far from that fervour of spirit which she possessed, would grow tired if the discourse were much prolonged; and overcome with the heaviness of the flesh, I sometimes fell asleep. At such times she, quite absorbed in God, would go on talking for some time without perceiving it, but when at length she discovered that I was sleeping, she would awake me by exclaiming in a loud voice: 'Alas, Father! why for the sake of a little sleep do you lose the profit of your soul? Am I speaking to a wall, or to you?' She often told us the thoughts of our hearts as clearly as we knew them ourselves, and frequently reproved me for some that had passed through my mind. And if I sought to excuse myself with a falsehood, 'O Father!' she would say, 'how can you say so? Will you deny that which I see more clearly than you see it yourself?' And then she would both tell me precisely what I had been thinking, and, moreover, give me a salutary lesson on the same." But this simplicity of their mutual relations diminished neither his regard nor her respect. He was at once her father and her son; her "dear Father, and negligent son," as she sometimes called him (Letter 92); and the absolute obedience which she rendered him in the one capacity did not prevent her labouring for his perfection in the other. In fact, her obedience to him as her spiritual director was absolute, and he sometimes thought good to put it to the test. One day after they had been conversing together for some time, Catherine rose to go on some charitable errand. He abruptly told her to sit down and remain where she was. She obeyed without the smallest gesture of surprise or hesitation, and was rewarded, says Caffarini, by a flood of ineffable consolation which made her eyes become, as it were, two fountains of sweet tears.[1] But she was his mother also, and was always trying to increase his fervour and his spirit of self-sacrifice. His chief fault seems to have been a certain repugnance to suffer, and the sum of all her exhortations tended to lead him to greater generosity. "I want to see you possessed with perfect zeal," she writes; "zeal makes us ready to sacrifice our own ease and comfort; no matter whence derived, we should renounce them for the sake of our neighbour. A servant of God once said to Him: 'Lord, what wouldst Thou have me to do?' and He replied, '*Honour Me and serve thy neighbour:* offer worship to Me, and sufferings for thy neighbour.' Let us then learn to suffer, my dear Father. God has called and chosen you: you thought it was moonlight when you were suffering, but believe me, in suffering you will find your true sunshine. Charity will only triumph in heaven: when she enters there she will bear the fruit of patience, for *patience is the very pith and marrow of charity*. . . Oh, I conjure you, for the love of Jesus, be detached from all creatures, and from me, the most of all. Clothe yourself with the love of God, and love creatures only for God's sake. Love them much, but have little to do with them, unless it be to labour for their souls. I desire to do this, if God gives me the grace. I would fain strip off the garments I have worn till now, and clothe myself anew in the Blood. That blood is, and shall be, the happiness of my soul; I deceived myself when I sought it in creatures. In all my labours I desire to have that Blood with me; in it to find all creatures, in it to quench my thirst for their love, and so to find peace in war, and sweetness in bitterness. And were I deprived of all creatures, and even of my father's tenderness, I should still find the Creator, the Eternal and Sovereign Father." (Letter 93.) When she received the news of his second appointment as Prior of the Minerva, she wrote exhorting him to govern his flock like a good Pastor, and not to be afraid of fatigues. "Accept them with joy, rather, and go to meet them, saying, 'Welcome!' Say moreover, 'What a grace this is which God gives me, by letting me suffer something for the glory of His name!'"

[1] Sup., Part I, Trat. 2, § 21.

Making due allowances for the immense fervour of Catherine's own soul, compared to which the infirmities of one cast in less heroic mould would naturally appear like pusillanimity, we may gather that in Raymund's character there was a certain deficiency of fire. It betrays itself in the Legend, which bears the stamp of being written by one, admirable rather for his humility and his scrupulous regard for truth, than for strength or ardour. When, therefore, circumstances placed him in the front of the battle, he did his duty on a motive of principle, but there can be no shadow of doubt that according to nature he would have greatly preferred his quiet cell at the Minerva, or even at Montepulciano, to the dignity of Papal Envoy to the King of France. Catherine, who knew him thoroughly, and his disposition to despond, kept ever sounding in his ears her trumpet-notes of encouragement. "I must not have you turn your head aside from any trouble or persecution; I want to see you glory in adversity, for it is only in trial we can show our constancy: we have no other means of giving glory to God. Dear Father, it is now the time for us utterly to forget ourselves; do not let me see you timid. Think of the necessities of the Church—alone, and, as it were, abandoned; and fight generously until death."

But it is in the letters that she addressed to him on the occasion of the failure of his embassy to France, that we best understand their mutual relations. When the news came of his return to Genoa, it moved her, as we have seen, to expressions which naturally disconcerted him to whom they were addressed. In his deep humility he was the first to admit that he could not rise to her level of enthusiasm; and he wrote a reply in which he seemed to doubt his fitness for the burden laid on him, and in his dejection expressed a fear lest he had lost something of Catherine's esteem. Between two hearts united in God by a friendship such as that which existed between Raymund and Catherine, however, no real misunderstanding could arise; and the humility and tenderness of her reply quickly healed the wound which had been caused by her former words. Her reproaches now are not for him, but for herself. "Without the light of Faith," she says, "no work or desire of ours will attain the end we wish, but everything we do remains imperfect.   And the reason is, as it seems to me, that love is the measure of faith, and faith of love.   He who really loves is always faithful to that which he loves, even until death. This makes me see that I do not truly love God, and creatures for God.   If I did, I should be faithful to Him, and ready to die a thousand deaths every day for His sake.   I should have confidence that God would be my defence as He was that of the glorious martyrs.   But because I do not love Him, I do not really trust Him; my love is tepid, and this is what hinders all the works He entrusts to me, and prevents their success.   Alas! dear Lord, shall I be ever thus miserable at all times and in all places?   Shall I always thus hinder the designs of Thy Providence by my infidelity?   Yes, most certainly I shall; unless, by Thy mercy, Thou destroy me, and make me anew.   Well then, destroy me; break the hardness of my heart, that I may no longer be an obstacle to Thy work.   And you, dear Father, pray, I conjure you, that both you and I may become strong in the Blood of the Lamb, and may effect something through His grace, instead of spoiling and ruining all.   It is with the same faith that we love the creature; for as charity to our neighbour proceeds from the love of God, so there is a faith which proceeds from the love we bear to creatures.   There is a general faith, and there is one more special between those who love each other more intimately, just as besides our general love for all, there is a special love which we bear to some.   And this love proves our faith, so that it is impossible for one to believe or understand that the other does not seek his good.   He who really loves has this faith, and nothing will change or diminish it, neither the words of men, the deceits of the devil, or change of place; otherwise he shows his love to be imperfect.

" It seems to me, from your letter, that you have suffered many interior conflicts from your sensitive nature; you thought that your burden was beyond your strength, and that I judged you according to my own measure.   You thought, too, that my affection for you was diminished, but you were deceived; you did but prove that *your* charity was diminished, and mine increased : for indeed I love you as I love myself, and I trust that God's goodness will supply what is wanting on your part. But it was not so, for you seemed ready to cast your burden to the ground, and were inclined to fall into weakness and distrust. I saw it clearly enough ; and I trust I may have been the only one who perceived it. So you see my love for you augmented instead of diminished. How could you suppose that I desired anything but the life of your soul? Where is the faith which you used to have, and ought always to have? And where that confidence which you did possess, that all events, both great and small, are in the hands of God? If you had been faithful, you would not have been so vacillating and timorous.

"But I know that it is my sins that caused it all. And I know that if there was a moment's weakness, yet you always have a good and holy desire to accomplish the will of God and of His Vicar. I did not wish that you should have been taken, but only that you should have gone on by the route that was pointed out. I, too, have been occupied day and night with affairs that have had no success, owing to the want of zeal of those to whom they were entrusted, but chiefly owing to my sins which prevent everything good. In the kingdom of Naples this last disaster has been worse than the first. I shall have much to say to you about all this, unless before you return, God, in His mercy, should call me out of this world. I certainly do wish you had continued your journey, but I do not trouble about it ; for I know all these things happen by the secret purpose of God. My conscience is at peace, for I have done what in me lay to communicate with the King of France. As to the embassy to the King of Hungary, the Holy Father greatly liked the idea, and had decided to send you and your companions. I do not know what changed him, but now he wishes you to remain where you are and do what good you can there. So have no anxiety about it.

" Abandon yourself therefore, and renounce your own sense and all desire of consolation. In Jesus crucified all things are possible to us, and God never lays a burden on us beyond our strength.

We ought to rejoice when we receive a heavy burden, for it is then that God bestows on us the gift of fortitude. It is by the love of suffering that we get to lose the feeling of suffering. Let us then give ourselves up to the false tongues and evil treatment of the wicked, as those did who, dead to themselves, laboured in this sweet Garden (Rome) on which they poured forth their blood, after first watering it with their sweat and their tears. How unhappy we are; for we have not shed our tears, or been counted worthy to pour forth our blood!

"You ask me to pray that God will give you the courage of St. Vincent and St. Lawrence, of St. Paul and the beloved Apostle, and then you say you will do great things: truly without such courage you will do nothing, little or great, and then you will not be my joy. It was because I knew this that I felt my solicitude for you increase in God's presence, and had you been near me I should have given you something more than words. But if you are faithful, you will do great things for God, and bring the affairs entrusted to you to a happy issue: it will not be your fault if they do not succeed. Believe me, I love your soul more than you can comprehend, and therefore I desire to see you perfect, and I would force you to be so if I could. I am always reproaching you in order to make you enter more into yourself; and I try, and shall always try to make you take up the burden of the perfect, and to obtain from God that you may reach the end of perfection, and shed your blood for the Holy Church, whether sensuality like it or not. You must bear patiently with my faults and with my words; and when you are shown your faults, rejoice in the goodness of God, Who has given you some one to occupy herself about you, and to watch over you in His presence. You say that Antichrist and his members are seeking to get possession of you with all diligence; but surely you cannot doubt that God is strong enough to prevent them from accomplishing their design. You ought to feel yourself unworthy of so great a happiness, and therefore to have no fear at all about it. God and our Sweet Lady will be ever with you. I feel like a vile slave on this ground on which has flowed the blood of martyrs: you left me here, and you have been with God, but I shall never cease to labour for you. Do not give me reason to blush for you. You are a man when you promise me to suffer for God ; do not be a woman when the time comes for you to keep your promises. Take care lest the same thing happen to you that happened to the Abbot of St. Anthimo; he left Siena and came to Rome, thinking to be safe here and to escape being put in prison, but he was put in prison at once, and has suffered as you know. That is the way in which cowardly people are caught. So be courageous and defy death. Pardon me if I have said anything contrary to the respect I owe you ; my love must be my excuse." (Letter 101.)

We have said this is the letter of a friend to a friend. Some one has remarked that it is a pity written letters cannot smile ; for on that account what is written in jest is too often read in earnest. This letter of St. Catherine's needs to be read with the memory in our mind of that smile which doubtless passed over her lips as she penned some of its passages ; its reproaches are more playful than serious, and do but testify to the confidence that existed between these two holy souls.

Here, then, we close these extracts from the more familiar portions of St. Catherine's correspondence. What remains will furnish us with materials for setting before the reader the narrative of her last victory.

CHAPTER VI.

CATHERINE'S LAST VICTORY.

JAN. AND FEB. 1380.

THE joy which had been caused in Rome by the victory of Marino, and the surrender of the Castle of St. Angelo, was of short duration. That double victory was indeed felt as so important a success, that it was announced by the Pope to all the sovereigns of Europe; but it was soon followed by disaffection on the part of the Romans themselves. "The ancient serpent," says Raymund, "finding it impossible to succeed by one means, tried another yet more dangerous. What he could not bring about by strangers and schismatics, he sought to effect by the hands of those who had hitherto remained faithful to the Holy See. He sowed divisions between the people of Rome and the Sovereign Pontiff; and things came to such a point, that at last the people openly threatened to put him to death." We have no precise information as to the cause of these disputes. No doubt the Antipope had his emissaries in Rome as elsewhere, and Catherine, who had long entertained fears that Urban's life was not secure in the city, had more than once warned him of his danger. "I beg of you to take all possible care to have your person well guarded," she writes, "for I know that the wicked do not sleep, and that they are seeking to lay snares against your life." (Letter 18.) In another letter,[1] she refers to some of the difficulties which surrounded his

---

[1] Letter 22. This is the last letter addressed by Catherine to Urban *which has been preserved;* but it is doubtful whether it was really the last which she ever wrote to him; and whether therefore it is identical with that which we shall find alluded to further on as written on the Monday after Sexagesima.

government, and offers her sagacious counsel. Francesco da Vico, Prefect of Rome, had usurped the lordship of Viterbo, and had given an insolent reply to certain ambassadors whom the Pope had sent to remonstrate with him. Francesco was an old offender, and even in the time of Gregory XI. had often been in arms against the Church, on which account he had incurred excommunication. When Gregory returned to Italy from Avignon he tried to win over this turbulent subject, and admitted him to favour. Urban treated him with more severity, and took measures for driving him out of Viterbo, and regaining possession of that city which was important for the security of Rome. Although in so doing he was amply justified, for the authority which Francesco had seized was utterly unlawful, yet it was a critical moment to choose for pushing his quarrel with so powerful an adversary; and Catherine, who understood the imprudence of such a line of conduct, advised the Pope at once to assemble a Council-general, calling together the chiefs of the city quarters, and other notables, that he might consult with them in this emergency. "I have learnt," she says, " the fierce and insolent reply which the Prefect has given to the Roman ambassadors. The best thing would be to call a Council-general, and for them to send you the chiefs of the quarters (*i Caporioni*) and some notables. I beg of you, most Holy Father, continue as before to see them often, and to keep on good terms with them. And I would suggest that when they come to tell you what the Council has decided, you should receive them with all possible condescension, explaining to them whatever may seem necessary to your Holiness. Pardon me if I say too much, but I think you ought to know the character of your Roman children, whom it is easier to lead by kindness than by harsh words. And you know that what is most necessary for you and for the Church just now, is to keep the people loyal and submissive to your Holiness. I would also most humbly suggest the prudence of your not promising more than you can perform, as much confusion ensues thereby. You will let me say thus much: your goodness and humility will not reject these counsels, though they come from the mouth of so miserable a woman; for the humble soul considers not who it is that speaks, but only what God's honour requires. Have courage! and as to the insolent reply which that rebel has dared to send your Holiness, fear nothing; God will provide for that as for all else, for He is the Master and Protector of the Ship of Holy Church and of your Holiness." She then refers to some affairs in connection with an embassy from Siena, the explanation of which has not been preserved, and concludes by again urging his Holiness "to condescend to human infirmity, otherwise the evil will only increase. Remember the ruin that ensued throughout Italy, owing to the bad governors not having been changed, who were bringing destruction on the Church of God." (Letter 22.)

No one can read this letter without gaining fresh insight into the character of St. Catherine. If any one has hitherto been disposed to regard her as a mere zealot, who blindly embraced the cause of the Roman Pontiff against that of the Antipope, thinking only of his claims and ignoring the grievances of those who opposed him, this letter is the reply. There is in it a plea for something very like popular government. If he is in difficulties, let him call a Council-general (*Consiglio Generale*) of the chief citizens and listen to their advice; a sound policy, full of good sense, as prudently conceived as it is humbly expressed. We are not informed whether it was adopted by Urban; and it is quite possible that, even if adopted, he did not carry it out in the spirit she would have advised; for the very next fact which comes to our knowledge is the dispute which broke out between the Pope and the Roman people.

Catherine had done her part as the Pope's councillor; if prudence and firmness could have averted the impending calamity, her words had pointed out the right way. Nothing was now left for her to do, save to offer her prayers and her sufferings, nay, to give her very life as a victim for the Church and its earthly Head. This was the sublime office reserved for the last days of her mortal life; she had often longed and prayed for martyrdom, and in a certain sense her prayer was to be granted.

When Catherine heard of the revolt of the Roman citizens,

and their threats against the life of the Pontiff, she was profoundly afflicted ; and having recourse to prayer, besought of God not to permit the accomplishment of so terrible a crime. " In a letter to me written at that time," says Raymund, " she told me that she had seen in spirit the city of Rome filled with demons who excited the people to parricide ; they poured forth the most horrible threats against the Saint, saying, ' Accursed wretch ! thou seekest to hinder us, but we will cause thee to die a terrible death !' She answered them nothing, but only prayed with greater fervour, entreating God, for the honour of His Name, and the salvation of His Church tossed about by such great tempests, to defeat the plots of the enemy, to save the Sovereign Pontiff, and not to suffer the people to commit so abominable a crime. Our Lord replied, ' Leave this people alone who daily blaspheme My Name, and when they have committed this crime, I will destroy them in My wrath, for My justice will no longer endure their iniquities.' But she cried with greater fervour, saying, ' O most merciful Lord ! Thou knowest how Thy Spouse, redeemed with Thy Blood, is outraged throughout the entire world ; and how few defenders she has, and how her enemies seek her humiliation and the death of Thy Vicar. If this calamity should happen, not the Romans only, but all the faithful will suffer much. Be appeased then, O Lord, and despise not Thy people for whom Thou hast paid so precious a ransom.'

" This struggle with her Divine Spouse lasted many days and nights, and her feeble body had much to suffer. God opposed His justice to her prayers, and the evil spirits continued their clamours against her. The struggle was so great that, to use her own expression, if God had not encircled her members she would have been annihilated by it. But in this obstinate combat, wherein her bodily strength was utterly wasted by protracted suffering, Catherine at last triumphed and obtained her petition. When God alleged His justice, she replied, ' O Lord, if Thy justice must needs be satisfied, inflict on my body the chastisement which this people deserves ; for the honour of Thy Name and of the Holy Church I will cheerfully drain the chalice of suffering and death ; for Thy Truth knows that I have always ardently desired this, and that Thy grace has kindled this desire in my soul.' When she had uttered these words from the bottom of her heart, she understood that her prayer had prevailed. And in fact from that moment the popular sedition gradually calmed down, but the Saint like a pure victim had borne its expiation. The powers of hell had permission to torment her holy body, and exerted their utmost rage against her, so that those who witnessed it assured me it would be impossible for any one who had not seen what passed to form any idea of what she endured at their hands.

" These terrible sufferings daily increased ; her skin seemed to adhere to her bones, and her body was reduced to a mere skeleton ; yet she walked, prayed, and laboured without intermission, though to those about her she appeared rather like a phantom than a living person. Far from discontinuing her prayers, Catherine only increased their length and their fervour ; her spiritual children saw most evident signs of the tortures heaped on her by the powers of darkness, but no one could apply a remedy. It was not the will of God ; and notwithstanding the decay of her bodily powers her soul rose joyously and courageously above all that she endured. The more she prayed, the more she suffered ; I was informed by those around her, and indeed by herself in a letter she wrote to me at that time, that in the midst of this martyrdom she heard the evil spirits shriek, ' Thou cursed wretch ! thou hast always pursued us, and thou pursuest us still : now we shall take our revenge on thee ; thou wouldst force us to depart hence, but we will first take thy life ;' and so saying they redoubled their blows." [1]

Maimbourg [2] says " that the disturbances in the city were at this time quelled through the interference of Catherine, who exerted herself with God by her prayers, and with the Roman people by her remonstrances. She was so successful that the citizens not only returned to their duty, but used in Urban's defence the very arms they had taken up against him." He also states that the

<hr>

[1] Legend, Part 3, ch. ii.
[2] Histoire du Grand Schisme, lib. i. p. 148.

Romans had first tried to poison the Pope, and then attacked him in the Vatican, when he courageously exhibited himself to the mob, clad in his Pontifical vestments, and overawed them by his presence.

In the meanwhile Catherine's sufferings continued daily to increase. We learn from the letter written by Barduccio Canigiani to his sister Maria Petriboni, a nun in the convent of St. Pietro di Monticella near Florence, that from the feast of the Circumcision of that year she had found it necessary completely to change her ordinary manner of living. The small amount of food she had hitherto been accustomed to take, caused her such suffering that it became impossible for her to touch it; and though consumed by a burning thirst, she was unable to swallow so much as a drop of water, though she seemed to be breathing fire. These sufferings were frightfully increased on Sexagesima Sunday, which fell that year on the 29th of January, from which day she never recovered her wonted state of health. We shall presently quote her own letters describing the extraordinary tortures of mind and body which she underwent at that time; but in order to render her words more intelligible, we shall first give the narrative as it is related by Raymund and her other biographers.

"From Sexagesima Sunday until the last day of April, when she passed out of this life," says Raymund, "her sufferings continued to increase. But one thing which she herself wrote to me was truly astonishing: up to that time, on account of the pain in her side and other infirmities which never left her, it had been her custom not to hear Mass until the hour of tierce; but through the whole of Lent she every morning went to the church of St. Peter's, heard Mass there, prayed for a long time afterwards, and returned home about the hour of vespers. Those who then saw her stretched on her bed thought she would never again be able to rise from it; but the next day, as soon as it was light, she would rise and set out again from her house in the Via del Papa, between the Minerva and the Campo di Fiore, and go to St. Peter's, walking quickly the whole way, a distance sufficient to fatigue a person in strong health."

The course here so exactly described will be familiar to many

of our readers.   Catherine must every day have passed by the
Minerva into the open market-place in front of the dark solemn
portico of the Pantheon ; thence pursuing her way along that
street where now stands the beautiful church dedicated to her
favourite patroness St. Mary Magdalen, until she found herself
in the Via St. Lucia.   Following its course she would come to
the bridge which now bears the name of St. Angelo, but which
at that time was called St. Peter's bridge ; she would have passed
under the walls of the castle, which presented much the same
appearance then as now ; for its marble walls had been levelled a
year before by the triumphant populace, when they took possession of it after the surrender of the French garrison ; and even
thence she would have had a further walk of some distance to
accomplish before reaching the Basilica of the apostles.   I need
not remind the reader that of the Basilica which she daily visited
not a vestige now remains.   It fell under the hammers of the
Renaissance, in order that Michael Angelo might realise his
magnificent promise—that " he would place the Pantheon in the
clouds."   He kept his word, and gave us the dome of St. Peter's ;
but he swept away the Basilica that had been founded by
Constantine, and dedicated by St. Sylvester, where Charlemagne
had been crowned Emperor of the West, and in which St. Catherine prayed.   Eight of the marble columns which may now be
seen in the balconies arranged above the pillars supporting the
cupola, and which are said by tradition to have stood in the
Temple of Solomon ; and the famous mosaic of the " Navicella,"
designed by Giotto and preserved in the porch of the present
building, are all that remain of the ancient Basilica.

Here it was, then, that on Sexagesima Sunday, as she was
praying at the hour of vespers, a mysterious circumstance occurred,
causing her such terrible agony that she never recovered its effects.
This event is not mentioned by Raymund, nor is it more than
obscurely alluded to by Barduccio in his narrative and by herself
in her letters ; but in the *Leggenda Minore*,[1] and again in his

---

[1] *Leg. Min.*, p. 156.   In the Process, after describing her sufferings from the
evil spirits and their threats of causing her death, he adds : *In cujus præsagium*

deposition, F. Thomas Caffarini gives us fuller particulars. It appears that whilst still in the Church of St. Peter's a mysterious vision or sign of her approaching death and of its cause was granted to her. She not only saw, but felt the Navicella, or Ship of the Church, laid on her shoulders. Crushed by the awful weight she sank fainting to the ground ; she understood that she was in some way to give her life for the Church as a true victim, and from that moment her bodily strength began visibly to consume away. This remarkable incident was followed on her return home by an attack or crisis of supernatural suffering. "On the night of Monday following," says Barduccio, "after dictating a letter to me, she had so violent a crisis that we mourned her as dead. She remained for a long time without giving the smallest sign of life ; then she suddenly arose, and seemed as though she had undergone no change whatever."

This "crisis" is more fully described in the Saint's own last letters to Raymund of Capua which shall now be quoted. The reader will observe the broken phraseology, and occasional confusion of sense, too clearly indicating the sufferings both mental and physical which were being endured by the writer.

"O my dearest Father!"[1] she writes, "I will not conceal from you the mysteries of God, but will relate them as briefly as I can, and as my weakness will permit. I will tell you also what I want you to do ; only do not afflict yourself on account of what I shall say, for I know not what the Divine Goodness is about to do with me, whether I shall stay, or whether He is about to call me away. My Father, my Father, my beloved son ! God has worked such wonderful things from the Feast of the Circumcision until

---

ostensum fuit in Sancto Petro de Urbe qualiter navicella ecclesi.? posita super spatulas virginis, in tantum Virginem ipsam compressit, quod moriendo in terram cecidit. (Process, 1299, 1300.) The same thing is affirmed by F. William Flete in his *Sermo in reverentiam Beatæ Katerinæ de Senis.*

[1] In the Aldine Edition this letter (No. 102) is dated Feb. 15, 1379 ; that is, according to our way of beginning the year, on January 1st, 1380, a fortnight after the events to which it refers. In this intervening fortnight the disputes between Urban and the Roman people must have broken out ; and the threatened danger have been dissipated.

now, that it would be impossible for me to relate them. But we will leave that time and come to Sexagesima Sunday (Jan. 29th), on which day happened those mysteries of which I am going to speak. Never before did anything similar occur to me. Such was the agony of my heart, that my very garments were torn. I fell writhing in the chapel [1] like one in convulsion ; had any one sought to restrain me, they would have caused my death.[2] On Monday evening I was much urged to write to the Christ on earth and to three Cardinals ; I procured help and went to my cell, but when I had written to the Christ on earth,[3] I could write no more, so intense was the bodily pain I suffered. Shortly afterwards there began terrible attacks from the evil spirits, who threw me down : they were furious against me, as though I, poor worm of the earth, had torn out of their grasp what they had so long held possession of in the Church ; and the terror I felt, joined to my other sufferings, was so great, that I wished to fly from my cell and go to the chapel, as though the cell had been the cause of my pains.

"I rose then, and being unable to walk, I leant on my son Barduccio ; but immediately I was thrown down again ; and lying on the ground it seemed as if my soul quitted the body ; not in the same way as it did that other time,[4] because *then* I tasted the joy of the Blessed, enjoying with them the Sovereign Good ; but now it seemed to me that I was a thing apart. I did not seem to be in my body, but I beheld my body as though it had

---

[1] The chapel ; that is the private chapel she was allowed to have in her house, in which this crisis took place.

[2] This passage is very obscure, and indicates a mysterious access of suffering, the cause of which was wholly supernatural, and which the Saint was unable to express in ordinary language : *Giammai uno simile caso non mi parbe portare.* M. Cartier translates *caso* as accident. But though *caso* often has the sense of accident, I do not think it at all conveys what is here meant, which is evidently intended to describe what one might call *an ecstasy of supernatural suffering.*

[3] This letter is supposed by Gigli to be the same as that (No. 22) which has been quoted above (p. 235), a letter of calm practical advice. It may have been so, but the fact seems questionable.

[4] At the time of her mystic death.

belonged to some other person; and my soul, seeing the distress of him who was with me (*i.e.* Barduccio), wished to know if I could use my body so as to be able to say to him: 'My son, be not afraid.' But I found I could not move my tongue, or any other member, any more than if my body had been utterly without life. So I left the body as it was, and fixed my understanding on the abyss of the Holy Trinity. I remembered distinctly the needs of the Holy Church and of the Christian people. I cried to God, and confidently implored His help, showing Him my desires, and seeking to do Him holy violence by offering the Blood of the Lamb and the sufferings He had endured. I prayed so earnestly that I felt certain He would not reject my prayer; and then I prayed for all of you, and conjured Him to accomplish in you His will and my desires. Then I implored Him to deliver me from eternal damnation; and I remained thus so long that all the family wept for me as dead.

"Meanwhile the terror of the evil spirits was somewhat dissipated, and the humble Lamb offered Himself to my soul, saying: 'Be sure that I will satisfy thy desires, and those of My other servants, and you shall see that I am a good Master. I act like the potter who destroys and refashions his vessels as he pleases; and so I act with My vessels. This is why I have taken the vessel of thy body, and have refashioned it in the Garden of Holy Church, so that it shall be other than it was in time past.' And He added other gracious words, which I cannot here repeat. Then my body began to breathe a little, showing that the soul had returned to it. I was full of wonder, and there remained such a pain in my heart that I still feel it. Then all joy, all consolation, and all strength seemed taken from me, and being carried into the room above, it seemed to me full of demons who began a fresh attack, the most terrible I ever sustained; for they sought to make me believe that it was not I that was in my body, but an unclean spirit. But I invoked the Divine help with the utmost tenderness, refusing no suffering, but repeating, *Deus in adjuorium meum intende, Domine ad adjuvandum me festina!*

"Two days and two nights passed in these conflicts, but my

mind and my desire underwent no change, my soul always remained fixed in its Object,[1] though my body seemed reduced to nothing.　On the feast of the Purification of Our Lady I wished to hear Mass: then all the mysteries were renewed, and God made known to me the great danger that was threatening the city and which has since appeared;[2] for Rome was on the point of revolting, and nothing was to be heard but blasphemies and irreverence; had He not pacified men's hearts, so that now, as I hope, all will end well.　Then He imposed on me this obedience, that during the whole time of Lent I was to offer the desires of the whole Family, and to cause Mass to be celebrated before them for the intention of Holy Church.　Moreover, every morning I was to hear a Mass at daybreak, which you know is to me *naturally* an impossible thing; but in obeying Him, all things become possible.　The desire to obey has taken such possession of me[3] that my memory retains no other thought, and my will desires no other thing; and not only does the soul refuse and reject all things here below, but even in conversing with the true citizens (*the Saints*) the soul cannot and will not share in their joys, but only in the hunger they had when they were pilgrims and sojourners in this life.　With these and other like feelings which I know not how to express, my life is consumed and distilled for the Sweet Spouse; I, in this way, and the glorious martyrs by their blood.　I pray the Divine Goodness that He may soon grant me to see the redemption of this people.

"When the hour of tierce comes, I rise from Mass, and you might see me going like one dead to St. Peter's, there to labour anew in the Ship of the Holy Church; and I remain thus until the hour of vespers; and I would fain remain in the same place day and night until I can see this people a little calmed, and reconciled with their Father.　My body remains without any kind

---

[1] *La mente sempre stava fisso nell' obietto suo;* that is united to God, the Object of the soul.

[2] From this passage we see that the revolt of the Romans broke out after the 2nd of February.

[3] This is far too feeble a translation: *tanto s'e incarnato questo desiderio.*

of food, not even so much as a drop of water, and its sweet sufferings are so great that I have never felt anything like them, and my life hangs, as it were, by a thread. I know not what the Divine Goodness intends to do with me. I do not mean as to what I feel within, for I understand in that respect what He wills for me; but as to what I suffer in my body, *it seems to me I am to crown it by a new kind of martyrdom in the sweetness of my soul, I mean the Holy Church.* Perhaps He will then cause me to rise again with Him, and terminate both my miseries and my crucified desires; or He may use the ordinary means of restoring my bodily strength. I pray His mercy to accomplish His will in me, and not to leave you and the others orphans; but ever to direct you in the doctrine of Truth with true and perfect light: and I am sure He will do so.

"I beg and conjure you, my Father and my son, who were given to me by the sweet Virgin Mary, that if you believe that God has cast the eye of His mercy on me, you will renew your life; and as one dead to all sense of self, cast yourself into this Ship of Holy Church.[1] Be ever cautious in your conversations. Your actual cell you can have but little of, but I would have you ever keep and bear with you everywhere the cell of your heart; for, as you well know, so long as we are shut up there, the enemy has no power to harm us. Then let everything you do be directed and ordered according to God. And I beg of you mature your heart with a true and holy prudence, that your life may be exemplary in the eyes of seculars, and not conformed to the ways of the world. Let your liberality to the poor and the voluntary poverty you have always professed be renewed and reinvigorated with true and perfect humility. Whatever position or dignity God may bestow on you, relax not, but rather go down lower into the valley of humility. Love the table of the Cross, and there feed on souls, embracing that sweet mother of humble, faithful and con-

---

[1] *Questa Navicella della Santa Chiesa.* These repeated allusions to the Navicella are easily understood when we bear in mind the vision with which this mysterious crisis began; in which the Ship of the Church (the representation of which was daily before her eyes) appeared laid upon her shoulders.

tinual prayer, with holy watching. Every day celebrate Holy Mass, unless absolutely prevented. Fly light and useless conversations; and always show yourself grave in your words and conduct. Cast from you all tenderness for yourself, and all servile fear; for the Holy Church needs not such servants, but rather those who are severe to themselves and devoted to her.

"These are the things to which I conjure you to apply yourself. I also request you to collect the Book, and every other writing of mine with which I have sometimes occupied myself, and which you, Father Thomas, F. Bartholomew, and the Master,[1] and Master Thomas also, may find; and do with them whatever you think most for God's glory. I recommend to you also this family, begging you that, as far as possible, you will be its pastor, director, and father; keep them all in the bonds of charity and perfect union, that they may not be scattered as sheep having no shepherd. As to myself, I hope to be more useful to them after death than ever I have been in life. I beg the Eternal Truth that all the abundance of gifts and graces which He has granted to my soul, may be poured out upon all of you, that you may be as lights set upon a candlestick. I entreat you ask the Eternal Spouse that He may enable me manfully to accomplish His obedience, and that He will pardon the multitude of my sins. And I beseech you also to forgive every disobedience, irreverence, and ingratitude of which I have been guilty, and every pain and distress I may ever have caused you; humbly asking your blessing. Pray earnestly for me, and get prayers for me for the love of Jesus. Pardon me if I have ever written anything to pain you. I do not say these things to distress you; but I wish to discharge my duty, because I am in doubt, and know not what the goodness of God is about to do with me. Do not be troubled

---

[1] The persons here named are all familiar to the reader. By F. Thomas may be understood either F. Thomas della Fonte, who for ten years collected notes of her graces and revelations, or F. Thomas Antonio Nacci Caffarini, who afterwards composed the Supplement to her life. The Master is F. John Tantucci. *Master Thomas* is either Thomas Buonconti, or Thomas Petra, the Pope's Pronotary and Secretary, with whom, during her residence in Rome, she had become very intimate.

because we are separated from each other as to the body; for though, indeed, it would have been a great consolation to me to have had you near me, it is a far greater one to know that you are labouring for the Church. Labour, I beseech you, with more zeal than ever, for her needs were never greater; and for no persecution depart without permission of our Lord the Pope. Courage, courage in Christ our Sweet Jesus! and never be cast down. Abide in the sweet and holy love of God; Jesus Sweetness, Jesus Love." (Letter 102.)

It would seem as though Catherine here brought her letter to a close, not having at the moment strength to finish all she had to say; and she takes up its thread in her next letter without any fresh introduction, so as to make of the two but one consecutive composition. She desired, while she was able, to say all that was in her heart to her spiritual Father; and having given her last earthly charges and directions, she now returns to the subject of what was passing in the interior of her soul.

"I was continually tormented by the ardent desire I had newly conceived in God's presence, because the eye of my understanding was fixed in the Eternal Trinity; and I beheld in that abyss the dignity of the rational creature, the misery which man incurs by mortal sin, and the necessities of the Holy Church, which God showed to me in His bosom. And I saw that no one can taste the Beauty of God in the abyss of the Holy Trinity, save by means of that sweet Spouse; wherefore all must· needs pass through the door of Jesus crucified, and that door is only to be found in the Holy Church. I saw then how the Church gives life, for there is so much life in her, that there is no one who can put her to death; and she gives strength and light, so that no one can weaken or darken her in herself; and ī saw that her fruit never fails or diminishes. Then the Eternal Deity said to me, 'All this dignity which your understanding cannot comprehend, is given to you from me. Look, then, with bitter sorrow, and you will see that men now only go to my Spouse for the sake of her outer vestment, that is her temporal substance; she is empty of those that seek her interior life, the fruit of the Blood.

He who does not bear that fruit which is the treasure of Charity with sincere humility, and in the light of holy faith, is not living, but dead.[1]   He acts like the thief who takes what is not his. The fruit of the Blood belongs to him who has the treasure of love; for the Church was founded in love, *She is Love Itself*,[2] and I desire that all should give themselves (to her) by love, even as I have charged my servants to give as freely as they have received.[3]   I complain that no one now serves the Church : on the contrary, all abandon her; but I shall know how to remedy this.'

"Then the grief and fire of my desires increasing, I cried to God, saying, 'O ineffable Love ! what can I do?'   And His goodness replied, 'Offer anew thy life, and give thyself no repose; IT IS FOR THIS THAT I HAVE CHOSEN THEE, AND ALL THOSE WHO FOLLOW THEE, OR WHO SHALL FOLLOW THEE HEREAFTER.   Apply thyself, then, never to relax, but always to increase thy desires. For, as to Me, I ever apply Myself with love to assist you with temporal and spiritual graces ; and in order that your souls may be occupied with no other thing, I have provided by kindling with great ardour her[4] whom I have chosen to direct you, training her and fitting her for the task by mysteries and hidden ways, so that she may consume herself in the service of My Church, and that you may serve it by humble, faithful, and continual prayers, and

[1] The language is obscure ; but the meaning evidently is, that though many may seem outwardly to belong to the Church, as covered by her exterior garment, yet they are not living, but dead members, unless they bear the fruit of the Blood, *i.e.*, unless they are in charity.

[2] *Ella è fondata in amore, ed è esso amore.*

[3] Freely you have received, freely give.—MATT. x. 8.

[4] *Quella ;* this certainly means St. Catherine herself, the Mother of the spiritual family to which this exhortation is really addressed, although the first part of the paragraph is addressed to her. But the difference may be observed between the *thy* and *thou* used at the beginning and end of the paragraph, denoting her only; and the *you* and *yours*, used in this small portion, in which her children are being spoken to.   A little further on, when Catherine is again individually addressed, the *thou* again appears.   I may observe that in none of her letters is the phraseology more obscure than in these two, requiring close attention to develop the sense.

all necessary exercises, which I inspire to each one according to his degree. Consecrate then thy life, thy heart, and thy whole affection to this my Spouse, for My sake, forgetting thyself (*per me, senza te*). Look on Me, and behold the Bridegroom of this Spouse, even the Sovereign Pontiff. See his good and holy intention which has no limits; and as the Spouse is one, so also is the Bridegroom. I permit that by the violent means he employs, and by the fear he inspires in his subjects, he should purge the Church, but another will come who will tend her with love. And it will be with the Spouse as with the soul, wherein fear enters first to strip her of vices, and then love follows, to fill and clothe her with virtues.

"'All this will be accomplished by patient endurance. Sufferings are sweet to those who truly feed at her breast; nevertheless, tell My Vicar, that so far as he can, he must show himself peaceable, granting peace to those who will receive it. And tell the Columns of the Holy Church, the Cardinals, that if they would repair all these ruins, they must be united, and be like a mantle to cover what may appear defective in their Father. Let them be regular in their lives and households, fearing and loving Me, agreeing together, and not following their own interests. If they act thus, I, Who am Light, will give them the light needful to Holy Church. And seeing what they have to do, let them promptly and ardently propose it to My Vicar, who cannot resist their good will, because his intentions are good and holy.'

"But no tongue can tell the mysteries which I saw in my understanding, and felt in my heart. I passed that day in ecstasy, and when evening came, I was so transported with the affection of love, which I could not resist, that I was unable to go to the place of prayer. And feeling that the hour of death was drawing near, I reproached myself bitterly for having served the Spouse of Christ so negligently and ignorantly, and for being the cause that others should have done the same. I was full of these thoughts when God placed Himself before me. He is indeed always present to me, forasmuch as He contains all things in Himself. But this was in a new way, as though memory, will, and understanding had nothing more to do with the body.   And I beheld the truth so clearly that in that abyss seemed to be renewed all the mysteries of Holy Church ; all the graces past and present which I had ever received in my whole life ; and *that day when God espoused my soul to Himself.*   Then all seemed swallowed up in the fire of love which constantly increased, and I thought no more of anything save how I might sacrifice myself to God for the Holy Church, and take away the ignorance and negligence of those whom God had put into my hands.   Then the demons were let loose on me, seeking to prevent me, and to diminish the fervour of my desire by their terrors.   They struck the poor husk of my body, but the desire of my soul only kindled the more, and I cried, ' *O Eternal God, accept the sacrifice of my life for the mystical body of Thy Holy Church.   I have nothing to give save that which Thou hast given to me.   Take my heart then, and press it out*[1] *over the face of Thy Spouse !* '

" Then the Eternal God, regarding me with an eye of clemency, took my heart, and pressed it out over the Holy Church.   And He took it with such force, that if He had not strengthened me, not willing that the vessel of my body should be destroyed, I must that moment have died.   Then the evil spirits cried with yet greater fury, as if they felt an intolerable pain ; they used their utmost efforts to terrify me, threatening me that they would find a way of rendering useless what I had done.   But because the powers of hell cannot resist humility joined to faith, the more they strove, the more ardently also I combated, as it were with weapons of fire ; and I heard words from the Divine Majesty so sweet and tender, and promises so full of joy, that in truth, I cannot speak of them.   Then I said, ' Thanks, thanks be to the Most High, the Eternal, Who has placed us like knights on a

---

[1] *Premilo ;* literally, *squeeze* it.   Observe also the expression, " I have nothing to give *save what Thou hast given to me ;* " alluding to the heart mystically given her by Our Lord.   In fact, this vision of her Heart is in some sense the complement of the earlier one, and helps us to see the mystical sense in which both are to be understood.   This pressing out of the heart of St. Catherine over the Church has been made the subject of one of the designs in Francesco Vanni's Pictorial Life of the Saint.

field of battle to combat for His Spouse, protected by the shield of holy faith. THE FIELD IS WON![1] THE VICTORY IS OURS! thanks to that virtue and power which has discomfited the devil, the tyrant of the human race, but who has been defeated, not by man, but by God. Yes! the Enemy is overcome! not by the suffering of our bodies, but only by the fire of the burning and inestimable Charity of God!'" (Letter 103.)

To complete this narrative we must add the prayer which on this same 15th day of February was uttered by Catherine in ecstasy, and taken down from her lips by some of her children; and which forms too interesting a monument of this time to be omitted here.

Certain words which the Blessed Virgin Catherine of Siena spoke in prayer after the terrible crisis which she had in the night of Monday after Sexagesima, when she was wept for as dead by her family, after which she never regained health, but continually grew worse until the end.[2]

"O Eternal God, my good Master, who hast formed the vessel of Thy creature's body out of the slime of the Earth! O sweetest Love! Of how vile a thing hast Thou formed it, and yet Thou hast placed within it a treasure so great as the soul which bears Thine image, O eternal God. Thou, good Master, my sweet Love, art the Master who destroys and makes anew; Thou breakest and repairest this vessel according to Thy good pleasure. To Thee, Eternal Father, I, most miserable, offer anew my life for Thy sweet Spouse; that as many times as it may please Thy Goodness Thou mayest drag it out of my body and restore it to my body, each time with more pain than before; in order that I may see the reformation of Thy sweet Spouse, the Holy Church. O Eternal God, I recommend to thee this Spouse.

"I also recommend to Thee my beloved children; and I pray thee, the Most High and Eternal Father, if it please Thee to take

---

[1] *El campo è rimaso a noi!*

[2] Our translation of this prayer, of the *Ultime parole*, and of the *Transito*, are all taken from the corrected edition of Signor Grottanelli.

me out of this body and not to let me return thither, that Thou wilt visit them with Thy grace, and when they are dead, make them to live again in true and perfect light.   Bind them together with the sweet bonds of charity, that they may die enamoured [1] of Thy sweetest Spouse.   And I pray that none of them may be snatched out of Thy hands, but that Thou wouldst deign to pardon them all their iniquities.   And pardon me also my great ignorance and negligence committed against Thy Church, and for not having accomplished all I might and should have done. *Peccavi Domine, miserere mei.*

"I offer and recommend to Thee my beloved children who are as my very soul.   And if it please Thy goodness to detain me yet longer in this vessel, do Thou, the Sovereign Physician, heal and sustain it, that it be not entirely torn to pieces.   O Eternal Father, give us Thy sweet benediction!

"*February* 15, 1380."

Who would dare to comment on such words as these?   They are as far above our criticism or our praise as the Divine mysteries they record are above our experience.   Here, then, we behold the handmaid of Christ crowned at last "with a new kind of martyrdom;" accepted as the victim of the Church; and giving to God the heart He had once given to her, that He might annihilate it for the renovation of His holy Spouse.   It is the completion of her course, the sublime consummation of her holocaust; there is now nothing more to relate than the story of her last passage.

But to you who read these words, are there none among them that have thrilled you through and through, as though the eyes of your glorious Mother had been turned and fixed on *you* as she uttered them?   When she cried to our Lord in loving agony, saying: "O ineffable Love! what can I do?" He replied, "Offer thy life anew, and give thyself no repose; IT IS FOR THIS THAT I HAVE CHOSEN THEE, AND ALL THOSE WHO FOLLOW THEE, OR WHO SHALL FOLLOW THEE HEREAFTER." Of whom was He

---

[1] *Spasimati,* a word expressive of the most intense and passionate love.

speaking, if not of the children of the Saint; *her family* then living on earth, and all those who were in time to come to be numbered among her children? And who are these? Oh, daughters of St. Dominic and St. Catherine, scattered over the wide world; you who wear her habit, and glory in calling her your Mother, whether it be in Italy or France, in England, or Holland, or America; you whose Order has given to the Church a white-robed company of saints, who became saints by treading in her footsteps, and whose names sound like sweetest music in our ears,—a Rose, "first flower of the new world," a Margaret, a Benvenuta, a Sybillina, a Lucy, and an Osanna;—you who in China have realised by hundreds her dearest wish of dyeing her white robe red in the blood of martyrdom, who in the Western Indies are reproducing her heroic work of tending the lepers;[1] whose companies are multiplying even on our English soil, engaged on a common work, under one watchword,—"God's honour, and the salvation of souls!"—it was of *you* she thought, it was to *you* she spoke in that supreme moment of her life. She would give you with her own lips the rule that was to guide you; she would point with her own hand to the path that you should follow. Nay, rather, she would have you hear, not from her lips alone, but from those of your Eternal Spouse, the meaning of your sublime vocation:

"OFFER YOURSELVES ANEW; GIVE YOURSELVES NO REPOSE; IT IS FOR THIS THAT I HAVE CHOSEN YOU!"

[1] The Hospital of Lepers at Cocorite, in the island of Trinidad, is now served by nuns of the Third Order, belonging to the (French) congregation of St. Catherine of Siena.

CHAPTER VII.

THE SHADOW OF DEATH.

ST. CATHERINE'S letters to Raymund of Capua quoted in the last chapter were written, as we have seen, on the 15th (and probably the 16th) of February; that is, on the Wednesday and Thursday that preceded the third Sunday of Lent. From the commencement of that holy season she had applied herself with so much fervour to meditation, notwithstanding her infirmities, that those about her were astonished at the abundance of her sighs and pious tears. Her prayer was at all times so fervent that one hour so spent weakened her frame more than two days of uninterrupted spiritual exercises would have exhausted any other person. Every morning after communion she had to be carried from her chapel and laid on her bed as one dead. Yet in an hour or two she would rise and go to St. Peter's, and stay there, as has been said, till vespers, returning home in almost a lifeless condition. And all this time her children marvelled to see with what a joyful countenance she would bear this fatigue, and with what sweet and affable courtesy she would welcome all who came to her, whether to consult her on the affairs of their souls, or on any business for the common good, though every one could see she was reduced to the last extremity. So she continued until the third Sunday in Lent, when she was forced to yield to the immense sufferings that overwhelmed her body, and the anguish that rent her soul in beholding the sins committed against God, and the dangers that threatened the Church. She was a mass of interior and exterior suffering, and thus she remained during eight entire weeks, being unable even to raise her head. In the midst of that martyrdom, she frequently said, "*These pains are physical, but they are not natural; God allows the demons to torment me thus.*" It was evident that what she stated was correct, and that her sufferings were wholly supernatural. But at each new torture she joyously raised her heart and her eyes to God, saying : "Thanks be to Thee, O my everliving Spouse, Who dost continually crown Thy poor and wretched handmaid with new proofs of Thy favour."

At this time her appearance was that of a skeleton covered with a transparent skin ; her countenance, however, beaming with an angelic expression ; whilst she was so entirely prostrate in strength that she could not so much as turn herself in her bed from one side to the other.[1]

It was in this state that she was found by F. Bartholomew Dominic, when, towards the close of Lent, he was despatched to Rome on business by command of his Provincial. He had been hitherto detained at Siena by the duties of his office as Prior of San Domenico, so that a year had probably passed since last they met. And thus during this long time of suffering and anxiety Catherine had been deprived of his company, as well as of that of so many others who enjoyed her closest confidence, God so permitting it for the increase of her sacrifice and her merit. He arrived in Rome on Holy Saturday, and at once hastened to Catherine's house, not being aware of the condition in which he should find her. His exact and beautiful account of what he witnessed shall be given in his own words :

"I found her lying on boards, surrounded by other boards, so that she seemed, as it were, in a coffin. I approached her, hoping to be able to converse with her as usual. Her body was so emaciated that it looked as though it had been dried in the sun, and no longer presented its former beauty. The sight was heart-breaking, and I said to her, weeping, ' Mother, how do you find yourself ? ' When she recognised me she tried to express her joy, but she could not speak, and I was obliged to put my ear close

---

[1] In the above account are blended together the accounts given by Barduccio in his Letter, and by Caffarini in the third part of his Supplement.

to her lips in order to catch her reply, that 'all was going on well, thanks to our merciful Saviour!' I then told her the business on which I had come, and added, 'Mother, to-morrow will be the Feast of the Pasch,[1] I should like to celebrate it here, so as to give Holy Communion to yourself and your spiritual children.' She replied, 'Oh! would that our sweet Saviour would indeed permit me to communicate!'

"I left her, and returned next day to fulfil my promise. I approached her in order to hear her confession and give her absolution; no one hoped to see her go to Holy Communion; for during several days she had been incapable of making the least movement. However I gave her for a penance to ask of God, for her consolation and ours, the grace of receiving Communion on so great a festival; and I then went to the Altar which was quite close to her bed. I prepared the Host and then commenced Mass. Catherine remained motionless until the Holy Communion; as soon as I had terminated and had taken the ablutions, she got up suddenly, to the great astonishment of all present, who shed tears of joy; she advanced unassisted as far as the Altar, knelt down with her eyes closed and her hands clasped, and remained thus until she had received the consecrated Host, and the wine which it is customary to present for washing the mouth. She afterwards fell into her ordinary ecstasy, and when she came forth from it, it was impossible for her to return to her bed; her companions carried her there, and she remained on it immovable as before. God permitted her, however, to converse with me during the few days that I still remained in Rome, and it was then that she explained to me the incredible pains and sufferings that the demons had forced her to undergo. She prayed with unabated ardour for the peace of the Church; she desired and asked of God to expiate in her person the sins of those who separated the faithful from the real Sovereign Pontiff, Urban VI. '*Be assured,*' said she, '*that if I die, the sole cause of my death is the zeal which burns and consumes me for the Holy Church. I suffer*

---

[1] This Easter Day must have fallen on March 25th, St. Catherine's 33d birthday.

gladly for her deliverance, and, if need be, I am ready to die for her.'

"'The affairs that led me to Rome being terminated, my companion pressed me to return. I constantly resisted, and I told this to Catherine. She said that I must go back to him that sent us. 'Mother,' said I, 'how can we go and leave you in such extremity? Were I absent and informed of your condition, I would quit all and hasten to your side. No, I cannot resolve to depart without seeing you better, or without at least having grounds for hope in your recovery.' Catherine said: 'My son, you well know what great consolation I experience in seeing those whom God has given me, and whom I love in the Truth. It would give me the greatest pleasure would our Lord grant me the presence of Father Raymund as well as yours; but it is His intention that I should be deprived of this, and as I desire not my will but His, you must depart. You know that at Bologna a Chapter of the Order will soon be celebrated for the election of a Master-General; Father Raymund will be nominated; I wish you to be there with him, and always to be obedient to him. I command you this as far as I have the power to do so.'

"I then told her that I would do whatever she commanded me, as soon as I saw her better in health, and I added: 'If it is God's will that I go, ask Him to restore you to health before my departure.' She promised me to do so, and when I returned on the following day, I found her so calm and cheerful, that I approached her full of hope. But she, who had hitherto remained motionless, extended her arms towards me and embraced me so affectionately that I could not refrain from shedding tears of joy; it was to make known to me God's will, and to exhort me to depart. 'The Lord had deceived me,' to speak like the Prophet —*Seduxisti me, Domine, et seductus sum; fortior me fuisti et invaluisti* (Jer. xx. 7). I left Rome. A short time after I had returned to Siena, a letter informed me that Catherine had quitted this life to be united to the Spouse Whose embraces she so ardently desired."

We have more than once named Master Thomas Petra, the

Pope's Secretary, who had first made Catherine's acquaintance at Avignon, and who had become very intimate with her during her residence in Rome. She had conceived a great affection for this good and loyal man whom she used to call her father. One day during the last few weeks of her life he found her in a garden belonging to a lady in Rome, whither her disciples had carried her by way of giving her some refreshment. He approached her, and observing her ghastly pallor and extreme emaciation, " Mother," he said, " it seems to me that your Spouse is about to take you out of this life; have you made all necessary dispositions?" "What dispositions," she replied, "can a poor woman like me make?" He replied, "It would be an admirable will and testament if you were to make known to each one of your disciples what he ought to do after your death. I beg of you, for the love of God, to do this; I am sure all will obey you as readily as I shall." " Willingly then," she replied, " I will do it with God's grace." Then he continued, "I have another favour to ask you, and I beseech you to grant it for the love of God. Obtain from your Divine Spouse that I may know the state of your soul after death." "That," she replied, "does not seem possible; for either the soul is saved, and then the bliss it enjoys makes it forget the miseries of this world: or it is lost, and then the torments it endures prevents its obtaining any such favour." However, she promised him to grant his request, if God would permit, and indeed she did do so, in the manner hereafter to be noticed.

Meanwhile the accounts which F. Bartholomew and others brought to Siena alarmed all her friends. Lapa had already rejoined her daughter, and Stephen was impatient to follow. The letters he received from the Saint's companions told him of her aggravated sufferings, of her combats with the demons, and the state of utter prostration to which she was reduced. He was now in haste to get his affairs terminated with all despatch, so that he might at once rejoin her: for her own words in some of her last letters to him kept recurring to his mind—" When will you come, Stephen? Oh, come soon!" One night as he was praying with the Brethren of the Company of La Scala, he distinctly heard these words: "Go to Rome! make haste! the departure of thy Mother is at hand!" When he told the others, they all agreed that it was a Divine warning, and that he ought to hasten to Rome without more delay. With his parents' permission, therefore, he set out at once, and reaching the city, proceeded at once to Catherine's residence. When he entered that beloved presence the sight of her wasted form and transfigured countenance told him that the end was indeed near at hand. And then once more he heard the sound of that voice, so well remembered and so dearly loved, and of which for eighteen weary months he had been deprived. "Thou hast come at last, my son," she said, "and hast been obedient to the voice of God, Who will not fail to make known to thee His will. Go therefore, and confess thy sins, and prepare with thy companions to give thy life for the Sovereign Pontiff, Urban VI." This, then, was their greeting, in which nature, truly, had no part; yet he had the satisfaction of once more discharging his old office of her secretary, for she bade him write a letter for her to F. Bartholomew Dominic to bid him a last farewell. "My son Stephen," she said, "write to Siena to F. Bartholomew, and tell him the Lord is exercising His mercy on me. Therefore, let him and the rest of his brethren at San Domenico beseech my Spouse Jesus that He would suffer me to lay down my life, even to the shedding of my blood, to manifest His glory in the face of the Church." [1]

We do not know the exact date of Stephen's arrival in Rome, and we cannot tell, therefore, for how many days he was permitted the sad happiness of watching by his Mother's dying couch. They cannot have been many; but few as they were, they did their work. They unveiled to him the secret of his own heart, and, setting the seal on all that had gone before, they accomplished that wondrous transformation of the natural man to which

---

[1] *Pro ejus gloria in faciem ecclesiæ illustrandum* (Vit. Step. Mac., ch. xi.). This expression may bear allusion to that mystic pressing out of her heart's blood over the face of the Church, spoken of in the last chapter.

can be given no other name than "the change of the right Hand of the most High." How could it be otherwise? They who know what it is to watch by the death-bed of one of God's servants, who have tasted the inexpressible sweetness of those last days, a sweetness so strange that at times we know not whether to call it joy or sorrow,—whether it be of earth or heaven,—can understand from their own memories something of what must have been passing in Stephen's soul. They will recall the quiet house, the gentle footsteps, the sense of Divine and angelic presences in that chamber from which all thoughts of earth, all clamour of human passions, all regrets, all resentments, all desires even, were banished. They will realise the calm and hush that must have fallen on every soul in the little family, as they stood round that bed of boards, and beheld the attenuated form and the countenance of their Mother, which, says Caffarini, shone, "as it had been the face of an angel."[1] The hours slipped by so gently, but alas! so fast; till feeling that few were now left her, Catherine, remembering the promise she had made to Thomas Petra, bid them all gather around her that she might give them a parting exhortation. It need hardly be matter of surprise that the words she then spoke were carefully noted and preserved by those present; and we shall give a faithful translation of them from what is regarded as the most authentic copy in existence.

THE LAST WORDS.

"The Blessed and most happy Virgin Catherine, feeling herself growing much worse on account of her many and grievous infirmities, called about her all her spiritual sons and daughters in Christ, and made them a devout and profitable exhortation, encouraging them in the practice of virtue; and specially to certain things which she said she had taken as the principle and foundation of all perfection; which were briefly these. First, she said that from the beginning she had understood that whoso would give himself wholly to God, must first strip his heart of all

[1] Sup., Part 3, Trat. 2, §. 2.

sensitive love of all created things out of God ; because the heart cannot be wholly given to God unless it be free, open, and without doubleness. And she declared that from her earliest days it had been her principal study to do this, desiring to seek God by the way of suffering.

"She said also that she had fixed the eye of her understanding in the light of living faith, holding it for certain that all whatsoever happened to her or to others proceeded from God, out of the great love He bears His creatures, and not out of hate. And thence she had conceived a great love and promptitude for holy obedience to the commands of God and of her superiors, remembering that all their commands proceeded from God, either for the needs of her salvation, or for the increase of virtue in her soul. And she added : 'This I will say in the presence of my Sweet Creator, that this point, by His goodness, I have never transgressed.'

"Next, she said that God had shown her that none can ever arrive at perfection nor acquire true virtue save by means of humble, faithful, and continual prayer, which she said is the mother that conceives and nourishes all virtues in the soul ; and without it, all languish and fade away. To which prayer she exhorted us most earnestly to apply ourselves, declaring that there were two kinds thereof, namely, vocal and mental prayer. To vocal prayer, she said, we should attend at the appointed hours ; but to mental prayer continually, striving always to know our selves and God's great goodness to us.

"And she said that in order to arrive at purity of heart, we should guard ourselves against all judgment of our neighbour, and all idle speaking of the doings of others, looking only to the will of God in His creatures ; and saying with much earnestness that for no cause ought we to judge another. For even if that which we should see were evident sin, yet we ought not to judge it, but with true and holy compassion, to offer it to God in humble and devout prayer.

"And speaking another time on this same subject, she rendered this witness of herself to her spiritual Father, that never, on account of any persecution, murmurs, detraction, injury, or evil-speaking, had she suffered herself to think anything in her mind, save that they who so treated her were moved thereto by charity and zeal for her salvation. And she gave thanks to the inestimable goodness of God, that by this light He had delivered her from the peril of judging her neighbour.

"Lastly, she said that she had ever placed a great hope and confidence in Divine Providence, and invited and urged us all to do the same, which she said she had found passing great and admirable even from her childhood; adding: 'And you yourselves have seen and experienced the same, and that so largely, that if our hearts were not harder than stones, our coldness and hardness must be dissolved thereby. Therefore, have a great love for this sweet Providence, which will never fail those who trust in it, and, specially, will never be wanting to you.'

"These, and many other things, she said, comforting and instructing us, and humbly exhorting us to that which our Saviour left as His testament to His disciples, namely, that we should love one another. And she repeated again and again with great fervour, 'Love one another, my children, love one another; for by this you will show that you are willing to have me for your Mother. And I will hold you to be my beloved children, and if you are virtuous, you will be my joy and my crown: and I will pray the Divine Goodness that the abundance of life, and all the gifts and graces which He has been pleased to pour into my soul, He will also bestow on each one of you.'

"Then she commanded us all, saying: 'My children, never relax your desires for the reformation and good estate of Holy Church; but always offer burning tears, together with humble and continual prayers in the sight of God for that most sweet Spouse, and for Pope Urban, the Vicar of Christ;' saying on her own part, 'For a long time have I cherished this burning desire; but chiefly about seven years ago it seemed to me that God Himself placed it in my heart. And from that time there has been no day that I have not offered myself before Him with sweet and sorrowful longings. And on that account has His Goodness been pleased to lay on this frail body so many pains and infirmities. But specially in this present time it seems that my sweet Creator has done with me as He did with Job, giving license to the demons to torment and persecute me as they please. For I never remember at any time to have endured such tortures as now I bear. Thanks be to His infinite Goodness which makes me worthy to endure something for the praise and glory of His Name, and for His sweet Spouse, the Church. And now, at last, it seems to me that my beloved Spouse, after so many earnest and burning desires and bodily pains, wills my soul to depart out of this darksome prison, and return to its final end. I say not that I see His will in this matter with any certainty, but so it seems to me;' and she added, 'hold this for certain, my sweetest and dearest children, that when I depart out of this body, I shall truly have consumed and given my life in the Church and for the Church; which thing is a most singular favour.' Then seeing us all weeping bitterly around her, she comforted us, saying: 'Dear children, let not this make you sad, but rather rejoice and be exceeding glad; considering that I am leaving a place of many sufferings, and that I go to rest in the peaceful sea,—the Eternal God; and to be for ever united with my most sweet and loving Spouse. And I promise you that I will be more perfectly with you, and of more use to you there, than ever I could be here: because I am leaving darkness, to pass into the true and Eternal light.

"'Nevertheless I leave both life and death to the will of my Creator. If He sees that abiding here, I can be of use to any one, I refuse neither labour, nor pain, nor torment; but I am ready, for His love and for the salvation of my neighbour, to give my life a thousand times a day, and each time, if that were possible, with greater suffering than before.'

"And so having finished these words, she called us her children to her, each one by name, and gave to each a charge what they should do when she should have departed out of this life: and each of us with reverence and humility received her obedience. Then she humbly prayed us to pardon her if she had not given us the holy doctrine, and the example of a virtuous life to which she was bound; and if she had not helped us with prayer before God as she should have done; and, moreover, if she had not sufficiently supplied our temporal necessities; as well as for any pain, distress, or trouble, of which she might have been the cause; saying: 'Every fault has been through ignorance; but I declare before God, I both have had and continue to have an ardent desire for your perfection and salvation, which if you attain, dear children, you will be my glory and my crown.' And then at last, whilst we all remained still weeping, she gave her blessing in Christ to each one of us, after her accustomed manner."

With regard to what is here stated concerning the separate charge which she delivered to each one of her disciples as to the state of life they should embrace after her death, more exact and interesting particulars have been left by her other disciples. She appointed Alexia to be the Mother and Superioress over the Sisters of Penance, in her place; commending her spiritual sons to the care of F. Raymund of Capua, whom she bade them regard and obey as their Father. She also sent a message to F. William Flete, bidding him not forget her children; and to the absent Neri di Landoccio, to whom she made known that his vocation was to the state of a hermit. "And lastly," says Stephen, "turning to me, and pointing to me with her finger, she said, 'As to *you*, I desire you, on the part of God, and in the name of holy obedience, to enter into the Order of the Carthusians, for it is there that God would have you to be, and it is there He calls you.'"

The place and the hour, when she was to speak to him that "Word of Christ," which until now she had withheld, were come at last: and when she uttered that word, a great light made itself sensible in Stephen's heart. "I say this to the honour of God and His servant Catherine," he writes, "that when she ordered me, in the name of holy obedience, to enter among the Carthusians, I had never once so much as thought of that or any other Order. Nevertheless, after her departure, I felt in my heart so great a desire to obey her, that if the whole world had opposed me, I should have made not the least account of it."

Caffarini tells us that during these last days she also gave her disciples other instructions, specially on the danger of self-love, the root of all evil; and that she acknowledged to them that she had once been filled with a most intense longing for solitude, desiring to live apart from all men in some grotto or forest; and that she had even prayed to our Lord with much earnestness that He would grant her this favour; but she felt Him reply within her, " Many live as to the body in their cell, and with their affections in the world : I will that thy cell should be the knowledge of thy sins and infirmities. Hollow out this cell in thy heart, and abide there in compunction. He who will do so will attain perfection, for wheresoever he goes, and with whomsoever he speaks, he will still remain retired, solitary, and enclosed."

And now there only remains for us to relate the end ; but not in our words shall the tale be told, but in those of the loving and broken hearts who stood by Catherine in her agony, and beheld her yield her glorious soul into the hands of her Creator. The narrative we are about to give is called the " Transito," or last passage. It is taken almost word for word from Barduccio's letter to his sister,[1] which has before been quoted; though the writer of this particular document in its existing form is believed by Gigli to be no other than Stephen Maconi ; and judging by the language used in the introductory paragraph, he would seem to have written it almost immediately after the orphaned family had sustained their unspeakable loss.

---

[1] In the footnotes we have indicated a few of the variations in the two accounts.

CHAPTER VIII.

THE TRANSITO.

April 29th, 1380.

We will now write the order of the glorious and happy end of this most sweet Virgin, according as our base intellects are able to comprehend the same, overcome as they are with immense grief.

"THE faithful Spouse of Jesus Christ having now lain eight weeks without being able to stand upright, suffering many unspeakable pains and torments, she came at last to such a state that she seemed almost to resemble those forms whereby painters depict death; that is, in her body and limbs, for as to her face, that remained up to the time of her burial, angelic and devout. And some days before her death she lost all power of motion, specially from her waist downwards, and could not so much as turn herself in the least degree.

"On the Sunday before the Ascension, being the 29th day of April, in the year 1380, there was a great change,[1] and it seemed to us that she was about to fall into her agony. She therefore caused all her family to be called, and with much humility and devotion, without speaking, made a sign to the priest that she desired the absolution from her faults and their penalties[2] which was given her by Master John the Third, of the Order of St.

---

[1] Barduccio says, "The night preceding the Sunday there was a great crisis two hours before dawn."

[2] *Da colpa e da pena*, that is, not the absolution given in the Sacrament of Penance, but that which enabled her to receive the Indulgence granted by the Pope at the hour of death. This is apparent from what follows a little later.

Augustine, Master in Theology. She continued consumed and sinking all day, until there seemed no sign of life left, but a continual, feeble, and painful breathing. It was therefore decided to give the Sacrament of Extreme Unction, and this was done by the hands of the Abbot of St. Anthimo, at which time she appeared to lie as one unconscious.

"Shortly after having received the holy unction, there appeared a great change in her; and by the movements of her countenance and of her arms she seemed to be enduring a grievous assault from the powers of darkness. She remained in terrible conflict with them for one hour and a half, making various signs, which we did not understand, with her eyes and her whole head. Having passed about half that dreadful time in silence, she at length began to speak, and to say: *Peccavi Domine, miserere mei.* And she said this more than sixty times, each time raising her right arm, and letting it fall again, striking the bed whereon she lay. Then she changed her words, and said, many times, 'O God, have mercy on me; take not from me the memory of Thee!' Then she said, 'O God, come to my assistance; O Lord, make haste to help me;'[1] and, saying this, she did not move her arm. Then she used other devout and humble words; and once, with holy boldness, she said, as though answering some one who accused her, 'Vainglory? never! but the true glory of Christ crucified.' When the space of time I have named had passed, her face suddenly changed, and from being dark and troubled, it became joyous and angelic, shining with such beautiful serenity that it was a great joy only to look on her. Her eyes, which before had appeared tearful and almost extinct, kindled, as it were, and became bright and resplendent. It seemed as though she had come forth out of some dark abyss; and the spectacle softened somewhat the grief of all her afflicted children, who stood weeping around her with a sorrow that may be imagined, for we thought at that moment that she was miraculously delivered from all her infirmity. She was then lying supported on the bosom of Monna

---

[1] Here Barduccio's account is rather different. He says she repeated the words *Sancte Deus, miserere mei.*

Alexia, her beloved daughter and disciple in Christ; but she now tried to rise, and we assisted her to sit upright, still leaning on Alexia. We had placed before her a little table on which were some relics of the Saints and certain beautiful images.[1] She immediately fixed her eyes on the crucifix which was in the centre, and began to pray; and as she prayed, to accuse herself generally before God of all her sins, and in particular she said, "*Mea culpa!* O Eternal Trinity, I have often and miserably offended Thee by my negligence, ignorance, ingratitude, disobedience, and many other faults. Woe is me! that I have not observed Thy general commands, nor those which Thy Goodness has laid on me in particular.' And often, as she thus accused herself, she struck her breast. 'Alas!' she exclaimed, 'I have not observed the command Thou gavest me to seek always Thy honour and the good of my neighbour; I have done the contrary, seeking my own honour and flying from labour, when I might have succoured others in their needs. O Eternal God! Thou didst command me to lose and abandon myself, and to seek nought save Thy glory and the salvation of souls; delighting in taking that sweet food upon the table of the most holy Cross. And I have ever sought my own consolation, and not cared to see souls in the hands of the demon. Thou, O most merciful Father! hast constantly invited me to oblige Thee by intense, sweet, loving, and crucified desires, with tears, and with humble, faithful, and continual prayer, to grant the salvation of the whole world, and the reformation of the Holy Church, promising by such means to show mercy to the world, and to reform Thy Spouse; and I, miserable that I am, have never responded to Thy call, but have slumbered on the bed of negligence. And therefore are all these evils come upon the world, and so much ruin on Thy Church. Woe, woe is me! O sweetest Lord! Thou hast set me to govern souls, and hast given me all these beloved sons and daughters, that I should love them with a passing great love, and guide them carefully in the way of truth; and I have been to them nothing but

---

[1] This had been given her at Avignon by a Cardinal. The frame of relics is still preserved in the Sacristy of San Dominico.

a mirror of misery. I have not taken care of them; I have not helped them with humble and continual prayer. I have not given them the example of a good and holy life, or fed them with the doctrine of the word in time of need. Oh, miserable soul of mine! I have not had the reverence I was bound to have for such innumerable gifts and graces; so many sweet pains and torments, that Thou hast been pleased to lay upon this frail body. I have had no regard to the ineffable love with which Thou hast given them to me, and so I have not received them with the loving affection that I ought.

"'Alas, my sweetest Love! Eternal Spouse of my soul, Thou, for Thine inestimable goodness, didst choose me, even in my childhood, to be Thy Spouse; and I have not been faithful to Thee, but most unfaithful: for I have not kept my memory full of Thee and of the remembrance of Thy benefits. My intellect has not been fixed in Thy truth, and in the sole knowledge of Thy Will; and my will has not been disposed to love and follow Thee with all my strength, as Thou didst require of me.'

"Of these and many other similar faults did this most pure dove accuse herself, more, perhaps, for our example than for her own need. Then she turned to the priest and said, 'Absolve me, for the love of Jesus crucified, from these sins which I have confessed before God, and from all others which I do not remember.' And he did so. Then she said, 'Now absolve me from my faults and their penalties;' he replied, 'You have been absolved.'[1] She said, 'I have had this indulgence granted me both by Pope Gregory and by Pope Urban; give me now Pope Urban's indulgence.' For like a soul athirst for the Blood, she seemed to seek by what means it might be poured over her head in yet greater abundance. Her wish was granted, and after this, still keeping her eyes fixed on the Crucifix, she began once more to pray, speaking to God high things, which for our sins we were not worthy to understand, save a little here and there; and also because of the pain which she had in her breast, which did not permit of her speaking very distinctly.[2]

---

[1] See p. 266.

[2] "We caught a few words, bending over her lips to listen, but my grief prevented me from hearing much." (Barduccio.)

" Then she addressed herself to some of her children who had not been present when she made her exhortation, and she imposed on them her obedience, as to what they were to do. And she asked pardon of them and of the others, not for her, but for our faults ; and after this she returned to her prayer.[1]

"Oh, how can I say what it was to see the humility and reverence with which, again and again, she asked and received the blessing of her weeping and afflicted mother, Lapa : most certainly it was a sweet sorrow ! What a devout spectacle to see that sorrowful mother recommending herself to her holy daughter, and asking and receiving her blessing in return ! Truly it pierced one's very soul to behold it ! And specially did the mother implore of her daughter to obtain fortitude for her from God, that in her deep affliction she might not offend Him. And certainly in this matter God both has wrought and still works wonderful things. But all this did not disturb her from her prayer, but she continued praying even while she spoke.

" And the end drawing nigh, she made a special prayer for the Church and for Pope Urban VI., whom she declared to be the true Pontiff and Vicar of Christ upon earth. And with great fervour she prayed for all her beloved children whom God had given her, and whom she loved with a passing great love ; using many of those words which our Lord spake when He prayed to His Eternal Father, imploring earnestly, and with most sweet words, that every hard heart might become softened. Then at last she said, ' Father, they are Thine, and Thou gavest them to me, and now I give them back Thee. Eternal Father, do Thou keep and guard them ; and I pray that none of them may be snatched out of Thy hands.' And so praying for us,[2] she signed and blessed us. Then once more making the sign of the Cross, she blessed all those who were not there corporally present. Then feeling the approach of her long and much-desired end,

---

[1] " She spoke a few words to Lucio and to me, and to another." (Barduccio.) This Lucio was one of her Roman disciples.

[2] "She spoke with such tenderness, we thought our hearts would cleave asunder." (Barduccio.)

still persevering in prayer, she said, ' Lord, Thou callest me to come to Thee, and I come; not in my own merits, but only in Thy mercy, which mercy I ask in virtue of the most Precious Blood of Thy dear Son!' At the last she exclaimed several times, 'BLOOD! BLOOD!' Then gently pronouncing the words, ' Father, into Thy hands I commend my spirit,' bowing her head, she gave up the ghost.

"Her death took place about the hour of sext, on the Sunday before named, being the Feast of St. Peter Martyr, of her Order. And we kept her precious body until Tuesday evening, during which time it remained fresh, of devout and angelic beauty, and emitting a sweet fragrance. Her arms, hands, fingers, feet, and neck, and all her other members, being as flexible as though her holy soul had not departed from the body. Deo gratias. Amen."

TOMB OF ST. CATHERINE.

CHAPTER IX.

MIGRAVIT AD SPONSUM! *1380.*

SHE had passed to her Spouse! the combat was over: the three and thirty years of labours and sufferings had been crowned with a loving martyrdom for the Church, and she had passed to her reward! The weeping children knelt a while round the sacred remains; "they were in great heaviness, for the loss of the good Mother who had departed from them," says the old legend, "and who had left them orphans in this wicked world. And they did what they could to conceal her death from the people, both to avoid the great press and tumult which they knew would be made if her death were once noised abroad; and also, that they might with more quietness confer together concerning the manner of her funeral." By general consent the direction of these last duties seems to have been committed to Stephen Maconi; and it was he who bore the sacred remains on his own shoulders, to the church of the Minerva, watching by them day and night until the moment came for their interment.

In a very short time the news of Catherine's death spread through the city, and vast crowds thronged the church, moving forward like great waves, says Raymund, that they might kiss the feet, or so much as touch the garments, of the Saint. The impetuous devotion exhibited by the people excited fears lest they might even seek to dismember the holy body in the church; for which reason it was judged prudent to place it behind the iron screen of the chapel of St. Dominic. There it remained for two days, during which time no change was observable in the countenance, and the limbs remained perfectly flexible, as in life. The people continued to pour into the church, bringing with them their sick and infirm friends, and recommending them to the prayers of the Saint. Many on touching the body, or even only articles that had been laid on it, received their cure; and the noise of these miracles spreading abroad, increased the eagerness of the multitudes, so that the whole population of Rome may be said to have collected in the church.

Meanwhile a circumstance occurred, to explain which we must return to the history of the previous day. On that Sunday morning when Catherine breathed her last, a certain devout matron of Rome, named Semia, who lived in the neighbourhood, and was much attached to the Saint, awoke, intending to rise and hear an early Mass, that she might return home in time to prepare dinner for her sons. Semia had not been to visit Catherine for several days, and so had not learned that her sickness had reached its last extremity. As she was preparing to rise from her bed, there appeared to her a child about the age of eight or ten years, who forbade her, saying, "Thou shalt not rise till thou hast seen what I have to show thee." Then taking her by her garments, he led her, as it seemed, to a large open place, where she saw an oratory, containing a fair tabernacle of silver, fast closed. The child bade her observe attentively what should happen, when lo! another child appeared with a golden key, who opened the tabernacle; whereupon there came forth a young and beautiful virgin, royally appareled in shining white, decked with jewels, and wearing on her head three crowns,—the first of silver; the second of silver mixed with gold, "showing a glistening red colour as when an orient red ground is wrought over with threads of gold;" the third of pure gold decked with precious stones.[1] Looking steadily on her, Semia recognised the countenance of Catherine of Siena, but her age not agreeing, she did not believe it to be her. Whereupon the young virgin, looking at the children, said, smiling, "Lo! she knoweth me not!" Then four other children came, carrying a kind of rich seat, in which they placed her, desiring, as it seemed, to carry her away therein. But she said to them, "Suffer me first to go and speak to her who sees, but does not know me;" and coming nearer she said, "Semia, do you not know me? I am Catherine of Siena: mark well what you will now see." Then Semia beheld how the children lifted the seat, and bore it up to heaven, where was a throne set, and on it a King, royally clad, holding in His hand an open book. As soon as the children had borne her to His presence, Semia beheld the young virgin descend from her seat and prostrate at the King's feet to adore Him; Who said to her, "Welcome, My beloved Spouse and daughter Catherine!" Then there approached a Queen, accompanied by a shining train of virgins; and when the holy maid saw her, she knelt upon her knees, and did her reverence. And the Queen also embraced her, saying lovingly, "Welcome, my dear daughter Catherine!" After which she passed among the virgins, and they received her with passing great joy, kissing and saluting her one by one. On this Semia began to pray aloud, and doing so she awoke, and found she had indeed fallen asleep again at the moment when she was intending to rise, and that all she had seen had been a dream. It was late, moreover, and she was in doubt if she should be in time to hear Mass; so in some disturbance of mind she made hasty preparations in her kitchen, and then set forth to the church, saying to herself, "If I lose Mass this day, I shall take all I have seen to be the work of the enemy; but otherwise I shall think it has been shown me for Catherine's sake." On reaching the church she found the gospel was over, and, much distressed, began to fear that the wicked fiend had deceived her. However, hearing

---

[1] These three crowns would seem to represent those of Virgin, Martyr, and Doctor, to the merits of all which states Catherine may be said, in a certain sense, to lay claim.

a bell ring for Mass at a convent of nuns hard by, she hastened thither, and was in time to fulfil her obligation, which somewhat comforted her. As soon as Mass was over, she hastened back, full of fear lest her sons should be home before her, and impatient for their dinner. They overtook her in the street, and begged her to let them have their dinner at once, as the hour was late. She unlocked the door and went straight to the kitchen, where, to her surprise, she found everything ready to be served. Full of wonder who could thus have come to her help, she was impatient that the meal should be over, that she might hasten to Catherine's house, and relate her dream. But when she came to the house she could make no one hear, though she knocked many times; for indeed all the inmates were at that moment absorbed in sorrow, the departure of their dear Mother having taken place shortly before; and they were still taking counsel how best to proceed in the matter of her burial. Semia, therefore, was forced to retire without seeing or speaking with any one; nor was it until the next day, that seeing the crowds hurrying towards the Minerva, and asking whither they were going, she learnt that Catherine had departed this life, and that her body had been carried to the church of the Friars. On this she also hastened to the church, and in a passion of grief reproached the Sisters for not having called her to be present at her dear Mother's last passage, inquiring at what hour she had breathed her last. Then she learned that Catherine had departed out of this life at the very hour when she had seen her so gloriously received into heaven, and relating the goodly vision which our Lord had shown her to the Sisters and others who stood about the bier, "they all gave glory to God, and took no small comfort."[1]

This narrative did not lessen the devotion of those who were present at Catherine's funeral; and during the whole of that and the following day the same extraordinary scenes continued. Many of the first preachers in Rome contended for the honour of celebrating from the pulpit the praises of the departed Saint; and among others, Master John the Third made an attempt to

---

[1] Abridged from Fen, Part 4, chap. ix.

deliver her panegyric in the church where she lay. But the tumult of the people coming and going, and their efforts to bring their sick and infirm near enough to touch the holy body, rendered it impossible for him to make himself heard. He contented himself therefore, with crying in a loud voice, "This holy virgin has no need of our preaching, she preaches sufficiently herself;" and so came down from the pulpit without saying another word. "It was truly a wonderful spectacle : the whole population of Rome came thither spontaneously," says Raymund, "to venerate the remains of the departed Saint, and recommend themselves to her prayers." Cardinals, prelates, nobles, and plebeians might be seen crowding round the bier, all speaking of her admirable life, trying to touch her body, or carry away portions of her garments. Many miraculous cures took place in the church; others followed after the body had been placed in the sepulchre prepared for it. During the two days and nights that elapsed before the interment, Stephen and his companions ceased not to watch by the beloved remains, and when at last the time came to deposit them in their last resting-place, it was Stephen who with his own hands laid the body in its coffin of cypress wood, reverently kissing it and watering it with his tears. He then closed the coffin, which was deposited in the cemetery of the religious, burial within the church being reserved for persons of the highest rank ; but it was not actually buried in the earth, but placed in a sarcophagus somewhat elevated above the ground. The funeral obsequies, which were of great magnificence, were celebrated on the 2nd of May, at the expense of Pope Urban, who commanded all the clergy of Rome, whether secular or regular, to assist at the ceremony. A few days later another funeral service of equal solemnity was celebrated by order of John Cenci, Senator of Rome, as a token of gratitude from the citizens to her who had proved their most powerful protectress. Although it had been Stephen's intention to leave Rome immediately after the funeral, yet he continued to linger from day to day, unable as it seemed to separate from the spot where reposed her mortal remains. He occupied himself in collecting every object she had ever used, and in writing accounts of her last moments to Raymund of Capua, to the Brethren of Our Lady at Siena, and to other pious persons; "which letters," says his biographer, "turned the mourning of those who read them into joy." Every night he watched for many hours by the tomb of the Saint; for this devotion was his only comfort, and he knew not how to give it up, though at the same time he felt moved to depart in order to fulfil her dying injunctions. However, he could not make up his mind to depart without some memorial of his beloved Mother. He debated in his mind whether he might not reopen the coffin and cut off some of her hair; or possess himself of a finger, or perhaps a hand. He remembered, however, what she had formerly predicted to Raymund as to the translation of her body, and prudently determined to wait till then, before taking any step of this kind. Nevertheless, after consulting with Alexia and the other Sisters, he reverently took a tooth, and gave one also to Alexia; Neri di Landoccio obtaining possession of a third. Raymund in his Legend relates the story of Cintio Tancancini, a young man of Rome, who was in the last extremity from quinsy, and whom Alexia cured by applying to his throat the tooth which had been given to her, and which she kept as her most precious treasure; and on one occasion when Raymund was speaking from the pulpit of the merits of the Saint, and relating this incident, Cintio himself stood up among the audience and attested the truth of the preacher's words. We shall not, however, dwell at any length on the miracles wrought at this time, or later, by the Saint's intercession. The reader will probably feel greater interest in hearing the manner in which the news of her death was communicated to some of her absent disciples. And first, we must speak of F. Raymund of Capua, who was just then preparing to leave Genoa for Pisa, on his way to Bologna, where the election of a new Master-General of the Order was about to be made. "The same morning that the blessed Catherine expired," he says, "I had gone to the church to celebrate the festival of St. Peter Martyr. After saying Mass, I again went up to the dormitory to prepare my little bundle for our intended journey, when passing by the image of our blessed Lady, which stood in the dormitory, I said an Ave Maria softly, after the manner of our religious, and remained kneeling there for a few minutes. At that moment I heard a Voice, which was not in the air, pronouncing words which I perceived, not orally, but mentally : yet I was more distinctly conscious of than if I had listened to them with my bodily ears, as though it had been a voice, yet without a sound. This Voice spoke, or at least presented to my mind these words : 'Fear not, I am here for your sake ; I am in heaven for you ; I will protect and defend you : be tranquil ; fear nothing, I am here *for you.*' At first these words threw me into great trouble and I tried to think what they could mean. At the moment I could only attribute them to the blessed Virgin whom I was in the act of saluting ; yet this I dared not think, because of my unworthiness. I feared some terrible calamity was at hand, and thought that perhaps as I had been invoking this good Mother of the afflicted, she had sent me this warning to prepare me for the coming event. For as I had been preaching at Genoa against the schismatics, I fancied some among them might be awaiting an opportunity to injure me. It was so I endeavoured to account for the prodigy which God had been pleased to work by the soul of His Spouse, in order to support my weakness."

Raymund was not the only person who, at the moment of Catherine's death, seems to have had an intimation of her blessedness. The reader will remember what had passed between her and Master Thomas Petra ; and this worthy man gave his testimony of what happened to himself after her death, in a letter which is to be found in the second deposition of F. Bartholomew Dominic, forming part of the Process. The responsible position, no less than the grave and accurate character of the writer, must be borne in mind while reading his extraordinary narrative.

"Eight days had elapsed after the death of Catherine," he says, "when early one morning a man of great piety, called John of Pisa, came and knocked at my door. I opened it directly. 'Catherine of Siena is coming,' he said. 'How can that be?'

I asked, 'she has been dead more than a week.' 'Nevertheless,' he replied, 'you may be sure that you will see her,' and, so saying, he departed, before I could call him back. The morrow, and the next day, and so on for nearly thirty days, I received a similar visit from men estimable for their virtues and their saintly lives. I presume they were angels from God, who took the forms of these persons to announce to me what was to take place. At last, one Sunday, after having recited my Matins, I disposed myself to take a little repose, when, towards daybreak, I saw in a cloudless sky, a multitude of blessed spirits who advanced in regular procession; they were clothed in white, and marched three by three, bearing ornaments, relics, crosses, silver chandeliers, lighted tapers, and musical instruments; and they sung, in several choirs, sacred hymns, the *Kyrie Eleison,* the *Gloria in Excelsis,* the *Sanctus,* the *Benedictus,* and the *Te Deum.*

"The magnificence of this spectacle completely rapt me out of myself; nevertheless, remembering the promise that had been given me, I took courage, and said to one of the Angels, 'What are you doing?' He answered me, 'We are conducting the soul of Catherine of Siena into the presence of the Divine Majesty.' When he had passed on, with those who accompanied him, I addressed another, and said, 'Where is she?' Directly he heard me, the whole procession formed an extended circle, in the centre of which was Catherine: she was clad like the Angels, and resembled Our Lord, as He is painted in the tribune of churches. Her hands were filled with palm-branches, her head was inclined, and her eyes modestly cast down. I recognised her perfectly well by her exterior. I then asked Almighty God to complete the vision, and to comfort my soul by allowing me to behold Catherine's countenance. I was heard ; she raised her head and looked at me *with that gracious smile which always expressed the joy of her soul.* The procession then resumed its onward march, continuing the heavenly chants."

What joy to those who beheld such spectacles ! The world is at liberty to call them dreams, and we are not careful to claim for them any other title. But happy they who have such dreams;

who, when the beloved ones of their souls have gone from them, are privileged thus to behold them "in the visions of the night when deep sleep falleth upon man;" with the old "gracious smile" upon their lips, and a new and heavenly joy on their shining countenances. If such be the dreams that follow the parting stroke, who would not so dream on for ever! Another revelation appears to have been granted to John of the Cells, who speaks of it in the following beautiful letter, addressed to his former disciple Barduccio.

"My Son Barduccio,—How can we any longer live, now that our Mother, our only consolation, is gone from us! What is now left us save to weep over our unhappiness! And we shall not be alone in our tears; for now is accomplished the word spoken by the prophet of old, '*There shall be a great weeping in Jerusalem.*' For now are weeping in the Church of our loving Lord the company of monks by themselves, and the company of devout friars by themselves, and the widows by themselves, and the virgins of the Church by themselves, and those who are married, and penitents, and all whom Catherine gained to God, they all weep by themselves, and the poor and the miserable, they also weep by themselves.[1] And after them, I also weep, although the angels are celebrating a joyful festivity in heaven for her; yet, nevertheless, nothing is so sweet to me as to weep. I do not weep for her, for she desired death, and is living now in the presence of her Creator: neither do I weep out of any diffidence (as to her state), but I weep because I am an orphan and abandoned; because the joy of my heart has been taken from me; and therefore my eyes are blinded with my tears, and nothing brings me comfort, for there is no comfort to be had. *And if it were not, that even now she has appeared to me, and consoled me with her devout and angelic presence,* I should, to use the words of the Patriarch Jacob, 'weeping, have gone down into the grave.' By the grace of God, I have for thirty days celebrated for her the holy Sacrifice of salvation. Come then, beloved son, come to your old Father, come to your brethren, who expect you impatiently, in such sort that when you

---

[1] The allusion here is to Zach. ii. 12.

come they will receive you as no other than an angel of God. And recommend me to Brother Raymund, and salute all the children of Catherine in my name. Farewell, my son, and may the Lord show thee His will, that thou mayest at all times know what is acceptable to Him."[1]

One other letter yet remains to be quoted. It is that which Nigi di Doccio addressed to Neri, still absent in Naples, on the subject of their recent bereavement.

"May 22, 1380.

"DEAREST BROTHER,—I think you know how our dearest and most venerable Mother departed to Paradise on the 29th of April last. Praised be our blessed and crucified Saviour, Jesus Christ! I seem left an orphan, for all my comfort was in her, and now I cannot stop from weeping. I weep not for her, but for myself, who have lost my only good. I could not, as you know, have suffered a greater loss. Pray her to obtain from God that He send me some comfort. As to our Mother herself, I rejoice and am glad, in 'so far as she is concerned; but for us, her children, who remain in this miserable world, there is cause indeed to weep over and to pity them. I cannot pour out my grief to any one except yourself, who were the means of my first acquiring so great a blessing. I feel some comfort in this, that our sweet Mother remains incarnated in my heart more than ever she was, and I seem now to know her as I never knew her before. How miserable we were to have so much of her company, whilst yet we never knew her rightly, or were worthy of her presence! And I take comfort in this also, that she said, as you know, that she would be more useful to us dead than living. Know, dearest brother, that my sorrow will greatly diminish when I can once more be with you; remembering, as I said, that you were the means of my first possessing so great a treasure. But the more the thing which we possess is good and holy, the greater is our sorrow in losing it. Dearest brother, I am so distracted in mind by my loss that I am writing to you incoherently, and so I will

---

[1] *Lettere di Santi Florentini.* No. xxvii.

bring my letter to a close. I greatly fear the orphaned children will be like sheep that have lost their shepherd. Our Mother left the Bachelor and Master Matthew in her place. Sano di Maco will be Prior of the Company next June. I shall never forget you. Write and say when you are coming to Siena. Sano di Maco, and Sano di Bartolomeo, and all the other orphans remember themselves to you. Paoloccio has taken a wife. I, your servant Nigi Doccio, the orphan, salute you as well as I can."

Meanwhile the election of a new General of the Order of Friar Preachers was proceeding at Bologna, where on the Feast of Pentecost, according to Catherine's prediction, Raymund of Capua was nominated to the vacant office by the *Motu Proprio* of the Sovereign Pontiff.   He made every effort to escape from so heavy and responsible a charge, but was at length constrained to accept it by obedience, as well as by the urgent solicitations of the Chapter. He determined in his mind that as soon as he should return to Rome he would cause the head of St. Catherine to be sent to the convent of St. Domenico at Siena, both as a token of affection to his brethren there, and also that this, the chief relic of her holy body, should repose in the city so dear to her in life, and which had been illustrated by so many of her most admirable actions. As soon therefore as he had entered on his office, and happily completed the visitation of the Ultramontane Provinces, he returned to Rome as would seem in the October of 1381 ; and once more took up his residence at the Minerva, where his first visit was to the sepulchre of her who, while she lived, had been at once his spiritual daughter and his Mother.   He caused it to be opened, a thing easily done, as in point of fact it was not actually buried beneath the ground ; and found that the clothes had suffered somewhat from the dampness of the place where the body was deposited, and where it was much exposed to the rain.   He therefore resolved immediately to transfer the remains to a stone sarcophagus, and to deposit them in a safe place on the right hand side of the high altar of the church.   When he had done this, he remembered, not without tears of tenderness, what Catherine had predicted to him on the eve of St. Francis, when they were together at Voragine on their journey back from Avignon;[1] namely, that he should on that same day, in a future year, cause such a translation of her body to be made; a prediction which was thus fulfilled in every particular.[2] As to his further design of sending her head to Siena, he could not venture on so important a step without obtaining the consent of the Sovereign Pontiff. He therefore solicited the necessary permission from Urban, who willingly consented, charging him, moreover, to omit nothing that could make known to the world the merits and glory of the Saint. Having received this permission, he once more visited the sacred body, and first prostrating on the ground and asking her assistance, he then with generous resolution separated the head from the body, enclosed it in a reliquary of gilded copper, and consigned it to the care of two friars of the Order, of whom one was F. Thomas della Fonte, and the other was F. Ambrose di Luigi Sansedoni, both Sienese by birth. F. Ambrose was a man of great learning, and *Socius* to the General, who reposed the utmost confidence in him, and on that account selected him for this business. The two Fathers performed their journey with the utmost secrecy, and succeeded in depositing their precious charge in the convent at the Campo Reggio, without its being known by the people; and as the holy relic could not be exposed to public veneration before the canonisation of the Saint, it was laid up in a chest, and placed in the sacristy, where the intention was carefully to conceal and guard it until such time as the decision of the Church should authorise their rendering it befitting honours.

But it was not destined that the head of St. Catherine should long remain in this obscurity. A few years later, Raymund was ordered by his physician to repair to Siena for the purpose of recruiting his health in the medical baths of that vicinity. According to the Carthusian biographer of Stephen Maconi this visit

---

[1] See p. 7.

[2] The account which follows is abridged from the rare little memoir, entitled "*Breve Relazione del modo come fu portata da Roma a Siena la Sacra Testa di Santa Caterina* (Siena, 1683). It does not bear the name of its author, but Carapelli informs us it was the work of F. Tommaso Angiolini.

took place in 1384 or 1385.[1]   Raymund was at that time engaged in compiling the life of the Saint, commonly known as the Legend ; a work to which he devoted such intervals of leisure as he could secure in the midst of his heavy official duties.   He took occasion of his visit to Siena to resume his labours on this book, and it was whilst thus occupied that his heart reproached him with having sent away from Rome the most noble of her relics in so secret a manner, and permitted it to have remained concealed so as to receive no signs of respect and veneration.   He was aware that in Venice the custom had been at once established of celebrating the anniversary of her death, and causing her praises to be published from the pulpit ; and reproaching himself for his own negligence, he resolved to repair it without loss of time, by taking measures that the sacred relic of her head should in future be treated with greater honour.   He therefore took counsel with the Fathers of the convent, and with several of the Saint's most intimate friends who were still resident in Siena ; among others with Master Matthew of the Misericordia, Neri di Landoccio, and Ser Christofano di Gano.   Stephen Maconi, then a professed Carthusian living in the monastery of Pontignano, about five miles out of the city, received a supernatural intimation to join them, as they were assembled in consultation in the church of San Domenico ; and it was through his influence that the consent of the Bishop was obtained for the plans which they proposed and laid before him.   It was agreed that Raymund should then present himself to the Consistory of the republic, and make known to them in what manner the head of their glorious fellow-country-woman had been brought to the city, and hitherto preserved concealed.   The Magistrates at once resolved that a grand public solemnity should be ordered, to be preceded by a week of spiritual exercises, during which time the most eminent preachers, whether

---

[1] Capecelatro, and some other writers, give 1385 as the date of Raymund's *first* translation of the body, in ignorance of the fact that this translation and the sending to Siena of the head of St. Catherine preceded by some years the public reception of the holy relic by the citizens, and the honours then rendered to it.   F. Gregorio Lombardelli even assigns to this latter event so late a date as 1388.

natives or foreigners, should be invited to proclaim the glories of St. Catherine.

This part of the festival Raymund made it his business to arrange. On the evening of Saturday the 23d of April, the bells announced the commencement of the great *predica*, which was opened next morning by Raymund himself. We shall not weary our readers with the list of all the preachers, but only notice the names of F. Bartholomew Dominic, F. Massimino of Salerno, F. Thomas Nacci Caffarini, F. John Piccolomini (son of the honest Gabriel), F. George of Naddi, whom the Saint had delivered from the thieves, and F. Bartholomew Montucci. On the following Sunday, May 1st (on which day was then kept what was called the "Solemnity" of the holy Virgin), the whole city flocked to San Domenico, and it was announced to them that on the following Thursday (May 5th) they should again repair to receive the head of their beloved fellow-citizen and protectress, Catherine Benincasa. Meanwhile, the fame of so many illustrious preachers who were collected in the city had drawn thither a great number of visitors from other parts. The Consistory moreover had written to all the bishops, abbots, and other prelates of the republic, inviting them to assist at the great procession which they had determined to celebrate on the following Thursday.

On the night, then, of the preceding Wednesday, Raymund took the relic with all possible privacy to the Hospital of St. Lazarus, outside the Porta Romana, where the procession was to begin, and where, says our historian, " St. Catherine was well known, and had worked many miracles." He placed it in a rich tabernacle, and prepared everything for the solemnity of the morrow. At dawn of day—a May day in the most delicious of Italian climates—the people, full of joyful devotion, came out into the streets, scattering flowers and sweet-smelling herbs, and burning perfumes in every place where the procession was to pass. When all was ready, the great bell of the Palazzo gave the signal from its lofty tower, and at that sound, as by magic, all the other bells of the churches rang out as by one consent, and continued doing so the whole time until the procession had reached its destination. It would seem that the Porta Romana had been chosen as the gate by which the procession was to enter, in order that thus they might traverse the entire length of the city; so they set forth at last, chanting with a thousand voices, and making the air resound with so many musical instruments, "that," says Angiolini, "you would have thought the gates of Paradise had been thrown open." First came two hundred girls and as many boys, all selected of equal heights, dressed in white, and adorned with gold, silver, and jewels. They carried in their hands huge bunches of roses, lilies, and other flowers, "in memory," says F. Angiolini, "of Catherine's words; for she was accustomed to say that every one should wear white garments, and carry flowers in their hands; meaning thereby that they should be pure and innocent in life, and adorned with virtues." Then came representatives chosen for each one of the *Contrade* of the city, and of the different arts, bearing lighted torches. The various Companies and Confraternities, both of the city and of the country for five miles, in like manner sent their deputies; and each of these societies represented in a kind of *tableau vivant* in the procession some mystery of the Saint's life, the dresses being provided at the public expense; while before each Company was borne its own banner and a vast number of torches. Then followed all the Hermits of the Sienese States, of whom there were great numbers, all supported by the republic, to the end that they might with less distraction pray, meditate, and afflict their bodies; and before them was borne the Crucifix. Next came the different religious communities, each with their cross. Then the secular priests of the diocese, followed by the canons, all carrying wax candles. Then the gentlemen, magistrates and officials, two and two according to their rank, and clad in robes of office. Then the illustrious Consistory, in their richest dresses of state; after them the abbots and other dignitaries; followed by the bishops, in their pontificals, all with their pastoral staves in their hands. Last of all came a Baldachin of gold brocade adorned with jewels, borne over the sacred relic, which was carried in a magnificent tabernacle of gold, adorned with pictures of St. Catherine's life, which had long before been prepared by Raymund. He himself, as Master-General of the Friar Preachers, walked on the left hand of the relic, while on the right appeared the Bishop of Siena.

It was a grand and solemn spectacle, but its most touching feature has yet to be described. Closely following the Baldachin came a long line of figures, walking two and two, clad in white robes and black mantles, on whom the eyes of all the citizens and of those who had come from distant parts rested with a peculiar interest. They were the Mantellate of St. Dominic, St. Catherine's own religious Sisters, many of them her chosen friends and companions in life. And their appearance recalled to every mind the days when she, too, clad in the same habit, went about those very streets on her missions of charity, ministering to the wants whether of soul or body, and diffusing around her the sweet perfume of her angelic presence.

And there, in the midst of them. assisting at this magnificent solemnity, wearing the habit of the Sisters of Penance, and walking in their ranks, appeared one venerable woman in extreme old age. *It was Lapa*, the mother of the Saint, who at eighty still survived to take part in the honours rendered to her beloved child. At the sight of her the beholders could not contain their tears, and many, breaking through the ranks, of the procession, crowded round to look at and congratulate her. exclaiming, " O happy you, who with your own eyes have beheld the glorious triumph of your daughter !" The procession having at last reached the Church of St. Dominic, at the further extremity of the city, and the *Te Deum* having been sung, Raymund delivered a brief concourse; the Bishop bestowed his benediction on the people; and the sacred relic was deposited in a becoming chest made for the purpose, and placed in the sacristy. Stephen Maconi bore his part in this procession, "and for many days afterwards," says his biographer, " he could not cease from weeping, and speaking of his blessed Mother." On the same day that her head was deposited in the Church of St Dominic, he himself received from Rome the finger on which had been placed the ring of her mystic espousals, and which had remained stiff and erect, whilst all the other fingers were perfectly flexible. It was preserved at Pontignano with great veneration, and some years later Stephen received the cure of a malady of his eyes by touching them with this precious relic.

We do not know what the reader will think of the devotion of the Sienese, when we add that not content with the Octave of preparation they celebrated another *"predica"* of fifteen days, after the conclusion of the solemnity, and the names of the preachers of each day are faithfully given by F. Angiolini. One of them was F. Matthew Tolomei, the brother of Master James, and the same who had accompanied the Saint to Rocca dell' Orcia; another was F. Augustine of Pisa, who had been in the Church of St. Christina when Catherine received the stigmas; another was F. Gregory of Cescena, whose discourse was so magnificent as to stupefy his audience with admiration. But I shall pass over other more illustrious names of Fathers gathered from every convent of the Order in Tuscany, as well as from Venice, France, and Spain, and only add the consoling fact that among the distinguished foreign Dominicans who during that fortnight filled the pulpit of San Domenico, are to be found the names of F. Peter Martyr of Ireland, and F. John of England, the first of whom was "a great Doctor of Paris," and the second "a man greatly renowned as learned, holy, devout, exemplary, and full of faith."

It is thus that the true narrative of this celebrated procession is carefully given by F. Thomas Angiolini; and we have quoted it here, both because his little work is extremely rare, and because the facts have been related by other historians with many variations from the truth. The procession is very commonly represented as having been made by command of the Magistrates of Siena, in order to receive the relic when first sent from Rome by Raymund; ignoring the fact that its original transmission to Siena had been made privately, and at least five years previous to the public reception above described.

Probably no such honours were ever decreed to any other servant of God within so short a time of their decease, and prior to their canonisation. They were rather civic than religious honours, for these last could not, strictly speaking, be permitted, according to the laws of the Church.   It was the welcome which Siena gave to the greatest and the holiest of her citizens.   And it was after this long day's festivity was over that the incident took place which Raymund has related in his Legend, though only accidentally, as it were, and in illustration of a totally different subject.

"It is now nearly five years ago,"[1] he says, "when I was in the city of Siena, where, at the earnest request of Catherine's spiritual children, I had commenced writing her life.   It occurred to me at that time *that the head of the Saint, which had been brought from Rome to Siena, and which I had ornamented to the best of my ability, had not yet been publicly exposed and honoured.* I thought that a day might be selected *for a solemn reception of this precious relic in the convent, as though it had just arrived,* and that the religious might chant the Office of the day, as a particular one could not be allowed as long as the Sovereign Pontiff had not yet inscribed her in the catalogue of the Saints.   The festival took place to the great satisfaction of the religious and the citizens, but especially of those persons of whom she had been the spiritual guide.   I invited her most faithful disciples to dine in the refectory, and recommended the lay brother to give an extra attention to the serving of the repast.

"When the Office was concluded, and the moment for break-fast arrived, the Brother in charge of the pantry came to the Prior and told him with much distress that there was not sufficient bread for the Brethren at the first table, and none at all for the twenty invited guests.   On this information, the Prior determined to ascertain the real situation of affairs, and having seen how it was, he immediately sent the steward, with Father Thomas (Catherine's first confessor) to several friends of the Order, to bring the bread required; but they delayed so long that the Prior

---

[1] This "five years ago" would be an admirable *point d'appui* for our chronology did we but know from what year we were to reckon back; but this Raymund has forgotten to mention. For the rest, his notice of the fact is valuable, and confirms the perfect accuracy of Angiolini's narrative. The words we have italicised show that the first sending of the head to Siena and its subsequent public reception happened at distinct times.

                                                                    T

desired that the loaves which were in the house should be set before the strangers who were with me, so that a very small quantity remained in the storeroom. But as those on the quest did not return, he bade the religious sit down to table and begin on this small quantity until more should be brought. Then it was found that either in the storeroom, or on the refectory table, or somewhere, the bread had so multiplied through Catherine's intercession, that the whole Community were abundantly supplied, both at the first and second tables, and plentiful fragments left over; in fact, fifty religious had been fed with what would barely have sufficed for five. When the Brethren who had been sent out returned with what they had procured, they were told that it would serve for another time, because God had amply supplied the wants of His servants. After dinner I was speaking with our guests at some length on the virtues of the blessed Catherine, when the Prior came in with some others of the religious, and told us the miracle that had just taken place. Then I said to those present, ' It is clear that the holy Mother would not refuse to work for our benefit the same miracle she so often worked in her lifetime; the prodigy of to-day shows that she has accepted our service, and that she is ever with us; let us then give thanks to God and to our good Mother.'"[1]

Having said thus much concerning the first procession of the holy head of St. Catherine, it may be well to add a few words as to the subsequent history of this precious relic. In 1468 it was transferred to a magnificent silver reliquary, representing the head and bust of the Saint, one of the keys of the same being delivered to the keeping of the Captain of the people, and the other to the Prior of the Convent. On the night of the 3rd of December, in the year 1531, a terrible fire broke out in the Church of San Domenico, which destroyed many of the sacred relics and other treasures preserved in the church and sacristy; but St. Catherine's head was saved, thanks to the devotion of a certain Florentine lay brother, named Brother Anslem, who, wrapping himself in clothes dipped in water, threw himself into the midst of the flames, and

---

[1] Leg., Part 2, ch. xi.

rescued the relic, though not without its having sustained considerable injury. At the beginning of last century it was again transferred from this silver reliquary to one of crystal, in order the more easily to be seen and venerated by the faithful. Dating from the time of its solemn reception by the citizens, the annual custom of celebrating the festival of the Saint by a procession of her relics through the city has always been observed; though since its transfer to the crystal reliquary, the head itself has not been carried, but only the silver bust, in front of which is placed another relic, namely, the thumb of her right hand; "that hand," says Gigli, "which held the pen that wrote so many marvels." This annual procession still forms the great *Festa* of Siena, in which not the clergy alone, but all the magistrates, nobles, and citizens take part. The streets are then adorned with tapestry and flowers, the Church of San Domenico and the little cell of the Fullonica blaze with lights, and are visited all day long by pious pilgrims; and at night the whole Contrada of Fontebranda is brilliantly illuminated, and resounds with hymns and pious songs which recall the life of her whose glory still sheds its radiance over her native city.[1]

We must not conclude this chapter without adding a few particulars concerning the other chief relics of St. Catherine. When Raymund removed her body from the cemetery to the Church of the Minerva, he placed it at the foot of a column facing the Rosary Chapel, where it remained until 1430. In that year St. Antominus (afterwards Archbishop of Florence) was Prior of the Minerva, and by his orders the body was placed in a new stone sarcophagus, richly carved and surmounted by a wooden statue of the Saint. The head of the figure rests on a pillow, on which are engraved the words, *Beata Katerina;* while on the sarcophagus itself appears the following inscription: SANCTA CATERINA VIRGO

---

[1] The head of St. Catherine is kept in the chapel dedicated to her in the Church of S. Domenico. An exact account of its present state will be found given in the Scientific Report quoted by Niccolo Tommaseo in the first vol. of his edition of St. Catherine's letters (Appendix XI.), in which the writer declares that in spite of the injuries of time, the countenance even yet retains an expression of "vigour and agreeable candour."

DE SENIS ORDINIS S. DOMINICI DE PÆNITENTIA. This sarcophagus has often been opened, and relics taken from it have been distributed among various churches and convents. Thus in 1487, F. Joachim Toriani, General of the Order, gave the right hand to the nuns of S. Domenico e Sisto, and at the same time sent a foot to the Church of SS. John and Paul, at Venice. In 1575, F. Sixtus Fabbri gave another large relic to the nuns of Santa Caterina of Rome, whose community descends from the disciples of the Saint. On the 17th of April, 1855, when the Church of the Minerva was undergoing restoration, the sarcophagus was again opened by F. Alexander Vincent Jandel, General of the Order, in presence of many ecclesiastics of high rank. On that occasion a considerable portion of the sacred relics was taken out by the General, and sent to the convent of St. Dominic's, Stone, the Mother-House of the English congregation of Sisters of Penance, which bears the name of St. Catherine. These relics, which fill two silver and crystal reliquaries each three and a half inches long, consist of portions of bone and skin presenting the appearance of grey ashes, among which appear mingled threads of gold, the remains, probably, of the cloth of gold in which the holy body was wrapped. One of these reliquaries is preserved at St. Dominic's, Stone ; the other at the convent of St. Catherine, at Bow, near London.

The Church of the Minerva was reopened after its restoration on the 3rd of August 1855. The relics of the Saint, still reposing in their ancient sarcophagus, were then deposited beneath the high altar which, on the day following, being the Feast of St. Dominic, was solemnly consecrated by Pope Pius IX., of holy and happy memory. The next day the shrine was visited by the Roman Senate, and the relics were borne through the neighbouring streets in a grand and solemn procession. On this occasion, as before at Siena, appeared the unusual feature of a number of Sisters of the Third Order, following the crowd of prelates and illustrious personages who were assembled to do honour to their great patroness. This is the event celebrated as the Translation of St. Catherine, which was decreed to be thenceforward observed as a *Totum Duplex* on the Thursday before Sexagesima Sunday, on which day had, until then, been kept the Commemoration, or Espousals of the Saint; and a Proper Office of nine lessons was granted to the Order to be on that day recited. A few years later Pius IX. adorned the tomb of the Saint with some precious jewels, in consequence of which it has been thought necessary to enclose the sarcophagus in a kind of lattice-work, yet so as still to leave it visible under the high altar.

We have already spoken of the right hand of St. Catherine which is preserved in the convent of San Domenico e Sisto; other relics of a different kind are, or were, preserved in various places. Gigli tells us that at Rome, in his time, a portion of her habit was to be seen at St. Niccolo in Carcere; a discipline and chain were at St. Cecilia in Trastevere; and a shoe of white leather at Santa Maddalena. This last-named convent is on the Pincian Hill, and was founded in 1582 by Sister Magdalen Orsini; but during the Pontificate of Gregory XVI., the Community, which was of strict observance, was broken up, and its members incorporated with those of Santa Caterina and another Dominican Community; the convent being assigned to the nuns of the Perpetual Adoration. The shoe mentioned by Gigli is probably, therefore, the same now in the possession of the nuns of Santa Caterina, who also have a crucifix said to have belonged to the Saint.

It is at Siena, however, that the greatest number of her memorials have been preserved, among which must be numbered the holy house of the Fullonica, which was her birthplace and home. It was purchased by the Signoria in 1464, and transformed into a devout oratory at the petition of the inhabitants of the Contrada di Fontebranda who were too poor to undertake the expense themselves. At that time we read of "the great number of foreigners who came thither on pilgrimage, devoutly kissing the stairs and floors, saying as they did so, 'Here lived the true Spouse of Christ,' and other similar words." The oratory when finished was given into the custody of the Confraternity of St. Catherine in Fontebranda. The house has happily been preserved in all its chief features unaltered, and the visitor may still see the workshop of Giacomo and the cellar where the wine was multiplied ; the staircase which Catherine so often ascended as a child, reciting a Hail Mary on every step ; the fireplace where she prepared the family meals ; the room she occupied with her brother Stephen, and that which afterwards served as her chapel, and in which Mass was celebrated after her return from Avignon. The altar still remains, and on it are reliquaries containing various objects used by her in her lifetime ; such as the lantern she carried when summoned to the sick during the hours of the night ; a phial of scent, given to her, probably, at the time of the plague ; and a stick on which she leaned when infirm. But by far the most interesting spot is the cell which was assigned to her own use, lighted by its little window, beneath which appear the remains of the brick steps on which she occasionally rested her head during her scanty hours of repose :[1] the walls and floors of this room remain unaltered, and the pilgrim may still kiss the ground where her feet once trod. The Church of Sta. Caterina occupies the site of the former garden ; and here is preserved the Crucifix brought from Pisa, before which she received the stigmata. From the top of her father's house Catherine could behold the neighbouring church of San Domenico, and here she is said by tradition to have been in the habit of resorting, as to a place of prayer and contemplation. Of the church itself we have already spoken. As at Sta. Caterina, the walls are everywhere adorned with paintings and sculptures representing the chief scenes of Catherine's life, executed by the best Sienese artists. Of these the most celebrated is the Swoon of the Saint, who appears supported in the arms of two of her Sisters. This painting, which is in the chapel of St. Catherine, is by Giovanni Antonio Razzi, of Verzelli, more commonly known as Sodoma, and is regarded as his masterpiece. Its grace and loveliness are beyond dispute, yet, as is so often to be remarked, the conception of the artist fails as a representation of the actual fact ; for this picture in no way corresponds with what we know to have been Catherine's real condition when

---

[1] Portions of these are preserved in St. Dominic's Convent, Stone.

in ecstasy. On the pavement of the church appear various inscriptions, placed there by F. Angiolo Carapelli, when sacristan, in order to show the exact spots where certain events in Catherine's life took place. Here, we read, her heart was exchanged for that of her Divine Spouse—there, she bestowed the silver cross upon the beggar; in another place she gave her garment to Christ under the form of a poor pilgrim; whilst another inscription marks the place where He was wont to recite with her the Psalms of the Divine Office.

Catherine's memory, then, still survives in the heart of her countrymen; and the events of her marvellous life form part of the classic history of Siena. Much might be said of the tributes which have been paid to the beauty of that life by literature and by art, but we purposely abstain from all such digressions as would present the reader with a mere human idealism of one of God's Saints. It is not with them as with the great ones of this world, whose histories may be woven into poems and dramas, and made the theme of fanciful conceptions. For, "the just are living for evermore." We cannot altogether relegate them to the past, and regard them through the dim medium of intervening centuries, as we regard many a hero and heroine whose historic existence is almost swallowed up in that with which they have been invested by the imagination. It is not to art or to poetry that the memory of the Saints owes its amazing and fructifying power, but to the fact that we hold with them a living intercommunion. In this sense St. Catherine lives as truly now as in the days of her mortal pilgrimage; nay, rather, endowed with a newer and more abundant life; and thousands of hearts at this moment turn to her as to a living Mother. In her own Order she has for five centuries held a position altogether exceptional, the undisputed model on which has been formed a countless progeny of Saints. Far from representing the ideas of a dead and obsolete past, her example and her words are as fresh and vigorous in this nineteenth century as they were in the fourteenth. As a living Mother, then, we will invoke her, and implore her, from her home in the highest heavens, where she joyfully reposes with her Eternal Spouse, that she will look down on the troubles and sorrows of us, her children, and assist us before God with her loving prayers!   *De excelso cœlorum habitaculo, in quo in jucunditate accumbis cum Sponso tuo, intuere, piisima Virgo, augustias et tribulationem generis tui, et subveni ante conspectum Dei nostri* (Off. Trans. S. Cath. Resp. ix.)

CHAPTER X.

THE DEVOTIONS OF ST. CATHERINE.

IT would be quite beyond the design proposed in these pages
to attempt, at the close of St. Catherine's history, anything
like a formal analysis of her character or spirit. If she has not
already herself revealed them, no comment from the pen of another
would help to make her better known. Yet before quite parting
with the glorious Saint, whose history has so long engaged us, it
may be well to cast one retrospective glance on the path we have
been following. In relating her story it has been the aim of the
writer, as far as possible, to make St. Catherine her own biographer,
specially when we have been required to study the inner movements of her heart. Few Saints have left behind them more
ample materials for such a study than we possess in the works and
letters of St. Catherine. They unveil her soul, as far as any soul
can be unveiled to human eyes; and it is in this, more even than
in the example of her great actions, that the value of her life consists. For her actions were, for the most part, on too colossal a
scale for imitation; we cannot even understand them aright
without an interpreter; and their interpretation must be sought
from a knowledge of the interior spirit, of which they were but
the outer shell. Incidentally, as the narrative of her life has proceeded, the quotations from her letters and the records of her
spoken words will, from time to time, have lifted portions of the
veil; but some may desire more than such accidental glimpses of
what lay behind it, or at any rate to be able to place such revelations before them in a coherent form. To do this may involve
something of recapitulation, for which the patience of the reader is

solicited; but it will also set before him some points which have of necessity been but briefly touched on in the course of our history.

There is perhaps no better way of reaching the end we have in view than by considering for a few moments the subject of *St. Catherine's Devotions.* Devotion is the blossom of Faith. Blossoms, as we all know, are of little value without fruit; but besides the obvious fact that they have a good deal to do with the production of fruit, they have another use, which is, that by their examination and dissection we recognise the tree from which they spring. We know what *style* is to an author or an artist; a something that betrays the irresistible, perhaps unconscious, tendency of his mind. It appears in certain words or locutions which perpetually recur on the written page; or certain forms—a subdued or splendid colouring, a grace of line, or a power of conception, which is always reappearing on the canvas, not only revealing to us the artist, but also giving us a key to the hidden emotions of his soul. And just what style is in art or literature, devotions are in the spiritual life. They mark the specialities of the souls in whom they appear, those specialities which make up the spiritual character. For, far from being all alike, we observe among the Saints that endless variety which (as St. Catherine has told us) so wonderfully increases the beauty of God's Paradise. And thus, when studying the character of any Saint, we require to know their special devotions, and to see them arranged in such an order as may show us their connection and coherence.

St. Catherine received from her Creator many great and glorious gifts, but, beyond all question, the most glorious of all was that which has been so often spoken of as "the Perfection of Faith." From the very dawn of her spiritual life she fixed the eye of her understanding on the great truths of Creation and Redemption, and fed her soul with the Eternal Verities of the Catholic Creed. One God in Three Persons; God the Son made Man for us, shedding His Precious Blood for our Redemption, and pouring It out over our souls through the Sacraments of Holy Church; these were the Verities which became to her the only realities in the world. They are the same truths which every child in every

Catholic poor school believes and professes ; but there is a difference between believing and professing them, as the common herd of men are used to do, and going down into their depths, exploring, tasting, and living upon them as Catherine did, until all else faded from her spiritual vision, and she became enamoured of the Truths of Faith. As the beauty of Faith grew upon her, she desired with increasing ardour to possess it more perfectly, and the gift of this Faith in its fullest measure was the foundation-stone of her sanctification. Thus the spiritual eye of her understanding became so illuminated that what others beheld in a dark manner, she gazed at almost without a veil; at any rate, the veil was so thin as not to impede her sight, and the spiritual world became far more real to her apprehension than the material and tangible world that surrounded her.

Among the Truths of Faith which she thus lovingly contemplated, the prime and principal one was God Himself. It has already been noticed how like her words are to those of the Catechism in speaking of the end of our creation : the same may be said of the expressions she uses regarding the Unity and Trinity of God. Her devotion to the Holy Trinity and her habitual contemplation of It appears on every page of her writings, which display her to us with the eye of her intellect fixed on that most Divine and exalted of all Mysteries, plunging into its depths, and delighting in its fathomless infinitude. "O Eternal Trinity !" she exclaims, "O Deity, Whose Divine nature gives the price to the Precious Blood of Thy Son ! Thou, Eternal Trinity, art the fathomless sea into which the deeper we enter, the more we find ; and the more we find, the more we seek. In that abyss the soul satiates herself, and is never satisfied ; but ever hungers and thirsts after Thee, the Eternal Trinity, even as the hart pants after the fountains of living water."[1] This, her habitual devotion, nowhere finds fuller expression than in her prayers, which are but a few specimens accidentally preserved of her daily communings with God. In these prayers she sometimes begins by invoking the " Eternal

---

[1] Dial., ch. clxvii.

Trinity, one God in three Persons" (23); sometimes she goes on to address each Person separately, distinguishing them with admirable precision; or she occupies herself with the attributes which she beholds in the Most Holy Trinity, and applies them to her own spiritual wants, asking light from Its Light, wisdom from Its Wisdom, and strength from Its Force (Prayer 24). Sometimes she contemplates the same mystery in another way, as displaying the love of God for man: as when she calls the adorable Trinity "our table, our food, and our servant." "For Thou, O Father, art the Table whereon is served to us the un-spotted Lamb, Thy only Son; and this Lamb is Himself our sweet and delicious food; and the Holy Ghost has made Himself our servant, serving to us the doctrine that enlightens our under-standing and attracts our heart" (*Ibid.*). And Caffarini tells us that when offering any special prayers for the souls of others, it was her custom to recommend them to each Person of the Holy Trinity.

She realised with astonishing precision, and dwelt on the thought with ever-increasing wonder and delight, that in the three powers of the reasonable soul there is impressed the image of the Most Holy Trinity. To her this was the most suggestive of all truths; and she drew from it a profound sense of the dignity of the human soul. "O Eternal Father!" she exclaims,[1] "Thou hast drawn man out of Thy holy thought, like a flower wherein are distinguished the three powers of the soul; and in each of these powers Thou hast placed a germ, that they may fructify in Thy garden and yield back to Thee the fruit which Thou hast bestowed. Thou hast given him *memory*, that he may retain the thought of Thy benefits; and *understanding*, that he may know Thy Truth and Thy will, which is his sanctification; and Thou hast given him *will*, that he may love that which his understanding perceives, and his memory retains." In her Dialogue she expresses the same truth even more precisely. After saying that it was uncreated charity which moved God to create man in His own image, she continues: "And this Thou

---

[1] Prayer 21.

didst, O Eternal Trinity, desiring that man should participate in Thee altogether. Therefore, Thou gavest him memory, that he might participate in the power of the Father; and understanding, that he might participate in the wisdom of the Son; and will, that he might participate in the clemency of the Holy Spirit."[1] Thus she passed from God to the creature, and from the creature back to God, whom she habitually recognised as the End and Object[2] of the creature, the only cause and explanation of how it came to be. Without God man is nothing, for God is He Who is, and the creature, of itself, is nothing. Out of this thought flowed the fountain of her humility. She marvelled that the creature, knowing itself to be a creature, should be capable of vainglory;[3] for as she expresses it in the Dialogue, "As soon as a soul knows itself, it has found humility."[4] Yet this same thought of God, as the one Object of the soul, taught her likewise to understand the soul's true greatness and dignity. If God were the Object for which man was created, nothing less than God could ever satisfy him : man's soul, having in it an appetite and capacity for the infinite, can never be appeased with finite things, which are all less and lower than himself. "For man," she says, "is placed above all other created things, and therefore he cannot rest or be satisfied save in something greater than himself. But there is nothing greater than man save God ; and therefore it is that God alone can satisfy him."[5] Hence, too, she understood the intolerable blindness and folly of pride. "It is impossible for us," she says, "even to comprehend the senseless ignorance of man when he trusts in himself and confides in his own wisdom. O foolish one! seest thou not that the wisdom that thou hast, thou hast from none save God!"[6]

---

[1] Dial., ch. xiii.

[2] In her first prayer she calls God *il proprio Obietto dell' anima ;* and the same expression is to be found in many parts of the Dialogue, as well as in her last letter to Raymund. It is unnecessary to point out the deep significance of such an expression, which summarises in a single word the relations between God and man.

[3] P. 260.

[4] Dial., ch. vii.

[5] Ibid., ch. xciii.

[6] Ibid. ch. cxl.

These truths, so simple, but so profound, she made the principles of her spiritual philosophy, and applied them in the guidance of souls.

St. Catherine, then, saw in God the Beginning and the End of man ; but between them yawned a vast abyss. Across that abyss there had once been a road, but it had been broken and ruined by the sin of Adam. To enable man once more to reach God, the Eternal Son of God took our nature upon Him and became THE BRIDGE. This thought forms the text of her Dialogue. "To enable you to enjoy eternal life and to reach your end, MY SON HAS MADE HIMSELF A BRIDGE." She understood that this was effected by the Incarnation. "For the greatness of the Divinity abased itself to the earth of your humanity, and by this union the Bridge was made, and the road repaired."[1] The amazing charity of God towards His creatures became in a manner sensible to her under this image. "My charity has been made visible in the person of My Son, Who has shown it to you by shedding His Blood for you. And this Blood nourishes you in the Sacraments. It is My Vicar who holds the key of the Blood, and who is charged to distribute It to you. You will find It in the hostelry which is established on the bridge, to feed the pilgrims who pass thereby."[2]

The abyss between God and man bridged over by the Word made Flesh ; we, the pilgrims between earth and heaven, only able to reach our end—the God for whom we were created—by passing over that Bridge ; but unable to pass, and fainting by the way without the Food that must sustain us on our journey ; that Food, the Precious Blood of Christ ; and that Blood applied to our souls by the Sacraments, and dispensed to us on earth by him who holds the key,—here are the sensible figures under which St. Catherine beheld the grand mysteries of the Catholic Faith : and here were the links of that wonderful chain which united together in her luminous devotion the Eternal God in Three Persons ; the Word made Flesh, and so becoming the Bridge between earth and heaven ; His Blood, the Price of our Redemp-

---

[1] Dial., ch. xxii.   [2] Ibid., chaps. xx., xxii., xlvi.

tion, and the Food of our souls; the Sacraments, Its channels; the Church, Its Tabernacle or Hostelry; and the Vicar of Christ and the priests of Holy Church, those who hold the key to unlock that Tabernacle, and who pour its priceless Treasure on our souls.

When, therefore, after naming the Most Holy Trinity, we say that St. Catherine's devotions of predilection were to all the mysteries of the Incarnation, but specially to the most Precious Blood as to the sum of them all, our meaning will be clear. It was the closely reasoned connection between all these adorable mysteries "cemented together as stones by the Precious Blood," which inspired her with her habitual ejaculation, "O Fire! O Blood!" and made those words to be, in fact, a brief and energetic profession of loving faith in all the articles of the Christian Creed; so that, even at the moment when she passed out of this life, the same accents still lingered on her lips, and she died murmuring the words, "Blood! Blood!" St. Catherine's devotion to the Precious Blood was not exclusively expressed in the phraseology of her writings and her prayers. Her frequent and fervent use of the Sacraments was an inherent part of this devotion. "She was as one famished for the Blood of Christ," says Caffarini, "ever seeking to be washed in It afresh." Her marked solicitude to procure from the Sovereign Pontiff privileges and indulgences for herself and others had the same origin. In one such Brief which she obtained from Gregory XI., an indulgence at the hour of death is granted to seventy-seven of her friends and disciples by name. On her deathbed, having received the indulgence granted her by Gregory, she was not satisfied until she had also received that of Urban. And, as we have seen, the disciple who wrote the account of her last moments comments on her continual request for absolution, saying, that "it was as though she desired that more and more of the Blood of Christ should be poured over her."[1] These things were evidences of

---

[1] In one of her prayers (9) St. Catherine uses the expression, "The Eternal Blood," which has been criticised by some as incorrect. She herself, however, adds her own explanation : "I call It Eternal, because it is united to the

that faith which filled her soul, and enable us faintly to realise the light in which she regarded the Sacraments and ordinances in Holy Church.

But further than this, it was the vivid comprehension she had of the dogmas of Creation and Redemption which was the origin of her immense love of souls. It is probably by her zeal for the conversion of sinners and the salvation of souls that St. Catherine is chiefly remembered. This sacred passion for souls sprang from the keen insight she had into the love which God bears them. In her Dialogue she represents the Eternal Father, after disclosing and explaining to her the mysteries of the Incarnation, as figured by the mystic Bridge, declaring to her that all she beheld had been the work of Love, and with amazing condescension soliciting her to pray for the souls He longed to save.[1] He made her understand that He chooses men to be His fellow-labourers, to take part in the great work of the salvation of the world; and that He asks and desires them by their prayers to move Him to show mercy to sinners. And then it was that in a rapture of love she exclaimed, "O Abyss of Charity! who can resist Thee! for Thou seemest to love Thy creatures even to folly, as though Thou couldst not live without them! . . . In mercy Thou didst first create them; in mercy Thou didst redeem them; in mercy Thou hast washed them in the Blood of Thy Son; in mercy Thou still desirest to converse with them. O folly of Love! it was not enough for Thy Son to become man, but He would even die for man. . . . We are the creatures whom Thou hast made, and I behold in our redemption in the Blood of Thy Son, that Thou art verily enamoured of the beauty of Thine own creature!"[2] In one passage of her Dialogue we have an intimation that the subject that drew from her the celebrated exclamation, *Vidi Arcana Dei!* was none other than the stupendous

Divine Nature;" and her commentators refer us to the words of St. Paul, *Per proprium sanguinem introivit semel in sancta, æterna redemptione inventa"* (Heb. ix. 12). And, again, to the passage in the Apocalypse, where we read, "*Agnus qui occisus est ab origine mundi"* (Apoc. xiii. 8).

[1] Dial., ch. xxix.   [2] Ibid., chaps. xxv., xxx., clxvii.

love of God for His creatures. "O Eternal, Infinite Good!" she exclaims, "O folly of Love! Dost Thou stand in need of Thy creature? It surely seems as though Thou couldst not live without him. He flies from Thee, and Thou followest after him, seeking him. He keeps away from Thee, and Thou drawest near. Nearer to him Thou couldst not come than to clothe Thyself with his humanity. I could say with St. Paul, 'The tongue cannot speak, nor the ear hear, nor the eye behold, nor the heart conceive that which I have seen.' What hast thou seen? *Vidi Arcana Dei!*"[1]

It was by the light of this revelation which she had received of the love which God bears His creatures, that St. Catherine came to contemplate souls; to measure their worth, and to appreciate that sin which alone can separate them from Him. We know that it was her intense realisation of God's love to man which broke her heart, and was the cause of her mystic death. When she returned from death to life, she found herself possessed and inebriated with two absorbing passions; the love of souls, and the hatred of sin; and henceforth her life became a long crusade undertaken to deliver the creatures so dear to God from the tyranny of His enemy.

God having been pleased to "elect her to be a labourer in the spiritual vineyard of the Church," communicated to her a special light for the guidance of souls. That exquisite purity of conscience which made sensible to her the least defect in her own conduct, enabled her to implant in the souls whom she trained in perfection a like horror of even the shadow of sin. With wonderful skill she used that insight which she possessed into the hearts of others, not merely to discover to them their hidden sins, but also to trace these sins to their fountain-heads, assuring her disciples that if they would be delivered from their habitual faults they must have patience to seek out, and courage to eradicate, the hidden root of self-love from which they sprang. Thus we read, that Sister Francesco di Marco, one of the Mantellate, came to her one day, complaining that her soul was full of uneasiness and

---

[1] Dial., ch. cliii.

obscurity, which she felt, without being able to explain. But Catherine told her that very often the smallest spark of an unmortified passion (*una piccola scintilla di passioncella*), if not promptly cast out of our hearts, may kindle within us a great fire which we cannot extinguish when we wish to do so; and made known to her the precise imperfection which she had unconsciously been cherishing, and to which her present sufferings were to be attributed.[1]

We have quoted this passage both for the sake of its intrinsic value, and also because it affords a proof that Catherine did not merely occupy herself with reclaiming great sinners, and rescuing them when on the verge of destruction. It is true that the stories which appear in her life, most often exhibit her to us engaged in this kind of work; but her power was no less wonderful in leading souls to perfection. A manual of spiritual direction might be compiled out of her letters, the key-note to which would certainly be *fidelity to conscience, based on the love of God.*

St Catherine's devotion to the Holy Eucharist, which may be said to have filled up so large a part of her daily existence, rested on precisely the same foundation. The Holy Eucharist is the extension of the Incarnation; and the clear perception with which her faith beheld "God the Son made man for us, truly present under the appearances of bread and wine," is the explanation of those long ecstasies, and all those other wonders of her Communions, which fill the pages of the Legend. But on this subject we have already sufficiently spoken in a former chapter; fully to illustrate it would be simply to rewrite her life.

One so devout to the Incarnation, so penetrated with a faith in the dogma, and a comprehension of all its bearings, could not but be a loving child of Mary. Accordingly we find St. Catherine addressing the Blessed Virgin as "The temple of the Holy Trinity," "The source of our peace," "The Mother of Mercy who has borne the fruit of life," "She who may be said to have saved the human race, inasmuch as she gave to Christ the flesh in which He redeemed us," "who (in a sense) redeemed us by her sorrowful

---

[1] Sup., Part 2, Trat. 5, § 10.

Compassion, whilst her Son was (actually) redeeming us by His Bloody passion," "The new tree which gives us the Fruit of Life," "The car of fire, preserving the Fire hidden under the ashes of our humanity," "She who drew the Divinity to descend upon her by the gentle force of her humility," "The book in which is written our rule," "She in whom is revealed the dignity, the force, and the liberty of man." For "the Almighty Himself knocked at the door of your will, O Mary, and if you had not opened to Him, He would not have taken on Him our nature." Finally, she says that "he who has recourse to Mary with love and respect will never become the prey of the infernal wolf;" and again, "O Mary, I address myself to thee with boldness, because I know that God can refuse thee nothing."[1] We shall scarcely find language more fervid or more tender than this; and from the moment when Catherine, as a little child, commended herself to Our Lady on each step of the staircase in her father's house, up to that Feast of the Annunciation, 1379, the very year before her death, when she wrote the prayer from which most of the above epithets have been extracted, her devotion to the Mother of God was of the same character, based on the same solid foundation of faith which inspired all her other devotions, and expressed in the same sweet and natural language.

It is almost needless to indicate St. Catherine's devotion to the

---

[1] The above extracts are almost all taken from St. Catherine's 11th prayer. Mgr. Rafaelle Maria Filamondo, in the learned "Considerations" on some of the expressions used in these prayers (printed in Gigli's 4th volume), examines and explains the sense in which she speaks of Our Lady as redeeming the world by her Compassion, and gives parallel passages from the Fathers. In some editions of her works a conclusion appears to her 14th prayer, containing expressions which contradict the dogma of the Immaculate Conception. The authenticity of the passage, however, has long since been disproved. It is admitted to be a literary forgery, and one not very creditable to its authors. The whole question has been critically examined by F. Hyppolito Marraccio, in his work entitled *Vindicatio S. Catherinæ Senensis a commentitia revelatione eidem S. Catharinæ adscripta contra Im. Conceptionem B.V. Mariæ.* (*Puteoli:* 1663). It would have been strange indeed if St. Catherine had given utterance to any expressions disparaging to a doctrine of which the Sienese were ever the most ardent defenders (See *Diario San.*, 2, 29, 520).

Church, as springing from the same root.   The Church is to her always the body of Christ.   It is Christ Himself: *è esso Christo.* Those who do not realise this truth with equal clearness, are naturally startled by the severity of her expressions in speaking of the enemies of the Church.   Even the Abbé Fleury is shocked at her calling the schismatics, "incarnate devils;" yet, as has been before observed, the language was rigorously logical.   If the Church be Christ Himself, the would-be dividers and destroyers of the Church are *His* enemies, and aim at His destruction ; and therefore she saw in them the likeness of the great enemy. Moreover, she had an eye to the ruin of souls, and those who caused that ruin she justly considered to be doing the work of demons.

St. Catherine's devotion to the Holy Church, the unspotted Spouse of Christ, is all the more apparent from the circumstance that at the time in which she lived, to use her own expression— repeated, and possibly even quoted by the English King—" her face had become pale."   Scandals were seldom darker, sanctity in the ministers of the Church never more rare.   The two Pontiffs, to whose cause she devoted herself with such unflinching loyalty, were both of them men of good-will and blameless lives ; but they were not without defects, and precisely such defects as ordinary minds observe and contemn ; and which, in such minds, diminish respect, and test the reality of faith.   In this, so far as Catherine was concerned, there was a peculiar Providence.   Had St. Gregory the Great or St. Pius V. sat on the chair of St. Peter instead of Gregory XI. and Urban VI., it might have been thought that some of St Catherine's impassioned loyalty was directed to the individual man.   We may safely say, however, that her conduct in that respect would have been entirely the same had the occupant of the Holy See been even less distinguished by personal qualities than those we have named.   She beheld in him nothing but the Vicar of Christ.   Exactly as she saw Christ in the poor pilgrim whom she clothed, did she behold Him in the persons of the Pontiffs whom she served ; so too in their inferior ministers. She had not the happiness of living in times when she might have seen the Episcopal thrones of Christendom filled by a St. Antoninus, a St. Charles, or a Bartholomew of the Martyrs; among the priests who ministered to the souls around her, she found neither a St. Vincent of Paul, nor an Olier, nor a Curé of Ars. In men like these, it would have required no extraordinary faith to recognise the " Ministers of the Blood." But St. Catherine lived in a sorrowful age, surrounded by scandals that would have tried a weaker faith, and to which, beyond all doubt, must in part be attributed the budding germ of that disaffection which two centuries later ripened in revolt. All the heresiarchs of that time began by taking scandal. There was plenty to cause it, and woe be to those by whom the scandals came! But while St. Catherine felt those scandals to the centre and marrow of her soul, so that they formed a part of that long anguish which was her life's martyrdom, they never dimmed her faith. This is much too weak an expression. They in a certain sense brought it into more dazzling light. " Let a man so account of us as the Ministers of Christ and the dispensers of the mysteries of God," says the apostle, and he adds : " Now it is required of dispensers that they be found faithful." It needed an eye illuminated by the Light of Faith to discern the Ministers of God in those so masked by human corruption as were some of those with whom St. Catherine had to do. Did she ever waver on this point, or rather, is not the very severity of her language the proof of her faith? for it was because they were "unworthy Ministers" of the Blood of Christ, that she so wrote and spoke. Hence her ardent longings for *reform*, though one need scarcely remark that a reform which struck at the very foundations of Faith could never have been welcomed by St. Catherine. Nevertheless, the peculiar magic which that word exercises over certain minds, and the fact that she not only *desired*, but even *predicted* its advent, has led some, who identify the word exclusively with the work effected by Luther and other sectaries, to claim St. Catherine as a morning star of the Protestant Reformation. That event (may we say it) must have been sadly in want of morning stars, if its votaries could find none better suited to the purpose than the Saint who, had she lived to witness the revolt of the sixteenth century, would certainly not have bestowed on its adherents a gentler name than she applied to the schismatics of the fourteenth. Such audacious suppositions could never have been put forth by any one familiar with her works. No doubt the word *reformation* occurs in them sufficiently often; her meaning in using it she has explained clearly enough, when she repeats again and again that "the Church herself can never need reform." And to conclude the matter we will say with Tantucci, that she meant neither more nor less than what the Councils of Constance and Trent intended by their canons of reform. When those Councils can be claimed by historians as Hussite or Lutheran assemblies, we shall cheerfully admit St. Catherine among the ranks of the "morning stars."

To come to another branch of the subject, St. Catherine's devotions to the Saints were all marked and characteristic. First in order we must place her devotion to St. Paul. Caffarini tells us that in one of her ecstasies it was made known to her that she had tasted the same degree of bliss as was granted to St. Paul when rapt to the third heaven. She loved him for his love of his Lord: it was just of that generous, fearless, self-forgetting character which her own soul so well comprehended. In the prayer she composed on the Feast of his Conversion, she says some wonderfully beautiful and profound things as to the nature of that love. "O Paul, holy Apostle, you well understood this truth, whence you came and whither you were going, and by what road you must travel to reach your end. On the day when the Divine Word converted you from error to truth, you saw in rapture the Divine Essence in Three Persons. Then when you returned to your bodily senses you beheld the Incarnate Word, and understood that He, by His sufferings, was to be the glory of His Father and our salvation. Then you became famished and athirst for suffering; you forgot all else; you confessed that you knew nothing but Jesus, and Jesus crucified. Neither in the Father nor the Holy Spirit could you find suffering; and therefore it was that you said you knew none but Jesus, who suffered such great things for us; Jesus and *Jesus crucified*." This generosity of the chosen Apostle was what so greatly endeared him to her, it was like the point of sympathy on which two friends meet and understand one another. His fervent words, his love for the very name of Jesus, his desire of suffering, his zeal for God's honour and the salvation of his brethren,—she felt and comprehended it all.

And next to him stood her glorious Father St. Dominic, the likeness and faithful pattern of the Son of God. She beheld him in vision resembling his Master even in his very person, no less than in his unalterable patience and his burning charity. From her earliest childhood it had been the dream of her imagination to serve God by the imitation of St. Dominic; and the fidelity with which she realised this idea is worthy of all admiration. In her nightly disciplines, in her desire of martyrdom, in her longing (like him) to give her body to torments, not once only, as she says, "but over and over again, each time with more pain than before," if by so doing she could win God some glory, or save one soul; in all this she was a faithful imitator of St. Dominic, as he was of Jesus Christ. So, too, in that profound humility which made him, before entering any town, kneel down and pray that his sins might not bring on it the Divine Judgment, Catherine followed closely on his track. For she believed all the evils in the world, all the woes of the Church, all the ruin of souls, over which she wept, to be the effect of her sins. "No more sin, O Lord, no more hell!" so she cried to God in prayer, asking that she might be placed in the mouth of hell to prevent sinners from going there. Such words are often enough regarded as pious exaggerations; but to understand them we must first understand *sin* as St. Catherine and St. Dominic understood it.

Of the other Saints of her own Order, St. Peter Martyr and St. Agnes of Montepulciano were her favourite patrons; she called St. Peter "the true knight without fear," and with St. Agnes, as we know, her relations were those of a familiar and holy friendship.

But what shall we say of her love of St. Magdalen, the saintly penitent, given her to be her mother by her Divine Spouse Himself? In all the lives of the Saints we shall scarcely find an example more striking of a special devotion to a chosen patron than that which St. Catherine displayed towards St. Mary Magdalen, the lover of our Lord. In one of his greatest works of art Fra Bartolomeo has depicted her side by side with St. Magdalen, contemplating the Eternal Trinity. He could hardly have better represented our idea of St. Catherine's fundamental devotion. Among the other Saints her preference was for the martyrs ; and of these we may name St. Stephen, St. Lawrence, St. Agnes, and St. Lucy of Rome ; the latter of whom, but little known, she specially loved, and was granted on her feast to share the merits of her martyrdom. In Rome she exulted in treading the ground consecrated by the blood of the martyrs. "They desired death," she says, "not to fly labour, but to attain their end. And why did they not fear death, from which man naturally so shrinks? Because they had vanquished the natural love of their own bodies by divine and supernatural love. How can such a man complain of the death of the body, he who desires to be set free from life which he finds both long and bitter ? How can he regret to lose that which he despises ? Nay, rather he desires to give his life for God Who is his Life, and to shed his blood for love of the Blood that was shed for him."[1]

Catherine comprehended the martyrs' spirit, because she shared it. For among her devotion we ought surely to number *her love of suffering.* Recalling in her Dialogue the memory of her own mystic death, she says : "When a soul that has been absorbed in God by love returns to her bodily senses, she endures life with difficulty, for she sees herself deprived of the union she had enjoyed with Him, and the desirable company of the Blessed. Yet, as her will is no longer her own, she can will nothing but His will. She desires to go to Him, yet she is content not to go, if so He ordain, but to remain and suffer for His glory. The more she suffers, the more she rejoices, for suffering soothes the desire she has of death, and the love of suffering sweetens the sorrow she feels not yet to be delivered from the body."[2] In Catherine's

---

[1] Dial., ch. 115.   [2] Dial., ch. lxxxiv.

mind suffering was identical with love: we cannot understand her practices of penance without remembering this. One in our own day has written that "to love is to suffer;" Catherine would have given those words her heartiest acceptance, and her profoundest interpretation; and she would also have reversed the terms and have said that "to suffer is to love;" indeed she does say so, repeating again and again, "The more we suffer, the more we prove our love."[1]

As to what are commonly called practices of devotion, her love of the Church Office certainly held the first place. The reader will remember her solicitude to be able to recite it, and knowing Who was wont to recite it with her, we do not need to be told that it could have been no common recitation of the Office that obtained so wondrous a favour. All the feasts and holy seasons were followed by her with a sympathy and depth of comprehension, which shows her feeding her soul on the language, the solemnities, and the order of the Sacred Ritual, which indeed supplies all true children of the Church with an ever-flowing torrent of spiritual recreation. Open the *Supplimento,* and you will see each new grace chronicled by no other date than the feast on which it occurred; and if sick, and unable to assist at the solemnities in which her soul delighted, she took comfort as she lay on her bed in gazing at the walls only of the distant cathedral. So long as she could use vocal prayers, which as time went on became impossible by reason of her ecstasies, she loved the Rosary and always wore it at her side. Her use of holy pictures and Crucifixes is apparent from the fact that in whatever place she sojourned some such object of piety is still shown which she is said to have used. Siena still keeps and venerates the miraculous *Madonna in Provenzana,* which according to tradition was first placed by her hands in the niche where it was discovered. She gave a Crucifix to the Convent of Monticella, and gladly received presents of crosses and images of the Holy Child. Her reception of the stigmas before the Crucifix at Pisa speaks for itself. Raymund tells us also that she had a

---

[1] *Quanto più sostiene, più dimostra che mi ami.* (Dial., ch. v).

great love for pious pilgrimages. We know that she made many such, and her daily pilgrimage to St. Peter's during the last ᵢLent of her mortal life, excruciated as she was with bodily and mental pain, stands before us as one of the sublimest pictures in her life.

Only one other point seems to deserve a word of notice. What devotion is more distinctive of the pious Catholic than the devotion to the holy souls in purgatory? With many it is a sort of special vocation to devote themselves to the relief of these suffering souls. To St. Catherine also this devotion was intensely dear. The charity of Christ pressed her, until she could obtain the deliverance of those for whom she prayed. And it is a significant fact that the long torture of that pain in the side, which never left her, was a voluntarily accepted suffering for the relief of her father's soul.

In this review of the devotions of St. Catherine we have purposely selected those which best express the immense power with which she held the mysteries of Faith, believed by her in common with all the children of Holy Church. Doubtless in the contemplation of those mysteries she was favoured with extraordinary lights such as no soul can attain by any human industry and which gave a sublimity to her doctrine, declared in the Bull of Canonisation to have been " not acquired but infused." Her eye, as it penetrated the truths of Faith, was permitted to behold in their amazing depths things which, in the very language of St. Paul, she declared to be unutterable ;—They were the *Arcana Dei*, the secrets of God. In those higher revelations— those " divine things " which " came upon her " from the hand of God, and seemed to transform her from a mere creature of flesh and blood into a seraph illuminated by a ray from the unapproachable Light—in these sublimer heights we cannot follow her. But there is a track left by her footsteps in which all may safely tread, a lesson which we can best express in her own admirable words : " The guide and support of the human will is the sacred light of Faith ; for that light is the beginning, middle, and end of all perfection." [1]

---

[1] Prayer 7.

CHAPTER XI.

A LAST GLANCE AT THE FAMILY.

AND now, before closing our narrative, it remains for us to take a last look at that little company of faithful disciples whom we have so often seen gathered round their Mother, taking part in her works, or gathering from her lips the maxims of perfection. On the event of her death they were scattered, as to their bodily presence, though the spiritual links that bound them together remained unbroken to the last. The first concerning whose after-career we naturally desire to know something, is Father Raymund of Capua. Elected to the chief office in his Order within a few weeks after Catherine's departure, the remaining nineteen years of his life were devoted to three duties : the defence of the Church against the schismatics, the reform of his Order, and the composition of the Legend, or biography of his holy penitent. Of the first of these we shall say little more than that Urban and his successors in the Holy See are declared to have found in Father Raymund "their right arm and eye." That in the midst of the unspeakable troubles of the Schism, he should have been able to have begun and successfully to have carried on a reform of those abuses in the Order which Catherine had in her lifetime deplored, speaks not a little for his courage and talent for government. According to the common sentiment of all historians of the Order, it is to St. Catherine herself that we must attribute that movement in the direction of reform which made itself sensible after her death, and which was mainly carried on by her disciples. " It was St. Catherine," says P Vincenzo Marchese, in his life of B. Lawrence of Ripafratta, "who by her earnest exhortation had moved Blessed Raymund of Capua resolutely to put his hand to the work of reformation; and it was her no less beneficial influence that gained to the Order that daughter of Peter Gambacorta of Pisa, who became the reformer of its religious women. And although Catherine herself, worn out by suffering, departed to the heavenly kingdom, yet Raymund, as soon as he was placed at the head of the Order of Preachers, delayed not to carry her wishes into effect. He made a pressing appeal for succour to all those who had a zeal for God and their holy Institute, which was quickly responded to in Germany by F. Conrad of Prussia, and in Italy by B. John Dominic, F. Thomas (Caffarini) of Siena, B. Lawrence of Ripafratta, and F. Thomas Ajutamicristo; the two last-named Fathers belonging to the convent of Sta. Caterina at Pisa. But long before they began their labours, Blessed Clara Gambacorta, impatient of delay, set on foot the reform among her own Sisters, enclosing herself with a few religious under a very strict rule in the convent of San Domenico, on the 29th of May, 1382. From this convent, as from a copious fountain-head, went forth those who reformed the communities of Genoa, Parma, and Venice. And not satisfied with this, by her prayers and counsels she greatly promoted the cause of reform even among the Friars themselves, so that the Dominican Order, with reason, regards Blessed Clara as another St. Teresa."

What is here said of the influence of Blessed Clara over the Friars, and her promotion of the reform no less among their convents than in those of her religious Sisters, is amply confirmed by a reference to the chronicle of Sta. Caterina of Pisa; from which we find that all the most holy religious of that community gathered round her as round a mother; and it is considered sufficient praise to bestow on Fra Niccolo Gittalebraccia, one of the pillars of the reform, to say that he was *de intimis filiis sororis Claræ de Gambacurtis.* Nevertheless, this very convent of Sta. Caterina of Pisa for a considerable time opposed itself to the reform, and Blessed Clara's disciples had to carry on the good work in more distant provinces. Raymund, on his part, laboured without ceasing to establish discipline and regular observance, but he invariably did so in the spirit of meekness. "He always exhibited the utmost gentleness in his government," says Caffarini, "being liberal and discreet to all, and severe only to himself. He lived in great poverty to the day of his death, which took place at Nuremburg, on the 5th of October, 1399." Though never beatified, he is always remembered in the Order by the title of "Blessed Raymund." He completed the Legend about the year 1395, having been engaged on it at intervals for fifteen years. Caffarini tells us that he himself assisted the author in his laborious task, in the course of which Raymund used great and praiseworthy diligence in collecting from their own lips the evidence of all those who had known Catherine most intimately, such as her mother Lapa, Lisa, Alexia, and the rest. In 1395, Raymund, coming from Sicily to Venice, brought the manuscript with him; and delivering it to Caffarini, who was then established in that city, desired him to have copies of it made and distributed into every province; a duty to which he and his companions devoted themselves with such ardour, that in an incredibly short space of time the Legend of St. Catherine was diffused throughout every country in Christendom. There are few things more remarkable in the history of literature than the rapid circulation of this book, unaided by the art of printing, and its translation into every known dialect. On its completion, Raymund applied himself to the translation of the Dialogue into Latin, carefully consulting the three secretaries to whom the original had been dictated, in order to secure perfect accuracy. The Abbé Fleury, in the truly astonishing remarks he has made on St. Catherine and her writings, has thought fit to express his surprise that her secretaries should have written in Latin what she dictated in Tuscan; but his words only betray his entire ignorance of the facts. The Dialogue was both dictated and written in Tuscan; that same Tuscan text which we still possess; and its Latin versions by Christofano and Raymund were not made until some years after her death.

From Raymund we will pass to St. Catherine's other Confessors. F. Thomas della Fonte survived her ten years, during part of which time he filled the office of Prior of San Domenico, and took great delight in causing paintings and images of the holy virgin to be made and placed in various parts both of the church and the city. Caffarini affirms[1] that he even placed in the Church of the Friars, and in a very conspicuous place (*in posto elevato*), a picture of the Saint receiving the Stigmata ; and after the great procession which has been described in the preceding chapter, he successfully exerted himself to obtain from the Magistrates that the same solemnity should be annually observed in their city.

F. William Flete is often said to have died in the same year as St. Catherine. His "Sermon," already referred to, and dated as having been delivered in 1382, proves this statement to be erroneous ; but it is probable that he did not long survive her. Master John the Third returned from Rome to Lecceto immediately after her death, and was still living in 1391.

F. Bartholomew Dominic took an active part in the reform of the Order under Raymund of Capua, a work for which his learning, holiness, and singular prudence specially qualified him. He filled many high offices in his Order, was for seven years Provincial of the Roman Province, Procurator for the Order in Rome, and finally became titular Bishop of Corona in the Morea. He had the happiness of labouring in concert with F. Thomas Caffarini for the reform and extension of that branch of the Order to which St. Catherine more particularly belonged ; and also of giving his most important evidence in that " Process of Venice," so often quoted in the preceding pages. As to F. Thomas Caffarini, his career was a yet more active and illustrious one. As a writer, he has certainly done more to illustrate the life of St. Catherine than any other of her disciples. We have seen that he assisted Raymund in the composition of the original Legend. When it was completed, he wrote his own *Leggenda Minore*, introducing many incidents which Raymund had omitted ; and finally he drew up his Supplement to the Legend, at the earnest solicitation of a vast number of religious persons, specially of the Camaldolese Hermits of Florence, and the Carthusians of Vienna.

[1] Sup., Part 3, § 1.

The letter addressed to him by the good hermits does them infinite credit as judicious readers and critics. They had both read the Legend and relished it, but they wanted more. "For our common and greater edification," they say, "we desire to be informed of all the daily, manual, and most minute actions of Catherine, of her conversations, her exercises, her particular ways of speaking, of whatsoever movements were noticeable in her gait, and the gestures of her hands and feet." We entirely sympathise with these their holy desires, and do not by any means accuse them as guilty of vain curiosity. We only wish that F. Thomas had more literally complied with their request, the rather that in one respect they set him an excellent example by dating their letter, August 26th, 1400. Not content with this first appeal, they sent him a second the following April, conjuring him to spare no pains in collecting the least little saying of the holy virgin, whether recorded in Latin or Italian; and to look very sharp after his copyists, lest, overcome with weariness, they should cheat, by leaving out some *minute cosarelle*, whereas he should oblige them to set down all with sincere fidelity. "For if you do otherwise," continues the Prior, "and are guilty of any negligence in this matter, be sure that you will have a rigorous account to give before the Tribunal of God." He adds that he has a few books about Catherine, one in particular which he has read over and over again *da capo a piedi*, namely, her wonderful Dialogue; and he concludes by spurring his friend on to expedition by reminding him of the shortness of life, and the fact that no one could be so fit to undertake the work as he.

As if this were not enough to drive F. Thomas to seize his pen and begin at once, the General of the Carthusians, who could have been none other than his old friend Stephen Maconi, forwarded him a letter on the 5th of August, written by another Don Stephen of the Certosa of Vienna, who relates to his Superior, by no means briefly, a tale of woe and of deliverance. It seems that on the night of Saturday, in the Octave of Pentecost, he had felt extremely ill, and was in such pain that he could neither stand, sit, nor lie down, nor rest either on his back or his side. When the signal for Matins was given, he was in great perplexity, not knowing whether to get up, or stay where he was. He felt sure he could not stand upright in choir, yet did not like to absent himself. So he bethought him that he would recite the Office of Our Lady, which he did, but could hardly remember if he did it mentally or vocally; indeed, he had very little voice left, and what there was, was extremely hoarse. Suddenly there came to his mind certain reports that he had heard of the wonderful assistance which the Blessed Catherine of Siena was used to give to those who invoked her. He began therefore to pray, that if what was commonly reported concerning her Sacred Espousals were true, he might, as a sign thereof, be immediately cured. Instantly he felt himself relieved of his pain; and going to the choir, was in time to sing the Lauds of the next day's solemnity in honour of the Holy Trinity, with his brethren. These letters seem to have made a great impression on F. Thomas, and the end of it was that he resolved to commence his Supplement without further delay. In one of the Prologues prefixed to the work, he apologises for thinking it necessary to add anything to Raymund's biography; but explains that though that holy man was the best authority who could be referred to for those years during which he acted as Catherine's director, yet these did not include the earlier portion of her life, the materials of which Raymund was obliged to gather from others, and concerning which he himself was better informed.

Thus much for Caffarini's written labours relating to the holy virgin. They formed but a small part of those to which he devoted himself in order to promote her honour. Soon after her death he undertook a pilgrimage to the Holy Land, returning whence he came to Venice, and was there lovingly captured by Blessed John Dominic, who by that time had taken the lead in the work of reform. He rightly judged that no one was better fitted to assist in that work than the chosen friend of St. Catherine; one who for long years had enjoyed her confidence, and who, as might well be believed, had imbibed her spirit. At Venice, therefore, Caffarini was thenceforward fixed; and there he effected many wonderful conversions, among which is specially noted that of a certain lady named Maria Storiona, who, from a life of worldly vanity, was so entirely changed by his preaching, that she embraced a course of austere penance, which merited for her after death the title of Blessed.

During the remainder of his life Caffarini laboured without ceasing to maintain or restore regular observance in the convents of the Friars, and to extend that Third Order which had been rendered so illustrious by the sanctity of St. Catherine. He re-wrote the Rule of the Sisters of Penance in Italian, and established several regular convents of their Order, in which work he was greatly assisted by F. Bartholomew Dominic, and the Blessed John Dominic. Indeed his zeal in this matter was so great that, as Ferdinand Castiglio tells us in his History of the Order, Caffarini was commonly, though inaccurately, called *the Founder of the Claustral Order of Penance;* that is, of those convents of the Sisters of Penance in which was established the regular religious and community life. Besides this, in concert with Stephen Maconi, he ceased not to copy, translate, and cause to be circulated, the Life, Letters, and Dialogue of the Saint. Applications were made to him for these books from many princes, and illustrious personages, among others from King Henry IV. of England; and he did his best to satisfy their demands, and to take every step which the difficulties of the time rendered possible to obtain her canonisation. On this point hope long deferred did not in the least abate his ardour. If he did not live to see his desires accomplished, it was he who prepared the way for their accomplishment, and like another David he was content to collect the materials out of which those who came after him were to raise the actual edifice. During the forty years of his residence at Venice he introduced there, and wherever his influence extended, the custom of celebrating the 29th of April as the anniversary of Catherine's death. On that day preachers pronounced her eulogy, her portrait was exhibited and decorated with a profusion of flowers, formed into crosses, bouquets, wreaths and crowns, this being the favourite manner of honouring the memory of her who in her lifetime was such a lover of flowers. And, says Caffarini, it was fitting that it should be so, for the Cross of Jesus was the flowery couch of her love; she was destined to collect a multitude of souls as a nosegay of sweet flowers to offer to God; her own words and works were like so many bouquets, and she herself blossomed in the Eternal Paradise in the month which is the season of flowers. For sixteen consecutive years he preached on this festival; and during one Lent we are assured that he preached daily, explaining the Gospel of the day, and illustrating it by examples drawn from the life of Catherine. Not the least remarkable incident connected with these honours rendered to the Saint, was the extra-ordinary multiplication of her portraits. The faithful who attended the celebration of her festival demanded them in such numbers that a process was devised by which they were struck off from wooden blocks, in a manner which seems to have anticipated the invention of wood-engraving.

But in 1411 objections were made to these celebrations of the anniversary of a person not yet canonised, though it would seem that at that time such proceedings were very commonly permitted. However, the affair was referred to Francis Bembo, Bishop of Venice, and Legate of the Holy See; and an inquiry was instituted, in the course of which twenty-five witnesses were examined with all possible formality. The proceedings were not closed until the 5th of January, 1413; and the depositions of the witnesses form that celebrated *Process of Venice* so often quoted in the foregoing pages. The result of the investigation was entirely to exonerate the Friars from all blame in what they had done to honour the memory of the holy Virgin of Siena; and the depositions, thus carefully collected, were afterwards used in the Process of her canonisation. That event Caffarini did not live to witness, though he survived to an advanced age. His death took place in the year 1434, and the veneration with which he was regarded by his brethren is shown by the title of "Blessed," which is commonly prefixed to his name.

Of the religious Sisters of St. Catherine, and their history subsequent to her death, few particulars have, unfortunately, been preserved. Those who were left in Rome formed themselves into a Community, of whom Alexia was the first Superioress; but she did not survive her beloved friend and Mother more than two years, and was succeeded in the government of the little family by Lisa. They at first continued to live in the house in the Via del Papa where the Saint had died, but some years later were transferred to a more suitable residence; and the Community, which now occupies the convent of Santa Caterina, not far from that of San Domenica e Sisto in Magnanapoli, derives its origin from St Catherine's own religious daughters.

The two worthy citizens of Siena, Master Matthew of the Misericordia, and Ser Christofano di Gano, must not be dismissed without a word. Of the first, we read that he continued the same kind, affable, and generous friend he had ever shown himself; regarding hospitality to the children and disciples of the holy virgin Catherine as a sacred duty. Anything that had belonged to her he gathered up and kept as a precious relic, were it no more than the smallest particle of her dress. He somehow got possession of one of her fingers, the index finger of the right hand; and placing it in a silver reliquary, he gave it to the Church of San Domenico. He survived until the arrival of Pope Gregory XII. at Siena, which was in the September of the year 1407, loving nothing so much as to speak of the virtues and recall the sayings of his beloved Mother. Being taken with his last sickness, he devoutly received all the Sacraments of Holy Church, and the Indulgence of which the Saint had received a grant from Pope Gregory XI. in favour of him and of seventy-seven of her other disciples. As to Ser Christofano, he lived to fill the important office of Lord Defender of the republic of Siena, and an excellent magistrate he no doubt made. This was in 1383 and 1384; and six years later his wife and all his seven children died of the plague within a few months of one another. After this domestic calamity, which freed him from those worldly shackles he had been half unwilling to assume, the old inclination revived in his heart to have done with the world altogether, and to seek a more perfect life. So, on the 14th of August, 1391, he took the habit of the oblates of St. Augustine, and dedicated himself, like a brave man as he was, to the service of the sick in the hospital of La Scala, where his exemplary character and business-like habits eventually procured for him the honourable office of Chancellor. The habit of these Brethren of La Scala was black, adorned at the side with the badge of a red ladder. And so our good Christofano appears in the painting which may still be seen in the "Pellegrinajo," as it is called ; that is, the hall where the pilgrims going to Rome are lodged and entertained. But besides his work in the hospital, there was another work to which Christofano devoted himself, and at which he continued to labour until his dying day. Conjointly with Master Paul Rector of the hospital, and Nicolas de Benvenuto, Archbishop of Ragusa, he tried to procure from Gregory XII. the canonisation of the Saint. The Archbishop had received from Christofano a copy of his Latin translation of the Dialogue, which so enchanted him that he never rested till he had translated it into Sclavonic for the benefit of his flock ; and leaving Ragusa, he came to Siena, where Gregory then was, with the express purpose of petitioning for Catherine's canonisation. Gregory was fully as devout to her memory as any of those who pressed him with their solicitations ; but at that time the grievous troubles of the Schism prevented the accomplishment of their wishes, and the Archbishop, dying at Siena, was buried in the church of San Domenico, "just on that spot," says Caffarini in the third part of his Supplement, "where Catherine had received from our Lord the gift of His Heart," leaving to Caffarini, with the permission of the Pope, all his writings, in which he had collected many things relative to the Saint.

The various devices conceived by Christofano for keeping up the memory of St. Catherine and promoting devotion to her were truly admirable. His veneration for her had first made him turn author; it now equally prompted him to become a patron of the arts. "Out of reverence to the said Catherine," he says, "I had her painted in the Duomo, near the Campanile, in the chapel of St. James Interciso, whom I also had painted there. I had a great devotion to St. James, because, when I went into Lombardy on the affairs of a certain senator, I saw him painted in a chapel. So I had him painted at Armaiuolo, in a corner of our vineyard, among other figures that are there." In no degree discouraged in the sacred duty he had imposed on himself, of obtaining the exaltation of his holy Mistress to the altars of the Church, he kept up an incessant agitation on the subject by means of letters addressed now to Caffarini, at Venice, and now to Stephen Maconi, who, as Prior-General of the Carthusians, had been called into Austria on the affairs of his Order. Christofano urged him to return, that with their united prayers and representations they might move the heart of the Pope. He was, however, doomed to disappointment. Gregory left Siena for Lucca ; and poor Christofano fell sick of a painful and tedious malady. Before he died, however, he had the consolation of once more greeting his old friend Stephen, who at last returned to Siena. " When Christofano saw him " (says the author of Stephen's life), " he embraced him lovingly, and exclaimed, ' Thou hast come at last, O Father, dear above all other friends : therefore I give thanks to God that He has heard my prayer, and suffered me once more to see thee ere I depart out of this life.' Then Stephen began to speak of the goodness of God, and the protection which the Seraphic Virgin of Siena displayed towards her sons who were still living in the world. As he spoke, Christofano's soul seemed to overflow with sweetness, and raising himself a little in his bed, he cast up his eyes to heaven, as though answering God Who called him, and so peacefully expired—all who stood by being full of wonder to see that the soul of Christofano should have been thus detained in his body, until he could die in the presence of his beloved Stephen." [1]

Francis Malevolti, concerning whom the reader will remember that Catherine had uttered a prophecy, and who in spite of his immense veneration for the holy virgin, had never, during her life, entirely overcome the fluctuations of his soul between the movements of nature and the pleadings of divine grace, shall tell his own story in his own words, for none can tell it better.

[1] Vit. Steph. Mac., lib. iv. cap. I.

On the occasion when some of the Sisters of Penance had complained of him and his want of perseverance in the ways of grace, Catherine had told them not to be troubled, for that the day would come when she would put such a yoke on his neck as he should never be able to shake off. When these words were spoken, both he and the Sisters standing by laughed merrily, having no notion what they might mean. He had at that time a wife and children, and seemed as unlikely a man to embrace a religious life as could well be imagined. "But after the holy virgin had departed to her Spouse," he says, "my wife and children also having paid the debt of nature, I found myself alone and free from all ties. I neither thought of, nor cared for the words above related ; but being alone, I found myself harassed by many who urged me again to enter into the state of matrimony. Nevertheless our Lord, Who would not that the words of His spouse should be falsified, found out a new way of binding me with the bonds she had foretold. One of my uncles, named Nicoluccio, who was considered to be a man of singular prudence, seeing my delight in horses and armour, said to me one day, 'Francesco, what do you intend to do? I should like you either to marry, or if that does not suit you, that you should do something else.' I asked him what he was thinking of, and he replied, 'I should like, as you are so fond of arms and horses, that you should become a Knight of St. John, and so indulge your taste without risking your salvation.' It was wonderful he should say this, and quite beyond human calculation, for he was not at all given to spiritual things, but much involved in worldly affairs. However, though I had never thought of the matter before, I at once gave my consent. It was agreed I should go to Genoa where the Chapter of the Knights was then being celebrated ; and there I was unanimously accepted, and a commission appointed to bestow on me the knightly dignity and the habit of the Order. I returned first to Siena, however, and busied myself collecting horses, arms, and other things required for my purpose. All being concluded, it came to the very day preceding that on which I was to be made a Knight. In the middle of the night as I lay on my bed, (I cannot say whether I was awake or asleep), behold, the glorious virgin Catherine appeared to me, and touching me, she said: 'Rise, negligent that thou art, and sleep no longer; seest thou not that I have found a way of breaking all thy bonds? and still thou followest nothing but the vanities of the world. Rise, and seek thy companion, Neri di Landoccio, and go both of you to the house of the Brethren of Mount Olivet, and there thou shalt without opposition be received. Dost thou not remember how I once said to thee that when thou shouldst think me to be far away from thee I should be nearer to thee than ever, and subject thy neck to such a yoke that thou shouldst never be able to shake it off?' When I answered: 'O my mother, do you not know how many and great things these monks do, and what long trials they require before they consent to receive any one into their Order?' and with many other words I tried to resist the Holy Spirit, and the glorious handmaid of Christ. But she said, 'If you do not fulfil what I have told you, you will not be able to accomplish what you now purpose doing; but will fall into great dangers,' and with that she disappeared. Now, when I came to myself and recalled what had passed, I was filled suddenly and miraculously with the most ardent desire of taking the habit of these brethren, so that the remainder of the night seemed intolerably long. When day dawned I went at once outside the city to Neri, whom I found already risen, for, as he afterwards told me, the same holy virgin had appeared to him, and had said, 'Expect thy friend Francesco Malevolti, and go with him to the house of Mount Olivet.' This Neri was at that time living near the city in the habit, and leading the life of a hermit. So we went both together to the monastery aforesaid, which is about fourteen miles from Siena, and is the principal house of the Order; where in the absence of the Abbot-General, the Prior of the house and the ancient Fathers, understanding my petition, with one accord agreed to receive me." After this nothing remained for Francesco save to return to the city in order to sell his horses and other property; and returning to the convent, he at once entered on the new life to which he had been so strangely called, and in which he persevered happily for many years, and died a holy death.

It remains to speak of Catherine's three secretaries, Neri, Stephen, and Barduccio Canigiani. Barduccio after her death, became a secular priest. "In her last moments," says Raymund, "Catherine enjoined him to attach himself to me and place himself under my direction; she did it without doubt because she was aware that he would not live long: in fact, a short time after he was attacked with consumption, and although he appeared at first to be convalescent, it soon became evident that there was no hope of his recovery. Fearing that the air of Rome was hurtful to him, I sent him to Siena, where he slept peacefully in the Lord. Those who witnessed his death, declare that at his last moments, he looked up to heaven smiling, and gave up his soul with such lively tokens of joy, that death itself could not efface their impression from his countenance: he probably saw her whom he had loved during life with such purity of heart, come forth to meet him, in the glory of triumph." His death took place little more than a year after that of his saintly Mother. Neri di Landoccio, to whom the merit certainly belongs of having been the means of introducing almost all his fellow-disciples to the Saint's acquaintance, returned from Naples to Rome in time to assist at her funeral, and witnessed all the wonderful events which then took place. He has told his own tale of sorrow and bereavement in two poems, in which he embalmed the holy memory of his saintly Mother, and gave vent to all the emotions which such an event would naturally elicit in his sensitive and loving heart. "O Spouse!" he exclaims, "elected to the throne of the blessed; O name, at the naming of which my heart is breaking, O refreshment in every grievous loss! Tell me what shall I do? for thy departure fills my afflicted heart with new and redoubled sorrows. Tell me who will now deliver me from an evil end? who will guard me from delusion? who will now point out to me the upward path? who will any longer comfort me in my troubles? who will any more say to me, 'Thou art not going on well'? who will encourage me? who will reprove me now? All these things make the tears to flow down my cheeks, until thou assurest me of that which thou didst promise me at Lucca."

Neri was not at once able to retire to his hermitage. He had hurried from Naples to attend the funeral before his business there was complete, and had to return thither immediately afterwards, for it was there he received the letter of Nigi di Doccio which has been already quoted. As soon as he could, he made his way back to Siena, in order to commence that solitary life to which his own inclination, no less than the Saint's commands, invited him.

His hermitage was outside the Porta Nuova of Siena. Here he gave himself up to a life of prayer and austerity, not however entirely neglecting literature and poetry. A letter followed him from Naples from his friend Giunta di Grazia, about a book which he had lent him, which was badly written and incorrect, begging him to procure a better one, and also to return "*quello pezo di Dante,*" which Giunta had left with him. In 1391 Stephen Maconi writes to him, "Those verses you sent me written with your own hand I have had copied on parchment in fine letters, well illuminated; and I gave them to the Duke's High Councillors, who were much pleased, and commended them greatly." No doubt these were some of the verses already quoted, or others on the same subject, for we learn from Caffarini in the third part of his "Supplement," that "he made many rhymes and devout songs in praise of the holy virgin, which *he wrote out with his own hand, and distributed to his friends.*" All his poems, however, were not on St. Catherine, and in the Bodleian Library is preserved at this time a MS. poem of his, a legend of St. Giosaffa, written in *ottava rima.* But besides his poems, he busied himself in other works connected with the memory of the Saint. Caffarini tells us that it was chiefly at his solicitation that F. Raymund wrote the Legend in Latin, and when finished, Neri, at the request of Caffarini, undertook and began its translation into Italian; but dying before the completion of the work, it was finished by another hand, Neri's translation only going as far as the fourth chapter of the second part.

By what has been already said, the reader will have gathered some idea of Neri's natural disposition. St. Catherine's letters have shown his habitual tendency to religious despondency, and in the retirement of his hermitage this constitutional infirmity at one time assumed an alarming form. For two years his dear friend Stephen received no tidings from him, and at last understood that the cause had been a temporary access of mental malady. Family troubles, and the threatened war between Siena and Florence, had come to the aid of long austerities, and for a time broke down the fine mind and sensitive organisation. "I hear from Leoncino," writes Stephen, "that you have been *alienato;*" but in his next letter he says, "It seems by your letter written on the Purification that you have recovered from that accidental derangement" (*alienazione*). In fact it was only a temporary attack, nor do we hear that it ever returned. For Neri was by no means a fanciful hypochondriac. Caffarini calls him a "*Vir mirabilis,*" and even in his hermitage he was looked up to as a man of influence and weight. Everybody wrote to him and consulted him—Maconi, Caffarini, Francis Malevolti, and the Carthusians of Lucca. It would seem he was not always very prompt in answering their letters, but in spite of that, they all looked up to him, and valued him as an adviser. His chief friends, however, were the Olivetan Monks, then enjoying a wide repute as living in great fervour and observance. He was also inseparably united with Gabriel Piccolomini (who with him had been an eyewitness of that prodigy described by F. Raymund, when St. Catherine fell into the fire and received no injury), and with his brother poet, Anastagio da Montalcino, whose poem on the Saint, written in her lifetime, has been so frequently quoted. Neri lived to a great age, and in his last sickness, out of motives of humility, he caused himself to be removed from his hermitage to the hospital of La Scala. There he placidly expired in 1406. We are half reluctant to quote the letter in which Luca di Benvenuto, one of the Olivetan Monks, communicates to a friend the intelligence of Neri's death. In it the tragic mingles with the comic, and the latter, it must be owned, prevails :

"Luca di Benvenuto to Ser Jacomo.

"*Ave Maria.*

"Dearest Father in Christ,—My negligence—I need say no more—but yet with grief and sorrow I write to you, how our Father, and our comfort, and our help, and our counsel, and our support, and our refreshment, and our guide, and our master, and our receiver, and our preparer, and our waiter, and our visitor, and he who thought for us, and our delight, and our only good, and our entertainer : and his meekness, and his holy life, and his holy conversation, and his holy teachings, and all his holy works, and his holy words, and his holy sayings, and his holy investigations. Alas, miserable ones ! alas, poor wretches ! alas, orphans ! where shall we go, to whom shall we have recourse? Alas ! well may we lament, since all our good is departed from us ! I will say no more, for I am not worthy to remember him, yet I beg of you that as it is the will of God, you will not let yourself be killed by the news; know then—alas ! I don't know how I can tell you—alas ! my dear Ser Jacomo; alas ! my Father and my Brother, I know not what to do, for I have lost all I cared for. I do not see you, and I know not how you are. Know, then, that our love and our Father—alas ! alas ! Neri di Landoccio, alas !—took sick on the 8th of March, Monday night, about daybreak, on account of the great cold,—and the cough increasing, he could not get over it, alas ! He passed out of this life, confessed, and with all the Sacraments of Holy Church, on the 12th of March, was buried by the Brethren of Mount Olivet outside the *Porta Tufi*, and died in the morning, at the Aurora, at break of day.[1] I know there is no need to recommend to you his blessed soul, and I, miserable as I am, am left to dispense all he left. I grieve you were not present at his end, and to undertake this business. It is left to me that you should have something; I don't know if it is the best, but I will keep your things, unless I die. Pray for Neri's

---

[1] Luca, as will be observed, buries him first, and makes him die afterwards. We endeavour to be literal, however, in the translation.

soul, and for me, Luca. And also to you, Ser Christofano, I must say something, but what I say to one I say to the other, may God keep us all in His grace! I beg of you, for God's sake, send me word how you are. Your parents are well. I need not say what a loss Neri is, you know it well. After Lent come, or send me word what I am to do with your things.—Your miserable

" LUCA DI BENVENUTO.

" *P.S.*—I, Luca, have given to Ceccanza . . . two new Capuces and a gown.

"To Neri de le Cancella, I gave a foot cover, and a pair of new stockings, and a pair of shoes, and a pair of leather stockings.

"To Monna Caterina (the Tertiary), I gave three chest preservers, and two old ones, and a pair of stockings, and socks, and also some old foot covers very much torn, and a gown, also torn; and the old cloak, and an old grey petticoat (!) and two old feather pillows, and a broken bed, and a pair of spectacles, and a shirt, and an old chair.

"To Monna Nera, a pair of torn sheets and a bed, very much broken, and a gown, mended and patched.

"To Dominic di Lorenzo, an old shirt.

"To Cecco, a sheath, and his spectacles.

"To Maltra, 10 soldi.

"To the Friars of Monte Oliveto, 62 soldi.

"To Tonghino, a bag, and an old torn towel."

In this very curious distribution of goods, the Friars of Monte Oliveto certainly came best off; but we must not be malicious. Neri left to them all his books, writings, and notes, as well regarding the holy virgin as on other matters. A picture of the Saint which he had caused to be painted, came into the possession of Padre Antonio Benedetto, of the same Order, and he made a graceful present of it to Master Paul, Rector of the Hospital of La Scala, and an old disciple of the Saint.

One member, and one only, of the little family remains to be spoken of, and we have reserved him to the last, because there is more to tell about him, and because he claims perhaps a larger share in our interest than any of his companions. First then, let us hear in what terms Stephen Maconi pours out his grief for their late bereavement in writing to his old friend Neri. The letter is dated from Rome, February 18th, 1381; whence we find that Stephen remained in that city for ten months after St. Catherine's death. Its style contrasts forcibly enough with the light-hearted and careless letters of former days, and tells of a blow which had struck to the heart; one of those touches by which God works out the sanctity of His servants, as the master sculptor fashions his statues by repeated blows of chisel and hammer. "Your return to Rome," he says, "was anxiously looked for by me, your useless and miserable brother. For as it has pleased the Divine Goodness so severely to punish my ingratitude, depriving you as well as me of that precious treasure which I did not rightly know or value, I desired to find myself once more with you, above all our brethren in Christ, that I might pour out my heart to so loving a brother, and confer with you on many things. But it seems that God did not so permit. Then I hoped to have met you at Siena, but that also was not allowed: and not only have I been deprived of your presence, but I have not even deserved to receive a short letter from you. Perhaps our good God wished to deprive me of the presence of all those with whom I thought to have taken a little comfort, in order that I might the better draw near to Him the Creator of all, and that without the intervention of any creature. In His inestimable charity may He grant me the grace to do this, and to do it manfully."

He met with no small difficulty on the part of his family to his resolution of becoming a Carthusian; but at last, some time in the April of 1381, he commenced his novitiate at Pontignano. During the whole of his time of probation he steadily refused to see any of his friends, but his Superiors insisted on his relaxing this rule in favour of St. Catherine's disciples. He wrote to Neri a few weeks after he had entered the monastery, beginning his letter, dated the 30th of May, "To my sweetest and most beloved Brother in Christ, *and in the holy memory.*"

"BELOVED BROTHER,—I write to inform you with great joy that our loving Lord in His goodness and not for my merits has cast the eye of His mercy on my misery, and has deigned that I should receive here the holy habit.   I write that you may share the joy with which my heart is full.   I do not relate the how and the why, only this I must tell you that our venerable Mother has amply fulfilled to me what she promised at the time of her happy death, that she would be more helpful after she was gone than ever she had been in life.   And though it would have been very sweet to have seen and spoken with you, yet I hold your peace of mind as dear as my own.   So I will not take amiss what, by God's grace, you are doing, since I firmly hope, as you say, that He, in His mercy, by the merits of the Blood of the Lamb, and the intercession of Mary (and of her in whom we are so closely bound together), will grant us the grace to see each other again in life eternal, provided that we follow on our way with manly hearts, without stopping or turning backwards.   May He grant it Who is blessed for ever.   Amen."

In December 1382 he writes again, no longer in the tone of a novice, for in fact, to his own great trouble, he had just been made Prior of Pontignano.

"DEAREST BROTHER IN JESUS CHRIST,—I shortly since received two letters from you, which were very welcome; reminding me of that holy time—by me so badly spent, so little understood or valued.   And not to be tedious I ask of you, my sweet brother, to have compassion on me, and help me with your prayers; and to pray that God will give me the grace to amend my life, and that I may remain His true servant to the end; and that the burden He has been pleased to lay on my shoulders (the office of Prior) I may know how to carry to His honour, and my own salvation.   When I took the holy habit, I thought, as I thanked God, to sing with the Psalmist, *Ecce elongavi fugiens et mansi in solitudine.*   But the spouse of obedience, which our holy Mother gave me, has chosen rather that I should sing, 'I am become, as it were, a beast of burden before Thee.'   So I must once more glory in the Cross of Christ, and rejoice in it, and desire nothing beside it. It would be a great happiness to speak to my dear brother, but not to write. I know I can be of no use to you because of my sins, yet I confess that I desire the salvation of all, and specially of those whom God has engrafted in the very centre of my heart."

We pass over a few years, and open another letter, written in 1391 by Maconi, then General of his Order, and just returned from a visitation of his convents, to Neri, who was recovering from a severe illness in his hermitage, brought on by excessive austerity. The letter is too long to quote, but he relates how he had been at Genoa 'and had dined there "with our common Father, Master Raymund, and Brother Thomas Antonio (Caffarini) and others, with many holy conversations on sweet subjects. . . . And our venerable Mother, Madonna Orietta Scotta, with great charity recognised me for her son, and many other things I could tell you which I doubt not you would like to hear." Who could doubt that Neri would indeed like to have heard of these things, and would read them with tears of tenderness, remembering the time when he and Stephen were lodging in Orietta's house with their holy Mother, and when both of them were restored to health by her in the long years that were past.

Stephen Maconi became celebrated after his entrance into religion for carrying on one of the Saint's good works with great success, namely, the reconciliation of enemies, and in this he was much assisted by F. William Flete. He never forgot his beloved Mother, but was always doing something to promote her honour— now sending a young man on pilgrimage to her tomb, who came back restored in body and soul, now agitating for her canonisation, now propagating copies of her life. He himself translated into Italian the *Leggenda Minore* of Caffarini, and sent a copy of it to the King of England. He always kept in his cell the gold reliquary containing the relics of many saints which had been given to St. Catherine at Avignon, and had been before her at the moment of her death. In little things and great he loved to keep alive her memory; and was particularly fond of *beans,* because they reminded him of a dinner he had had with her one Easter Day shortly before her death, when there was nothing else in the house, "for," says his biographer, Don Bartholomew, "the remembrance of that banquet stuck fast to the marrow of his spirit, so that when he was Superior he always adorned the table of his religious on Easter Day with the delicacy of beans; and the same pious custom flourished in several convents of the Order for many years."[1]

In 1401 he was elected General over that part of his Order which remained faithful to the obedience of Gregory XII., successor to Urban VI. The chief seat of this part of the Order was fixed in Austria, but when Gregory came to Siena, Stephen was summoned thither to join him, and accompanied him in many of his journeys. He exerted himself to induce the Pontiff to resign his dignity with a view to secure the peace of the Church; and what he advised, he himself put in practice; for going into France he succeeded in gathering together the disunited members of the Order; he induced Raymund Ferrer (brother to St. Vincent) who was General over the other half, to resign his office, doing the same himself; and so the two branches being reunited, elected a Superior who was accepted by all. This new General appointed Stephen his Vicar over all the convents of the Order in Italy, an office he held till his death. He resided at Pavia, at the splendid Certosa which had been founded in 1396 by Gian Galeazzo Visconti, in expiation of his crime in murdering his uncle and father-in-law, Bernabò Visconti, and all his family. The monastery of " Our Lady of Graces " is supposed to be the most splendid monastery in the world, though its splendour is rather that of a palace than a religious house. Here then Stephen Maconi spent the evening of his days, ever loving to speak of

---

[1] Either Don Bartholomew relates the circumstance of the bean banquet with several inaccuracies, or there were two such repasts. The one we have narrated (p. 176) took place in Siena on Ascension Day, 1373, before Stephen knew the Saint. Bartholomew places the scene of *his* story in Rome, on Easter Day, and very shortly before St. Catherine's death. However it may have been, the result was, that Stephen's Carthusian brethren always had beans to eat on Easter Day.

Catherine, and to repeat what he remembered of her instructions. Indeed, his biographer gives a sort of abstract of these instructions which the old man was accustomed to give to his monks. Towards the close of his life he became intimate with St. Bernardine of Siena, who was born in the very year of Catherine's death, and who delighted in nothing so much as to sit and hear Stephen pour out his recollections of their glorious fellow-citizen. And while Stephen found a sweet consolation mingled with sadness in thus dwelling on the memories of the past, the youthful friar felt his heart kindle as he listened, with holy emulation, and an increase of ardent charity.

Stephen died at Pavia on the 7th of August, 1424. At his last moments he repeated the verse *Maria, Mater gratiæ*, and then invoking the intercession of Catherine, he expired with her beloved name upon his lips.

And now our task is ended, and the time has come when to all these holy souls and loving hearts we must bid a last farewell. Not as the shadowless characters of a poem or drama have they come before us, the creatures of imagination demanding our sympathy with their fictitious sorrows and skilfully depicted passions. Far different from this has been our acquaintance with St. Catherine and her companions. For *she* is as truly a living and loving mother to us as any of the beings of flesh and blood by whom we are surrounded : and they who held her company, and who laid up for our benefit the treasures of their testimony, are our brethren and sisters also. There is between us the fellowship of sympathy : we understand their language, and they have opened to us their hearts.

Farewell, then, to you, faithful Lisa, and Alexia, beloved and privileged to the very end ; farewell, Barduccio, found worthy to stand by thy Mother in her last combat and to hear her call thee "Son ;"[1] to Neri, with his grave and pallid brow, the inspired poet, and the true-hearted friend ; to Stephen, the careless one, but the best-beloved of all ; to Matthew and Christofano, in whose company we have seemed to go about the streets of the old city,

____

[1] See p. 243.

and to mingle in all the ways and "doings" of their blameless lives; to each and all of you, farewell !

Farewell to all the scenes amid which we have seen you passing for so many a day; to the oaks of Lecceto, the vineyards of Montalcino, and the chestnut woods of Monte Amiata; to the streets and the churches which once you peopled in the grand old days of Siena's freedom; to the graves in San Domenico, where so many of you are laid to rest. It is well with you now, for the time of bitter separation is over, and the hour of reunion has come. We envy not your happiness, though we would gladly share it; and the thought of you and of "the holy memory" will help us through many a troublous day. Five long centuries have passed, since all of you, under the guidance of a Saint, fought out your combat and went to your reward. You lived human lives of common vicissitude, and were made of common mould like us; you were weak, and you stumbled; you fell, and you rose again. And now, all is over, and you are reunited with your Mother in the Eternal Presence; and you understand the tangled web of your past lives, and the meaning of all that once seemed so strange. As we think of you and think of her, time seems to vanish "like a needle's point," and we, too, look to a day not far distant, when parting shall be no more; and falling from the heavens like the echo of church bells, we seem to hear a chant in which your voices mingle with the voices of others who have gone before:

"*Absterget Deus omnem lacrymam ab oculis Sanctorum; et jam non erit amplius neque luctus, neque clamor, sed nec ullus dolor; quoniam priora transierunt.*"

CHAPTER XII.

URBAN VI. died in 1389, and was succeeded in the line of the Roman Pontiffs by Boniface IX. and Innocent VII., both of whose Pontificates were of short duration. On the death of Innocent in 1406, Cardinal Angelo Corario of Venice, titular Patriarch of Constantinople, was elected Pope under the title of Gregory XII. The Antipope Clement VII. continued to reign at Avignon until 1394, and on his death the Cardinals of his obedience elected as his successor Cardinal Peter de Luna, who took the title of Benedict XIII. Both Gregory and Benedict were elected by their respective partisans under the promise of abdicating the Papal dignity, should a similar resignation be obtained from the rival Pontiff. The sincere desire on the part of all good men on either side was to extinguish the unhappy schism; and it was with this view and intention that in 1409 the Cardinals of both obediences assembled in council at Pisa, to confer on the necessary steps to be taken for restoring the peace of the Church. Their decision, unfortunately, only introduced greater disorder: for they took on themselves to declare both the reigning Popes deposed, and proceeded to elect a successor to the vacant dignity. The Pontiff thus irregularly elected, took the name of Alexander V., but dying almost immediately, a fresh election was made at Bologna, the newly-chosen Pope being known as John XXIII. As, however, neither Gregory nor Benedict acknowledged the Cardinals as possessing the lawful authority to depose them, this ill-advised proceeding only increased the existing disorders, by adding a *third* claimant to the chair of

St. Peter.   This miserable state of things lasted until 1417, when a General Council of the Church assembled at Constance.   The voluntary abdication of Gregory XII. having been first obtained, the two other pretenders to the Papacy were deposed ; and the election of a Pope, the validity of whose title should be universally acknowledged, became at last possible.   On the 11th of November 1417, Otho Colonna was accordingly elected, taking the title of Martin V. ; and thus Christendom was once more united under the obedience of one Supreme Head.   The man who had probably the greatest share in bringing about this happy result was the Blessed John Dominic, then Cardinal Archbishop of Ragusa.   He had already laboured nobly in carrying out one of St. Catherine's great desires, the reform of the Dominican Order ; and it was his lot to be the chief instrument in realising another, by restoring peace to the Church.

But more than this, the Fathers of Constance, by the election of a *Roman* Pontiff, had brought about the permanent restoration of the Holy See to Rome.   They also entered vigorously on the work of reform : in their 43rd Session they published many ordinances, having for their sole object the reform of the clergy ; nor did they separate without declaring that another Council should shortly be called, for the express purpose of carrying out this great work more effectually.   St. Catherine therefore had not lived in vain ; the cause for which she had given her life was vindicated before the eyes of Christendom ; and it is little wonder that Pope Martin and his successors should have been besieged by petitions from every quarter, to delay no longer in raising to the altars of the Church the holy maiden of Siena.

But this glory was reserved to a Pope, her countryman by birth, and the member of one of those noble families of Siena whose name had been borne by more than one of her disciples. Æneas Sylvius Piccolomini was probably the greatest scholar of his time, and had received the laurel crown from the hands of the Emperor Frederick III.   He had travelled through every European country, including Scotland, whither he was sent as ambassador to King James I. from the Council of Basle.   He had filled the post of Secretary to the two Popes Eugenius IV. and Nicholas V.; he was created Bishop of Siena and Cardinal of Santa Sabina by Calixtus III.; and finally, in 1458, he was elected successor to the last-named Pontiff, taking the title of Pius II.

In the year following his election Pius II. came on a visit to Siena, where he remained two months, during which time he lavished favours on his countrymen with a liberal hand. Corsigni, his native place, was given the dignity of an Episcopal city, and received the new name of *Pienza;* the Pope bestowed the golden rose on the Signoria of Siena; he made several Sienese Cardinals; he raised the See of Siena to the rank of an Archbishopric; he restored to the nobles their municipal rights; and last, but not least, he resolved on the Canonisation of St. Catherine. Few contrasts could be greater than those which existed between these two illustrious fellow-citizens, or their respective claims to celebrity; between the ambassador of Frederick, and the ambassadress of Gregory; between the scholar of the Renaissance, and the author of the *Dialogo;* between the letters of Æneas Sylvius, and the letters of St. Catherine. Yet there was one point of closest sympathy between them, and the Pope who was to decree to Catherine the supreme honours of the Church, was one whose Pontificate was to be spent in strenuous, but unavailing, efforts to organise a fresh Crusade.

In fact, at that juncture, the rapid advance of the Turkish arms was threatening the safety of all Europe. In 1453 Constantinople had fallen, and the boundaries of the empire now began to be assaulted. True to their traditions, the Popes, as the Fathers of Christendom, had continued to warn the Christian sovereigns of their danger, and had laboured vigorously to concert measures of defence. Two men only had responded to their call; Huniades, the brave Regent of Hungary, who repulsed Mahomet II. from the walls of Belgrade; and George Castriot, better known as Scanderbeg, who chased the Turks out of Epirus, and restoring the independence of his native country, became its prince. For many years he upheld the cause of Christendom unsupported by any other allies than the Roman Pontiffs. "Had the efforts of Calixtus III. been seconded by the princes of Christendom," says Platina, the contemporary and historian of that Pope, "the success of the Turks would have been rendered impossible ; but in spite of the fair words which they gave to his ambassadors, none of them showed themselves ready to act, when there was question of their sacrificing their selfish interests."

Pius II., before his elevation to the chair of St. Peter, had taken an active part in all the measures concerted by the Sovereign Pontiffs for the defence of Christendom. He now devoted to the same cause all the talents and energies with which he was so remarkably endowed. He had conceived the design of calling a European Congress at Mantua for the purpose of forming a common league against the infidels; and on leaving Siena, he repaired to that city and opened the assembly in person, delivering an address so eloquent and touching as to move his audience to tears. The insane spirit of intestine dissension hindered the realisation of his hopes. Civil wars broke out simultaneously in Spain, England, Germany, and Italy ; and though the Crusade was indeed proclaimed, the Pope was left to carry it on as best he could, unaided by a single European sovereign.

From Mantua he again returned to Siena, where he made a long sojourn, receiving there a crowd of embassies from the afflicted provinces of the East, who in the moment of supreme anguish looked to the Vicar of Christ as to their only hope. There was a singular suitability in the fact that these dying echoes of the crusading war-cry should have been heard in the native city of St. Catherine ; nor was the coincidence lost on Pius II. On his return to Rome he took measures for proceeding without delay to her solemn canonisation ; and the necessary formalities having been concluded, the Bull which raised her to the Altars of the Church was finally published on the 29th of June, being the Feast of the Holy Apostles, 1461. To mark his special devotion to the Saint of Siena, the Pope drew up her Office with his own pen. Nor is this the only composition in which Pius II. has celebrated her praises ; for besides the hymns of that Office which were written by him, we possess another little poem in which he may be said to have briefly epitomised her history: and it is worthy of notice that in this poem every one of the special and supernatural graces of St. Catherine's life are distinctly named: as her holy Espousals; the exchange of her heart with that of Christ; her mystic death and return to life, and her reception of the Stigmata.

The Pontificate of Pius II. terminated three years later, whilst he was engaged in a last supreme effort to organise the Crusade. He had succeeded in gaining to the cause Philip, Duke of Burgundy, the Doge of Venice, and several of the Italian rulers; and in the month of October 1463, he published an Encyclical letter addressed to all Christian princes and prelates, declaring his intention of proceeding in the year following to Ancona, where the fleet of the allies was then preparing to assemble, and of himself accompanying it to the shores of Greece and Asia. He kept his word, arriving at Ancona about the middle of July. There, however, he was attacked with fever, and expired on the 14th of August, 1464, and with him expired also the last hopes of the Crusade.

In the Piccolomini library, attached to the Duomo of Siena, may still be seen the ten grand frescoes, in the execution of which Pinturicchio is said to have been assisted by the youthful Raphael, representing the chief events in the life of this celebrated Pope. Among them we see the Proclamation of the Crusade at Mantua, the Canonisation of St. Catherine, and the preparations for the departure of the fleet from Ancona; and thus the name of the Saint in whose heart survived the spirit which had animated the first Crusaders, is indissolubly linked with the memory of the Pope by whose lips the holy war was for the last time proclaimed.

In the Bull of St. Catherine's canonisation the first Sunday in May was assigned as the day on which her feast was to be celebrated. In 1630, however, by a decree of Pope Urban VIII., this was changed to the 30th of April: the 29th of that month (on which day her death actually took place) being already occupied by the Feast of St. Peter Martyr. The same Pontiff brought to a close a vexatious controversy which had been raised on the subject of the Saint's stigmas, by declaring them to have been "not bloody, but luminous." This declaration was in exact conformity with the narrative of Blessed Raymund; and the lessons of the Office, as approved by Pope Urban, so commemorate the fact. At a later period Pope Benedict XIII. granted to the whole Dominican Order, as well as to all the clergy of Tuscany, an Office of the Stigmas of St. Catherine; the 3rd of April being set apart to be kept as a feast in their honour. On the Thursday before Quinquagesima Sunday was formerly kept the commemoration of her holy Espousals; but this has been merged in the Feast of her Translation, which is now celebrated on that day, a new Office of the Translation having been granted to the Order by Pope Pius IX. in the year 1855. A few years later an additional honour was rendered to the Saint by the same holy Pontiff, who, by a decree dated April 13th, 1866, declared the Seraphic virgin, St. Catherine of Siena, secondary Patroness of the city of Rome; and her feast was thenceforth ordered to be celebrated throughout the Order with a solemn Octave.

THE END.

ON CONSUMMATED PERFECTION.

A brief Dialogue by St. Catherine of Siena.[1]

A CERTAIN soul being one day illuminated by a ray of light received from the Author of Life, entered into the consciousness of her own misery and weakness, that is to say, of her ignorance and natural propensity to sin. Borne on still further to contemplate something of the greatness of her God, of His Wisdom, Power, and Goodness, and all the other perfections of His Divine Majesty, she perceived with great clearness how absolutely just and necessary it is that He should be served and honoured with all possible perfection and sanctity. It is *just*, because He is the Creator and Lord of the universe, and has created all things, that all may after their manner incessantly praise His holy name and be directed to His glory ; therefore it is but right and fitting that the servant full of respect towards his Lord should faithfully serve Him and dutifully obey Him. She saw that it is *necessary*, because the good God has been pleased to make man for Himself, a rational creature, composed of body and soul, on this condition, that, if he shall make good use of his free will, and persevere in fidelity to Him until death, he shall be rewarded with an eternal life, rich in every manner of blessing, to which he can in no other way attain. But, notwithstanding this condition of their being, she saw that few indeed are those who fulfil their duties and therefore very few who will be saved ; for nearly all " seek the things which are their own ; not the things

---

1 The original Italian Text of this Treatise is not now in existence ; that published by Gigli being a translation from the Latin Copy preserved in the Vatican Library.

which are Jesus Christ's" (Phil. ii. 21). She saw besides that the life of man is very short, and the hour and moment which will close the brief time in which it is possible for him to gain merit, very uncertain ; that, in the future life, those rewards and punishments will be given to each one in just retribution by an inevitable and irrevocable sentence, which he shall have merited by the tenor of his past life ; and that thenceforward there shall be no more escape from hell for ever ! She saw further, that, though many discourse much and in various ways of the virtues by which God may be faithfully honoured and served, yet the capacity of the reasonable creature is so limited, the intellect so obtuse, the memory so weak, that it can neither apprehend many things, nor faithfully retain those which it has apprehended ; and therefore, that though many are continually trying with all eagerness to instruct themselves, there are very few who arrive at that perfection of life with which God both ought to be and must be served. She saw that almost every one was on this account disquieted by a thousand cares and fluctuating amid a thousand agitations of spirit ; and so living in a state of extreme peril for the soul. At the sight of all these things, that soul was deeply moved ; then with a sudden resolution she prostrated herself before our Lord, and with vehement desire and love besought His Divine Majesty that He would be pleased to teach her some brief rules of perfection in which might be condensed all the truths taught both by the Holy Scriptures and by all kinds of spiritual writings ; by the observance of which God might be served and honoured in a fitting manner, and men might lead so holy and perfect a life, that, after passing through this brief and miserable mortality, they might attain the immortal happiness prepared for them in Paradise. And God, who never fails to accomplish those holy desires He puts into the heart, rapt her in an ecstasy, and making Himself present to her spirit, thus spoke to her :—"My Beloved, these desires are above all things pleasing unto Me ; and My inclination to satisfy thee is stronger than thy greatest longings to be satisfied. It is My good pleasure, since thou so wishest, to pour out upon thee all those favours that may be necessary, or useful, or even helpful for thy eternal salvation. Listen then, and fix thy mind on what I am about to tell thee. I, the ineffable Truth, condescending to thy request, will briefly explain to thee that which fully contains within itself the sum of all virtues, and the most sublime and perfect sanctity; which comprehends in itself the teaching of all the masters of the spiritual life and the volumes of the Divine Scriptures; so that, if thou wilt behold thyself therein as in a mirror; and wilt persevere in conforming thy practice to it, thou shalt arrive at the perfect fulfilment of all that is contained whether clearly or obscurely in the Holy Books, and shalt be made worthy to enjoy henceforward a perpetual peace and an ineffable and continual joy. Know, therefore, that the salvation of My servants and all their perfection depends upon this one thing, that they do in all things My will only; and to that end that every moment of their life they use every effort to seek Me alone, to honour Me alone, to please Me alone. The more diligently they apply themselves to this, the nearer do they approach perfection; because by this means they draw nearer to Me, in Whom by pre-eminence all perfections dwell. But, that thou mayest better understand this sublime truth which I have laid open to thee in few words, look upon the face of My Christ, in whom I am well pleased. He annihilated Himself by taking the form of a servant and being made in the likeness of sinners, that you, who were buried in the thickest darkness and had utterly forsaken the way of truth, might be illuminated with His words, His example, the splendour of His Divine light, and be brought back to the right path. Observe that He continued in one unceasing exercise of obedience even unto death to teach you that your salvation entirely depends on a firm and efficacious resolution to do My will alone. And whoever will diligently examine and meditate upon His life and doctrine, will see clearly that all perfection and sanctity consists in nothing else than in persevering obedience to My Will. Therefore does He, your Divine Leader, repeat so often : " Not every one that saith to Me Lord, Lord, shall enter into the kingdom of heaven ; but he that doth the will of My Father who is in heaven" (St. Matt. vii. 21).   And it is not without reason that He twice repeats "Lord," since all the transitory conditions of persons in the world may be reduced to two kinds, religious and secular; and He desires to signify by this double repetition, that no one, of whatsoever condition he may be, can attain eternal beatitude by rendering Me any sort of external homage, if he does not also do in all things My Divine Will.   So in another place He says: "I came down from heaven, not to do My own will, but the will of Him that sent Me" (S. John vi. 38); and in another place: "My meat is to do the will of Him that sent Me;" and further on: "Not My will but Thine be done;" and finally: "As the Father hath given Me commandment, so do I." (S. John iv. 34; S. Luke xxii. 42; S. John xiv. 31.)   If thou desirest, therefore, in imitation of thy Saviour, to perform perfectly My Will, in which all thy happiness consists, it is necessary that thou shouldst make no account at all of thine own will, but that thou shouldst contradict and crush it in all things, until at last it dies within thee.   The more utterly thou diest to thyself, the more perfectly shalt thou live in Me; and the more thou dost empty thy heart of all which is thine own, the more abundantly will I fill it with that which is Mine."

Now when that soul had heard these most salutary doctrines of truth, she replied full of joy :—"It rejoices me more than I am able to express that Thou hast been pleased to instruct Thy most humble servant; and, as much as in me lies, I render thanks for it to Thy most gracious Majesty.   Truly, as far as I can comprehend with my limited understanding, the thing cannot be otherwise than as Thou hast taught me and so well explained by the example of my blessed Saviour.   For Thou, being the highest good and the only good, Who can'st not will sin, but only that which is just and right, I must infallibly do all that ought to be done if I fulfil Thy Will; and I shall fulfil Thy Will if for Thy love I contradict my own, which Thou wilt not in any way constrain, but dost leave it perfectly free, that I, by voluntarily and constantly subjecting it to Thine, may become dearer and more full in Thy sight.   I desire greatly to begin to do that which Thou hast told me; but as yet I understand not well in what Thy Will is found, and by what faithful service I can best consecrate myself wholly to its fulfilment. I humbly pray Thee, therefore, if I be not importunate, and if my boldness trespass not on Thy condescension, to instruct me briefly upon this also, which above all things I desire to know."

And the Lord said to her:—"If thou seekest to know My Will, that thou mayest perfectly fulfil it, behold in one word that which it is:—that thou shouldst love Me to the utmost of thy power without ceasing; that thou shouldst love Me with all thy heart, and all thy soul, and all thy strength. It is on the performance of this precept that all thy perfection depends; and therefore it is written that 'the end of the commandment is charity,' and that 'love is the fulfilling of the law'" (1 Tim. i. 5 ; Rom. xiii. 10).

To these things that soul replied:—"I understand well that Thy Will and my perfection consists in loving Thee truly as I ought with ardent love and sovereign charity; but I comprehend not well how I am to do this. I beseech Thee, instruct me also briefly on this point."

And God said to her: " Hear then and be attentive with all the application of thy mind to what I am about to tell thee. If thou desirest to love Me perfectly, thou hast three things to do. First, thy will must be detached, removed, and separated from every carnal and earthly affection, so that in this life thou shouldst love nothing temporal, fading, and transitory, except for Me. And what is yet more and above all, thou must not love Me, or thy neighbour, or thyself for thyself, but thou must love all for Me alone. For Divine love cannot tolerate any other affection with it or any earthly love. Therefore, so far as thou shalt permit thy heart to be infected with any contagion of earthly things, so far thou wilt sin against My love and fail of thy perfection; for a pure and holy soul should hold in abhorrence all that gives pleasure and enjoyment to sense. Never suffer any of the things My bounty has created for the use of men to hinder thee from loving Me. For to this end have I created all things and given them to man, that he, knowing more fully through them the richness of My bounty, may love Me in return with a larger affection. Bridle therefore with a strong hand thy appetites and carnal concupiscence; keep perpetual guard over thyself; and courageously resist all those earthly desires which Thy corrupt nature and this miserable mortal life excite in thy heart, that thou mayest be able to sing with the prophet: 'Blessed be God, who hath given strength and agility to my feet,' *i.e.* to the feet of the soul, which are the affections; 'who hath made my feet like the feet of harts, that they may flee from the dogs;' *i.e.* the snares of concupiscence of earthly things; 'and setteth me upon high places;' (Ps. xvii. 34), *i.e.* raiseth me to contemplation.

"When thou shalt have fully executed all this, thou mayest proceed to the exercise of the second thing, which is of yet higher perfection. And this is, that thou shouldst direct all thy affections, all thy thoughts, and all thy actions to My glory and honour alone, and employ thyself continually with all earnestness in praising and glorifying Me, by prayers, by words, by example, and in whatever way thou canst. And this thou must endeavour so to do as to excite in all others, as well as in thyself, these same affections and sentiments towards Me. Now this practice is yet more pleasing to Me than the first, because My Divine Will is thereby more perfectly and more directly fulfilled. There yet remains the third thing, which when thou shalt have achieved, thou mayest rest assured that nothing more is wanting to thee, and that thou hast reached perfect sanctity. This is, that thou shalt use thy utmost endeavour to attain such a disposition of spirit that thou mayest become one thing with Me, and thy will may become so entirely assimilated and conformed to My all-perfect Will, that not only shalt thou never desire that which is evil, but not even that which is good, if it be not according to My Will; so that whatever shall befall thee in this miserable life, from whatsoever quarter it may come, whether in things temporal or things spiritual, nothing shall ever disturb thy peace or trouble thy quietness of spirit; but thou shalt be established in a firm belief that I, thine omnipotent God, love thee with a dearer love and take of thee more watchful care than thou canst for thyself.

And the more perfectly thou dost abandon and resign thyself to Me, the more will I console thee with My grace, and make thee feel My presence; and thus thou wilt ever know more and more, and experience more fully, the tenderness of My love for thee. But thou wilt never reach this measure of perfection except by a firm, constant, and absolute denial of self-will. He who neglects to acquire this, neglects at the same time the most sublime perfection; and he who cheerfully embraces it, executes at the same time My most holy Will, pleases Me in the highest degree, and has Me continually with him. For there is nothing more pleasing to Me than to abide within you and work in you by My grace: 'for My delights are to be with the children of men' (Prov. viii. 31), to transform them into Myself (if only they desire it, for I will in no way do violence to their free will); in such a manner that they may become one with Me in the participation of My infinite perfections, and especially My unchangeable peace and My most perfect tranquillity. But, that thou mayest better comprehend how ardent are My desires to dwell with you, and mayest kindle in thyself a more fervent longing to subject and unite thy will with Mine, consider attentively that I have willed that My only begotten Son should become incarnate, that My Divinity, despoiled of every token of greatness or glory, should be united to humanity; in order that by this great act of benevolence and charity, by this ineffable demonstration of love, I might draw and constrain you in like manner to unite your will to Mine and to remain perpetually bound to Me alone. Consider that I have willed further that this My Son should suffer the cruel, painful, and most fearful death of the Cross, to the end that by these torments He might destroy your sin, that sin which had raised a barrier of division between you and Me so effectually that I could in no way look upon you; that further in the highest of the Sacraments I have prepared for you a table, too little appreciated, of the Body and Blood of this My Son, in order that by partaking of it you may become transformed and changed into Me. Even as the bread and wine of which you partake is changed into the substance of your body, so you, by feeding under the species of bread and wine upon this My Son, who is one with Me, shall become spiritually transformed into Me. And this is what I have already spoken to my servant Augustine in these words :—' I am the food of grown men ; grow, and thou shalt feed on Me ; nor shalt thou convert Me into thee, but I will convert thee into Myself.' "

And, when that soul had heard what the will of God was, that to execute it faithfully a perfect charity was required, and that this could only be obtained by an entire annihilation of self-will, she spoke thus to the Lord :—" Thou hast manifested to me, O my Lord and God, Thy Will, and hast shown me, that, if I love Thee perfectly, I shall love nothing transitory and earthly, nor even my own self for myself, but all alone for Thee and in Thee. Thou hast added, that, in order to love Thee, I must seek with earnest care to praise and glorify Thee in all things and at all times ; and that in such a manner as that others may do so likewise ; that I must endeavour further to bear with a peaceful, cheerful, tranquil heart whatever may befall one in this miserable life. And now, since I gather from what Thou hast hitherto said that all these things are to be done by the abnegation of my own will, since the more I die to myself, the more perfectly I shall live in Thee ; I beseech Thee to teach me in what manner I may acquire this great virtue of the perfect abnegation of myself."

And God, who is so good that He can deny nothing to the pious desires of His servants, thus replied to her :—" It is certain that everything depends upon the perfect abnegation of thyself, since the more thou dost empty thyself of thy own will, the more will I fill thee with My grace. And all thy perfection comes from the participation of My Divine goodness by means of grace, without which the human creature, in all that concerns its true dignity and perfection, is absolutely nothing. If thou dost indeed desire to attain this perfect abnegation of self, thou must prostrate thyself before Me in the most profound humility, with a thorough conviction of thine own poverty and misery ; and thou must at all times eagerly seek this one thing, to obey Me alone and to do My Will only. And to this end thou must make in thy soul as it were a little spiritual cell, closed in with the material of My Will, in which thou must enclose thyself and make therein thy constant dwelling-place; so that, wherever thou goest, thou mayest never go forth from it, and, wherever thou lookest, thou mayest never see anything beyond it; but My Will must so encompass every faculty of thy body and soul, that thou shalt never speak of anything but what thou deemest pleasing unto Me, nor think, nor do anything, but what thou believest agreeable to My Will. And it shall be that the Holy Spirit shall teach thee what thou shalt do in all things. Moreover thou mayest attain this abnegation of thine own will by another road, if thou canst obtain those who are able to guide and instruct thee according to My Spirit; namely, by subjecting thy will to them, by obediently following their counsels, and by trusting thyself and thy concerns fully to them; since he who hears My faithful and prudent servants "heareth Me" (S. Luke x. 16). But I desire further that thou shouldst consider with firm faith and profound meditation that I, thy most glorious God, I, who have created thee for eternal beatitude, am eternal, sovereign, omnipotent; that I can do with you whatever pleaseth Me; and there is none who can oppose himself in the least degree to My Will; that no good can happen to you unless sent by Me; nor can any evil befall you except by that same Will of Mine, as I have already told you by My Prophet Amos: "shall there be evil in a city which the Lord hath not done?" (Amos iii. 6), that is, which I have not permitted. In the second place, I wilt that thou seriously meditate that in Me, thy God, dwell the most perfect intelligence, and knowledge, and infinite wisdom; that, therefore, I behold all things with the utmost clearness and acutest penetration; so that in My government of thee, the heavens, and the earth, and the entire universe, I cannot be deceived in any way or misled by any error. Were it otherwise, I should neither be all wise, nor should I be God. And, that thou mayest acknowledge the more the power of My infinite Wisdom, know that even from the evil of guilt and punishment I am able to draw a good greater than the evil. In the third place, consider attentively that, as I am thy God, so am I infinitely good, yea, charity itself by My Essence; that, therefore, I cannot will anything but that which is useful and salutary to thee and to all men; nor can I wish any evil to My creatures; that, as man was created by My bounty, so is he loved by Me with inestimable charity. When with a firm faith thou shalt have received and pondered in thy mind these truths, thou shalt see that I only suffer tribulations, temptations, difficulties, sicknesses, and all other forms of adversity to befall men for the greater advantage of their eternal salvation; that through the very things which to you seem evils, the true evil of your bad habits may be corrected, and firm resolutions made to attain that virtue which can alone guide you to that true and ultimate good which as yet you know not. Thus illuminated by the living light of faith, thou wilt perceive that I, thy God, have infinitely more knowledge, power, and will to advance thy happiness than thou hast; and further, that thy own knowledge, power, and will for thine own good depends entirely on My grace. For this cause, seek with all diligence to submit thyself totally to My Will; so shalt thou take thy rest and abide in continual tranquillity of spirit, and shalt have Me for ever with thee, for My "place is in peace" (Ps. lxxv. 3). Nothing will then agitate or irritate thee; nothing shall be to thee an occasion of sin or scandal, for "much peace have they who love My law; and to them there is no stumbling-block" (Ps. cxviii. 165). For they so love My law, that is, My Will which is My law by which all things are directed, they are so intimately united by it to Me, and experience such great delight in observing it, that (sin only excepted, which is offensive to God) nothing has power to disturb them, from whatsoever quarter it may come, or of whatsoever weight or quality it may be. For the eyes of their soul are clear and undefiled; and therefore they see that from Me, the sovereign Ruler of the world, Who govern all things with infinite Wisdom, Order, and Charity, nothing but good can spring; and that I can take care of them and their affairs far better and more successfully than they could of themselves. And thus considering that I and none other am the Author of all that they have to endure, they are strong with an invincible patience, and suffer all things, not only with resignation, but with cheerfulness and joy, tasting in all things which befall them externally or internally the sweetness of My ineffable charity. And this is to " think of the Lord in goodness " (Wis. i. 1), that is, to believe, and meditate with a cheerful and grateful spirit, even in the midst of tribulations and difficulties, that it is I who sweetly dispose all things, and that whatever happens springs from the inexhaustible fountain of My goodness. But the great good which this holy consideration and blessed disposition of heart would effect, is hindered, corrupted, and destroyed solely by this one thing, the love of yourselves and of your own will. If you destroy this within you, there shall be no more hell for you, neither the eternal torment of body and soul prepared for the damned, nor that other hell of interior turmoil which you make for yourselves and suffer during your mortal life, through your perpetual agitations and anxious cares about many things. If, therefore, thou wouldst live in grace in this world which passes rapidly away, and if thou wouldst live in glory in that world which has no end, seek to die to thyself, denying thyself and laying down thine own will. For " blessed are the dead who die in the Lord " (Apoc. xiv. 13), and " blessed also are the poor in spirit " (S. Matt. v. 3), since they already see Me in a manner in this their pilgrimage by reciprocal love, and shall behold Me hereafter in glory and honour in their true home.

SO BE IT.

APPENDICES.

APPENDIX A.

RELATION OF A DOCTRINE, OR SPIRITUAL INSTRUCTION.

Written in the year of our Lord 1376, on the seventh day of the month of January, by Brother William Flete, an Englishman, of the Hermits of St. Augustine in Lecceto, a man of great learning and sanctity ; which doctrine and document received *vivâ voce* from the Seraphic Virgin, St. Catherine of Siena, of whom he was a disciple, was by him reduced to writing in Latin, and has lately been translated into the vulgar tongue in the following manner, from an ancient manuscript, still preserved in the Archives of the Fathers of St. Dominic of Siena, similar to the other ancient text preserved in the Chartreuse of Pontignano near Siena, amongst the memorials of the Blessed Stephen Maconi, another disciple, and secretary of the Saint.

The holy Mother, speaking of herself as of a third person, said that in the beginning of her illumination she placed as the foundation of her whole life, in opposition to self-love, the stone or self-knowledge, which she separated into the three following little stones :

The first was the consideration of her creation ; that is to say, how she had no existence whatever of herself, but one solely dependent on the Creator, as well in its production as in its preservation, and that all this the Creator had done, and was still doing, through His grace and mercy.

The second was the consideration of her redemption ; *i.e.*, how the Redeemer had restored with His own Blood the life of grace which was before destroyed; and this through His pure and fervent love, unmerited by man.

The third was the consideration of her own sins, committed after baptism, and the graces therein received, through which she, having deserved eternal damnation, was astonished that out of the eternal goodness of God, He had not commanded the earth to swallow her up.

From these three considerations there arose within her so great a hatred against herself, that she desired nothing whatever conformable to her own will, but only to the will of God, Who, as she already knew, willed nothing but her good. From this it followed that every tribulation or trial was to her a matter of pleasure and delight, not only because it came through the will of God, but also because she saw herself to be thereby punished and chastised. She began likewise to have the greatest dislike to those things in which she used formerly to take pleasure, and great delight in what formerly displeased her; thus the caresses of her mother, in which she had once found so much pleasure, she now shunned as she would sword or poison, whilst at the same time she joyfully embraced all the abuse and insults that were bestowed upon her.

And she also welcomed what at the same time she abhorred— the temptations of Satan; she welcomed them for the suffering they brought, and abhorred them inasmuch as they offered her sensual enjoyments. After these things there was kindled within her an immense desire for purity, and after having made continual prayer during many months to obtain it, and that it might be bestowed on her in its highest perfection, our Lord at last appearing to her said: "Beloved daughter, if thou wouldest obtain the purity thou desirest, thou must needs first become perfectly united to Me, Who am purity itself, which thou shalt obtain if thou observe three things. In the first place, thou must turn thyself wholly towards Me with thine intention, and have Me alone for thine end in all thine actions, and make it thy sole study to keep Me ever before thine eyes. Secondly, denying thine own will, and paying no regard to that of any creature soever, thou must have respect and consideration for Mine, which wills thy sanctification, since I neither wish nor permit anything except for thy good. If thou attentively observe this, nothing shall sadden or disturb thee even for an hour, but rather thou wilt esteem thyself obliged to any who insult thee. Moreover, thou shalt not judge anything to be sinful unless thou knowest it manifestly to be so, and then thou shalt be indignant against the sin, but shalt compassionate the sinner. The third thing is, that thou judge the actions of My servants, not according to thine own inclination and taste, but according to My judgment; because thou knowest full well that I have said, ' In my Father's house are many mansions,' and because the mansion of glory corresponds with the merit of the way; so, as there are many mansions in that Fatherland, there are also many roads leading thereto. It is therefore My will that thou judge not My servants in any way, but that thou shouldst have the highest respect for all their actions, provided they be not expressly against My teaching. If thou observe these three things, thou shalt become well regulated in thyself towards Me by means of the first, and towards thy neighbour, be he good or evil, by means of the second and third. In this way thou shalt not through vices quit the way of virtue, and consequently shalt have and shalt perfectly preserve purity, by the aid and operation of My grace.

For the better explanation of the foregoing, she also said that self-love is the occasion of every evil and the ruin of every good; and that it is of two sorts; namely, sensitive and spiritual. The first is the cause of all sensual sins, as well as of all others that are open and manifest, and that are committed through affection towards earthly and created things; that is to say, when for the sake of such things the commandments of the Creator are despised and transgressed. The second kind of self-love, called spiritual, is that which causes a man who has a contempt for earthly things, for all creatures, and even for his own sensuality, to be, in spite of all this, so tenaciously attached to his own spiritual sense and to his own opinion, that he will neither serve God nor walk in

His ways, unless according to his own inclination and sentiments. Hence it follows, since God will have man to be absolutely destitute of self-will, that such an one can neither remain where he is, nor continue going on his way, so he must needs fall, because he adheres more to his own will than to that of God.

Of this sort are all those who will choose for themselves a state of life and occupation agreeable to their own notions, and not according to the vocation of God, decided by the counsel of prudent and discreet men. Such again are those who attach themselves too much to any spiritual practice or exercise, for instance, fasting and the like, in which they place, as it were, their end, so that if perchance it happen that they are unable to practise it, they give way at once to despair, and abandon everything. In this class may also be numbered souls who have an excessive love for consolations and spiritual sweetnesses, for when these are wanting, they at once fall into discouragement. For true spiritual love loves God alone, and the salvation of souls for God's sake. Let all things then be made use of in due order for this end, nor let the means, whatever they be, trouble us, provided that their end be the honour of God and the salvation of our neighbour. Whosoever then possesses true spiritual love, must judge all things and accept all things according to the will of God, and not according to the will of men : and when deprived of any spiritual consolation, he should at once reflect and say: "This happens through the Divine plan; by the permission of God, Who, in all the adversities He sends me, seeks and wills nothing but my justification and sanctification;" and with this thought all that is bitter will become sweet. Thus spoke the Saint.

The same Brother William Flete adds further the following words : "Our Mother, Blessed Catherine, asked our Lord for solitude, and he replied to her : Many people remain in their cell who live out of their cell; My will is that thy cell be the knowledge of thyself and of thy sins. From this cell Catherine never issued forth, and every servant of God should act in the same way, because in this manner he would keep within his cell in whatever place he might be."

APPENDIX B.

FATHER WILLIAM FLETE.

(From Pitt's " De Illustribus Angliæ Scriptoribus," p. 521.)

Joseph Pamphili calls him William Flete, and several foreign writers also call him Flete. He was an English monk of the Order of the Hermits of St. Augustine; a lover of solitude and heavenly contemplation, and very famous for his sanctity. Ever ascending from virtue to virtue, and growing every day more holy, he found by his own experience that no perfection in this world is so great as that, by the help of the Divine grace, we may not attain to a greater. When he heard that some of his brethren in Italy had been reformed and had embraced a stricter discipline in their monasteries, he hastened thither and persevered among them (as Ambrose Coriolanus and James of Bergamo testify) in wonderful innocence and integrity of morals even to the last day of his life. He is said to have received divine revelations in his prayers and contemplations, especially about the future calamities of England, on which subject he wrote various epistles, full of varied learning and Christian zeal, addressed chiefly to the members of his own Order and Institute. The following list is preserved of his writings :

1. To the Provincial of his Order in England, one Epistle. *Obsecro in Domino Jesu.*

2. To the Doctors of the Province, one Epistle. *Cum timore Dei, et reverentia.*

3. To the Brethren in general, *Ait enim Apostolus, Spectaculum.*

4. Predictions to the English of calamities coming upon England. One book.

5. Divers Epistles. One book.

6. Of Remedies against Temptations. One book.

Some or all of these were preserved in Pitts' time among the Norwich MSS. in the Public Library of Cambridge. The same writer represents him as dying in Italy in 1380, in the reign of Richard II., a date which is proved to be incorrect by the fact of his sermon on St. Catherine having been delivered in 1382. Pitts also quotes Sabellicus, who affirms that he was finally enrolled among the number of the Saints, which, however, would seem to mean no more than that he enjoyed among his own Brethren the repute of sanctity.

APPENDIX C.

BULL OF BONIFACE IX.

(*From the Bullarium of the Order*, p. 352.)

September 8, A.D. 1395.

BONIFACE IX.

To Richard, King of England, that the Clerks who recite the Daily Office with him according to the rite of the Friars-Preachers, may retain the same rite when they are absent, for two months only.

LXIX.

Boniface, Bishop, Servant of the Servants of God, to his most dear son in Christ, Richard, the illustrious King of England, Health and Apostolic Benediction.

The special and sincere devotion which thou hast proved thyself to bear towards Ourselves and the Roman Church, deservedly induces Us graciously and favourably to grant thee those things which thou suppliantly asked of us. As, therefore, formerly We judged it fitting to grant to thy Majesty by the authority of our letters,[1] as is more fully contained in the said letters, that as thou

---

[1] These letters are missing.

didst allege thou wast accustomed to recite the Canonical Hours according to the rite of the Friar-Preachers, the Clerks, Priests, and even the secular attendants of thy Majesty, should be allowed to recite the Canonical Hours in this manner according to the rite of the Friar-Preachers, which, it was asserted, differed but little from that of the Roman Church, and should not be bound, if they did not wish it, to observe any other rite or order in this matter ; so, being willing now to grant thee a still greater favour, We, by the authority of these present letters, as a special grace, concede to thy Majesty, that, as often as it shall happen that one or more of the said Clerks, Priests, or Religious, who have been accustomed to say the hours wtth thee in this manner, shall be absent from thee, with the intention of returning to thee, they, while thus absent, may, for the space of two months only, to be reckoned from the day on which they left thee, be allowed to say their Hours according to the said rite of the Order of Friar-Preachers, nor shall they be bound against their will to observe any other rite or order.

It shall not, therefore, be lawful for any man to infringe this Our grant, or, &c.

Given at Rome, at St. Peter's, on the 6th of the Ides of September, in the sixth year of our Pontificate.

INDEX.

www.ingramcontent.com/pod-product-compliance
Lightning Source LLC
Chambersburg PA
CBHW021543110726
47902CB00004B/1003